The World Since 1945
A Brief History

Second Edition

Daniel R. Brower

PEARSON

Prentice
Hall

Upper Saddle River, New Jersey 07458

Library of Congress Cataloging-in-Publication Data

Brower, Daniel R.
  The world since 1945 : a brief history / Daniel R. Brower.—2nd ed.
     p. cm.
  Includes bibliographical references and index.
  ISBN 0-13-189705-5
     1. History, Modern—1945-1989. 2. History, Modern—1989– I. Title.

D840.B68 2005
909.82'5—dc22   2004040019

VP, Editorial Director: Charlyce Jones Owen
Executive Editor: Charles Cavaliere
Associate Editor: Emsal Hasan
Editorial Assistant: Shannon Corliss
Marketing Manager: Heather Shelstad
Marketing Assistant: Jennifer Bryant
Production Editor: Laura A. Lawrie
Manufacturing Buyer: Tricia Kenny
Art Director: Jayne Conte
Cover Design: Bruce Kenselaar
Composition: This book was set in 10/12 Times by ICC.
Printer/Binder: The interior was printed by Courier Companies, Inc.
The cover was printed by Phoenix Color Corp.

Credits and acknowledgments borrowed from other sources and reproduced, with
permission, in this textbook appear on appropriate page within text.

Pearson Education LTD.
Pearson Education Singapore, Pte. Ltd.
Pearson Education Canada, Ltd.
Pearson Education–Japan
Pearson Education Australia PTY, Limited
Pearson Education North Asia, Ltd.
Pearson Educación de Mexico, S.A. de C.V.
Pearson Education Malaysia, Pte. Ltd.

10 9 8 7 6 5 4
ISBN 0-13-189705-5

Contents

Maps

Preface

Priding ourselves on shaping history, we function day to day as slaves of the events that inexorably unroll themselves before our eyes, and fear possesses us and hatred follows in its train.

—Jawaharlal Nehru, 1949

The moment in August 1947 when the British Empire liberated its Indian colony was a time of triumph and celebration for Nehru, who was India's first prime minister. There, as in other colonies that achieved independence in the postwar years, nationalist leaders hoped that liberation would open an era of freedom and progress for the former subject peoples. But Nehru discovered that the transition of power brought human tragedy as well as triumph. He gave voice to that disillusionment two years later, recalling the anguish, helplessness, and despair that he experienced in the first months of independence. Nehru's confession is a timely warning not to exaggerate the achievements or minimize the destruction brought by the postimperial age.

Forging a national community has been a fundamental, complex task following the fall of the Western empires in the years after the Second World War. The challenge was to create new political foundations for public life, and to forge new bonds of trust to hold together the peoples of the new states. These daunting tasks suggest the great scope of renewal that has been attempted in our postcolonial age. There exists as well a dark side to this story of transformation, for hostility and fear among peoples at times produced bitter conflict in the decades following colonial liberation. This ethnic and social unrest has undermined new governments and created political chaos within these states.

Nehru had imagined a far happier time for his newly liberated country. These shattered dreams are as much a part of the history of the world since 1945 as the achievements that countries such as India actually did experience. Knowledge of these events can help us to reach a balanced, sober understanding of human relations in our complex world.

Destruction and creation are inseparable parts of the history of the late twentieth century. The bitterness and suffering generated by this struggle of ideals and interests have made the world an uneasy, violent place. Perhaps the most appropriate—certainly the most optimistic—image of contemporary world history is provided by the Greek myth of the phoenix, the bird reborn from the ashes of its own destruction. To discern essential signs of the emerging new era represents the most challenging historical task of any survey of turbulent periods of change, particularly one so close to us.

The emergence of a world consisting of states claiming to be nations is the major theme of this textbook. The process has generated powerful new political ideals and created problems of human relations unknown to previous generations. It has thrust some peoples into unexpected prominence as a result of the violent history of this period. The textbook's chronological coverage extends from the closing years of the Second World War, when the Axis empires were close to defeat, and reaches forward beyond the collapse of the Soviet Union and the end of the Cold War to a new era when nation-states gave shape to the political map of the entire world. In the same period, the power in the hands of a few states, especially the United States, gave them opportunities to shape the course of global relations. At the same time, that power and prosperity attracted enemies, some of whom took the path of terrorism to attack these states. Violence is an integral part of the story told here.

The world-historical perspective adopted in this text is especially meaningful to make clear the increasing interaction among states and peoples since the close of the Second World War. The principal questions I seek to answer follow directly from this premise: What have been the most significant trends shaping this interaction? How can we explain the emergence of these global trends? What has been their impact on peoples throughout the world? This brief survey cannot possibly explore in detail all the dimensions of this interaction; of necessity, it is very selective. To draw the reader's attention to important issues, each chapter contains a "Highlight" essay that addresses a key issue, and a "Spotlight" essay offering a biographical sketch of an individual whose life encapsulates an essential trend in contemporary world history. Throughout the text, three subjects have guided the selection of the major trends and events to be addressed. These are the international history of states; the role of ideology in shaping political movements and reshaping cultural and social values, and the evolution of world economic relations.

All three emphasize related aspects of global interaction. International history examines the essential factors that have shaped the foreign policies of governments and the relations among states. These include, first, the political ideals and national interests of states, second, the economic and political influence of states in global affairs, and third, the balance of power among countries. These three factors taken together explain in large measure the evolution of global conflict and cooperation from great confrontation of the Second World War to the Cold War conflict between superpowers following the world war, and finally to wars and peacekeeping after the end of the Cold War. International history offers crucial insight into the global forces that shaped the world as we know it.

The potent force of political ideology emerges from deeply felt convictions of right and wrong, justice and injustice, giving rise to powerful mass movements and guiding the policies of governments. The importance of these aspirations in our time is such that some scholars have suggested calling the twentieth century the "age of ideology." Liberalism was the dominant political faith among Western countries in the early century and it appeared in the late century to have won greater support around the world than ever before. During most of the century, Marxism provided the ideological guidelines for state policy-making and cultural controls in the socialist countries of the communist bloc and in the Third World. Nationalism, of Western origin but without any single intellectual source or text, places the emergence of national communities and the formation of the nation-state at the center of human endeavor. It is undoubtedly the single strongest political bond among peoples in the world today. In the late twentieth century, influential political movements claiming to defend the Muslim religious community drew strength from their ideological coherence. In studying these ideologies we can appreciate better the motives of important political leaders and the manner in which social discontent has been articulated and expressed in political movements.

Finally, economic history stresses the significance of productive resources, of new technology, and of ownership of these means of production. These factors have determined the profound differences separating developed and developing nations and the dispersion across the globe of wealth and poverty. Vital natural resources, such petroleum, have become essential to the well-being of the global economy. Countries possessing these resources have acquired vast wealth, and have attracted the attention, both helpful and destructive, of foreign powers.

These three realms of inquiry—international, ideological, and economic history—are guides to interpreting the global forces of change. They suggest where and how powerful new historical trends have emerged. In simplest terms, they illuminate the process by which human power in various forms has, for good and ill, reshaped the modern world.

The story told here adheres to the simple principle that history is a tale of the past revealed over the passage of time. Its emphasis on international, political, and economic trends focuses that tale on the formative influences that have made the world as we know it. Its frequent use of historical quotations and images of these trends, in the form of quotes from political leaders and observers, or reproductions of political posters and photographs, is inspired by the belief that the proper subject-matter of history is the lived experience of the past. The meaning and purpose that participants attributed to those events are as much a part of our history as the events themselves. The tale retold here is one that they first wrote. We may praise or condemn what they did, but first we need to understand what they sought to do.

The judgments that we bring to a past as close as the twentieth century are inescapably influenced by our immediate perception of the world about us. To those who might object that such interpretations commit the sin of "presentism," that is, of distorting the past to make it fit the needs of the present, I would respond that history as we teach and write it is necessarily a dialogue between the present and the past. The essential requirement for historical understanding is to allow the voices from the past to answer in their own terms the questions and concerns that we judge to be historically meaningful.

The thematic focus of this text is in large measure drawn from my experience as lecturer and textbook author in the field of modern world history. This undertaking has occupied me during nearly three decades of teaching this subject, and has benefitted from innumerable discussions with colleagues who have proven generous with their time and indulgent of my endeavor. The sober understanding of the past that we acquire with the passing of time is a privilege largely denied this text, whose last chapters touch on events that occurred only yesterday on a historical scale. Students in my twentieth-century world history course at the University of California-Davis have lived through the many stages of this work. The yearly renewal of this student audience has constantly challenged my conclusions and incited me to rethink the meaning of events for those who are creating the history of the twenty-first century.

I would like to thank the reviewers of this book, Frederick Dotolo, St. John Fisher College (NY), and Guoqiang Zheng, Angelo State University.

This book is dedicated to Matthew, Michael, and Natalie, with the wish that they may find the world a place to say "Fanfare for the Makers!"

Daniel R. Brower
September 20, 2003
Berkeley, California

Chapter 1

Toward the Second Twentieth Century: The Last World War

Outline

The Empires of Germany and Japan

The Alliance against the Axis

The Fall of the German and Japanese Empires

Highlight

Internationalism

Spotlight

John Maynard Keynes

World history after the Second World War differed so fundamentally from earlier decades that it deserves to be called the "Second Twentieth Century." The spread of nation-states, among all the historical changes that marked the half-century after 1945, has had the greatest impact on the lives of people throughout the world. In the history of humanity, the rise and fall of great empires provided a clear indication of the emergence and decline of civilizations. In modern times, the most influential empires were those of European states. Their age passed quickly, though. By the late twentieth century, none were left. Taking their place were nation-states. The transition had first begun in the early nineteenth century when Latin American nation-states emerged from the ruins of the Spanish Empire. It ended when, in the early 1990s, the Soviet Union fell apart, leaving in its place nation-states throughout its Eurasian realm. The decades following the end of the Second World War were the crucial moment when empires fell and nations replaced colonial territories. The story of this process is the major theme of this book.

Although new state borders spread across the map of the world to mark the frontiers of nations, international economic forces created regional and global links that transcended these barriers. An international economy, born of the industrial revolution, had emerged in the late nineteenth century out of the trading and investment activities of the Western countries. With the fall in the last decades of the twentieth century of the command economies of communist states, this economy penetrated deeply into the lives of peoples around the world. "Globalization" is the term used to describe its impact. Its driving power was the search for profit, for it operated as a market,

1

capitalist economy. Those regions that did not share in the benefits of this economic system belonged to a "Third World" where poverty and hunger were the lot of its inhabitants. The fate of these regions, although governed by independent nation-states, depended still on decisions made in far-away, prosperous centers of the global economy. The emergence of this new economic system after war's end is our second theme.

The outcome of the Second World War itself led directly to the Cold War, which is the third major theme of this book. The war of 1939 to 1945 bore little resemblance to the First World War. The earlier conflict had been largely European in origins, and its armies and major battlefields were European as well. Only twenty years separated the end of one world war and the beginning of the next war, launched by the aggression of the Japanese Empire in East Asia and Nazi Germany in Europe. This war was followed in turn by a global ideological, political, and diplomatic conflict between the victorious western powers and their former ally, the Soviet Union. It lasted until the late 1980s. The impact of this so-called Cold War shaped in many ways the evolution of global relations among the world's most powerful states; its end opened a new era in international affairs. All three trends—the appearance of nation-states throughout the world, the spread of a global economy, and the Cold War—emerged out of the turmoil of the Second World War.

This world war was truly global, for it came closer than ever in human history to uniting the peoples of the world in one vast, terrible, human endeavor. Involved in the conflict were countries from every continent, and its battlefields were scattered around the globe. Heroism was no longer the sole privilege of soldiers in battle. Resistance movements in countries occupied by the Axis powers kept alive visions of a better life to follow liberation. For the first time armies opened their ranks to women, who were not yet warriors but were no longer merely temporary workers and protectors of the home. The scope of death and destruction extended throughout the civilian population. New military technology gave mobility to armies, and made military aircraft the key element in naval battles and the means to carry the war far behind the front lines. At the end of the war, one single explosive device revealed the capacity of atomic energy to lay waste to an entire city. Human ingenuity put in the hands of statesmen and their military commanders fantastic weapons of destruction.

German and Japanese victories in the first stages of the war destroyed the old global balance of power. The conquests by the Axis powers marked deeply the population within those areas, obliterating old frontiers and overturning established governments. The Nazi New Order in Europe and the Asian empire of Japan both found supporters among their conquered peoples. The Nazis recruited fascists and sympathizers in the conquered areas for military service and administration, while the Japanese selected anti-Western nationalists to govern former European colonies. Opposition to the Axis empires centered on an international coalition of Allied states united for the defeat the aggressors.

Allied military victory proved, in the end, easier to achieve than political agreement on the postwar peace. By 1944 these victories had made clear that the forces of Great Britain, the Soviet Union, and the United States would soon defeat the German and Japanese empires. The war leaders of these nations—Winston Churchill, Joseph Stalin, and Franklin Roosevelt—agreed on the short-term objective of complete destruction of the Axis. But their wartime discussions revealed the great difficulties that they faced in shaping a stable peace. Later, Western critics condemned the failure of British and American leaders to force Stalin, deeply suspicious of his Western allies, to accept the restoration of prewar state borders in Europe and Asia. But these critics overlooked the limits to Western power, the new might of the Soviet Union, and the powerful revolutionary movements that emerged out of resistance forces in formerly occupied lands. At war's end, a new boundary was taking shape that divided the lands freed by Soviet troops and those freed by the Western Allies. The peace, like the war that preceded it, bore no resemblance to the First World War.

THE EMPIRES OF GERMANY AND JAPAN

By 1944 the outcome of the war was no longer in doubt. Both in East Asia and in Europe, the Axis coalition was falling apart, and its remaining military forces were in full retreat. Japan and Germany, the pillars of this coalition, had conquered vast territories. Their years of domination had provoked widespread opposition to their rule, yet among the conquered peoples were some who had chosen to collaborate with the conquerors. Each had created a vast empire, that is, a state whose peoples are gathered together by a conquering army and whose leaders govern these peoples in last resort by force of arms. In these terms their empires were heirs to a long tradition, as old as human civilization, of empire building.

But their leaders had justified their conquests in terms of nationalism. They claimed that the people in their homelands, Germany and Japan, were united as one nation under their leadership. They understood "nation" to refer to a population joined together by a presumed common ancestry and by a shared culture. Both Japanese and German leaders proclaimed the superiority of their own people, who they believed possessed a "natural" right to dominate other peoples. Both regimes welcomed the collaborators from among these peoples; the Japanese even asserted that they sought to free Asian colonial peoples from Western rule. But racism lay at the heart of these two conquering empires. The Nazis carried to monstrous lengths their assertion of racial superiority, branding certain conquered peoples (Jews, Gypsies) "subhuman" and creating a system of mass execution (termed "genocide") to exterminate them. The empires of Japan and Germany were unlike any that came before them.

The Japanese Empire

At its largest, the Japanese Empire extended from China through the lands of southeast Asia and across the Pacific Ocean from the Philippines to Indonesia. Its expansion had begun in the 1930s, and culminated in the great offensives of 1941–42 that swept through southeast Asia and the eastern Pacific. It was the work of aggressive generals, backed by the emperor. Their domination of Japanese politics grew in the 1930s until they had created a militaristic regime. Civilian government never completely disappeared, for politicians continued to run important ministries, yet it was merely window dressing for rule by the generals. Militarism spread so deeply into the Japanese state and society that it resembled closely European fascism (but without the charismatic leader and single-party state). The emperor remained an object of worship; his compliance with the militaristic regime strengthened the power of the generals. From late 1941 until the end of the war, General Tojo was prime minister. The military ruled Japan.

In East Asia, China had been Japan's first and greatest conquest, but remained still only partially under firm control. The great Chinese Empire had vanished decades earlier, but in its place new political movements had emerged that refused to submit to Japanese rule. In the western areas of China, the Nationalist People's Party (Kuomintang, or KMT, in Chinese) led the forces of the Republic of China. Their leader, General Chiang Kai-shek, had refused to concede defeat despite the loss of the most populated coastal regions of his country. His government claimed to lead and to speak for the nation of China. But it was terribly weakened by the war, and held together largely by Chiang's authoritarian rule and by the army under his command. The United States supported

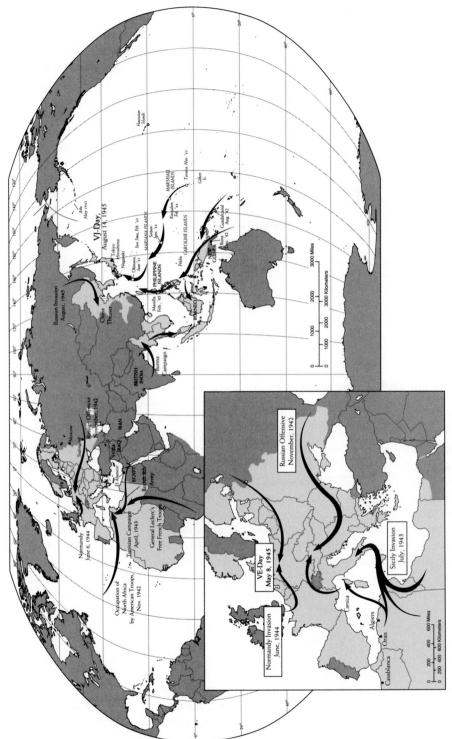

The Second World War in Europe and Asia

4

Japanese Militarism for School Children: Tokyo High School Students at National Spiritual Mobilization Week, 1938 (*Hoover Institution*)

Chiang's state, but its forces were far away and it was incapable of delivering adequate military aid. The Republic of China could hope to govern all China only after the U.S. forces had defeated Japan.

The other Chinese movement fighting the Japanese was the Chinese Communist Party. Its leader, Mao Zedong, was an inspired revolutionary who had created a mass political movement and a peasant army. Fighting a guerrilla war, the Communists had been able to take control of large areas in northern and central China. They were allies with the Nationalist government in the fight against Japan. But their goal was ultimately to unite the country under their leadership and to bring to its peoples the revolutionary program of state socialism that Stalin had imposed on the peoples of the Soviet Union. At heart, the Nationalists and the Communists were bitter enemies. Their antagonism was only temporarily held in check by the war with Japanese forces.

The Japanese Empire encompassed almost all of southeast Asia. Indochina, Burma, and Malaysia lay under their occupation. There, as in the Philippines and Indonesia, Japanese authorities encouraged anticolonial nationalists to collaborate in governing the population. Everywhere

they were partially successful, though their ruthless economic exploitation of the conquered lands stirred up resistance.

The Japanese were even able to recruit, from prisoners of war, an entire army group made up of soldiers from the British colony of India. Baptized the Indian National Army, its troops fought for the liberation of India from British rule. The British forces whom they confronted were Indians like themselves, who remained loyal to the British Empire. The British government of Winston Churchill proclaimed that its war against Japan sought to maintain the empire. Nationalist Indians, Malaysians, and Burmese, whether collaborating, neutral, or still loyal to the British Empire, expected liberation after war's end. They were proven correct.

The German Empire

Since Germany's great conquests of 1940–42, a New Order had reigned throughout the enormous territories of their "Third Reich" ("third empire"), from the shores of the Atlantic Ocean to the center of the Soviet Union. At its core was the Nazi Party, whose brutal nationalist ideology set the guidelines for rule over the entire empire. Nazism

Nazism on Display: Hitler Addressing Party Rally, Approximately 1935 (*National Archives*)

is one variation of the extreme nationalist ideology described as "fascism." The latter turned ethnic nationalism into a militaristic creed, for it idealized warriors as the embodiment of the mythical greatness of a nation. Fascist leaders believed it their right and duty to unify the nation under their command. Democracy tolerated diversity and dissent, both of which fascists despised. Hitler made this ideology his own. To it he added his own virulent hatred of the "subhuman" Jews. Anti-Semitism (anti-Jewish prejudice) infused the entire Nazi movement to such an extent that it made Nazism a uniquely brutal form of fascism.

Backed by his Nazi Party, Hitler had imposed on the German state and its people a dictatorial regime. The Nazi Party was the sole political movement, and it obeyed Hitler as its adored "Leader." "Hitler is the Party, the Party is Hitler," exclaimed one zealous Nazi leader. Nazis were the choice recruits for the state's secret police, the Gestapo, and for the elite special military force, the SS. All its members swore an oath of absolute obedience to the Leader: "The word of Hitler has the force of law." It controlled the prison camps, including the camps of mass execution of the "subhuman" subjects of the empire.

The Nazi empire's principal characteristic was exploitation of the conquered lands. After 1941, all Europe lay at the disposal of the Nazi leaders: French agriculture helped to feed German armies and to sustain a comfortable standard of living in Germany; the industrial production of occupied Europe augmented German economic resources and supplied military equipment to German armies. German authorities considered the working population of Europe to be available for their needs. German workers had to serve in the armed forces.

This repressive policy hit with greatest brutality the Polish nation and the Jews of occupied Europe. Poland once again ceased to exist. Much of its western territory was incorporated into Germany and the Polish inhabitants forced to abandon everything to move to the east. The central region became simply the Government-General, which was an area under German rule open to exploitation by German businessmen provided with Polish forced labor.

These racist policies reached their most inhuman level in the extermination of the Jews of Europe. Nazi anti-Semitism constituted a powerful bond among all party members and found supporters among peoples in eastern Europe, where most of Europe's six million Jews lived. Hitler sought a way to eliminate them all. His solution was to undertake the systematic mass extermination of an entire people. In late 1941 he had given his approval to the policy called by Nazi leaders the Final Solution. Its implementation began in 1942. His instrument for this inhuman policy was at hand—the SS organization, whose members were sworn to absolute obedience to his orders. The entire Jewish population of Europe was to be shipped by train in cattle cars to special camps in Polish territories. These were extermination camps, organized according to the same standards of industrial efficiency as slaughterhouses for animals. All that was left were mountains of clothing, gold teeth, hair, and other items taken from the victims. A few prisoners survived for a time to work as forced laborers, only to be killed in their turn.

The Final Solution remained in operation to the end of the war. By then more than five million Jews had been exterminated, the victims of insane Nazi racism and the moral cowardice of Germans. Historians still debate the circumstances and causes of this policy of genocide, a phenomenon so complex and terrifying that it defies adequate explanation. Germany's New Order tore apart the old Europe, its peoples and its states. Nothing could return the continent to its previous condition.

THE ALLIANCE AGAINST THE AXIS

The alliance opposing the Axis states had formed gradually in reaction to Axis aggression. Nationalist China had fought alone against Japan for four years, and Great Britain had fought alone in Europe against Nazi Germany, until 1941. That year the German attack in June on the Soviet Union brought the British their first major ally. The Japanese attack on U.S. naval forces in Pearl Harbor gave the Chinese a U.S. alliance, and Hitler's declaration of war on the United States sealed the alliance for the war in Europe. Military collaboration between the Soviet Union and the Western states was founded on a common enemy, Germany, against whom they had promised to fight until complete victory. But the Soviet Union and its Western allies were unlike one another in many respects: They fought on different battlefronts; they pursued differing aims for peace; their political systems were the product of antagonistic ideologies of communism and democracy. They had agreed through negotiations at international conferences on a set of short-term common objectives for victory in war and the reconstruction of Europe and East Asia. But their different long-term goals created enormous barriers to a stable post-war settlement.

The Soviet Union and the European War

The Soviet Union was a vital yet mysterious member of the Grand Alliance. Western statesmen realized from the start that the U.S.S.R. would occupy a dominant position in central Europe when Germany was defeated. The greatest mystery for Westerners surrounded the international objectives pursued by the Soviet Union.

The Soviet Union, like Nazi Germany, was a dictatorship in which a single ruling party was led by an all-powerful dictator assisted by a vast secret police network. But Joseph Stalin and his Communist Party justified their regime on ideological principles absolutely contrary to those of the Nazis. When the Communists had seized power in Russia in 1917, their leader, Vladimir Lenin, had declared that his revolutionary regime sought to destroy international capitalism and imperialism. Their goal, he proclaimed, was to liberate the oppressed masses and to build a socialist society, as Karl Marx had forecast a century earlier.

Following Lenin's death in the mid-1920s, Joseph Stalin had become the leader of the Communist Party and of the Soviet Union. In size and ethnic diversity, his country resembled the Russian Empire, for it stretched from eastern Europe to the Pacific Ocean, from the Arctic Ocean to Inner Asia. He had put in place in the early 1930s an intensive program, revolutionary in its impact, for the creation of a highly industrialized economy completely under the control of the state, of which he was the supreme leader. Later in the decade, he had proudly announced that the Soviet Union had, first of any land, created a socialist society. To him, this achievement meant that Soviet society had entered a higher stage of historical development that any other country in the world. Stalin spoke out against capitalism and imperialism and urged colonial peoples to revolt against their oppressors.

Soviet political realities under Stalin were the product of his dictatorial rule and of the state's commitment to mobilize the population and the country's resources to strengthen the state's power. This multi-national land, termed officially a "union" of national republics, was in fact a communist empire. Stalin employed an enormous

secret police network to eradicate any form of opposition to, or even suspected defiance toward, the dogmatic truths of the state ideology, baptised Marxism-Leninism-Stalinism and to his personal rule. His government exploited the country's economic resources and labor by means of what is best described as a command economy, that is, an economy whose operations were commanded by the state and that lacked any legal market for investment, labor, land, or goods. All industrial and commercial enterprises were "nationalized," that is, they were the property of the state; all farm land was "collectivized," which in reality meant that the land was controlled by the state and that the farmers received only what meager income that the state chose to give them. Controlling this vast economic operation was a system of state command planning, whose orders had the force of law. It was totally unlike the market economy of western countries.

From the moment he seized power, Stalin had claimed that his country was surrounded by enemies of socialism. It needed to be ruthless in its vigilance and its preparedness for war. Stalin himself referred to Western states as a "capitalist jungle" where "might made right" and powerful states became strong at the expense of the weak. Believing this the way of the capitalist enemies, he made these principles the guidelines of his own foreign policy until his death in 1953. He had conducted Soviet foreign policy from the moment he took power until 1941 on the principle that whatever was in the interest of Soviet territorial security and power had first priority for his country, and for world communism. When the opportunity arose in 1939–40 to seize territory from small states along the Soviet Union's western borders, he did not hesitate to take it. Revolutionary expansion played no part in these foreign dealings. In appearance the Soviet Union was a revolutionary communist regime, but its policies were those of a great power. In both respects it constituted a troubling presence in the coalition.

Soviet objectives since the outbreak of war with Germany in mid-1941 had concentrated on the defense of the country. The war had begun with disastrous military defeats and the loss of most of western Russia and the Ukraine. In this crisis the country mobilized for total war. Stalin took direct control of political and military affairs. His dictatorial powers obliterated the distinction between political and military leadership; later they permitted him to adjust military operations to diplomatic interests of state.

The vast powers of the state and the Communist Party had turned to the war effort. The apparatus of the police state was directed to stiffening the will of the population to fight. Most of the population responded to war demands with extraordinary patriotic fervor. Among the Russian population, the war against Germany became a national cause for which they were prepared to sacrifice their well-being and their lives. The greatest sacrifice came from the front-line soldiers. In the first two years of war, the Red Army lacked sufficient military equipment and skilled officers to match the powerful German army. Soviet generals replaced the missing armaments by demanding suicidal heroism from their soldiers. By war's end, Soviet military dead had reached ten million.

Soviet War Poster, 1944 (*Poster Collection/Hoover Institution*)

The battle that foretold the outcome of the German-Russian war had occurred in mid-1943 on the plains of central Russia. That summer Hitler made one last attempt to defeat the Soviet Union. His offensive produced the biggest tank battle in the entire war. But the Red Army was prepared this time with sufficient equipment, troops, and competent generals. The Soviet military machine proved mightier than the German army, which not only lost the battle but was forced into full retreat. By the late fall the German withdrawal had reached western Russia. Victory was at last becoming a tangible reality for the Soviet leaders.

The United States in the Grand Alliance

Throughout the 1930s the United States had taken no active role in European or Asian affairs. Its economy was in the grip of the depression, which left factories idle, farm land uncultivated, and millions of Americans unemployed. The people and their leaders had in these circumstances little concern for foreign conflicts; isolationism, that is, the refusal to take an active role in international affairs, was their preferred foreign policy. It had retained a powerful hold on America in the first years of war in East Asia, and even after war broke out in 1939 in Europe. The initial reaction of the U.S. Congress to the outbreak of the wars in East Asia and Europe was to adhere strictly to the isolationist policy. President Franklin Roosevelt had to declare the United States neutral in the war in East Asia, and later in the war in Europe.

Gradually U.S. isolationism had weakened as German power grew. Franklin Roosevelt had never shared the revulsion felt by many Americans at U.S. involvement in the First World War. He had begun his political career as a supporter of President Woodrow Wilson's domestic and foreign policies and had been active in the war effort as secretary of the navy during the First World War. He shared the belief, first defended by his elder cousin Theodore Roosevelt in the early

1900s, that the United States had to take an active role in world politics. As German conquests multiplied, he began to speak out frequently against isolationism and in support of the British. He feared the Nazi threat to U.S. security, especially after German victories in western Europe in 1940. But his most successful speeches on international affairs discussed the war in Europe in idealistic terms. Roosevelt himself abhorred Nazism and believed deeply in democracy. Yet his measures directed against Germany were based primarily on considerations of security and power. The American public understood far more readily, however, the rhetoric of internationalism (see "Highlight," this chapter). The president explained the European conflict to the American public in terms that emphasized the defense of democracy and that largely omitted issues of U.S. national security. In the summer of 1941 he obtained Churchill's approval for the Atlantic Charter, which committed both nations to "a better future for the world" following the "final destruction of Nazi tyranny."

The Japanese attack in December 1941, had suddenly thrust the United States into the midst of the world war. U.S. participation gave the alliance a central focus for the global conflict. Decisions made in Washington were influential both in the course of the war in Europe and Asia and in the elaboration of the diplomatic aims of the Allies. This situation was the result primarily of the global military presence of U.S. forces and of the economic aid provided by the United States to its allies.

Early in the war, the United States had come to possess the greatest array of modern armaments of any belligerent. The U.S. fleets in the two oceans constituted the largest number of fighting vessels ever to sail under one flag. Only the United States had access through its naval forces to the shores of every continent and island where the war was being fought. The U.S. Air Force grew to surpass in size that of Great Britain. Only

U.S. Homefront Recruitment Poster, 1942
(*Poster Collection/Hoover Institution*)

the U.S. Army was outnumbered by another ally. The Soviet Red Army constituted the largest land army in the world, a fact of crucial importance for the ultimate fate of the states of eastern and central Europe.

The second reason for U.S. primacy in the Allied coalition lay in its enormous economic resources. After remaining partially unused throughout the depression, factories and farmland resumed full operation when war production began. The nine million unemployed in 1940 found jobs, and business boomed. Mobilized for the war effort, the U.S. economy not only equipped its own military forces on land, sea, and air, but also provided great quantities of supplies to its allies. Roosevelt had started a program of military assistance to Great Britain even before

the United States entered the war. This "Lend-Lease" aid began to go to the Soviet Union shortly after the German invasion of Russia.

Throughout the war Roosevelt was guided in making strategic military decisions by the determination to minimize U.S. casualties as much as possible. To do so, he sought to mobilize overwhelming superiority in armaments before launching major military campaigns. For this reason, he had to defer approval of the attack on Germany's continental empire until 1944. Until then only the Red Army prevented total German victory on the European continent. Without an eastern front, the Western Allies would confront the bulk of German forces when they attempted their European invasion. The U.S. government judged the alliance with the Soviet Union indispensable also for military victory in East Asia. In both the European and Asian wars the Soviet Union was an extremely valuable ally.

The Alliance at War

By late 1943, the collaboration between the Soviet Union and the Western allies had become a real diplomatic alliance. At the conference of Teheran in the fall of 1943 Stalin finally met with Churchill and Roosevelt. The Western leaders made at that time a firm commitment to open a second front in Europe by invading France in the spring of 1944. That conference marked the high point of good relations among the Allies. The three leaders formulated there the basic terms of their Grand Alliance, focusing on three important objectives. First, they repeated their intent to pursue the war against Germany to total victory. Following German surrender, the country would be divided temporarily into occupation zones. Policies of demilitarization, denazification, and reparations payments would be imposed on the German population.

Second, Western leaders accepted Stalin's demand that the Soviet Union retain its new western

Leaders of the Great Powers: Stalin and Roosevelt at the Teheran Conference, 1943 (*National Archives*)

lands. Informally, they also agreed that Poland, having lost eastern territory to the Soviet Union, would receive German lands along its western border. They reluctantly accepted Soviet territorial annexation and new Polish frontiers for the sake of the alliance, though in doing so they contributed to the creation of a new postwar Soviet sphere of domination in eastern Europe.

Third, the Soviet Union consented to enter the Asian conflict following victory in Europe. Roosevelt, heeding the advice of his military, was convinced that the Red Army was the only military force in position to defeat Japan in China and thus ease American casualties and bring the Asian war to a quick end. Stalin's promise of military assistance constituted for the U.S. president a major achievement, for which he was ready to pay a high diplomatic price.

That price became terribly clear when the Allied leaders met at Yalta in February 1945 to discuss the future peace as well as the end of the war. Agreement on the disposition of German lands once the Nazis were defeated posed no problem; zones of occupation for the four European powers (including France) had emerged from discussions the previous year. Berlin was also divided among the Allied forces, though the city itself lay within the Soviet zone of eastern Germany that extended as far west as the Elbe River. Regardless of where troops from east and west met at war's end, these zones set the limits to the area they would subsequently occupy.

Collaboration in the war in East Asia also raised no serious disagreements. In exchange for a Soviet offensive in northern China and Korea, Stalin requested Japanese territory (Sakhalin, the Kuril Islands) and concessions in Chinese territory (the same as those the Russian Empire had possessed before the 1917 revolution). Roosevelt promised to obtain agreement to these concessions from Chiang's Nationalist government. He had become Stalin's collaborator in redrawing the boundaries of other states to satisfy Soviet territorial demands. Even the question of Soviet participation in the United Nations did not create serious problems, probably because Stalin concluded that Roosevelt's project, although useless to Soviet interests, posed no real threat. To this extent the Grand Alliance continued to function effectively.

Its limits were apparent when Poland was discussed. Roosevelt asked for Soviet acceptance of the principle of national self-determination and democratic elections. Stalin did agree to a Declaration on Liberated Europe promising free elections. But the statement left so many holes for Soviet evasion that, as one of Roosevelt's advisers told him, "you can drive a truck through it." Soviet domination in Poland could not be shaken by diplomatic declarations. Roosevelt asked for no more, however, so important to him was Soviet collaboration in the war against Japan. Historical debate continues on the failure of the United States to insist on real national self-determination for Poland. The imposition of a Soviet-backed communist regime in that country was probably not negotiable. When Roosevelt talked of a world of peace and great power collaboration, Stalin understood great power hegemony and spheres of influence. No real meeting of minds or permanent agreement could exist between statesmen of such differing convictions.

THE FALL OF THE GERMAN AND JAPANESE EMPIRES

The great battles of 1944 made the Alliance's power apparent to Allied and Axis states alike. In June the combined naval and land forces of the Western Allies opened a front on the Normandy coast of France. After weeks of fighting, American armored columns were able to begin a rapid offensive through central France, capturing along the way several hundred thousand German prisoners. In August Allied forces liberated Paris. The hope that Allied armies would be able to penetrate German territory that fall was frustrated by the failure of the British offensive through Belgium and the Netherlands. Germany had suffered a major defeat in the west, but the war remained still outside German territory.

In the east Germany suffered a defeat as overwhelming as the Normandy battle. Stalin assisted the Allied invasion by ordering a major Soviet offensive that June along the entire Central Front, then in western Russia. Hitler's instructions to the German Army were to fight without retreat, a hopeless task but one that his generals obeyed. The result was that the Red Army was able to defeat and to encircle most of the German military forces on the front, approximately three hundred thousand men. The destruction of the Central Front opened the Soviet path to Poland and to eastern Germany. By August its advance divisions had reached the outskirts of Warsaw. Despite Nazi fanaticism and the grim determination of German troops, Axis defeat was by then inevitable.

Reconstructing a war-torn Europe and East Asia was an Allied preoccupation in the last years of the war. The Soviet Union had its own plans to establish a sphere of influence over its neighboring states. Stalin talked of postwar "democracy" for these lands, but meant Soviet domination. The British government, under Winston Churchill, clung to the goal of reestablishing the British

Empire in territories lost during the war. The objectives of the United States were different as well. For President Roosevelt, the policy of "internationalism," first defended by President Wilson at the end of the First World War, set the guidelines for the postwar world order.

HIGHLIGHT: Internationalism

The dream that peace should reign among countries has existed for as long as modern states have waged war. In the nineteenth century, Western writers and political leaders committed to human rights and democracy formulated a new project for insuring peace among nations. Their theory, termed "internationalism," became the basis of President Woodrow Wilson's peace program to end the First World War. The tragic destruction and loss of life brought by that war convinced many Westerners that such a conflict must never again occur. It had to be "the war to end all wars." But for the dream to come true, it had to be based on a new system of international relations. Despite Wilson's failure, President Franklin Roosevelt revived in a modified form this view of a world at peace. It guided him in laying plans for the postwar international order.

Roosevelt's peace proposals drew inspiration from the core arguments of internationalism. With some reservations, he set out to end reliance on the principles of balance of power and "reason of state" to resolve conflicts among states. These guidelines had governed diplomatic relations since the seventeenth century. To change this system meant altering the very process by which states settled disputes and maintained peaceful international relations.

Those who defended the traditional system called themselves "realists." They argued that the foreign policy of states had to pay attention to the real power possessed by independent countries, not to programs for peace presented by visionaries and idealists. They observed that the process of international relations was often a struggle among sovereign states, since no higher law or binding moral code restrained the behavior of states. A government might hope for good will and cooperation from other states, but it had to be prepared for the possibility that one or several of them would prove a threat to its well-being.

The reasons for war that these "realists" cited were, first, that some leaders are always tempted to abuse their political power, particularly at the expense of foreign countries. Second, each state has a certain array of special needs and objectives that at times compete with those of other states. These interests of state dictate the guidelines of the foreign policy of any country, which is bound at times to have to confront another country whose interests clash with its own. A government might hope that negotiation and compromise would settle these disputes, but the ultimate defense of its interests, and first of all the defense of its people and territory, had to depend on its ability to defend itself in war. Realists for centuries had argued that individual states had to be the final arbiters of these interests. What they called "reason of state" was the only rational foundation of international relations. They recognized that powerful aggressive states might seek to dominate or even destroy other states by using the brutal methods of "power politics." To counter this danger they believed that alliances among states opposing this aggressor would maintain a stable balance of power, that is, counterbalance the might of the dominant state. Still, war remained an eventuality for which states had to be prepared.

Internationalist critics judged this defense of war intolerable and immoral. Long before the First World War had proven the destructiveness of modern war, they had condemned the realists for assuming that states were forever destined to struggle among themselves. They found inspiration in the liberal democratic ideology, especially its emphasis on human rights, and in economic trends of the nineteenth century that strengthened trade and financial cooperation among states. The First World War reinforced their conviction that they had to succeed in bringing a halt to wars that had become so destructive there could be no real victors or vanquished. Their belief in liberal democracy persuaded them that most human beings were reasonable and capable of understanding the importance of common interests shared by states and peoples. If the right democratic institutions and diplomatic methods of collective action were put in place, wars could be halted. Modern states had brought an end to feudal wars; internationalists proposed to do the same for wars among states.

The nineteenth century had given them special reasons to believe that their project was realizable. The spread of democracy placed power in the hands of masses of voters. They argued that the people had solid grounds to oppose a political leader who plotted military aggression, since their own lives and property would suffer most in the event of war. Internationalists believed that the interests of economic leaders also lay in the preservation of peace, particularly in conditions of a growing international economy. They expected that economic interests and common sense would combine to create an enlightened public opinion throughout Western countries. Generals or dictators, unaccountable to the people, were the likely source of conflict. They had to be restrained, but the means to that end was international cooperation. All peaceable states ought to agree among themselves to insure the security of each state, for by standing together, they would dissuade aggression. They had to be prepared to act collectively, however. Their individual sovereignty (the right to act independently) would at times have to be subordinated to the need for collective action against aggressors. The preservation of peace among nations was certainly worth this sacrifice.

President Woodrow Wilson had been the first leader of a great power to make internationalism the core of his foreign policy. When at the close of 1916 he had called on the warring European states to end their fighting, he made clear his vision for the future. A "just and secure peace," he had argued, would end the "organized rivalries" of the balance of power. Most important, it had to recognize the right of peoples to choose their own governments, whose "just powers derive from the consent of the governed." "National self-determination" was the foundation for peaceful governments. Finally, these governments had to be prepared to cooperate in an organized "community of nations" charged with settling international disputes. It was an extraordinary proposal, called for by the catastrophe brought on the West by the war.

"United Nations" in War: Wartime Poster, 1943 (*Poster Collection/Hoover Institution*)

Wilson created a visionary plan for international relations that did not vanish with his political defeat after the war. "Wilsonianism" was the term by which political leaders in the United States often referred to internationalism. Franklin Roosevelt revived its essential elements. He appealed in the name of world peace to the American people to accept the terrible sacrifices of the new war. He promised that its victorious outcome would restore freedom and allow peoples around the world to proceed with the creation of their own nation-states. The League of Nations ceased to exist at the outbreak of the Second World War, but the Allies agreed to create at war's end the United Nations (U.N.). Once again, the U.S. took the lead. At the founding of the U.N. in 1945, President Truman reaffirmed his state's commitment to internationalism, which in his folksy words meant that "no matter how great our strength, we must deny ourselves the license to do always as we please" in decisions of war and peace.

Wilson's vision appeared closer than ever to fulfillment in the reordering of global relations that followed the collapse of Western empires, then the end of the Cold War. The U.N.'s membership grew rapidly with the entry of new nation-states. The dream of an international concert of states to protect peace grew stronger when, in the last decade of the twentieth century, peacekeeping forces operating under the United Nations flag and at the orders of the Security Council appeared in country after country where civil wars or regional conflicts threatened the lives of the population and the security of the region.

The United Nations's most ambitious peacekeeping effort came in Iraq. Following its defeat in 1991 by a coalition of states fighting under the U.N. flag, it took charge of destroying Iraq's weapons of mass destruction and supervising the economic embargo placed on the country's international trade. The 2003 war against Iraq ended that attempt at international containment of an aggressive state. Claiming that the United Nations was incapable of controlling Iraq's armaments and that Iraq was a threat to peace, President George W. Bush ordered U.S. armed forces (aided by those of Great Britain) to invade Iraq to overthrow the regime of Saddam Hussein (see Chapter 8). At the beginning of the twenty-first century, internationalism was a still a contested doctrine for international peace.

The Liberation of Europe

The Grand Alliance had promised cooperation both for war and for the peace to follow. More important than agreements among the Allies, however, was the location of Allied troops at war's end. Europe was divided between Soviet and Western armies. While new Allied plans were laid for a common future for Europe, a kind of partition of Europe had already begun to emerge. In the background, the United States and Great Britain proceeded on their own to set up new institutions for international trade that they judged vital for the recovery of the market economies of the West. In economic terms, the communist and capitalist world remained deeply divided.

Among Western statesmen, Roosevelt had the greatest potential influence for the rebuilding of postwar Europe. The American political system placed the formulation of foreign policy in his hands alone, although it left to Congress and the voters the decision to allocate the funds needed for foreign ventures. He was an astute politician who had lived through the hopes and the deceptions of President Woodrow Wilson's peace policies at the end of the First World War. The lesson he drew from that experience was that U.S. wartime influence would not extend into peacetime. The American people, through their elected representatives, would demand an immediate return to peacetime conditions—the demobilization of U.S. troops and an end to foreign aid. In these circumstances the best Roosevelt could achieve would be a peace that was self-enforcing, that is, one that did not require permanent U.S. military commitments. He held out the promise of national self-determination for lands occupied by the Axis, even when these areas had previously been Western colonies. He looked forward to collaboration among the Great Powers within the framework of a new international peacekeeping organization, to be called the United Nations.

Roosevelt's internationalist peace plans included the establishment of an international economy based on free trade and a stable financial system. The industrial regions of the world had suffered greatly in the global depression of the 1930s. It became clear to economists and government leaders in Britain and the United States that one major cause of the depression had been the collapse of international trade, brought about by high tariffs and the absence of international funding. In the midst of war, U.S. leaders looked ahead to peacetime when they hoped to promote stable global economic expansion. The growth of trade would stimulate production and new technology, which were of benefit both to the war-torn countries and to the American economy. Meeting in the United States in late 1944, British and American officials reached agreement for the development after the war of new institutions for the support of international trade. This "Bretton Woods system" promised a reinvigorated global market economy, buttressed by U.S. economic wealth.

As Allied forces moved toward central Europe, the key role of occupation authorities in restoring or founding nation-states became evident. France was the most important country liberated by the Normandy invasion. After its defeat by Germany in 1940, it had lost its independence. Its economy was in the service of the German war machine and its people were subject to German exploitation. As the years of occupation passed, opposition to the Germans grew and underground resistance forces gathered together in the Free French movement. Its leader was General Charles de Gaulle, a traitor to his army in 1940 when he refused to accept the armistice with Germany and fled to London. By 1944 his dedication and eloquence in the cause of French freedom had placed him at the head of the noncommunist movement opposing the Germans.

De Gaulle had much greater difficulty obtaining the recognition of Roosevelt. The American president believed that "national self-determination" meant the choice of new leadership by free elections, not by self-proclamation. Yet de Gaulle was the major noncommunist political leader in France, committed to free democratic government. This agreement on basic political principles, plus the popularity of de Gaulle among the French people and Resistance forces, finally earned him the diplomatic backing of the Western Allies. The French resistance forces also accepted his leadership. He in turn had to agree to their demand for substantial internal reforms in what they hoped would be a new France. In a manner consistent with the principle of national self-determination, France recovered its independence.

SPOTLIGHT: John Maynard Keynes

Until the Englishman John Maynard Keynes (1883–1946) revolutionized economic theory, economists devoted themselves to the scholarly study of what was known as the "dismal science." Classical economics had no role to play in public life, and its specialists sought no place there. They referred to their theory as "laissez-faire" (meaning to "let alone") capitalism, because they believed that the laws governing economics operated, and had to operate, without any outside intervention. Prosperity and depression followed one another in a natural cycle as inevitable

Lord Keynes addressing Conference meeting

Preaching the International Economy: John Maynard Keynes Addressing the Bretton Woods Conference 1944 (*UPI/Bettman*)

as the seasons. When depression hit, bankruptcies and unemployment spread widely. Recovery would again lead to renewed prosperity, businesses would again prosper and the laboring population would enjoy better times. But no one could alter the cycle.

Keynes challenged that theory and made economic well-being a central concern for governments. He was a rebel in his chosen career, just as he was a rebel in his personal life. He belonged as a young man to the Bloomsbury circle of bohemian intellectuals in London, who defied Victorian moral conventions for the sake of personal liberty. Among them, Keynes had no need to hide his homosexuality. His brilliance as an economist earned him a place among English negotiators at the Versailles peace settlement in 1919. Afterward, he taught quietly at Cambridge University, marrying a Russian ballerina and now and then speculating (and usually winning) on the stock market.

His real achievement came when he sought to explain the fundamental economic problems caused by the depression of the 1930s. In those grim years he challenged classical economical theory by arguing that the cyclical evolution of capitalist economies did not necessarily (or even ordinarily) lead to full employment and long-term stability. The promise of laissez-faire capitalism to restore prosperity after major declines in economic activity was false. He spelled out his own theory in a book titled *The General Theory of Employment,* published in 1936. It created an uproar among economists, for it proposed that governments had the responsibility to use their financial resources (and the advice of economists like himself) to reform the imperfect capitalist system. His theory quickly attracted political leaders looking desperately for a solution to the social crisis caused by the depression. Like President Roosevelt, Keynes sought to protect the freedom of the market economy and liberal democracy on which it depended. At a time when communism and fascism were attracting supporters everywhere (including students at Cambridge University where he taught), he wished to find a "middle way between the anarchy of laissez-faire and the tyranny of totalitarianism."

The Second World War carried him one step further to consider the entire global economic system. Recovery from depression and war required a new system of international trade and financial cooperation. The United States had to occupy the central position if the postwar world was to avoid the chaotic, destructive protectionism and economic stagnation of the 1930s. The British and U.S. governments welcomed his help. He was, they recognized, a "true genius." At negotiations in 1944 during the Bretton Woods conference in New Hampshire, he played a key role in bringing agreement on the international institutions to stimulate reconstruction and multilateral trade after the war. That system did not begin full operation until after his death. It grew in importance to become a central feature of the late-twentieth-century global economy. Keynes had helped build that "middle way" on which the Western world depended.

The Soviet Union in Eastern Europe

Although the Western leaders urged national self-determination throughout occupied Europe, Stalin accepted it only where it suited Soviet power politics. His objectives and methods of building peace differed fundamentally from those of Roosevelt. The difference lay in the use of power. Whereas the U.S. authorities set out to create a new world order that would require the least possible U.S. international intervention, the Soviet leader proceeded to deploy his military power to ensure diplomatic or political domination in the areas around the Soviet Union liberated by the Red Army. As in the 1930s, Stalin honored the principle of power politics to "respect only the strong" and remained as suspicious as before of the "capitalist jungle." The war against Germany had temporarily allied capitalist states and the Soviet Union, but in his opinion the fundamental antagonism between the two social systems remained. In Stalin's world view, applied even more ruthlessly in his dealings with fellow Communists, no one could be trusted of their own free will to work for the common good. He recognized only political and military power.

He was true to these convictions in his dealings with his wartime allied states. He had to respect the might of the West, especially the United States with its undamaged, productive economy, great navies, and enormous air power. The Soviet Union had been bled dry and strained to the utmost to support the Red Army. For that reason, however, he assigned first priority to the strengthening of the Soviet international position. Even before the war was over Soviet scientists had begun work on nuclear weapons (spies in the United States had passed on word of the development of an American nuclear bomb). Of immediate importance to Allied relations, Stalin judged indispensable the creation of a Soviet sphere of domination around his country.

By 1943 he had begun to assemble the political and diplomatic parts of a postwar protective zone on the Soviet western borders. Its essential condition was that the small neighboring states renounce their independence in foreign relations. The Czech government-in-exile in London understood the future shape of central Europe. In 1943, it proposed to the Soviet Union diplomatic agreements by which the Czechs accepted Soviet international leadership in exchange for their internal freedom. Stalin agreed to the proposal. When the Red Army liberated Czechoslovakia, it passed control over to this government, which proceeded to reconstruct a parliamentary democracy and coalition government. In 1945 Stalin looked for diplomatic recognition of Soviet power, not communist revolution in Czechoslovakia. Realism, not communist ideology, dictated these agreements.

Where communist forces enjoyed substantial power Stalin was prepared to accept their rule on the condition that they too submit to Soviet leadership. Yugoslavia had by 1945 come under the control of the guerrilla forces under the leadership of Tito and his Yugoslav Communist Party. From their mountain bases they proceeded to occupy the country following the passage of the Red Army. Implementing their revolutionary plans, they immediately set up, on the Soviet model, a one-party dictatorship and a federal state made up of national republics to govern their multiethnic population. At Soviet insistence they accepted economic agreements providing cheap raw materials from their land for the reconstruction of the Soviet Union.

Events in Poland clearly revealed to the West Soviet aims in eastern Europe. Poland provoked the greatest controversy among the Allies even before war's end. When the Red Army reached Polish territory in 1944, the Soviet occupation authorities immediately began eliminating the remnants of the noncommunist resistance forces. At the end of the year they placed the Polish Communist Party at the head of a new provisional government. The U.S. and British governments protested this mockery of national self-determination in

Poland. Their diplomatic efforts to protect Polish democracy were half-hearted, but they probably had no means to force a change in Soviet policy. Stalin's determination to dominate Poland was non-negotiable.

In the spring of 1945, the Allied armies defeated the remnants of the once-mighty German army. German generals kept the bulk of their troops in the east in an effort to halt the Soviet offensive. By April Western armies were advancing rapidly through central and northern Germany. Churchill, already foreseeing competition with the Soviet Union over European spheres, urged that Western troops occupy Berlin and Prague. These were politically important cities far within areas designated for Soviet liberation. General Dwight Eisenhower, Supreme Allied Commander, refused to alter his military priorities to make room for political calculations. In April Roosevelt died, replaced by his vice president, Harry Truman, an inexperienced former senator from the Middle West. The only course of action open to the new president was to follow Roosevelt's guidelines. After Hitler's suicide in late April, German leaders capitulated to the Allies. The European war ended in early May 1945, with Soviet troops in Berlin.

In July, Western forces in eastern Germany pulled back to allow the Soviet army to occupy its full zone. Carrying out their part of the occupation agreement, Soviet authorities opened to Western troops access to their half of Berlin, which became their occupied zones of the city. Demilitarization and denazification started, and arrangements for the imposition of reparations began in all areas of the defeated land. The German state had ceased to exist. What took its place depended on the four occupying powers, for the time being cooperating still as Allies.

Victory in East Asia

The war in the Pacific followed a very different course. It continued until the end to be primarily a

Allied Victory in Europe: Soviet Red Flag Atop the Reichstag, Berlin, May 1945 (*Hoover Institution*)

naval war. In early 1945 the British finally launched an offensive into Japanese-occupied Burma from India. The British Empire's greatest colony was India. In the century since the British conquest, Indians had become an integral part of colonial rule, serving both throughout the civil service and at all ranks of the Indian Army.

Nationalist opposition in India to British rule had by then become a powerful force. It was centered around the coalition movement called the Indian National Congress, led by Mohandas Gandhi and Jawaharlal Nehru. Gandhi was responsible for giving the Congress its mass following, drawn to his inspirational teachings of national rebirth of India. He had successfully argued in the Congress against Indian participation in the war against Japan. For that he and the other

Congress leaders were kept in jail throughout the war.

But taking their place in aiding the British was a movement that spoke for the millions of Muslims in India. This Muslim League feared that Congress, made up largely of people of Hindu background, would worsen the condition of the minority Muslims. In collaborating with the British, the League looked forward to a free, but divided Indian subcontinent where a Muslim state they wished to call Pakistan would govern the areas where most Muslims lived. The impending, tragic partition of India was already moving forward.

While the war continued, Indians serving the British remained loyal to their imperial rulers. The Indian Army fought for its British commanders in

Asia, the Middle East, and Europe. The Indian civil service performed its duties as expected. Operating from India, the supreme commander of Southeast Asia, Lord Mountbatten, prepared for the offensives that would retake the lost British, Dutch, and French colonies of Burma, Indonesia, and Indochina. Before his forces could proceed beyond Burma, U.S. nuclear bombs exploded over two Japanese cities and Japan capitulated unconditionally.

The U.S. naval offensive had begun in 1943. The previous year U.S. naval forces, in battles in the Coral Sea and west of Hawaii near Midway Island, had blocked Japanese efforts to destroy the U.S. fleet in the Pacific. Instead, the Japanese navy suffered serious losses in those battles, especially to the aircraft carriers that proved the decisive weapon in that far-flung war. Within a few months the U.S. Pacific fleet was superior in number and power to the Japanese ships. Gradually, U.S. naval and marine forces moved westward back across the Pacific, "island hopping" to establish ports and air bases closer and closer to Japan. In 1944 they controlled the seas as far west as the Philippine archipelago. That year, army divisions under General MacArthur's command reconquered the former U.S. colony. By the end of 1944 the U.S. Air Force controlled the skies over the islands and operated from bases close enough for massive bomber attacks of Japan. Maritime commerce had been destroyed by U.S. submarines, depriving the Japanese military of vital raw materials. General MacArthur's next objective was the invasion of Japan itself, where bitter fighting was expected before the Japanese surrendered.

In July 1945, the Japanese war cabinet began to consider peace negotiations. Military leaders defended a policy of war to the death to protect the honor of their country and their emperor. Other leaders sympathetic to peace negotiations continued to count on Soviet neutrality and Soviet mediation to obtain from the United States essential peace conditions, principally the protection of

the emperor. They were misguided on all counts. Stalin was preparing for Asian war and the United States adhered to its demand of "unconditional surrender."

The U.S. war in the Pacific was in its own way total war. Hatred of the Japanese was high, particularly when stories of Japanese mistreatment of Allied prisoners of war appeared. In the battles of 1944, many Japanese soldiers fought to the death, refusing to surrender in the face of hopeless odds. Their determination further strengthened the U.S. policy of total war. Japan's defeat was to come in part through massive land offensives by the Soviet Union in north China and by the United States in Japan. But in the summer of 1945, the U.S. Air Force acquired a weapon of unimaginable power.

American development of the atomic bomb had first begun out of fear that Nazi Germany would develop the bomb. Germany's defeat in May and the successful testing of the bomb in July 1945 presented the U.S. leaders with a new choice. A weapon of unprecedented power was available for use in the war on Japan. Its use was no longer a matter of deterring the enemy, but an opportunity to destroy an opponent defenseless against air attack but prepared to fight a land war to the death. The U.S. government chose with little hesitation (only some of the scientists advising restraint) to authorize its use by the U.S. Air Force. On August 6, one bomb obliterated the city of Hiroshima, killing more than one hundred thousand people; a second destroyed much of Nagasaki on August 9. The world had entered the age of nuclear war.

The Soviet land war against Japan ended almost as soon as it began. On August 8, the Red Army invaded Manchuria. Stalin had respected to the letter his agreement with Roosevelt at the Yalta Conference to begin war in Asia three months after hostilities ceased in Europe. Japanese forces were overwhelmed by the Soviet invasion, which swept down Manchuria and into Korea. Despite inevitable defeat, a week elapsed before the Japanese war cabinet accepted surrender. On August 14 Emperor Hirohito personally ordered the empire's armed forces to capitulate for, in his words, "the unendurable must be endured."

The Soviet offensive and the nuclear bombing brought the Asian war to an abrupt end. U.S. invasion of the Main Islands proved unnecessary. The debate still continues whether the use of the atomic bomb was needed to avoid that invasion. Historical evidence now suggests that it was. The emperor and his advisers, in whose hands lay the choice of war or peace, continued to reiterate their demand that the Japanese people "smash the enemy nations." Their appeals to carry on the war resembled Hitler's refusal to accept defeat. The Japanese population appeared ready to obey. The two atomic bomb attacks, coupled with the Soviet invasion of Korea and Manchuria, forced the emperor to change sides and order the surrender. The concern of American military experts that without use of the bomb the war might endure for months, bringing with it enormous U.S. casualties, was well founded.

The Second World War had ended. The Allied countries had defeated the mightiest military empires in history, but at a terrible cost.

SUMMARY

The Second World War completed the slow process, begun in the previous war and the depression, that ended the era of empires. The defeat of Japan brought down its overseas empire; its destruction was followed soon by the collapse of the empires of the Western states in southeast Asia. Japanese authorities had exploited and mistreated the peoples of their empire; yet their initial victory, coupled with their claim to defend "Asians" from Western imperialism, proved an effective means to undermine the authority of the Western colonial regimes that had once ruled these lands. In August of 1945 nothing was left of the Dutch and French empires. The British Empire was weakened and discredited in the eyes of many of its former subjects. The capitulation of the Japanese Empire was complete. Everywhere its troops prepared to leave the conquered lands where they had ruled until the war's end. A vacuum of power opened up in that enormous area, and no one knew what its future would be.

The destruction produced by Nazi rule in Europe and the long war was appalling. Many millions of people had been reduced to misery, and governments lacked the means to help them. Nearly fifty million civilians and military personnel died in the war, a grim measure of the scale of devastation. The United States, which suffered relatively few casualties, emerged the most prosperous and powerful country in the world. But the Soviet Union, despite the suffering of its peoples, possessed the military and diplomatic strength of an international power. The war had created a worldwide division of spheres of influence dominated by the two states, each of whom had very different plans for a new global order.

DATES WORTH REMEMBERING

1937 Sino-Japanese war
1939 German war in Europe
1940 German conquest of western Europe
1941 German-Soviet war
1941 U.S. entry into European and Asian wars
1942–43 Stalingrad battle
1943 Teheran Conference
1944 Normandy landing
1944 Warsaw uprising
1944 Liberation of the Philippines
1944 Bretton Woods agreement on international trade
1945 Yalta Conference
1945 Soviet war on Japan
1945 Hiroshima atomic bomb explosion
1945 End of Second World War

RECOMMENDED READING

Twentieth-Century World

Raymond Betts, *Uncertain Dimensions: Western Overseas Empires in the Twentieth Century* (1985). A thematic study of the development in the twentieth century of European colonial empires until their collapse.

Eric Hobsbawm, *The Age of Extremes: A History of the World, 1914–1991* (1995). A personal, critical view of this century.

War in Europe

*Robert Conquest, *Stalin: Breaker of Nations* (1991). The best short biography of the secretive dictator, stressing his political life.

*Robert Devine, *Roosevelt and World War II* (1969). A brief study of Roosevelt's wartime foreign policy.

Lloyd Gardner, *Spheres of Influence: The Great Powers Partition Europe, from Munich to Yalta* (1993). Despite the lurid title, a careful study of European diplomacy from 1938 to 1945.

Charles Hession, *John Maynard Keynes: A Personal Biography of the Man Who Revolutionized Capitalism and the Way We Live* (1984). A respectful life history of the great economist.

John Keegan, *The Second World War* (1989). A succinct military history, beautifully illustrated, of the war in Europe and Asia.

*Voytech Mastny, *Russia's Road to the Cold War: Diplomacy, Warfare, and the Politics of Communism,* *1941–45* (1979). The best study of Stalin's wartime foreign policy.

War in Asia

Herbert Bix, *Hirohito and Modern Japan* (2000). A new, very critical story of Emperor Hirohito's responsibility for the Japanese war.

*John Toland, *The Rising Sun: The Decline and Fall of the Japanese Empire, 1936–1945* (1970). A critical history of the Japanese military's effort to conquer and hold an East Asian empire.

Memoirs, Novels, and Visual Aids

*Thomas Keneally, *Schindler's List* (1982). The dramatized story of an ordinary German manufacturer at Auschwitz who became a hero to the Jews (subject of a 1993 movie).

Primo Levi, *Survival in Auschwitz* (1959); and *Moments of Reprieve* (1986). Memoirs of one prisoner's terrible year at Auschwitz.

Guy Sajer, *The Forgotten Soldier* (1971). The vivid memoirs of an Alsatian volunteer in the German army, who survived the army's great retreat from Russia to the Baltic.

Saving Private Ryan (1999). The best movie version to date of the Normandy Landing and the chaos of the enormous battle that followed.

The World at War. Outstanding BBC series (in sixteen parts) on the Second World War (available through <http://www.shop.pbs.org>).

(*Indicates book available in paperback.)

Chapter 2

The Cold War and the End of Western Empires

Outline

Highlight

Spotlight

The Second World War left in its wake the ruins of Western empires. Across much of the world, recovery from war meant rebuilding lives, rethinking human relations, and reconstructing economic and political institutions on new foundations. The human scale of suffering defied imagination, and its impact was felt throughout Europe and East Asia. The political disorder at war's end called for new solutions. Nationalist parties in lands freed from Japanese occupation demanded more forcefully than ever before the end of colonial rule. In some cases, they were able to negotiate independence with their colonial rulers; in other areas, their demands were rejected by imperial authorities. The result was the outbreak of new conflicts, called by their anticolonial leaders "wars of national liberation." In those tumultuous years, reform and revolution dominated political life in Europe and Asia.

The vacuum of power left in Europe after the collapse of the Axis states opened the way for the United States and the Soviet Union to take the lead in reordering European relations. In eastern Europe, reconstruction proceeded in large measure according to the wishes of Soviet authorities and the political goals of communist parties. In western Europe, severe economic shortages and fears of Soviet domination combined to make these countries diplomatically and economically dependent on the United States. Political and human conflicts added to diplomatic insecurity to complicate enormously the peacemaking. Latent fears of a global communist revolutionary conspiracy reemerged in the West, replacing the idealized wartime picture of a loyal Soviet ally. In the Soviet Union, official pronouncements revived the specter of the capitalist-imperialist menace from the Western states. On both sides, the reappearance of this hostile language indicated the breakdown of wartime good relations and reinforced the barriers standing in the way of constructive agreements for postwar peacemaking.

The new conflict between the Soviet Union and the United States produced its own grim vocabulary. The term "Iron Curtain" suggested that an impenetrable wall divided Europe, split apart by communist seizure of power in the states of eastern Europe. The overwhelming military and economic superiority of the United States and the Soviet Union in their respective spheres earned them the label of "superpowers." Soon, the expression "Cold War" captured the ominous character of the hostile relations between the two sides, not actually at war but mobilizing their military and diplomatic forces in anticipation of a new conflict in Europe or East Asia. This global confrontation presented U.S. political leaders, little experienced in power politics and global relations, with complex questions. What was the nature of the conflict? Was the threat communism or was it Soviet power? What areas constituted a vital interest to the United States, and where should U.S. support be directed?

The U.S. response to these new circumstances was a peacetime strategy of foreign involvement in the diplomatic and economic reconstruction of Europe and Asia. Baptized "containment," it set the guidelines for U.S. diplomatic and political policies for more than forty years. The Cold War fueled an arms race between the two superpowers. Although the acute phase of hostility ended in the mid-1950s, the failure of postwar peacemaking and the continued U.S.-Soviet rivalry in later decades gave a warlike character to the relations between the superpowers for almost a half-century.

POSTWAR EUROPE

The empires of France and Great Britain survived the war, but their decline had already begun. The real victors in the war, the United States and the

Soviet Union, were opposed to colonial empires. They had given encouragement to anticolonial movements during the war. When they joined in helping create the United Nations, their representatives insisted on full representation for non-Western states. They both repeated, in very different terms, their support for the liberation of the colonies of the Western empires. Their cooperation quickly ended, but the impetus to decolonization remained.

The hopes nurtured during the years of war for rapid peacemaking proved short-lived. They rested on the assumption that the Allies would continue to cooperate once victory was won. The United States under Roosevelt had anticipated that a modified version of internationalism would govern relations among the victors, that is, that they would recognize a common goal in collaborating both to encourage national self-determination in liberated lands and to work within the United Nations to help preserve the peace. The Soviet policy of a postwar sphere of influence depended for its full success on Western agreement for communist domination of an area around the Soviet Union so vast it resembled a new Soviet empire. Neither plan was effective. The alliance fell apart, and conflict replaced cooperation.

The End of Western Empires

The remaining Western empires lost their colonies one after another in the postwar period. The dramatic change came swiftly in Asia, more slowly in Africa. Pressure for decolonization came from the colonial peoples, from Soviet and U.S. political leaders, from the United Nations, and from within the imperial states themselves. After centuries of power, the British and French colonial empires disappeared. The long-term consequences altered the very nature of global relations.

The United Nations became, in the years after its formation in 1945, a forum for defenders of

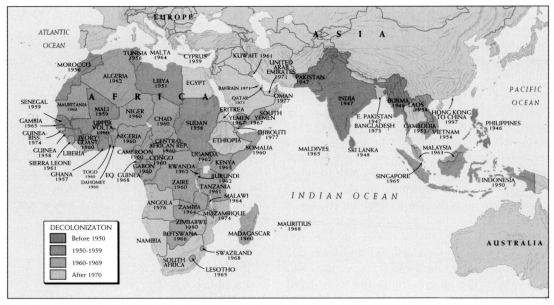

Decolonization of Western Empires since 1945

national liberation. It came into being through agreement among the Allied states. President Franklin Roosevelt was instrumental in obtaining the cooperation of the Allies for this undertaking. His views on decolonization guaranteed that the Preamble of the U.N.'s Charter recognized formally the "equal rights of nations large and small" and repeated the commitment, made by the League of Nations, to support "self-government or independence" for the mandated (now called "trustee") territories. He did, though, insist that the Charter give special powers to the major states. Roosevelt hoped that cooperation among the Allies would insure a long-lasting peace.

Although Roosevelt died before the United Nations came into existence, President Truman carried forward his initiative. Peacekeeping responsibilities belonged to the Security Council. There, Soviet and American delegates, along with the other permanent members, decided on key U.N. policies. These could also be proposed by the General Assembly, where delegates from all the world's sovereign states had seats. When the British government decided in 1946 it could no longer govern the Middle Eastern area of Palestine (a "mandated" territory), it let the U.N. decide how Palestine should be divided between Jewish and Arab states. Nationalist movements in non-Western lands found a sympathetic audience in the United Nations.

But the U.N. was vulnerable to antagonism between the Soviet Union and the Western states. The "veto" power given to the Security Council members (enabling any one of them to block U.N. action) opened the way for the U.S.–Soviet rivalry to paralyze the United Nations. Its only effective action to stop aggression came in 1950 when the Security Council, minus its Soviet member, condemned North Korea for its invasion of South Korea. Soldiers from twenty states fought North Korea under the U.N. flag, with the goal of keeping the Communists out of South Korea. Its intervention placed it squarely on the side of the West in the Cold War.

The recovery from war of the Western states created pressures as well for loosening colonial ties. The participation of the United States government in that reconstruction gave U.S. leaders an influential voice in the foreign policy of these states. The reconstruction of countries that had been liberated by the Western Allies lay in the hands of their elected governments. Western postwar policy in Europe rested on the principle of national self-determination, that is, that self-rule and political liberties offered the right path to stable recovery from war. It did not dictate the social and economic reforms that these governments should introduce and assumed that outside powers ought not meddle in their internal affairs. But U.S. foreign aid, especially the Marshall Plan launched in 1947, was a potent means to influence their foreign affairs. The government of the Netherlands discovered this unpleasant fact after it had launched a military campaign in the East Indies to defeat nationalist forces and restore colonial rule there. The U.S. threatened to cut off all foreign aid to that wartorn country unless the Dutch negotiated a peaceful withdrawal from their most valuable colony. For a few years, U.S. leaders made decolonization one of their highest priorities. Seeking to help create a new world order, they enlarged Wilson's 1919 internationalist program by insisting that colonial peoples should enjoy the "right to national self-determination."

Among the Allied governments, sympathy toward colonial peoples (and reluctance to continue imperial rule) was strong at war's end. Before the war the U.S. had promised its Philippines colony independence. In Great Britain, the Labor Party won national elections in 1945 on a program that included freeing colonial peoples of the empire. Similar views emerged in France. Defenders of imperial glory and power, such as Britain's elder statesman Winston Churchill, condemned this "betrayal" of empire. In France, the opponents of decolonization were able to call a halt (temporarily) to colonial liberation. Within European countries opinions were deeply divided on the pace and even desirability of freeing colonial peoples.

Both Great Britain and the United States intended that independence come to their Asian colonies by treaty agreement with their colonial subjects, and that the population be given the opportunity to vote on new leaders. In other words, liberation was to come according to Western principles of national self-determination. In Burma, a unified nationalist movement (strengthened by Japan's recognition of Burmese independence in 1942) accepted the offer of the British government to participate in the process. A similar situation existed in the Philippines, where supporters of independence agreed on the terms proposed by the United States.

The British discovered quickly that their withdrawal from colonial areas could bring bitter conflicts. The difficulties arose partly from an animosity toward the British imperialists, partly from deep divisions among the population on the future independent state. Palestine became an arena of irreconcilable disagreement between Jewish settlers, seeking a homeland there, and the Arab population opposed to any Jewish state (see Chapter 6). The British departure in 1948 left in its wake the makings of war between Arab states and the new state of Israel. Similarly, the British negotiators in India could not bring the two major nationalist parties, the National Congress and the Muslim League, to agree on terms for independence (see Chapter 4). Unable to keep the peace, the British forces left their great colony in 1947 in the throes of civil war.

Yet these tragic sequels to negotiated decolonization were hardly more destructive than the colonial wars of European states attempting to hold onto Asian colonies. The Netherlands had governed the East Indies for four centuries; its state-owned oil company, Royal Dutch, had discovered vast petroleum deposits there. In 1945, the Dutch were not prepared to yield this valuable colonial possession, and sent troops to reoccupy the vast archipelago. Indonesian nationalists organized guerrilla resistance; a colonial war dragged on for three years until the Netherlands accepted the inevitable, granting Indonesia its independence in 1949.

Twice France became embroiled in similar colonial conflicts. The first erupted in the French colony of Indochina, where nationalists and communists had in 1945 renounced all ties to France. Negotiations began with the French government, but in 1946 French military forces, backed by pro-empire politicians in France, set out to destroy the independence movement. That war lasted until 1954, when in its turn the French government acknowledged that it could not defeat the communist rebels. France's second, and bloodiest war was still to come. The Algerian war, begun in 1954 to repress an anticolonial rebellion, was the last attempt to preserve one small part of the French Empire. France's army generals were so committed to this cause that they became key players in organizing a revolt against their government when they learned of negotiations with the Algerian rebels in 1958. Their rebellion ended the short life of the Fourth Republic, created in 1945, and brought to power Charles de Gaulle.

Wartime leader of the French struggle against Germany, General de Gaulle agreed to return to power on the condition the French parliament write a new constitution for a presidential regime (somewhat like the U.S. system). Once this Fifth Republic began to function, he turned to the Algerian war. He was convinced that this colonial conflict undermined French unity and international prestige, both crucial to his plans for a new France. He sought for France the stature of great power in Europe and Africa, welcoming collaboration among nationalist leaders in France's colonies where he could find it, renouncing efforts to forcibly retain ties to lands where nationalists refused any ties. In 1960, his government launched plans for a "French Community" among France's African colonies, most of whose leaders agreed to cooperate. In North Africa, he concluded that, since his army could not defeat the Algerian rebels, he had to accept their demand for complete independence. Despite terrorist attacks by settlers and attempted revolts by forces within the French army, de Gaulle carried out his project to end French rule in Algeria in 1963.

Decolonization of the once-mighty European overseas empires continued until the 1970s. Colonial lands in Africa were last to reach the point of massive decolonization (see Chapter 5). The reason lay partly in the weakness of nationalist movements there, and partly in the reluctance of European imperial leaders to accept the possibility that African peoples were prepared for independence. One British colonial official painted a bleak picture of a population scarred by "ignorance and poverty, disease and widespread malnutrition, primitive cultivation and harsh natural conditions, hopelessly inadequate revenues and need for services of every kind." His argument was in many ways justified, but it was also a self-serving claim to continued colonial rule. Without intending it, he revealed how inadequate imperial rule had been to meet the human needs of these colonies.

But international and economic priorities in Europe dictated liberation for all the colonies, even African. In 1961, Belgium abandoned its Congo colony, largest of all African holdings. Great Britain and France pulled out of Africa in the same period. The Asian and African holdings of the Portugese Empire, the first European overseas empire, were the last to obtain independence. Ruled by a dictator, General Salazar, until 1975, Portugal had sent troops to suppress nationalist rebellions in its African colonies of Angola and Mozambique, and its East Indies colony of East Timor. But when a democratic government took over from Salazar in the mid-1970s, one of its first acts was to free these lands. By then, the only reminder in Europe of that imperial age was the presence of migrants from their former colonies. They left their homes in search of better jobs in Europe with, as their most important entry card, a knowledge of the languages of their former colonial rulers. Slowly, in conditions of either peaceful negotiation or war, the European colonial empires in Asia and Africa gave way to nation-states.

Western Europe's "New Deal"

At war's end the European peoples had to turn their principal efforts to their own recovery. The terrible destruction left in the wake of liberation called for ambitious reconstruction, not just of the physical framework of an industrial economy but also of social relations in a more humane society. Hopes and plans looked to a better life for the entire population, and political leaders sought to satisfy these expectations for social welfare. As a result, labor obtained a greater voice in industrial affairs.

Women became active political leaders and new family policies provided state support for child care. The postwar economic reforms in countries such as Great Britain and France created what is known as "mixed economies," that is, productive property partially nationalized (i.e., state-owned), partially in private hands. Expensive in the best of times, these reforms exceeded the financial resources of their still impoverished populations. Yet political leaders could not back down. They deeply believed in social justice for their people, whose demand for a "new deal" brought strong pressure for quick action. In those postwar years the governments in western Europe were concerned above all with rebuilding their own countries.

Ruins of European War: Budapest, Hungary, 1945 (*Hoover Institution*)

In Great Britain, the close of the war marked the beginning of momentous political and social changes under the leadership of the Labor Party. It called on British voters in 1945 to "face the future" by supporting its plan for democratic socialism. In the national elections that year, it overwhelmed the Conservative Party led by Winston Churchill. It took power at a critical time, for the war had resulted in the death of a million British citizens and had caused tremendous property loss, both to foreign investments and to domestic capital. A year later, it had to ask Washington for a four-billion-dollar loan, most of which paid for food and fuel imports. By the winter of 1946–47, the British government faced such a serious budgetary crisis that it could no longer pay for both its domestic reforms and its foreign obligations in India and the Middle East. Decolonization came, in part, out of this near bankruptcy. Social welfare and nationalization of basic industries had highest priority for the Labor government. Domestic interests came first.

Similar reform movements took power in other western European countries. The need to care for the health, education, and welfare of their populations put a heavy burden on their budgets and required careful planning. Foreign aid from the United States began to arrive by 1948, but it had to be spent with great care. In several countries, the urgent need for guidance in reconstruction led to greater government intervention in economic life than ever before. In France, this took the shape of state forecast planning. It did not seek, as in the Soviet Union, to replace free market forces by state command planning. Instead, its goal was rational use of the scarce resources for optimal economic growth. Railroads had to be rebuilt, and became the property of the French state. Their reconstruction followed the guidelines for modernization and electrification spelled out in the plan. Capitalism and state-run industries operated side by side in this new French mixed economy.

This reform movement in western European countries enjoyed the support of the majority of the population. It owed little to the example of Soviet socialism, which before the war had stood out as the only alternative to Western capitalism. After the war, the Soviet command economy and the prestige brought by Soviet victory over Nazi Germany won support from large numbers of Europeans. But Soviet expansionism and the revolutionary communist ideology appeared to most Europeans a new threat as dangerous as that Nazism had once posed. The Cold War was never far from the concerns of Europeans in the postwar years.

These fears were especially great in countries to the south of the Soviet Union. Immediately after the war the Soviet government demanded of Iran and Turkey special territorial concessions— land in northwestern Iran, and in Turkey control over the Straits from the Black Sea to the Mediterranean Sea. Stalin's expansionist ambitions extended to these southern borderlands. Land on the Iranian border would open to the Soviet petroleum industry greater access to the great oil fields of the southern Caspian. Forcing Turkey to give Soviet authorities oversight on ship passage through the strategic sea passage would satisfy a centuries-old tsarist objective. The leaders of both countries begged for support and aid from the Western Allies against their powerful northern neighbor. In 1946, Western protests ended Soviet pressure in Iran. Soviet interests there were not important enough to risk conflict with the West.

In Greece, the Cold War began with the revolutionary plans of the strong guerrilla movement led by the Greek Communist Party. In 1946, it mobilized its troops, armed and trained in the war against the Germans, in a civil war to seize power from the conservative government. The Greek Communists took inspiration and received military aid from Tito's communist regime in Yugoslavia. The Greek government obtained military and economic aid first from Great Britain, whose troops had fought there in the war. Then, when the British government concluded in late 1946 that it lacked the means to help, the Greek leaders turned to the United States. In this case, as in China, Stalin had serious doubts about the uprising. On his geopolitical map, both China and Greece belonged within the Western sphere. In early 1947, he privately warned visiting Yugoslavs that the Greek Communists were foolhardy to attack a government that could rely on the help of "the most powerful nation in the world." Revolutionary zealotry was not his approach to postwar global politics. Western observers imagined that Stalin ruled like a tyrant over the foreign communist parties as he did over the Soviet Union. It was a mistaken assumption but found justification in Stalin's ideological bombast and the communist uprisings in Europe and Asia.

The Making of the New Soviet Empire

At the close of the war, the Soviet Union was second only to the United States in military might. It was at the head of an international communist movement more vigorous than ever before. Its victory over Germany gave its leaders enormous influence in lands liberated by the Red Army. The war, however, had weakened terribly the Soviet people and their country. These two contradictory features—Soviet international strength and internal weakness—dictated Soviet international and domestic postwar policy.

Victory created the conditions for Soviet expansion, limited only by the strategic priorities of the Soviet Union and Stalin's recognition of U.S. military might. Recovery from the devastation of war called for massive Soviet investments and brought economic exploitation of the Soviet sphere as well as the continued sacrifices of the Soviet people. Stalin's determination to maintain Soviet military and diplomatic power was as great as before.

Although Stalin does not seem to have had a master plan for Soviet expansion, he did have certain minimum objectives. These included diplo-matic domination in the states along the new Soviet western and eastern frontiers. Soviet policy was expansionist within these limits. Stalin's foreign goals were opportunistic as well, for he was prepared to take advantage of communist revolutionary gains. His policies unsettled the balance of power in Europe and Asia and forced the Western states to reconsider their wartime practice of collaboration.

He remained deeply suspicious of the "capitalist camp." The United States had become, at war's end, the most powerful country among the democratic states. The techniques of power politics, that is, reliance on Soviet military and economic might to insure his country's security, continued to guide his foreign policy. He remained convinced, as he had stated first in 1931, that the "law of the jungle" dictated relations between the West and the Soviet Union. His country had emerged victorious in the war, and for this reason he had grounds to hope that the capitalist states would acquiesce in his new zone of domination. Still, he relied on the protection that his large land army gave him in East Asia and Europe.

His confidence in Soviet postwar might was undermined by the successful construction and deployment of the atomic bomb in the U.S. war on Japan. Faced with a potential enemy possessing such a devastating weapon, he could not assume that his armies would guarantee control of the new Soviet sphere in Europe and Asia. The lesson he drew from the Hiroshima explosion was a simple one. Gathering the Soviet scientists who had already begun nuclear weapon research, he exclaimed: "Hiroshima has shaken the world. The balance has been destroyed." Their secret instructions were to build a Soviet bomb immediately. The chances for peaceful relations between the former allies were dwindling even at the close of the war.

In the period between 1945 and 1947, Stalin had to take account of the political strength and revolutionary militancy of foreign communist parties. In Yugoslavia, Tito's forces immediately set up a party dictatorship and openly flaunted their admiration for Soviet socialism. Twice they attacked Western military planes flying over their western frontiers; Stalin suggested this was imprudent but said no more. Tito lent active support to the Greek Communist Party in its guerrilla war, despite Stalin's warnings of possible conflict with the West. In the early postwar years, Stalin gave only general guidance to foreign communist parties, some of whose leaders behaved in a far more revolutionary manner than he. Crucial to his cautious action was his knowledge of the devastation that the war had caused his country, and his determination to protect his country's newly won dominance on its western and eastern borderlands.

The war had caused great suffering among the Soviet people. The losses in life were so great no one has ever been able to calculate them accurately. The figure of twenty-seven million civilian and military dead, commonly repeated now, suggests the extent of suffering inflicted on the country. Large areas of western Russia were devastated, the cities reduced to rubble, the countryside stripped of its livestock, the mines flooded. So scarce were food reserves that when the 1946 harvest failed, famine swept the eastern regions. The Soviet government had to request Western food shipments (provided by the United Nations Relief and Recovery Administration) to feed its people.

Recovery required workers for rebuilding. Millions of men never returned from the war or came back disabled and unfit for work. One half of the draft-age men had either died or been seriously wounded in the war. Soviet troops, eleven million strong in 1945, were rapidly demobilized to provide labor for reconstruction. The Red Army declined to three million in 1948, smaller than Western observers believed at the time but still by far the most powerful army in the world. Stalin ended hopes in 1946 for better living conditions for the Soviet population when he proclaimed rapid growth of heavy industry the first priority. Industry was power, and it came before material comfort of the population. Women had to

Soviet Propaganda Poster for Eastern Europe: "For Peace, For a People's Democracy," 1948 (*National Archives*)

take on the heavy physical work of men, in the cities and in the countryside. Collectivization of all arable land remained the basis of Soviet agriculture, permitting the Soviet state to drain the resources of the collectivized farms (*kolkhoz*). Industrial growth did begin again, but at great cost to the people.

The lands occupied by the Red Army or dominated after the war by the Soviet Union had to provide resources for Soviet economic reconstruction. Before reparations ended East Germany alone furnished approximately $5 billion in agricultural and industrial supplies. Factories in the northern Chinese province of Manchuria, seized in the Soviet war against Japan, were dismantled and shipped back to the Soviet Union before the

Soviet troops withdrew in 1946, leaving behind an industrial wasteland. The states within the Soviet sphere had to accept Soviet purchase of their raw materials such as coal at prices far below cost. The Soviet authorities imposed a policy of economic exploitation within their sphere of domination regardless of whether the country was a former enemy, such as East Germany, or a postwar ally, like Poland and Yugoslavia.

Partition of Germany

The acute problems of reconstruction in central Europe brought together the human, political, and diplomatic conflicts that lead to the partition of postwar Europe. The hatred of other Europeans toward Germany extended beyond Nazism to the Germans themselves. Throughout eastern Europe, the new governments forcibly expelled in 1945–46 most Germans who had not already fled. The total number of German refugees probably exceeded ten million; most of them sought refuge in the western zones of Germany. At the same time, the millions of forced laborers taken into Germany during the war sought to return to their homelands or to emigrate to a new country. The Jewish survivors of the extermination camps looked to Palestine, while most Ukrainian and Russian deportees hoped for a new home in the West. These destitute peoples were concentrated in central Europe. Their care fell on the United Nations and the occupying powers, who were also obliged to prevent the inhabitants of the ruined German cities from dying of hunger and cold.

In 1945, the victorious Allies set about destroying the Nazi political and military system before constructing a new Germany. The wartime agreements included the dissolution of the Nazi movement, demilitarization, and an unspecified amount of reparations. The most prominent Nazis were put on trial in Nuremberg in the winter of 1945–46. Accused of crimes against humanity, all were found guilty by an international tribunal and most were executed.

The first serious East-West disagreement arose over issues of reparations. In their eastern zone of Germany, Soviet authorities claimed the region's agricultural production and mining output for their own desperate needs. Having seen their own palaces and museums destroyed and their contents shipped to Nazi Germany, they proceeded to seize as war booty valuable art collections belonging to German museums and to civilians. They demanded that Western authorities deliver to them large amounts of German industrial equipment as well. In the spring of 1946, the impoverishment of the German economy and growing suspicion of Soviet policies led the Western powers to refuse the Soviet authorities any additional goods from their zones. This conflict over the economic spoils of war revealed the importance each side attached to Germany. It was becoming less the enemy and more a front line between East and West. The zones were becoming territorial divisions.

In these circumstances U.S. authorities decided in 1946 to alter their German policy from punishment to reconstruction. This sudden change resulted both from their growing awareness of Soviet power in central Europe and from the economic burden of occupation. The cost of administering the zones grew as German living conditions worsened. A barter economy, in which cigarettes and soap were the most widely accepted medium of exchange, provided the essential items for those Germans with anything at all to trade. Prostitution flourished as desperate German war widows turned to the well-nourished occupation troops. The high cost of supplying the Germans in the American zone with minimum food, clothing, and heating—$700 million in 1946—made restoring German economic production an urgent affair for the U.S. government. The British state, faced with near-bankruptcy later that year, agreed to the new objectives.

In early 1947, the British and American occupying authorities united their two zones into one economic unit. Later that year, the French brought their zone in as well. The Western governments put into place a new economic policy for reconstructing that part of Germany under their control, disregarding the vehement objections of Soviet occupation authorities. That year the U.S. government declared that "an orderly and prosperous Europe requires the economic contribution of a stable and productive Germany." One-fourth of the country was excluded from that new policy. Translated into plain language, the new policy of the Western allies effectively partitioned Germany and marked the end of cooperation with the Soviet Union.

The paths of eastern and western Germany increasingly diverged. In the east, the Soviet authorities created a one-party regime dominated by the so-called Socialist Unity Party, run in fact by German Communists. Their treatment of their German subjects was brutal. Soviet occupation troops, knowing that no punishment would follow, were responsible for the rape of an untold number German women. These women were treated as war booty. Elections continued to be held but the Communists, backed by the Russians, held power in their hands.

Political reform in the western zones looked toward restoring parliamentary democracy. In provincial elections in 1947, voters preferred either the Social Democratic Party, which defended socialist reforms and favored a unified, neutral Germany, or the Christian Democratic Party, which advocated free-enterprise capitalism and reliance on the Western powers to prevent Soviet domination. Political life in eastern and western Germany was increasingly divergent, though in theory the country remained united.

Allied negotiations over Germany's future collapsed in mutual recriminations and accusations. The foreign ministers from the victorious powers met in 1947 to write peace treaties for the Axis countries. They could agree only on a treaty for Italy, never partitioned into occupation zones. Germany represented, for both Soviet Russia and the Western powers, a position of strength neither would concede. Responsibility for the failure to complete the German peacemaking process was shared by East and West, for neither side originally sought partition. Stalin may have looked forward to a united German state under Soviet influence but, failing in that objective, he resolved to keep hold of his eastern zone. The Western Allies sought a united democratic Germany outside Soviet control. When that goal appeared threatened by Soviet domination in eastern Europe, they clung to their zones. Partition came by default. It was a product of mutual hostility and the very unstable balance of power in central Europe.

Iron Curtain and Containment

In the two years following the end of the Second World War, American leaders became increasingly conscious that their wartime expectations for a postwar settlement in Europe were unrealistic. The U.S. policy of collaboration with the Soviets was incapable of yielding satisfactory agreements. The issue causing particular concern among western diplomats was the political reconstruction of eastern Europe. They had looked forward to a postwar settlement in which occupation forces would withdraw everywhere to permit democratic elections and the restoration of independent states. But the Soviet sphere of domination in eastern Europe stood in the way of a return to the independent nation-states of the 1920s. The manipulation of democratic elections by Communists in the East also heightened their concern. Communist parties were undermining rival political movements there to ensure their own political supremacy. Both diplomatically and politically, the fate of eastern Europe lay in Soviet hands.

In 1946, Winston Churchill set out to stir up U.S. public concern about Soviet expansion. He came to the United States that year as the guest of the U.S. president, Harry Truman, to speak out against a return to American isolationism. In his eyes, Soviet political and military might in

Europe was so overwhelming that no balance of power was possible without a U.S. commitment to help western European countries. A master of the English language, he drew a picture for his American audience of a continent cut in two by an "Iron Curtain" erected by communist forces in the east. His appeal for support won widespread backing among a U.S. public hostile toward communism and increasingly fearful of Soviet military strength. Churchill's aim was U.S. involvement in European affairs to counterbalance the political and diplomatic preponderance of the Soviet Union's armies and allied political parties in eastern Europe. He looked for a new balance of power in Europe. Only the United States could help.

Churchill's call came at a time when U.S. diplomats in Moscow were proposing a new policy toward the Soviet Union. The most influential spokesman was George Kennan, since 1944 stationed in the Moscow embassy and an outspoken critic of the wartime internationalist policy of conciliation and collaboration with the Soviet state. Kennan proposed a strategy, which he called "containment," to deal with the Soviet Union (see "Highlight," this chapter). His assessment of Soviet objectives appeared to fit Soviet postwar diplomacy in places such as Poland and Germany. His proposals coincided with deepening concern among U.S. leaders at the failure of negotiations with the Soviet Union.

In the spring of 1947, President Truman finally turned his back on the internationalist program to implement Kennan's policy of containment. To do so, he needed the approval of Congress and the American people. In those postwar years the public in the United States was immersed in dismantling the economy of war and returning to peacetime living conditions. The economy boomed, and foreign conflicts appeared distant affairs. Isolationism remained a strong presence in the country and in Washington.

To counter this force, Truman made his public appeal for a new global policy in the spirit of internationalism defended by Wilson and Franklin Roosevelt. He spoke out for the defense of political liberty and self-determination for peoples threatened by "aggressive movements that seek to impose upon them totalitarian regimes." He did not explain what strategic interests required the new policy, or what realistic limits he put to U.S. intervention in distant lands. He emphasized Western internationalist objectives, not U.S. national security, because of his need to win public and congressional backing for the new policy of containment. Its implementation required an end to isolationism and the readiness by Congress to approve peacetime foreign alliances and massive amounts of foreign aid. The American public remained more attuned to issues of democracy and self-determination for oppressed peoples than to problems of global balance of power. Nothing like Truman's policy of foreign alliances and aid had ever occurred in U.S. history.

In concrete terms, the new policy sought two diplomatic objectives. One was to strengthen particular states which were of strategic importance to the West and in need of outside economic and military assistance. In March 1947, President Truman proposed a program of foreign aid to the Greek and Turkish governments. Greece was in the midst of a civil war in which the Greek Communists were gaining ground. Turkey was threatened by Soviet diplomatic and military pressure. His "Truman Doctrine," intended to protect a Western sphere of influence, took on the appearance of a battle for democracy and against communism, not at all what diplomats such as Kennan sought. It did win public support, and the funds were voted quickly.

The second objective was the economic reconstruction of Europe and Japan. Speaking in mid-1947, Secretary of State George Marshall proposed that the United States, for the first time in its history, offer foreign aid to countries devastated by war. That year, the economic recovery of western Europe was progressing but at such a high cost it could not continue without outside help. The poor living conditions of the population there contributed significantly to social unrest, an important factor in the electoral strength of communist parties. In 1947, Japan and western Germany looked like important frontline areas along the borders of the Soviet Union's sphere.

The immediate goal of providing aid was economic recovery. The larger aim was to encourage the stabilization of economic conditions in independent states within a global economy. Marshall proposed that the United States provide large sums of monetary aid as well as economic supplies to those governments ready to meet certain conditions. The most important was that they coordinate their use of the U.S. funds and supplies, and make public their financial and economic needs. The Marshall Plan committed the United States to the expansion of the international economy and to the improvement of economic conditions of distant countries without any specific diplomatic rewards or expectation of repayment.

The new policies turned the United States away from isolationism and toward involvement in the international affairs of Europe and Asia.

Although the U.S. Congress did not approve the Marshall Plan until mid-1948, the offer received immediate support from all Western countries. The Soviet Union and its satellites refused, although not before both the Polish and Czechoslovak governments, under communist leadership, had publicly accepted the U.S. offer. Stalin's orders were outright refusal. The Marshall Plan was not overtly anticommunist; the Truman Doctrine was. Together they altered the very basis of relations with the Soviet Union. They brought the economic resources and potential military might of the United States to bear on areas where the line between Soviet and Western spheres of influence remained ill-defined. The rejection of Marshall Plan aid by eastern European states made clear that Europe was split in two.

HIGHLIGHT: Containment and Anti-Communism

The Soviet Union appeared to many Westerners a mysterious and threatening presence among the victorious powers of the Second World War. Its history had followed a very different path from that of the liberal democracies. Its leaders explained international relations using a language of class conflict completely unfamiliar to the western public. Winston Churchill had been so puzzled in 1939 by Soviet policies that he called the country "a riddle wrapped in a mystery inside an enigma." Its actions remained equally difficult to understand after the defeat of the Axis powers, when it had become a key player in global politics.

One solution to the riddle pointed to the role of communist ideology in Soviet politics. Communist leaders extolled Marxism-Leninism-Stalinism as the source of truth in history, politics, and human relations. Revolution was, in theory, the only path to progress. Since 1917, enemies of communism in America and elsewhere in the West had warned that the Soviet Union was the homeland of a revolution that, unless resisted, would destroy Western civilization. Their anticommunist persuasion made them fear an inevitable confrontation between the Soviet Union and the West. Preparations were urgent to resist the revolutionary offensive of the Soviet state and its supporters. It was not clear whether that attack would come from Soviet armies or a series of communist political conspiracies and insurrections. Whatever methods the communists used, the threat remained real as long as the Soviet Union existed. The anticommunist theory of Soviet international behavior foresaw inescapable conflict, even war, with the homeland of communism.

Another answer to the mystery of Soviet expansion came from lessons drawn from the history of the rise and fall of empires. In the past, aggressive new states had expanded by conquering and taking control of territories and peoples beyond their borders. Their leaders sought power and wealth through territorial aggrandizement and were prepared to use threats and force to achieve this goal. But these great empires had invariably met obstacles to their aggressive growth. Other states had by diplomatic or military means put up barriers to their rise to power, and their own internal weaknesses had with time forced them to contract and ultimately to fall. From this historical perspective, the Soviet Union had acquired the might and size of a great empire because its leaders were expansionist, like others before them. The communist ideology strengthened their suspicion of other states, but was not the explanation for Soviet territorial expansion. Their foreign policy did constitute a threat to the security and interests of independent neighboring states and to the hope for a stable peace. But a historical approach suggested that the reasonable response, as in earlier times, was to put together diplomatic and political restraints to contain this new imperial power.

The historical explanation of Soviet aggressiveness was the key idea behind the new U.S. foreign policy of containment. It appeared in the late 1940s at a time when Franklin Roosevelt's policy of collaboration and conciliation (termed "internationalism," since it relied on international negotiation and peacekeeping) had failed to bring fundamental agreements with the Soviet Union on peace in Europe and Asia. George Kennan, the principal architect of the new policy, argued that the old internationalist approach could not possibly produce satisfactory results. His observations and understanding of what he called "Soviet conduct" convinced him that Soviet leaders were deeply suspicious of the West and fanatically determined to overcome the perils that they believed threatened their rule.

In Kennan's opinion, the origins of their hostility lay in the historical experience of Russia. It had, time and again, confronted aggressive foreign enemies, whom only military might could repulse. He never made clear how the memories of this long past had shaped the suspicious world view of Soviet leaders. At times, he argued that their communist ideology bore a large measure of responsibility for their particular antagonism toward the capitalist states in the West, and that Stalin's own ruthless personality shaped Soviet political life. But his understanding of the Soviet Union drew above all on his conviction that it showed the historical traits of an expansionist empire. It relied on despotic authority within its borders, and was prepared to expand its diplomatic and political influence beyond those borders whenever weaknesses appeared in neighboring states.

Soviet hostility and expansionism stood in the way of a permanent peace settlement. Conciliatory gestures from the West had no chance of moderating the Soviet leadership's suspicions. They relied only on their country's military and diplomatic might, not international agreements, to protect Soviet interests. They were unresponsive, in Kennan's words, to the "logic of reason." But his long years of study of Soviet conduct convinced him also that they were not "adventuristic" in seeking to expand the power of their state and were prepared to avoid "unnecessary risks" when they encountered resistance. In other words, they understood the "logic of force." This formula gave Kennan the key to formulating a new long-term U.S. policy less appeasing than Roosevelt's internationalist approach, but less belligerent than the anticommunist agenda.

In the short term, his containment strategy called for resistance to, not conciliation of, the Soviet leaders' efforts to expand their sphere of domination around the borders of the U.S.S.R. Kennan had seen firsthand the consequences of appeasement of Nazi Germany in 1938 (he was stationed in Czechoslovakia during the Munich crisis). Containment was his answer to the danger of appeasement. It called for U.S. diplomatic backing and economic aid to certain strong, independent states that were capable of resisting Soviet expansionism. With U.S. support, these countries would become secure allies of the West and centers of regional stability. They included states in western Europe, the Middle East, as well as Japan. The threat from the Soviet Union was not military aggression. Kennan was persuaded that Soviet leaders recognized their military and economic weakness relative to the United States. He urged that diplomatic alliances and economic prosperity become the principal barriers to contain the Soviet Union.

This policy did not promise a quick solution to the conflict with the Soviet Union. International peace, as he understood the term, was a dream that could never be fully achieved. The protection of human rights was an ideal that for him ought not prevent collaboration with authoritarian states vital to containment. Allies ought not be excluded on grounds of their internal politics. Kennan did not believe that U.S. foreign policy had to respond to the communist ideology with an anticommunist crusade. He disagreed with anticommunists about the nature of the Soviet threat, and he disagreed with them as well about the correct U.S. response. His policy was in some respects too realistic. Presidents Wilson and Roosevelt had promised that the U.S. involvement in foreign wars furthered the cause of democracy and national self-determination. In other ways it was too restrained to win complete approval. Some U.S. leaders were sympathetic to the warnings of the anticommunists and favored a vast rearmament program and a system of global military alliances.

Yet his program remained the core of U.S. policy toward the Soviet Union. Despite moments of anticommunist fervor and crises that threatened nuclear war, the U.S. government did not attempt to force a Soviet retreat and resigned itself to the existence of a vast Soviet sphere of domination. It also initiated or accepted negotiated settlements, occurring more and more frequently after Stalin's death. Kennan had foreseen the day when this patience would be rewarded by the internal decline of Soviet power. Forty years after he proposed his policy, that decline began. It culminated a few years later with the complete collapse of the Soviet Union and the end of the Cold War. Containment succeeded beyond his wildest dreams.

THE COLD WAR IN THE WEST

By the winter of 1947–48, nothing remained of the Grand Alliance. Negotiations had ceased and had been replaced on both sides by public denunciations. The United States launched a massive program of economic aid to Europe, coupled with shipments of armaments to Greece and Turkey. Stalin remade the Soviet sphere of domination into a Soviet empire, where all important policies were decided in Moscow. Actual military conflict did not occur, but the talk was of war between the superpowers. From the perspective of several decades later, clearly Stalin never intended a military offensive against the West. To that extent, Western fears were exaggerated. He did, however, use the international position of strength acquired in the German war to impose the diplomatic and political domination of his state beyond its borders. In pursuing this expansionist policy, he must bear principal responsibility for the failure of the peace.

Western fears of Soviet military aggression played a part as well in the growing hostility between East and West. American leaders magnified Soviet military strength beyond its real level and argued that it, plus Soviet communism, was proof of Soviet aggressive intentions. Partly because they needed to win American support, partly because they mistook Soviet power politics for revolutionary communism, their new policy appeared a global struggle against communist expansionism. Out of this climate of hostility and fear emerged military alliances and the arms race.

Soviet Satellites and the Berlin Blockade

The new U.S. containment policies of 1947 brought a swift reaction from the Soviet Union. Predictably, Stalin pronounced these initiatives to be a threat to his sphere of domination in Europe. He responded by drastically strengthening Soviet control over the states in his sphere and by calling on other communist parties to resist the "aggressive" U.S. initiatives. Late in 1947, Soviet leaders organized a meeting of European communist parties, ostensibly to create a new international organization, the Communist Information Bureau (Cominform). Its real purpose was to make clear Moscow's somber view of the new threat from the West and to mobilize communist parties and governments within and outside the socialist camp for action. Reviving the rhetoric of war, Stalin's aide Andrei Zhdanov called for opposition to the Marshall Plan and to the "expansionist and reactionary policy" of the United States. He warned that a new "struggle against the U.S.S.R." had begun. His warning was clear: War by the capitalist powers on the socialist camp was possible. Communists had to rally to the defense of the socialist motherland.

The mobilization of international support for the Soviet Union moved in three directions. It brought Soviet control over communist parties and governments; it led to the elimination from power in the eastern European governments of the remaining noncommunists; it called for militant campaigns by communist guerrilla forces to

establish their own revolutionary regimes in areas where they had seized control. Czechoslovakia experienced the most dramatic political upheaval as a result of Stalin's Cold War policy in eastern Europe. In February 1948, the Czech Communist Party forced the democratic parties in the coalition government out of power, destroying parliamentary democracy and creating a single-party, communist dictatorship. It happened at the orders of Moscow. Behind the Iron Curtain, there could be no national self-determination.

Increased Soviet power within its sphere brought with it a secret campaign to dominate the communist parties in the area. It succeeded everywhere except in Yugoslavia. In that country the Yugoslav leaders understood national independence to be the fundamental condition of their revolution. Tito had protested in 1946 that his state was not part of anyone's "sphere of influence," though he did explain later that of course he did not have the Soviet Union in mind. The Yugoslav Communists were revolutionaries, committed to one-party dictatorship and social revolution. They were also nationalists, unwilling to accept Soviet domination. When, in early 1948, Stalin's agents attempted to replace Tito with a compliant Yugoslav leader, they were powerless against a united Yugoslav party leadership. Failing in his secret maneuvers, Stalin made the conflict public. In the spring of 1948, the Soviet Union withdrew its economic and military advisers from Yugoslavia. It was a warning of Moscow's displeasure.

That summer the Cominform expelled the Yugoslav party from its membership. It accused Tito of confusing Soviet international policy with "the foreign policy of the imperialist powers" and of "boundless ambition, arrogance, and conceit." Its goal was the overthrow of the Yugoslav leader. Stalin privately boasted that "I will move my little finger and Tito will fall." He did more than that, for the Soviet Union and its satellite states imposed an economic blockade on Yugoslavia. The Yugoslav party rallied around Tito. For the first time, Communists loyal to their own country had defied Stalin and the Soviet Union. It was an unequal conflict that Western observers compared to the biblical contest between David and Goliath.

Germany was the location of the first open conflict between the United States and the Soviet Union. The dispute originated in the new Allied policy toward the three western German zones. In 1947, their occupation authorities joined the three to make one economic unit. This union was an important step in their efforts to revive the west German economy. It was still suffering from the destruction of war, serious shortages of food and other vital goods, and an inflation so rampant that the German currency ceased to have real value. No longer were economic policies formulated for all Germany; negotiations with the Russians had broken down. The western Allies' ultimate objective was the creation of a new German state (leaving aside the problem of Berlin). To achieve this, they were prepared to disregard the wartime agreements on Germany. In the spring of 1948 the Western occupying powers announced the introduction in their zones of a new German currency. This was an important step toward an independent West Germany.

West and East had split in the middle of Europe. The West was in the process of rebuilding a new Germany. Even without the eastern German lands this state would have a population of fifty million and an industrial base sufficient to make it a major economic power in Europe. Supported by the United States, it became a frontline region. The Western occupation forces no longer protected the Allies against Germany. Instead, they protected the German areas they controlled against the Soviet Union.

Stalin opposed the creation of a unified western Germany as strongly as he objected to an independent Yugoslavia. Once again, he turned to economic blockade to get his way. To stop unification required halting the currency reform, and to achieve that goal he ordered the Berlin blockade. When the new currency first appeared in June 1948, Soviet troops stopped all rail, road, and canal traffic into west Berlin along the three narrow land passages from the western zones. They cut off electric power from the east to the 2.5 million inhabitants of west Berlin. The Soviet objective was not to seize all Berlin, which was only a pawn. Stalin's goal was to block the formation of a united western Germany by imposing hunger and cold on west Berliners. They had become hostages in the Cold War. They were completely dependent on supplies from the West. Stalin expected that, faced with the suffering of helpless Berliners, the Western powers would abandon their unification plans in exchange for an end to the blockade.

He did not take into account the capabilities of modern air transport, since his state had few of its own. The Western powers kept supplies moving along the air corridors, which the Soviets could not block without an act of war. The airlift worked. At its peak that winter one plane arrived every two minutes in Berlin. The blockade failed, and in May 1949, Soviet officials finally opened the passages to Berlin. Neither side had used military force, for both sought to keep the conflict within political and diplomatic limits. Yet the blockade greatly heightened Western fears of war. Stalin's clumsy policy had succeeded only in accelerating the unification of the Western zones and the formation of a Western military alliance.

Western European Recovery

The German Federal Republic came into existence in 1949. German politicians and lawyers wrote the constitution under Allied supervision. It gave West Germany a federal structure under parliamentary rule. In the first national elections of 1949 the Christian Democratic Party obtained the majority of the votes, and selected the Republic's new chancellor (head of the government). He was Konrad Adenauer, a prisoner during the Nazi years and a strong believer in Germany's rightful place within a unified Western political and military community.

Gradually the West German state recovered its full sovereign powers. In 1951, Adenauer obtained full control over German foreign policy. He was instrumental in bringing his country within the European Common Market, alongside Germany's age-old enemy France. In 1955, his state entered the western military alliance, the North Atlantic Treaty Organization (NATO), and recovered the right to form a German army. A nationalist and a conservative, Adenauer did not recognize the legality of the new western borders of Poland, far within old German lands, nor did he accept the permanent partition of the German lands. In his opinion, West Germany had to speak for the real German nation, as its people were free. His state welcomed the 3.5 million refugees who fled East Germany over the next decade, and subsidized West Berlin's reconstruction to make it a showplace of prosperity in the middle of gray, drab East Germany.

Western Europe underwent a remarkably rapid economic recovery from the war. The Marshall Plan went into effect in mid-1948. By 1952, it had supplied more than $10 billion in financial and economic assistance to European countries, the largest shares going to Great Britain ($3.2 billion), France ($2.7 billion), and West Germany ($1.5 billion). Each government chose the appropriate use of the aid. In Britain, it helped rebuild old industries. In France, it provided the means for modernizing French industry and transportation. The West German government used the funds to lay the foundations of a free-enterprise industrial system (called the "social market economy"), in which the state encouraged capitalists to reinvest their profits and asked workers to accept low wages and long hours. The result was what came to be known as the German economic miracle. By 1952, German production climbed to 50 percent above the prewar level.

By then, Western European economic growth averaged 5 percent a year. This growth came with large imports from the United States and increased trade among the European states. The European and U.S. economies were becoming increasingly interdependent. Gradually they adapted to the new system of international monetary exchange,

conducting foreign trade in dollars. The U.S. formula for economic aid to promote political stability and industrial expansion among western European countries proved a resounding success.

The economic recovery of the West was due in part to the new institutions for international finance and multilateral trade created during the war. At the 1944 Bretton Woods conference in the United States, representatives from Western governments had agreed on guidelines for postwar international trade and financial cooperation among the major industrial states. The misery brought by the 1930s depression, when protectionism was rampant and countries found their own resources inadequate for recovery, had taught Western leaders a lesson. They had agreed in 1944 that an international bank, the World Bank of Development, should become a source of long-term loans to nations requiring assistance for economic growth. At the same time, they created a special reserve of funds, held by the International Monetary Fund (IMF), to facilitate trade through short-term loans to states lacking adequate foreign currency to pay for needed imports. Finally, they had laid plans to encourage governments to participate in multilateral trade agreements to lower tariffs and encourage trade on a global scale. This plan ultimately became the General Agreement on Tariffs and Trade (GATT).

All three reforms were intended to meet the need for an institutional basis on which an international free market could function. The goal was economic growth on a global scale. The system's international currency was the dollar, just as its principal banker had to be the United States. Although the Bretton Woods plans were of less help in postwar recovery than U.S. economic aid, they did become a permanent part of the new global economy of following decades.

Containment and Military Alliances

In 1948, the U.S. government moved beyond its containment policies of military and economic aid to consider rebuilding its own military arsenal.

Western European leaders encouraged this reversal of postwar U.S. demobilization to overcome, in George Kennan's words, "their own military helplessness" and their "lack of confidence in themselves." Military conscription began again in the United States. In 1949, U.S. international obligations widened with the creation of a collective security pact uniting North American and western Europe states. This North Atlantic Treaty Organization (NATO) obligated each member to assist in the defense of the others against any aggression. The presumed enemy was the Soviet Union, and the principal defender of the NATO states was the United States.

Large amounts of U.S. military supplies were already going to the Greek government to help in its civil war against the communist-led guerrillas. Outnumbered by the regular Greek army and deprived after 1948 of Yugoslav support, the insurgents finally gave up the struggle in 1949. Their leaders and the remnants of their army fled to Soviet satellite countries, taking with them thousands of Greek civilians. Western military and economic aid was probably the decisive factor in preventing that country from becoming a communist dictatorship and Soviet satellite.

Primarily political and diplomatic in 1947, the U.S.-Soviet rivalry focused in the next years increasingly on issues of military balance of power and the development of new nuclear weapons. In the context of the Cold War, scientists became warriors and laboratories the key places where future wars were planned. Neither side envisioned this armaments race to be the means of launching an aggressive war, but each feared the power new weapons would give the other. This logic was as true in the Soviet Union as in the United States.

In 1949, the Soviet Union exploded its first atomic bomb. Soviet scientists had succeeded, far more quickly than anyone in the West anticipated, in carrying out Stalin's orders in 1945 for the development of Soviet nuclear weapons. They already had begun research on the hydrogen bomb. The destructive capacity of this weapon exceeded by a thousand times that of the atomic bomb. In those years they set out to develop ballistic missiles as well. These rockets were capable of carrying nuclear weapons in a matter of minutes from the Soviet Union to the United States and were a greatly improved substitute for long-distance bombers, of which the Russians had very few. Each new Soviet step heightened pressure in the United States for new armaments in a cycle that appeared endless.

Deeply suspicious of Soviet intentions, the U.S. government undertook an intensive program to expand its armed forces in 1950 (even before the outbreak of the Korean War). Its crucial ingredient was to be an enormous arsenal of nuclear weapons, including the hydrogen bomb. U.S. military leaders ordered aboveground tests of nuclear bombs on Pacific islands and in the western United States. They turned the tests into experiments in destructive might, positioning entire naval fleets near the Pacific bomb sites and building mock towns for the land tests. They encouraged U.S. citizens to build backyard air raid shelters and to lay in supplies to survive weeks below ground. A third world war became an imaginable event.

Convinced of the aggressive intent of Stalin, the U.S. government decided that national security lay in military superiority over the Soviet Union. In Allied countries near Soviet borders, the United States built air bases for its Strategic Air Command, whose bombers were in position to attack the Soviet Union. By the early 1950s, military preparedness came to dominate U.S. Cold War thinking. Tragically, both Soviet and U.S. leaders could find no other way to ensure their countries' ultimate protection than to apply nuclear power to military use.

U.S. leaders revised the containment strategy in those years to include military alliances with countries near the Soviet Union or in areas of communist insurgency. They offered the inducement of foreign aid in the form of armaments to strengthen the military forces of allied countries. These global anti-Soviet policies extended through the Middle East and Asia. The United States signed alliances with a number of states individually, including the Philippines and Taiwan. In the 1950s, the U.S. and British governments each organized military alliances in these regions. The South East Asia Treaty Organization (SEATO) included states extending from Pakistan to New Zealand; the Baghdad Pact included Turkey, Iraq, and Iran. The most visible effect of these alliances was the distribution of armaments to dictators and democratic governments alike and the formation of a vast U.S. sphere of influence.

SPOTLIGHT: Eleni Gatzoyiannis

The tragedy of Eleni Gatzoyiannis (1912–48) was to find herself on the front lines of the Cold War. She knew that she and her children were caught in the middle of a civil war, but terms such as "socialist camp" or the "Truman Doctrine" meant nothing to her. The communist guerrillas occupying the remote mountainous region of northern Greece where she lived believed their real enemy to be the forces of capitalism, not the Greek government troops in the valley below. In such a war, everyone had to join the battle, and those who disobeyed had to be punished. Eleni understood the struggle differently and defied their orders. She did so to save her children but at the price of her life.

The village where she lived was close to the borders of Albania and Yugoslavia. The Greek king and his government were far away in Athens. Politics had no place in the lives of the

Escapees From the "Gathering Up of Children": Greek Refugee Children and Mothers, Athens, 1948 (*Christopher Emmett/Hoover Institution*)

mountain villagers. Living was very hard there, and the men of the village traveled far away, even to America, to earn enough to support their families. Her husband made his living working in America. He came back often, but never for very long. He was scarcely more than a visitor with gifts and stories about a faraway land. In the first eight years of their marriage, they had five children, four girls and a boy. It was the law of the village that wives and children stay behind. The stern moral code of the mountain people dictated that women care for their children and serve their own parents, keeping together the family while the men were away. Eleni obeyed that code.

When the war came to Greece in 1940, her family helped her stay alive. Her husband could not return and could not even continue sending money since mail from America no longer reached their village. Her father brought the food that kept the family from starving. Young men from her village joined the guerrillas fighting the Germans. German army units swept through the area, pursuing the guerrillas and burning the villages suspected of helping them. She was lucky, for her farmhouse survived while many others around it were destroyed. At war's end, she had kept her family intact. Peace returned, and Eleni begged her husband to bring the family to America. He promised to do so, just as soon as he had saved enough money. In the meantime, she had to stay.

And then the civil war began. In 1945, the communist guerrillas had fled to Yugoslavia to escape the army of the Greek government. Then in 1946, they came back. War, not political campaigns and elections, was to be their path to power. They followed the example of the Yugoslav Communists, who helped train and provided arms to their forces. Their Democratic Army faced a strong Greek army trained and equipped by the British and the Americans. They were not strong enough to move out of the mountains. In 1947, with Stalin's encouragement they organized their own provisional government in what they called their liberated area of northern Greece.

The villagers became the citizens of this tiny, infant state and its unwilling laborers. Children learned in school to salute the portraits of Stalin, and to sing "Onward to the struggle for our precious freedom!" The Communist Party promised the villagers to protect "our friends who work with us," but swore punishment for any who collaborated with the "monarcho-fascist" enemies. The only immediate change to the villagers' well-being was the loss of grain that the new government collected as taxes, and the time they had to give to work brigades organized by the new authorities. Eleni herself was often ordered to work harvesting the grain in the fields that the guerrillas had taken for themselves.

Soon, the Communists ordered young women to serve in their army. Eleni saved her eldest daughter from that service by pouring boiling water on her foot and then burning it with a hot branding iron. The local authorities suspected her of having defied them. There was nothing she could do, without being arrested, to prevent her second daughter from being conscripted. It was harder and harder to protect her children.

Then in the spring of 1948, the Communists decided to transport to Albania and Yugoslavia the children between five and fourteen years old living in the villages in their territory. They called it the "gathering up of children," explaining that they only wished to provide a haven from the devastation of war. But it was really their way of forcibly enlisting new followers for the long combat to come. Their struggle was not going well. Their leaders refused to admit defeat, though, and anticipated retreating north beyond the Greek borders to find a refuge for themselves and their followers in nearby communist-controlled countries and to prepare for new war. They knew parents would resist the abduction of their children. Their police had to seize the children by force. Within a few months they had rounded up twenty-five thousand involuntary young refugees.

Eleni refused to let this happen. The front lines of the government forces were just a few miles away, and behind the lines were her parents and brothers. Secretly, she and neighboring women found guides to take a group of twenty women and children down the mountain and through the front lines to the valley and safety. Just before they were to leave, the guerrillas ordered her again to work in the fields. She had to go, for had she tried to join the fugitives the security police would have been alerted and caught them. So in the end she had to abandon her children.

The authorities were furious that so many people had escaped. They had never trusted her, calling her the "Amerikana." They blamed her for conspiring with the enemy and put her on trial. They tortured her to make her confess, and forced neighbors to testify against her at the little show trial in the village organized by the chief of the area. They had decided in advance that she was guilty. She was shot by a firing squad two months after her children had fled.

Stalin's Empire

In eastern Europe, Stalin ruled the small communist countries on the Soviet Union's western borders through his ambassadors and secret police officials. These governments became "satellites," that is, states whose decisions on leadership and key policies were made in Moscow. In the years after 1948, all were miniature replicas of the communist regime in the Soviet Union. Their leaders ruled with the same dictatorial power as Stalin, employing similar repressive police methods. In some countries, little "show trials" put on display leading Communists accused of "national deviation" and "Titoism." These mockeries of justice repeated the experience of the Soviet trials of the 1930s. All the accused confessed their guilt, and most were executed.

The Soviet socialist model was applied by force to eastern European societies. Industry and commerce were nationalized. Peasant farmers were forced to sell their produce to the state at low prices. State plans set ambitious targets for industrial growth, achieved at the cost of miserable living conditions for the population. The Stalinist literary style of socialist realism was imposed on writers and artists who had to glorify Soviet

socialism and Stalin's "genius." A gray uniformity colored public life, forced into the Stalinist mold.

Of all the eastern European states, only Yugoslavia escaped Stalinist domination. The expulsion of the Yugoslav Communist Party from the Cominform in 1948 was followed by the political and economic isolation of the Yugoslav state. Its trade with all other communist states ceased, and Soviet and all eastern European states broke diplomatic relations. For a year, Tito continued to claim his fidelity to Stalinism and to Soviet socialism. Finally disillusioned, he took apart bit by bit the framework of Stalinism which he had used to guide Yugoslavia's foreign and domestic policies. He joined the leaders of newly independent Asian states in founding the so-called nonaligned movement of countries refusing to join either Western or Soviet military alliances. But the Yugoslav one-party dictatorship remained, a remnant of his years of loyalty to Soviet communism.

His country kept its constitutional order as a federation of national republics (modeled on the Soviet Union). Tito maintained peace among the many peoples who lived there by giving each a small degree of political autonomy. The Serbian people were the most numerous and the peoples living in the north of the country (Slovenes and Croats) were the most prosperous. He made sure that all shared the available income and economic resources. His authority and the power of his party made this formula work. A rebel against Stalinism, he even loosened slightly his dictatorial powers in the early 1950s. Among the satellite countries his state alone enjoyed real independence and his people were spared Stalinist terror.

Despite Tito's public defiance of Soviet hegemony, Stalin chose not to invade Yugoslavia. Although Red Army forces surrounded Yugoslavia and made threatening moves, they never attacked. Perhaps Stalin feared prolonged Yugoslav resistance; perhaps he was determined to avoid any risk of war with the United States. In matters of European security the dictator pursued a very cautious policy. Tito's revolt did not disrupt Soviet domination elsewhere along its borders. After 1949, the Soviet Union could deploy a few nuclear weapons, but it remained militarily inferior to the United States. It possessed only a few long-range bombers and its navy was little more than a coast guard protecting its shores. Whether through prudence or fear, Stalin pursued a foreign policy of domination but not aggression.

The Soviet leader was growing old. In 1949, he celebrated his seventieth birthday, receiving so many gifts from within the Soviet Union and around the world that they filled two entire warehouses. He continued to rule with dictatorial powers, feared by his subordinates within the ruling party committee, the Presidium (formerly called the Politburo). His successor, Khrushchev, remembered later how Stalin could "without warning turn on you with real viciousness." His suspiciousness remained acute. Violent public denunciations of "Zionists" foretold a worsening of Soviet persecution of the Jews, more numerous there than in any other country. These signs of a new wave of terror suddenly ceased in March 1953. That month a cerebral hemorrhage brought Stalin's life to an end (hastened, perhaps, by the Presidium's willful

delay in ordering emergency medical care). His death closed an extraordinary, terrible period of Russian history and of Soviet communism.

THE COLD WAR IN ASIA

Like Europe, the lands of East Asia became an arena for the Cold War. There, too, Soviet and U.S. troops took up in key areas the role of occupying forces. In other lands liberated from the Japanese, nationalist forces emerged after the war claiming the right to construct new nation-states. There, the fall of the Japanese Empire took place in conditions of such disorder that the peaceful transfer of power was nearly impossible. Though the influence of the Soviet Union and United States was great, they could not control the course of local wars. In the late 1940s their growing conflict extended to East Asia. The Cold War had become a global conflict.

Wars in East Asia

The collapse of the Japanese Empire left vast areas of East Asia without effective rule. The Japanese home islands became a part of the U.S. Pacific zone of occupation. Manchuria was occupied by Soviet forces, and Korea was partitioned between Soviet and American occupation troops. Elsewhere, no Allied occupation forces were present to take the place of the Japanese troops. In many areas, guerrilla forces emerged from the countryside, claiming the right to create independent states. Communists had collaborated in the anti-Japanese struggle, and they had their own plans for leadership after the war. To keep order, the Allied Commander of southeast Asia, headquartered in India, was forced to call on Japanese soldiers in distant parts of his area to serve as police until Allied troops arrived.

In Indochina, French army and naval units returned in strength in 1946. They confronted a strong communist-led nationalist movement under Ho Chi Minh. He had proclaimed the creation of the independent state of Vietnam at the time of the Japanese retreat in 1945. The French refused to recognize his new state. They set out to reconquer their former colony. Ho's forces retreated to the rural and mountainous areas of Indochina to begin a new guerrilla war. With a brief interruption, it lasted thirty more years.

In China, the Nationalist government claimed sovereign powers in the Republic of China. Chiang Kai-shek, president of the republic and heir to Sun Yat-sen as the head of the Nationalist Party, was more determined than ever to take control of the entire country. He had enjoyed the backing of the United States during the war and had received substantial amounts of military and economic aid. President Roosevelt's plans for postwar East Asia relied on Nationalist China to be a regional center of stability and authority. He hoped China would become one of the "four policemen" collaborating in a new world order. His plan could not become reality. Chiang's forces had failed to win any major battles against the Japanese and remained confined at the close of the war to the mountainous interior. Communist guerrilla forces had conquered large rural areas within the Japanese puppet states on the coast. Their troops were too weak, though, to seize control of major cities.

The U.S. government continued after the war to place its hopes on the Nationalists. President Truman ordered fifty thousand marines to the northern coast of China to keep order while U.S. planes and ships transported Nationalist troops into the areas being evacuated by the Japanese.

Chinese Communist Leaders (far right, Mao Zedong; far left, Zhou Enlai) with General George Marshall in Yenan, 1945 (*Philip Sprouse Collection/Hoover Institution*)

He also made available surplus military supplies worth $1 billion to the Nationalists. In no other wartorn country did the United States become so directly involved in the task of postwar recovery.

The burden of rebuilding China lay in the Nationalists' hands. It proved a task they could not handle. Behind a facade of power, the Nationalist state was weak. Chiang's government was incapable of administering the country in an efficient manner. Nationalist generals in command of newly reoccupied provinces conducted their affairs like the old warlords, interested above all in enhancing their own power. They did little for the people. The inefficient Nationalist state and expensive army proved an obstacle to economic recovery. Exorbitant government spending fueled rapid inflation, which became ruinous in the postwar years. The most serious weakness of the Nationalist regime was its inability to win the confidence of the Chinese people. Corruption and abuse of power discredited its claim to national leadership. Its failure to implement land reform for the peasantry deprived it of support among the masses of the population.

The war had swelled the power and authority of the Communists. Their army had grown to one million and their liberated territories held a population numbering fifty million. Mao Zedong and Chiang had been rivals for power in the decade before war began with Japan, and they resumed their contest as soon as peace returned. The U.S. government, faithful to the same principle of national self-determination that it followed in Europe, encouraged the two sides to form a coalition government. It was an arduous task. The U.S. Secretary of State, General George Marshall, traveled personally to China to persuade the two leaders to reach agreement.

He had the assistance of Joseph Stalin. The Soviet leader practiced the same power politics in Asia as in Europe. He considered that China belonged to the American sphere of influence. In late 1945, he signed a ten-year treaty of friendship with the Nationalist government. In exchange, he obtained important economic concessions in Manchuria (including control of a seaport). With these spoils in hand, he urged the Chinese Communists to give up their hopes of seizing power by force and to accept instead a political coalition with the Nationalists. He later recalled that, when a Chinese Communist delegation came to Moscow in 1945, "we told them that we considered the development of the uprising in China had no prospect, and that the Chinese comrades should join the Chiang government and dissolve their army." The combined pressure of the United States and the Soviet Union brought together the former enemies. In January 1946, the Nationalists and Communists signed a cease-fire and began discussions to form a joint government.

The agreement quickly collapsed. Outside intervention proved incapable of effacing the bitter rivalry between the two contenders for power. The United States could not force Chiang to put aside his deadly hatred of the Communists. The Soviet Union had no means to impose on Mao Zedong the dissolution of his peasant army and the abandonment of his liberated areas. These were twin elements to the policy on which Mao had based his revolutionary hopes ever since 1928. At the end of 1946, fighting between Nationalist and Communist troops began again over the perennial issue of territorial control. Manchuria was the prize, occupied by Soviet troops until late that year. Their withdrawal began a contest between Nationalists and Communists to take over that once-prosperous region.

In the battle for control of Manchurian cities, the Nationalists had the initial advantage. The Communists, less well equipped and fewer in number, had to retreat to the countryside to resume guerrilla war once again against their old enemy. In late 1946, the United States finally abandoned efforts to bring the two sides together. General Marshall declared impossible an agreement between, in his words, "the dominant reactionary group in the [Nationalist] government and the irreconcilable Communists." By late 1947, communist forces were two million strong and had succeeded in cutting off north China from the central regions. Only force of arms would decide the victor.

Communist Victory in China

That conflict became one of the greatest wars of the twentieth century. On one side was the Nationalist state, with more than three million troops equipped with U.S. armaments. It appeared the dominant political movement in the country, but its strength was rapidly declining. The weaknesses apparent in 1945 became more serious with each passing year. The army was poorly led and, with the exception of several crack divisions sent to Manchuria, consisted of conscripts who deserted at the first opportunity. The population was increasingly hostile to the Nationalist government, incapable of assuring public order and of preventing the collapse of commerce and industry. When forced to choose, more and more Chinese turned to the Communists.

Their forces were fewer in number in 1948 than the Nationalists, but the balance was beginning to shift in their favor. Social, political, and military factors explain their increasing power. The party leadership under Mao Zedong proved effective and skillful in mobilizing popular support and in forming a military and political organization capable of governing large areas of the country. The Communists had to rely on their own resources, for no aid came from the Soviet Union. They fixed their own political objectives, paying polite attention to Stalin's recommendations but never obeying him blindly.

In 1947, Stalin's new aggressive policy for the international communist movement encouraged Mao in his revolutionary communist crusade in China. That year Mao began a social revolution in the rural areas under communist control. Farms of landlords and wealthy peasants were confiscated and the land was redistributed among poor peasants. The Communists ordered the end of hired labor and promised all peasants a modest amount

of land. A new revolutionary order was emerging in the Chinese countryside, and support among the masses of the peasantry grew correspondingly. Ten years before, Mao had proclaimed that "political power grows out of the barrel of a gun." That gun was held in the late 1940s by peasants who believed that they were fighting for their own land as well as for a liberated Chinese nation.

The communist cadres enforced these reforms ruthlessly, often brutally. Still, they proved effective administrators capable of maintaining order in the "liberated areas." After decades of war, firm and orderly rule appealed to many Chinese. Another factor behind the growing strength of the Communists was military leadership. The commanders of the People's Liberation Army (PLA) had, after years of guerrilla fighting, learned to lead massive army groups in battles increasingly resembling a regular war. They proved superior to the Nationalist generals. Their soldiers (among whom were growing numbers of Nationalist deserters) remained disciplined, increasingly confident of victory and convinced of the justice of their cause. The power of the Chinese Communists lay principally in their morale and leadership, not in numbers.

In 1948, the communist objective became the conquest of all Manchuria. That spring communist armies blockaded Nationalist garrisons throughout the region. In mid-1948, they began the systematic destruction of the best troops the Nationalists could field. By the end of 1948, the Nationalists had lost thirty divisions. Half these forces had deserted or surrendered without fighting. All Manchuria lay under communist rule, and panic was spreading among Chiang's troops in China.

In early 1949, the balance of military force between the two sides had swung toward the Communists. The U.S. government had done as much as possible to help the Nationalist government with economic and military aid. President Truman refused to send U.S. troops to fight in place of Chiang's demoralized army. The Communists, unaided by the Soviet Union, obtained most of their arms from American supplies captured from the Nationalists. The U.S. government condemned the military offensive of the Communists, and Stalin may have warned the Chinese comrades to show caution, but to no avail. In the Chinese civil war, no outside powers could contain the conflict.

In the winter and spring of 1948–49, the PLA launched massive military offensives all through north and central China. One Nationalist army, surrounded in the capital city of Beijing, surrendered in January 1949, with the loss of half a million troops. A few months earlier, armies of the Communists, numbering five hundred thousand soldiers, attacked the main defensive line protecting Nationalist areas in central China. By February 1949 the defenses there were breached and the Nationalist armies routed. Between the spring and fall of 1949, Mao's forces moved south across the Yangtze River and into southern China. That summer entire Nationalist armies, generals as well as troops, deserted to the Communists. By the fall of 1949, no important areas of resistance remained.

In October 1949, the Communist Party leadership proclaimed in Beijing the formation of the Chinese People's Republic. The most populous country in the world, land of the world's oldest civilization, had passed under communist rule. A successor state had taken power, ending the long period of disorders in China following the fall of the Chinese Empire in 1911. The Communist Party leaders did not consider the war at an end until they captured the island of Formosa (Taiwan), where Chiang and remnants of his Nationalist forces had fled. Their People's Liberation Army prepared for an amphibious invasion of the island, planned for the summer of 1950. Nothing appeared to stand in its way.

The U.S. government had no clear idea of the intentions of the new Chinese leadership. Seeking to make clear what part of East Asia lay in its security zone, it publicly outlined in 1949 its military forces' "defense perimeter." This strategic area included Japan; it excluded all lands on the Asian continent (including Korea) as well as Formosa. That statement made clear that the United States took no responsibility on the Asian mainland to send its own military forces to fight communist states. At the same time, new Asian nationalist regimes from South Korea to the Philippines obtained U.S. economic and military aid. Early in 1950, the U.S. government agreed to assist the new Indochinese state of Vietnam, largely a French creation to win the backing of nationalist groups in the war with the Vietnamese communist guerrillas. These anticommunist policies did not appear in late 1949 to exclude recognition of the new People's Republic of China. Secret talks began that winter between Chinese leaders and the United States in preparation for the possible opening of diplomatic relations.

To Mao Zedong, the Chinese People's Republic needed first of all to establish good relations with the Soviet Union. He traveled to Moscow in the winter of 1949–50 on his first trip outside China to begin lengthy and difficult negotiations with Stalin. The Chinese Communists requested a military alliance, economic assistance, and the end to Soviet occupation of Chinese territory. These Soviet-controlled areas included a port and railroad in Manchuria and a large area of Chinese Central Asia. The Chinese were in effect requesting the end to Soviet imperial domination in East Asia. Chinese and Russians shared a common Marxist-Leninist ideology, and Mao revered the wisdom and achievements of the Soviet party. Though the Chinese desperately needed Soviet help rebuilding their wartorn country, they were determined to obtain Stalin's recognition of their new revolutionary state.

For his part, Stalin persisted in treating China, even though communist, as a subordinate member of the Soviet sphere of influence. He apparently distrusted the Chinese Communists, whose independent behavior must have reminded him of the Yugoslav Communists. Mao later recalled that "Stalin feared that China might degenerate into another Yugoslavia and that I might become another Tito." Stalin certainly was concerned at the

Stalin, Mao, and the Spirit of Leninism: Fragment of 1950 Painting "In the Name of Peace (Signature of Sino-Soviet Treaty)," 14' × 9' (*Russian Museum, St. Petersburg*)

possible weakening of the Soviet sphere of influence in East Asia, which extended from Central Asia through Mongolia to North Korea. Alongside the Chinese leaders in the negotiations were Communist representatives from these lands. The negotiations dragged on for two months.

In the end, Stalin agreed to Mao's request for a military alliance and economic aid. He promised the withdrawal Soviet forces from Manchuria in a few years. In exchange, Mao had to recognize the independence (under Soviet protection) of Mongolia and to tolerate the existence of a special autonomous region in Manchuria under a Chinese communist leader taking orders from Moscow. Between these two enormous states, relations remained friendly, and the Chinese honored Stalin's ideological leadership. Yet Communist China did not join the ranks of Soviet satellites.

Divided Korea

The border dividing the superpowers in the Cold War reached as far east as the country of Korea. In 1945, Soviet invasion forces had taken control of Korea just as the Japanese Empire capitulated. They had withdrawn into the northern half of the peninsula, respecting the wartime agreement with the United States. This partition of Korea between United States and Soviet occupation troops would end when an Allied peace treaty with Japan restored Korean independence.

The desire for national unity was strong among Koreans after a half-century of Japanese rule. But the occupation zones became an insurmountable obstacle to unification. The U.S. authorities opened their southern half of Korea to exiled nationalists under the leadership of Syngman Rhee. In 1948, he became head of the Republic of Korea. U.S. army forces withdrew from the south. Their military base was to be Japan, which the U.S. government made into its East Asian strong point in the Cold War. Rhee governed South Korea with dictatorial powers, suppressing the Korean Communist Party and its labor unions and

damning the Communists as traitors to the nation. He vowed that national unification would be his doing, warning that his army was prepared to seize by force the northern half of the peninsula unless the Communists agreed to his terms for unification. The U.S. government, as opposed there as in China to becoming directly involved in civil war, took seriously the threat of war. To restrain Rhee's nationalist fervor, it provided the South Korean army with only defensive weapons.

Soviet occupation authorities in the north created a civilian government under the control of the Korean Communist Party. Following the example of the United States, in 1948 it permitted the Communists to create their own state, the Korean Democratic Republic, and withdrew its occupation forces. North Korea's leader was Kim Il Sung, a veteran Communist who had learned his revolutionary lessons in Moscow in the 1930s, then had acquired military skills fighting alongside the Chinese Communists in the war against Japan. He admired Mao's revolutionary exploits, especially his defeat of the Nationalists and his unification of all China. Kim hoped to do the same for Korea, for (like Mao and Ho Chi Minh in Vietnam) he was a nationalist as well as communist revolutionary. But unlike these other Asian Communists, he could not on his own begin a war for Korean unity. His devotion to Stalin was reinforced by his reliance on economic and military aid from the Soviet Union. North Korea was a new Soviet satellite.

Armed by the Soviet Union, his army was ready for war. He still needed Stalin's approval to undertake the conquest of southern Korea. Through the winter and spring of 1949–50, he bombarded Moscow with telegrams begging for the Great Leader's backing. His army had already fought in the Chinese civil war and was better armed than the South Korean forces. He assured Stalin that military victory would come in four weeks. All Korea would be under the Communists. The moment was right. Though Rhee talked of war against the north, his military forces were weak. Unstated but understood by both Kim and Stalin was the argument that what the Chinese Communists had already achieved, Kim's forces should be permitted to do in their turn. Revolution was his goal, and no U.S. troops stood in his way.

SUMMARY

The Cold War could not provide a permanent settlement to the Second World War. Stalin's intent to create a diplomatic and political sphere of domination around the Soviet Union ensured a partition of Europe that followed the approximate line of farthest advance of Soviet armies. His warning after 1946 of the inevitability of war with the capitalist powers kept his country in virtual wartime conditions. Privately he admitted that this war would not come soon. "Respecting the powerful" dictated that he avoid risky actions that might provoke the mighty United States, for his country would take years to recover from the terrible wartime destruction. West Berlin was blockaded, not seized, by his troops; Yugoslavia was isolated, not invaded. Although political leaders in the West feared the diplomatic and military might of the Soviet Union, Stalin was intent on consolidating his new empire on the Soviet Union's borders, not on launching a new war. But the Soviet dictator's limited expansionist aims stood in the way of enduring peace treaties and undermined a stable balance of power in Europe. Peace could not be ensured in these conditions.

The U.S. policy of containment encouraged the formation of politically and economically strong allied states in strategic areas around this Soviet empire. In these terms it constituted a creative and ultimately successful global strategy. Still, the U.S. government's fear of Soviet aggression produced a policy of military containment. It rebuilt its own armaments and supported anti-Soviet military alliances even where the Soviet Union posed no real threat. This revision of the containment policy accelerated the nuclear arms race, and led to the creation of military alliances

that gave the U.S. hegemonic influence so great that it seemed to be building its own global empire.

Both the massive destruction of war and international tensions contributed to the emergence of two distinct new global systems in the decade after the war. In the East, one-party regimes imposed command economies on their lands, following the Soviet model of collectivized agriculture and nationalized industry run by a mammoth state and party bureaucracy. In the West, countries were bound together through trade and investment in an international capitalist economy. The United States was the center of this Western system. The dollar was the stable currency of exchange, and U.S. technology provided key tools of modern production. U.S. foreign aid and private investments were vital ingredients for economic growth in foreign lands. The economic crisis of the depression appeared resolved for the time being. The new challenge was to avoid a war between the superpowers, each possessing nuclear weapons whose use would bring civilization to an end.

In the background to the Cold War, new political and social forces were reshaping the world. Both superpowers proclaimed that the age of colonial empires had ended, and expressed opposition to Dutch and French military reoccupation of their Asian colonies. Yet in a real sense the Soviet victory in the Second World War had brought that country an enlarged empire around its borders, where national frontiers were meaningless divisions within a vast territory governed from Moscow. The old age of empires had disappeared in the turmoil of the Second World War. The new world of nations had only begun to take shape.

DATES WORTH REMEMBERING

1945 Formation of United Nations
1945 Partition of Korea and Germany
1945 Victory of Labor Party in British elections
1946 Philippine independence

1946–49 Civil war in China
1946–49 Greek civil war
1946–54 French colonial war in Indochina
1946–49 Dutch colonial war in East Indies
1947 Indian independence and partition
1947 Marshall Plan and Truman Doctrine
1947 Start of Cold War
1948 Communist seizure of power in Czechoslovakia
1948 Yugoslavia resistance to Soviet domination
1948–49 Berlin blockade
1949 Founding of Chinese People's Republic
1949 Creation of North Atlantic Treaty Organization
1949 Creation of German Federal Republic (West Germany) and German Democratic Republic (East Germany)
1950 Sino-Soviet treaties of aid and alliance
1953 Death of Joseph Stalin

RECOMMENDED READING

The Fall of European Empires

Raymond Betts, *Decolonization* (1998). A useful essay surveying the process by which Europe's overseas empires vanished.

The Cold War

*John Lewis Gaddis, *Strategies of Containment: A Critical Appraisal of Postwar American National Security Policy* (1982). A very perceptive study of U.S. containment policy from its origins to the late 1970s; also, *We Now Know: Rethinking Cold War History* (1997), for the author's views on the Cold War in light of secret Soviet documents from the Cold War period.

Anders Stephanson, *Kennan and the Art of Foreign Policy* (1989). An intellectual biography of the diplomat, stressing the cultural forces that shaped his world view.

Daniel Yergin, *The Shattered Peace: The Origins of the Cold War and the National Security State* (1977). A study of the disturbing transformation of U.S. political life under the impact of the Cold War.

Soviet Foreign Policy

David Holloway, *Stalin and the Bomb: The Soviet Union and Atomic Energy, 1939–56* (1994). The engrossing story of the start of the nuclear weapons race from the Soviet side.

Voytech Mastny, *Cold War and Soviet Insecurity: The Stalin Years* (1996). A convincing interpretation of Stalin's postwar foreign policy.

Memoirs and Novels

*Milovan Djilas, *Conversations with Stalin* (1958). Unique personal record of three secret meetings between Yugoslav communist leaders and Stalin between 1944 and 1947.

Nicholas Gage, *Eleni* (1983). The story of a Greek mother as told by her son after he had become a correspondent for *The New York Times* and had returned to Greece to reconstruct her life and tragic death in the Greek civil war.

*Czeslaw Milosz, *The Captive Mind* (1953). Enthralling real-life portraits, by an eyewitness (later emigre) Polish poet, of intellectuals who collaborated in the formation of communist Poland.

Chapter 3

Revolutions and Recovery in East Asia, 1950–1990

Outline

Communist China

War and Revolution in Indochina

Japan's Recovery from Defeat

Highlight

Revolution and Command Economies

Spotlight

The Fourteenth Dalai Lama

Last of the empires in East Asia, the Japanese Empire lost all its colonial lands in the cataclysm of defeat at the end of the Second World War. Its troops departed from the Asian mainland, abandoning Indonesia, Burma, Indochina, China, and Korea. Disorder sustained by terrible poverty was widespread and contenders in those lands to the title of national leadership were bitterly divided. Left with only their archipelago of main islands, the Japanese people had to remake their lives in the ruins of cities and under American occupation. In many respects East Asia had to be remade.

The countries of the region retained the boundaries drawn by Western imperial powers. The revolutionary armies of the Chinese Communist Party never recovered all the outlying lands that the empire had once ruled, but the new state did keep by negotiation and force of arms the bulk of its territory and population. It was still a multieth-nic country, with large Turkic and Tibetan minorities in its western regions. The preponderance of Han-speaking people gave it greater claim than ever before to be the land of the Chinese nation. Still, its size and diversity left it in appearance like the old empire, whose lands the new communist rulers still hoped to recover. The new China appeared in many ways an empire-nation.

The leadership and character of new states in Korea and in Indochina were shaped by bitter civil wars in which Communists and noncommunists, each backed by a superpower, struggled for control. The settlement of the Korean conflict left that country partitioned between communist and noncommunist states, like Germany a reminder of the Cold War. In Indochina, on the contrary, the war lasted far longer and had a very different outcome. For three decades civil war and foreign intervention tore apart the former French colony.

In the end, the military triumph of the Vietnamese Communist Party made it the ruling force throughout that land, still separated from its neighbors by the borders drawn by the French in the nineteenth century. The existence of these frontiers was one visible sign of the permanent impact of the West on East Asia.

The Soviet Union and the United States were a constant and important presence, both by the influence they exerted and by the opposition they encountered, in the evolution of the East Asian countries. Chinese Communists depended in the early years of their revolution on the Soviet Union for ideological inspiration and military support. Later, when they denounced their Soviet neighbor, the conflict led to a profound alteration in the Asian balance of power. The United States played a key role in the reconstruction of Japan, both as occupying power and as a source of economic aid, until for a time the Japanese economic "miracle" became a model for American industry. To understand the evolution of those states we must pay attention both to internal political forces in each country and to the policies of the two superpowers. Their global ascendancy made post-1945 world history in some measure a product of their actions.

COMMUNIST CHINA

In 1950 the future of China, the oldest existing civilization in the world, was the responsibility of the Communist Party. The long years of civil war had divided the population and devastated much of the country. Despite the destruction that the Japanese war had produced, it proved a unifying influence. The Communists' struggle against a hated foreign enemy brought the party the support of Chinese patriots and nationalists. It paved the way for political unification of the country following the military victory of the communist forces. Mao Zedong came to power both as the "Great Helmsman" of his party and as the heir to an ancient imperial state.

Mao Zedong and Communist Dictatorship

The Chinese Communist Party undertook after 1949 the revolutionary task of transforming the Chinese state and society and of remaking the behavior and attitudes of the Chinese people. Mao Zedong's influence had grown until he became the object of a semireligious cult resembling the hero worship in the Soviet Union surrounding Stalin. His dominance infused Chinese communism in its first decades with unique revolutionary traits. Ever since the 1920s, Mao had placed his hope for revolution in China above all in the peasant masses. He preserved that faith when he set about, as he explained in his peculiar Marxist vocabulary, to "destroy feudalism" and to "build socialism." What to skeptics appeared impossible was attainable, he believed, since "the masses of the Chinese people" were capable of "miracles," provided they received correct communist inspiration and party guidance. This extraordinary confidence in the Chinese masses remained with him throughout his years in power and inspired grandiose—and ultimately disastrous—experiments in Chinese communism.

Mao believed that his understanding of communism and socialist revolution offered the country a unified body of revolutionary wisdom. The message incorporated two principal lessons: (1) The revolutionary ideology of Marxism-Leninism had to be adapted to Chinese conditions; (2) Mao possessed the creative knowledge to discover the Chinese path to the socialist society and to lead the party and the country to this glorious life. He gave to the People's Liberation Army (PLA) a special, and crucial place in the Chinese communist movement. It had been the spearhead of the party in the seizure of power. He believed that its discipline and dedication set the model for the whole revolutionary vanguard, of which it was, in some respects, the elite. No earlier communist movement had placed such heavy responsibilities on its military organization in the struggle for political power. Taken as a whole, these fundamental precepts of Chinese communism define what is called "Maoism." Mao's beliefs were utopian. For a quarter-century they marked China's path to the future.

In the early years, the Chinese Communists conceived of their country's immediate future as a literal repetition of the construction of socialism in the early decades of Soviet development. They idolized Soviet achievements and made the Soviet Union their model of political dictatorship and economic revolution. They believed (although not for long) that the Soviet Union had successfully achieved a socialist society. China's revolutionaries had to follow the Soviet model on its own road to socialism. Mao declared on his visit to Moscow in the winter of 1949–50 that Soviet farm collectivization, nationalized industry, and command planning were "models for construction in New China." While the Japanese were in those same years reconstructing their state and economy on the basis of Western democratic and capitalist institutions, China's path followed that of Soviet communism.

China, Stalin, and the Korean War

The bonds uniting communist China and the Soviet Union became a military alliance in the Korean War. Soviet, Chinese, and Korean Communists launched and sustained a local conflict that deeply marked the Cold War and changed the course of East Asian history. Throughout the winter of 1949–50 Kim Il Sung had begged Stalin to approve an invasion of South Korea. Without Stalin's word he could not act. In his telegrams to the Great Leader, his arguments emphasized the strength of his army, capable in his opinion of victory within a few weeks. That spring, Stalin gave his consent. In June 1950, North Korean troops invaded South Korea. A unified Korea, like its neighbor China, seemed destined to become another triumph for revolutionary communism.

Stalin's readiness to allow that war came only after he had obtained the support of the Chinese Communists. Mao showed no hesitation in backing his Korean comrades. Moved by a sort of revolutionary conceit, he seems to have believed that his forces could conquer Taiwan that summer, and North Korea could conquer the south, without U.S. military opposition. He too credited North Koreans with sufficient armed might to overwhelm their enemies in the south. Even if the United States did reverse its policy of keeping troops off the Asian mainland, Kim Il Sung was certain of a rapid victory, making it unlikely U.S. forces could intervene in Korea in time to prevent communist victory.

The Korean conflict ceased being a local war two days after the invasion, when President Truman declared that his country would defend South Korea. This sudden reversal of U.S. policy was because of two factors. First, the U.S. leaders realized that a communist Korea would extend the ring of Soviet satellites to within a short distance of Japan, the kingpin of U.S. Asian defenses. Second, U.S. failure to resist the North Korean offensive would convey a message throughout the world that the policy of containment hid military weakness, reviving memories of the 1930s appeasement policies toward Nazi Germany. Having emphasized the military dimension of containment, the United States had to prove its readiness to resist military expansion backed by the Soviet Union.

The Korean fighting quickly became a full-scale war. North Korean forces routed the South Korean army. This forced the United States immediately to send troops from Japan to stop the offensive. The U.S. government appointed General Douglas MacArthur commander of the forces in Korea. He fought under the United Nations' flag when the U.N. Security Council (minus the Soviet representative, away protesting the failure of the United Nations to seat communist China) approved the defense of South Korea in a formal motion condemning North Korea's aggression. MacArthur's own vision of the war extended as far as the ultimate destruction of communism in the Far East, in China as well as Korea. The U.S.

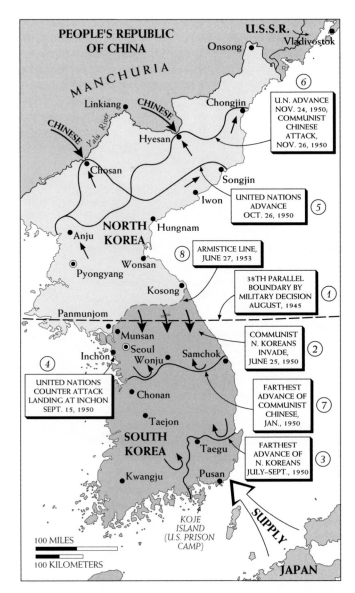

PEOPLE'S REPUBLIC
OF CHINA

U.S.S.R.
Vladivostok

MANCHURIA

Onsong

CHINESE

Linkiang

CHINESE

Chongjin

CHINESE

Yalu River

Hyesan

Chosan

Songjin

Iwon

6 U.N. ADVANCE
NOV. 24, 1950;
COMMUNIST
CHINESE
ATTACK,
NOV. 26, 1950

5 UNITED NATIONS
ADVANCE
OCT. 26, 1950

NORTH
KOREA

Anju

Hungnam

Pyongyang

Wonsan

8 ARMISTICE LINE,
JUNE 27, 1953

Kosong

1 38TH PARALLEL
BOUNDARY BY
MILITARY DECISION
AUGUST, 1945

Panmunjom

Munsan
Seoul
Wonju

Inchon

4 UNITED NATIONS
COUNTER ATTACK
LANDING AT INCHON
SEPT. 15, 1950

Samchok

2 COMMUNIST
N. KOREANS
INVADE,
JUNE 25, 1950

Chonan

7 FARTHEST
ADVANCE OF
COMMUNIST
CHINESE,
JAN., 1950

Taejon

SOUTH
KOREA

Taegu

3 FARTHEST
ADVANCE OF
N. KOREANS
JULY–SEPT., 1950

Kwangju

Pusan

SUPPLY

100 MILES

100 KILOMETERS

KOJE
ISLAND
(U.S. PRISON
CAMP)

JAPAN

Korean War 1950–53

government lent some support to that idea when in July it reversed its decision not to defend Taiwan. U.S. naval forces of the Seventh Fleet sailed into the Straits of Formosa to block Chinese troops preparing to invade the island. Suddenly, the front lines of the Cold War extended around communist China.

U.S. objectives in the Korean conflict did not become clear until late that fall. General MacArthur's immediate goal was the defense of South Korea. Two months after the invasion, U.N. troops launched a surprise landing in the middle of the peninsula, forcing the North Korean army to flee north to escape encirclement. Supported by

New War in Asia: U.S. Counteroffensive against North Korean Army, September 1950 (*National Archives*)

President Truman, MacArthur pushed U.N. troops beyond the line of partition that September into North Korea. His forces quickly reached the very borders of China. His goal was complete military victory and the capitulation of North Korea. The U.S. government had already received Chinese warnings of military intervention if U.S. land forces approached Chinese territory. MacArthur dismissed these warnings, believing mistakenly that his armed forces could defeat Chinese troops (and perhaps welcoming the possibility to bring the war into China).

The Chinese leaders carried out their threat. Their reasons for intervening appear mainly strategic. U.S. troops occupying territory on the very borders of their country constituted a serious threat to the stability of their regime. In November, three hundred thousand Chinese troops attacked the U.N. forces, which were quickly overwhelmed and forced to retreat back into South Korea. There the front soon stabilized in the region of the old border. The war dragged on for almost three years. The United States suffered more than one hundred thousand casualties and the Chinese nearly one million. China and the United States had become enemies. In 1951, the U.S. government dismissed MacArthur from his position of commander-in-chief. His dreams of military victory were out of touch with the limited objectives of U.S. military strategy. The U.S. government sought only to

撲滅戰火，拯救和平！

Chinese Communist Korean War Poster "Extinguish
Fire of War, Save Peace!" 1952 (*Poster Collection/
Hoover Institution*)

protect South Korea, refusing to use its nuclear
weapons in a war for the containment of North
Korea, not conquest.

The Korean War continued for another two
years. It was marked by bloody, inconclusive battles that failed to break the stalemate. In the course
of the war, North Korean cities were destroyed by
intensive U.S. aerial bombardments. Responsible
for the outbreak of hostilities, Stalin apparently
prevented a compromise settlement. The Korean
conflict confirmed his grim view of the inevitability of capitalist war, and forced communist China
to depend on the Soviet alliance and Stalin's leadership. In 1951 the first peace negotiations began,

only to stall over minor issues of prisoner repatri-
ation raised by the Communists.

Shortly after his death in 1953 the prisoner
issue no longer mattered to the communist negotiators. Stalin's disappearance made possible the
end to the Korean War (and soon that in
Indochina). Chinese and Soviet governments
undoubtedly knew of the threat by President
Eisenhower's new administration to increase its
military effort in Korea. They probably heard the
rumors (spread intentionally by the U.S. government) that it was even considering the use of
nuclear weapons. The Korean War ended in 1953
in an armistice, but that was sufficient for the

Chinese, Soviet, and U.S. negotiators. The leaders of North and South Korea had to accept the decision.

North Korea remained under the rule of Kim Il Sung and the Communist Party. For the next half-century, he forced his country to conform to a dogmatic Stalinist ideology. Kim became North Korea's Great Leader and the subject of public adulation. He maintained a brutal dictatorship, and kept industry and agriculture in a rigid command economy long after it was abandoned in China. The army prospered, sending infiltrators over the demilitarized zone into the south and periodically threatening to resume the crusade for national unification. The Communists forbade any communications with the south. Until the end of the century, Stalinism had a secure home in North Korea.

In the south, the country lay under Syngman Rhee's authoritarian rule. After his death in 1965, a series of military rulers seized control of the government. After overseeing the recovery from war, they threw the country's meager resources into building a modern industrial economy. Their statist methods of "guided capitalism" closely resembled the Japanese model. To increase savings (and funds for investment), they imposed stringent controls on consumption, even forbidding Koreans to take their vacations outside the country. By the 1980s, their methods and the people's industriousness succeeded in creating a South Korean "economic miracle." Their troops, assisted by an entire U.S. Army division, were permanently stationed along the demilitarized zone that separated their state from communist Korea. The division of the globe into rival armed camps was a visible part of the Korean peninsula.

Revolutionary China

The Chinese leaders faced enormous problems implementing their revolutionary plans. They had extensive experience governing comparatively small areas during their years of guerrilla war.

Suddenly they found themselves in control of a land larger than the continental United States with a population approaching six hundred million. Among these people were many who had fought for or supported the Communists' enemies. Political convictions and self-interest had incited many Chinese to work with the Nationalists, while others had collaborated with the Japanese. China remained an impoverished country, severely damaged by decades of war, whose new leaders dreamed of building a socialist society of abundance and equality. The revolution had a great distance to go, and some of its leaders, especially Mao, were very impatient.

The formation of a new state came first. The ruling organs of the Chinese People's Republic copied the Soviet one-party system. When the new constitution went into effect in 1954, it gave the Chinese state a National Assembly, chosen by popular election, whose responsibilities included selection of the president of the Republic and of the Council of Ministers. The new order formally acknowledged the existence of national minorities by creating an "autonomous region" for each non-Han people. Tibetans, Turks, and Mongols possessed (in theory) the right to their own local government, schools, and culture. Behind this democratic facade lay, as in the Soviet Union, the monopoly of power of the Communist Party. All candidates to elected political positions had the advance approval of party authorities. Only one candidate for any office ever appeared on electoral ballots. Voters merely registered their approval of the party's decisions. Communists appointed in Beijing kept firm control over the autonomous regions, where units of the PLA were ready to repress national unrest. This "people's democracy" meant in fact that the leaders of the Chinese Communist Party could claim to speak for the people in deciding what was best for the revolution and for their own power.

The Communist Party itself followed the Leninist principle of centralization of command in the hands of the Central Committee and the

Politburo. Mao Zedong was chairman of these powerful committees. He held also the positions of president of the Republic and head of the People's Liberation Army. Taken altogether, these responsibilities confirmed his preeminence over the state and the party. His authority was uncontested in those years. Like Stalin, whose power and eminence Mao admired, he set the guidelines for state and party policy. The fate of China lay in his hands, to the extent that any man could exercise supreme power in so enormous and complex a country. Around the great square in Beijing were hung the portraits of the intellectual giants of revolutionary Marxism, beginning with Marx and Engels, then Lenin and Stalin, and finally Mao.

This picture of the "apostolic succession" of world communism elevated Mao to the rank of world leader.

Making a socialist revolution on the ruins of the oldest civilization in the world required the purging of enemies and the elimination of rival ideologies. The Communists began the "repression of the enemy classes," conducted by the army, the courts, and the secret police (the National Security Forces). In 1951, a new law against "counterrevolutionaries" called for mass meetings and public denunciations of anticommunists. No one knows the number of Chinese arrested and sentenced; moderate estimates mention one to three million executions. A vast system of

Cult of Mao: Bust of Mao Zedong, 1970 (*Poster Collection/Hoover Institution*)

prison camps emerged in remote parts of the country to "reeducate" the prisoners, many of whom spent decades as forced laborers. The party-state did not tolerate diversity of religion or political persuasion. Following the Soviet example, it imposed its own ideological mold on the country's intellectual and cultural life.

The social reforms undertaken in those years were directed against the "five bonds" that had constituted the core of imperial Chinese society. The Communists' attack on old China included among their targets the traditional family, which was the bastion of Confucianism and ancestor worship. They championed the principle of the equality of rights of women. Applied to Chinese society, it required the abolition of the old marriage practices, including infant and forced marriage, concubinage, and infanticide. Divorce became legal, as did abortion. The new regime wiped out the practice of foot binding, which had been a symbol of women's subjugation and a relic of that "feudal" past whose destruction was key to the success of the revolution. All these reforms were contained in the family law of 1950. It challenged the customs of centuries.

These reforms became effective only after massive propaganda campaigns and new edicts drove home the message that the revolution would not spare the family. In those years, the regime promoted birth-control methods to limit the rapid growth of the population. Other new social policies included a ruthless campaign against drug addiction, which was virtually wiped out within a few years. Political dictatorship and sweeping social reforms brought the power of the new state and of the party into the personal lives of the Chinese population.

The Great Leap Forward

Stalin's death in early 1953 opened a new period in Soviet relations with China. The new Soviet leaders publicly acknowledged China's status as an equal in the socialist camp. They renounced the special territorial concessions that Stalin had

obtained. They expanded their economic aid program, providing China in the following five years with machinery, credits, and technical assistance worth billions of dollars. The next few years were a honeymoon in the relations between the Soviet Union and China.

Using the Stalinist economic system as their model, the Chinese leaders adopted the principal institutions of the Soviet command economy, that is, command planning, collectivized agriculture, and rapid development of nationalized industry. In 1955, they launched their first Five-Year Plan for economic development. That same year Mao ordered the party to begin a rapid campaign for farm collectivization. In 1955 the state nationalized the remaining private commercial and industrial enterprises. Imitating Soviet practices, the Chinese leaders strictly limited peasant consumption in order to turn agricultural production to the benefit of the cities and the industrial population.

By 1956, the entire Chinese economy was under state control. Mao expected miracles of socialist development, pointing to the Soviet experience to justify his claim. "The Soviet Union's great historical experience in building socialism inspires our people," he wrote that year, "and gives them full confidence that they can build socialism in their country." Never again did he refer in such glowing terms to Soviet socialism.

Within a year Mao denounced (at first in private, then publicly) the Soviet leaders for abject failure in their commitment to socialism. It is not clear what brought him to that startling reversal of opinion. He revealed later that he judged the Soviet leaders guilty of permitting the existence in their country of substantial inequalities in salaries and incomes. To him, this amounted to the revival of capitalism and the decay of socialism. He attacked the Soviet bureaucracy, whom he believed guilty of corruption and profiteering. In Marxist terms, he was right on both counts, but later events proved that his own utopian socialism was equally flawed.

The dispute between the two communist states quickly assumed the proportions of a religious

schism. In the spirit of a Protestant church reformer challenging the Catholic papacy during
the Reformation in sixteenth-century Europe,
Mao believed that he, better than any other Communist, understood how to achieve a just, egalitarian socialist society. The conflict began in the
tones of a doctrinal quarrel. United until then by
their universal vision and shared ideals, they proceeded to condemn each other as sinful heretics.

In early 1958, Mao set out to prove that the
Chinese way to socialism was the correct path. He
based his hopes on his conviction that the Chinese
masses were capable of such prodigies of work, of
such superhuman efforts, and of such radical improvements in their collective institutions that
their willpower and his leadership would bring to
China in a few years both abundance and social
equality. He wrote that the "six hundred million
people of China" were like a "clean sheet of
paper" on which "the newest and most beautiful
pictures [could] be painted." He asked that they
assist him in a "Great Leap Forward."

In concrete terms, his new plans required that
China abandon the Soviet-type economic policies
that it had just adopted a few years before. Command planning had to end, for it was misguided
and harmful. He argued that in a year Chinese
workers and peasants could by their own efforts
raise economic production by 100 percent, could
complete enormous dams and flood control projects, and could transform collective farming into
communistic farming. He demanded the creation
of "people's communes" in the countryside, relatively few in number and grouping up to one hundred thousand peasant households, to replace the
collective farms. They were to be organized on
egalitarian principles, with no special benefits to
good workers and no separate garden plots or private houses. Families would organize their lives
collectively, with meals and childcare provided
by the commune. Mao wrote just before the campaign got underway that "there is no difficulty in
the world" the masses cannot overcome "if only
they take their destiny into their own hands." Because mass work was required, more Chinese

were needed, and birth control had to end (it did
not return until twenty years later when the country's population had grown by another three hundred million). The Great Leap Forward revealed
Mao's extraordinary revolutionary populism and
utopianism.

The reality was disaster. The worst consequences resulted from the radical reorganization
of agriculture. Peasant farmers lost the incentive
to work, were taken from their farming for great
irrigation and flood prevention projects, and spent
long hours in political indoctrination meetings.
Agricultural production in 1959 and 1960 declined so seriously that famine spread through the
Chinese countryside. The full extent of the catastrophe of the early 1960s became public knowledge decades later. Despite severe rationing and
the decision in 1961 to import large quantities of
grain, millions of Chinese rural inhabitants died
(recent estimates suggest more than forty million)
as a result of famine and disease. Mao's disastrous
experiment in mass mobilization was the cause.
The crisis gave Mao's opponents in the party
leadership the incentive to force an end to the
Great Leap Forward. They publicly criticized
"guerrilla methods" in governing the country.
They took control of the government, pushing
aside Mao despite his complaint that he was being
treated like a "dead ancestor." He was, temporarily, dethroned. Still, his authority as Great
Helmsman of the Chinese revolution ensured his
stature in the party. For a few years, he had to suppress his dissatisfaction with the course of his
country's development. His vision of egalitarian
socialism no longer set policy, and his influence
dwindled among the party leadership.

His revolutionary policies hastened the
breakup of the Sino-Soviet alliance. Many issues
of national interest were a source of disagreement
between China and the Soviet Union in the late
1950s. Disputes over territorial questions and
differing policies toward the United States were
bound to strain the ties between the two most
powerful communist states. In 1960, Mao accused
the Soviet Communists of betraying Leninism

and selling out the cause of world revolution by not promising its military backing in case of war with the U.S. over Taiwan. In retaliation, the Soviet leaders stopped all Soviet assistance, refusing any further help in Chinese nuclear development and breaking the economic aid agreement. Within a few weeks, all Soviet technicians left and factories being built by the Russians stood abandoned. To Soviet leaders, good relations with neutral Third World countries became as important as their relations with China. At about the same time as their quarrel erupted with China, they agreed to sell arms to India. In the circumstances, it was a hostile act toward China.

India and China were divided by a long-standing territorial dispute on their long Himalayan frontier. In 1950, Chinese troops had conquered and annexed the kingdom of Tibet. Rebellious peoples, Turkic in western China (Xinjiang) and Tibetan in the southwest, lived on this borderland of the new state. The Chinese government wanted rapid access to these lands in the event of unrest. They began building a strategic highway linking Tibet and Xinjiang through mountainous territory claimed by India. In 1959 the Tibetan people did rebel against the Chinese, requiring prolonged military repression. Tibet had become a Chinese colony. The strategic highway's use in keeping together this new Chinese empire was clear.

The Chinese government was determined to establish its control over the strip of territory claimed by India. By 1960, the quarrel turned into a military confrontation. The Indian government refused to cede the area needed and began to move its own troops there. The Chinese leaders prepared for war. In 1962, their troops, operating in difficult mountainous areas all along the Indian border, attacked and defeated Indian forces in a brief border war (see Chapter 4). Having occupied the area along the highway, they halted the war. Without any outside support (the Soviet Union remained neutral) the Chinese regime had proven that it was a major power in Asia.

SPOTLIGHT: The Fourteenth Dalai Lama

For most of his life, the Fourteenth Dalai Lama, born in 1937, has been a political refugee. He remains the legitimate leader of the Buddhists of Tibet, though he had to flee the country in 1959 to escape imprisonment by the Chinese Communists who rule his land. He, like many millions of other political refugees in the twentieth century, became the victim of war and revolution.

As practiced in Tibet, the Buddhist religion had for many centuries formed the core of the life of the population in that remote mountainous kingdom. The Dalai Lama is the name given to the person, chosen while still an infant, who is believed to be the reincarnation (reappearance after death) of the spirit of the Buddha himself. The Fourteenth Dalai Lama was the spiritual descendant of the First Dalai Lama of the sixteenth century, when this Tibetan Buddhist practice began. Monks in Tibet's many monasteries preserved the religious teachings of the Buddha. They regarded the Dalai Lama as the source of wisdom and guidance in religions and political affairs. Until the twentieth century, these monasteries were the center of Tibetan life, and the source of law and public order. The Dalai Lama was, in effect, absolute ruler as well as religious leader, a "God-King." For a time, Tibetan leaders had recognized Chinese suzerainty (political authority) over the country. Still, nothing that the Chinese Empire did threatened their way of life and religion.

When the Western world (in the form first of British explorers) discovered Tibet, they brought with them tools of modern life unknown to Tibetans. Electric power and steam engines suddenly

XIVth Dalai Lama (*Stillwell Collection/Hoover Institution*)

became tangible, and desirable items. The Tibetan rulers had need of a foreign policy, ambassadors, and a postal system. In 1911, the collapse of the Chinese Empire was their chance to proclaim Tibet an independent country.

That peaceful period ended when the Chinese Communists invaded their land in 1950. As soon as the People's Liberation Army had conquered the central regions of China, their troops invaded the western borderlands. They claimed the area by right of imperial heritage. Tibet, with a tiny army and primitive weapons, was an easy conquest. The Communists claimed to have "liberated" Tibet from the imperialists. But their conquest and subjugation of the land resembled the policies of a conquering empire. They brought to the Buddhist people of Tibet their own version of modernity. It included war on religion, the end to monastic rule, and the exploitation of the natural resources (including uranium) hidden in the remote region. The life of Tibetans was never the same again.

In the first years of Chinese rule, the Fourteenth Dalai Lama (still a young man) tried to conciliate the Communists and to preserve Buddhist practices. He had had little contact with foreigners, but had begun to learn of the world beyond the Himalayas from occasional visitors (and from two German prisoners-of-war who had fled captivity in India). India was Tibet's other powerful neighbor, and a land where respect for the Buddhist religion was widespread. The Dalai Lama could expect moral support from Indians, and even might hope for diplomatic backing from the Indian government. Until the border war erupted between India and China, the Indian leaders discouraged him from challenging the Chinese invaders. He had become a player in the "great game" of power politics in those crisis years.

Mao's Great Leap Forward brought the full force of the Communists' antireligious campaign to Tibet. In early 1957, Chinese Communists and PLA soldiers began systematically weakening Tibetan Buddhism, attacking the monasteries, expelling the monks, destroying religious relics, and tearing down the ancient buildings. The Dalai Lama's deepest religious and political convictions required that he speak out against these vicious measures. They aimed, in his words, at the "extermination of the religion and culture of the Tibetan race." He publicly condemned the anti-Buddhist measures, though he risked his own life in doing so. In 1957, Tibetans joined in a massive revolt against their Chinese rulers. The PLA was there to suppress the rebellion. But it took the occupation forces fourteen years to do so.

The Dalai Lama could no longer remain in his country. In the midst of the violence, he secretly fled across the high mountain passes to India in 1959. There, with more than one hundred thousand Tibetan refugees, he asked for political asylum. Although the Chinese Communists protested India's "imperialist" intervention in their affairs, the Indian government agreed to his request. The Chinese victory in the Sino-Indian war of 1962 insured that the Dalai Lama's exile would last for a long time.

He and his followers created what they called "Tibet in exile," located in one of the old British hill stations in the Himalayan foothills. He continued to act as the true leader of the Tibetan community, heading a government-in-exile and receiving foreign statesmen. Prime Minister Nehru was the first to visit. His was a discouraging message, for the Indian government would not back the cause of Tibetan independence. Secret messengers kept the Dalai Lama in touch with Tibetans living in Tibet. He devoted his time largely to religious matters, but politics kept intruding in his life. The agonies of the Buddhists during Mao's Great Cultural Revolution brought from him expressions of sympathy and pleas to the Chinese for toleration, all to no avail. Tibetans again revolted against the Chinese, and for several years fought a desperate guerrilla war. But the Chinese were too strong.

In 1974, the Dalai Lama begged his followers to cease armed resistance. He presented to Tibetans a pacifist program of opposition, arguing for nonviolence in defense of the rights and liberties of his people. At first, he called for a neutral Tibet that would take no part in the power politics of Asian states; later he asked only for full autonomy for Tibet within the People's Republic. For his courage and moral strength, the Dalai Lama won the Nobel Peace Prize in 1989. The Chinese leaders paid no attention to his proposals and denounced his "subversive" activities. Exile was to be his fate.

The Cultural Revolution

The years between 1960 and 1966 were a period of temporary calm before Mao and his supporters launched a new and even more violent revolutionary offensive. The people's communes were disbanded and smaller collective farms reinstalled. The recovery of agriculture required a large investment of state funds, allocated in those years according to pragmatic criteria of need and productivity.

Although powerless to prevent these changes, Mao refused to compromise. He rebuked his colleagues for their "bourgeois" spirit. He publicized his version of revolutionary communism—and his cult—in a little red book entitled *Quotations from Chairman Mao*. Its distribution was assured by the People's Liberation Army, which printed one billion copies to make sure it was available to the entire Chinese population and to foreign supporters. Its most ardent readers were China's youth, among whom admiration for the Great Helmsman was deep and unquestioning. Mao welcomed what he called their "socialist education" and their support for his ideals.

In the mid-1960s, he seems to have become convinced that his revolution was caught in an ongoing conflict between forces of evil—his enemies—and of good—the masses, the army, and the students. He imagined Chinese youth to be uncorrupted by avarice or ambition, and ready for combat against the "enemy classes" whom he imagined had penetrated his country. His immediate objective was to end the "counterrevolutionary restoration" of those he called a new "exploiting bourgeoisie," including well-paid professionals, intellectuals, and party bureaucrats. In a manner recalling Stalin's Great Terror, he prepared to undertake a new class war against his own party and the educated elite of his country.

The decade of turmoil that began in 1966 had no parallel in the history of earlier revolutions. It involved both the Chinese state and society. It undermined party institutions and rule, produced a prolonged upheaval in education, industry, and agriculture, and destroyed precious works of traditional Chinese culture. So chaotic were conditions that the full story remains obscure. In 1966, Mao was still the revered leader of his people, able to mobilize supporters among the students, workers, and soldiers to participate in what he referred to as a Cultural Revolution. That year he made clear whom the enemies were, warning that "the bourgeois agents who have infiltrated the party, the government, the army, and all sectors of cultural life constitute a gang of counterrevolutionary revisionists."

Mao's principal weapon in this class war was a mass movement to promote what he baptized his "Great Proletarian Cultural Revolution." His immediate goal was nothing less than the destruction of the old party leadership and the creation of a new revolutionary regime, consisting of "revolutionary mass organizations" running a country rid of greedy bureaucrats, profit seekers, and egotistical intellectuals. Somehow he managed to win sufficient backing from party leaders to begin a campaign that they must have known threatened their policies and their power. In 1966 he obtained the authority to create and to lead a special committee charged with organizing his Cultural Revolution.

This organization started a propaganda campaign in mid-1966 calling on all 700 million Chinese to "destroy the old world." The first recruits for the Cultural Revolution came from the student youth, organized in units called Red Guards. That fall all regular university and high school studies ceased (the interruption lasted nearly ten years). Students had better things to do than to study, for Mao called them to lead his new revolution.

The Red Guards were the revolutionary organization of Chinese youth. Their appearance coincided with Mao's emergence at the head of the Cultural Revolution. That August, he gathered together one million Red Guard youth at the Gate of Heavenly Peace in Beijing, appearing before them just as the sun rose in the east. His message was simple: "Destroy the old and construct the new." That fall and winter violence swept the country as these self-proclaimed revolutionaries organized mass demonstrations, attacked alleged counterrevolutionaries, imprisoned party officials, and destroyed old monuments and precious relics of China's past. Centers of resistance emerged when party officials mobilized their own supporters to oppose this children's crusade. Street demonstrations often degenerated into open fighting between rival political factions.

The next ten years were a time of extraordinary turmoil. Serious disorders accompanied the attack on party officials and factory administrations. Rival groups of Red Guards fought for leadership and battled with worker organizations claiming to defend the true Maoist line. Punishment inflicted on "class enemies" included public humiliation, exile to the countryside, imprisonment, even death by beating. Cities like Canton and Shanghai experienced so much violence that the conditions there resembled civil war.

Soon units of the People's Liberation Army began to intervene to enforce a minimum of public order in China's cities and towns. In 1967, Mao authorized the army to supervise the economic and political affairs of the provinces. The army commanders did not seek to militarize the

Chinese state. Instead, they organized revolutionary committees, grouping representatives of workers, students, and the military in very disorderly and unstable coalitions. They replaced the old regional and city party committees, which were a prime target in the Cultural Revolution. The guiding principle of action of these committees was the "three loyalties": loyalty to the "person, the thought, and the policies" of Mao Zedong. Maoism was the very essence of the Cultural Revolution.

Mao's revolutionary regime proved incapable either of governing the country effectively or of establishing new institutions for socialist revolution. The PLA became by default the backbone of political rule throughout the country. At a party congress held in early 1969 the head of the PLA, Lin Biao, who was second only to Mao in political power, proclaimed that the Great Cultural Revolution had triumphed. The reality was endemic disorder and continued witch hunts of supposed enemies. PLA provincial military commanders held onto meager remnants of political authority in the country. The tasks of industrial construction, training of professionals, and scientific research had all been abandoned in the upheaval. Hundreds of thousands of scientists, specialists, and teachers were forced to accept "reeducation" by performing menial tasks in agricultural communes. China had entered a period of permanent revolution from which it did not finally emerge until after Mao's death in 1976.

In those years, relations with the Soviet Union became so strained that war appeared likely. Mao's supporters treated the Soviet Union as if it had become the principal enemy of China. The Chinese press published maps that claimed for China most of eastern Siberia (the Chinese Empire had exercised a remote and sporadic suzerainty over these lands before the nineteenth century). Pitched battles erupted with Soviet forces on the Manchurian border in 1969; sporadic violence erupted all along the enormous Chinese-Soviet frontier that year and the next.

The Soviet government concluded that Mao was as dangerous and aggressive as Hitler had once been. They believed the threat of war with China so serious that they moved large military forces, including nuclear missiles, to their eastern region bordering China. The conflict between the Soviet Union and China became a new cold war.

Gradually other party leaders, appalled by the internal turmoil and foreign danger Mao had created, brought an end to the period of revolutionary zealotry of the Cultural Revolution. Zhou Enlai, the chairman of the council of ministers and the most influential moderate party leader, resumed his role in policy making. The process by which power changed hands again remains unclear. In 1972, the party leaders formally disbanded the Red Guards. Most of its members were sent to work in the countryside, where they could no longer champion Mao's Cultural Revolution. But as long as Mao remained alive, no one challenged his utopian vision of Chinese socialism, and no new reforms appeared to remedy the havoc that his policies had created.

"To Get Rich Is Glorious"

In the late 1970s, this Maoist revolutionary order fell apart. The event that opened the way to sweeping changes in China's economic system was Mao's death in 1976. He received all the honors due the founding father of the new China. He was elevated to the status of "venerated ancestor" for citizens of the People's Republic. His heirs could do no less, for their power ultimately rested on the revolution that he had launched. But Mao's successors had learned by painful experience from their leader's terrible utopian experiments. Abiding poverty for over one half of the population, who still had barely enough food for survival, was too great a price to pay for socialist egalitarianism. The future development of China, and their own authority, depended on putting China on the road to economic growth.

By 1978, all Maoist supporters had fallen from power. A new party leadership, headed by Deng Xiaoping, was in a position to bring to an end the quarter-century of Mao's destructive revolutionary experiments. That year Deng declared publicly that Maoism was "wrong in its theories, policies, and slogans." After a quarter-century of utopian experiments, communist dreams ceased to have any role in economic policies.

The new leadership sought pragmatic reforms that would give the Chinese population the opportunity and incentive to get to work. Education, science, and technology became a high priority. Command planning was drastically weakened. Foreigners obtained the right to open their own businesses. Private stores could offer goods that consumers desired and at prices that the market could bear.

Deng drew the line at nationalized industry. He was unwilling to abandon the enormous network of state-run factories. These remained a foundation of China's socialist economy and an assurance of worker support. Their guarantee of work, housing, and welfare to their employees and workers created what observers called China's "iron rice bowl." Deng did order that these nationalized enterprises, notoriously inefficient, earn profits on their production. Events proved his hope to be misplaced, for the factories continued to lose money, surviving only on state subsidies.

Deng's immediate concern was to give to the Chinese rural population the economic incentive to raise food production. China's very survival depended on their efforts. In 1978, the new leaders revised so thoroughly the regulations that had kept farmland under state supervision that they in effect returned farms to individual ownership. Prices on farm produce were largely freed from state control, permitting the farmers to make profits from their work. In the years that followed, the government opened private commercial networks to bring to the countryside consumer goods desired by the farmers. These soon included expensive durable items like refrigerators, television sets, and motorcycles imported from Japan. The formula was remarkably successful.

The end of collective farming had an enormous impact on the lives of the Chinese masses, most of whom still lived in the countryside. Within a short time, Chinese farmers were able to double the country's agricultural production. They introduced new, highly productive strains of rice and wheat that had been developed a decade before in the West as part of the "Green Revolution." By the mid-1980s, China had a surplus of food for export. By then, the economy was expanding by the remarkable rate of 10 percent each year. At the end of the decade, only one tenth of the population (still one hundred million people) were still living in poverty. Deng Xiaoping himself proclaimed that the motto for the new China was: "To get rich is glorious!" It was a slogan that bore no resemblance to Maoism. Later the communist leaders toned down his exuberant message to promise Chinese people the more attainable goal of "a moderately well-off society." It was still a far more appealing ideal for the Chinese people than Mao's permanent revolution.

Chinese socialism survived in the rhetoric of the Communist Party. Most important of all, the party-state was sacred. Its powers grew even greater when in 1980 it dictated a birth-control policy restricting each family to only one child. Penalties for violations were very strict, at times brutal. At the extreme, local officials could force a pregnant woman who had exceeded the limit of children to have an abortion. The leaders could find no alternative to controlling the rapid rise in population, which by then had passed one billion.

The Chinese Communist Party possessed the repressive apparatus of a dictatorship. The secret police operated when need be outside the law; prison camps in remote regions kept prisoners in miserable conditions for long periods; when disorder threatened, the state called upon the military might of the PLA. China's leaders were prepared to wield these brutal methods when their power was challenged by the democracy movement in the late 1980s. The supporters of democratic reforms, drawn largely from China's intellectual elite and student population, asked for representative government and free speech. They drew their ideas from Western liberal institutions and from the political reforms under way in the Soviet Union (see Chapter 7). The movement grew so powerful that in the spring of 1989 its supporters organized massive demonstrations in Beijing against the party dictatorship. They were backed by many workers, but had no encouragement from the country's rural population. Political liberty remained an affair of China's urban population. Symbolizing their goal was a statue baptized the Goddess of Democracy, which demonstrators constructed in the center of Beijing, in Tiananmen Square.

The party leaders refused any compromise with those they considered "counterrevolutionaries." They could not conceive of any weakening of the communist dictatorship. It was the essence of their power, which they refused to weaken in the belief, like Stalin and Mao, that history was on their side. In early June 1989, they called in reliable army units to disperse the demonstrators, thousands of whom were killed or injured.

The leaders insisted that the Communist Party alone possessed the wisdom to lead the people to socialism. But no one claimed to know what a real socialist society was or when it would emerge in China. The Chinese government increasingly emphasized its nationalist program for a united China. Chinese migrants moved, with state support, into borderland territories of non-Han peoples in the western regions of Tibet and Xinjiang. The influx of ethnic Chinese threatened to overwhelm these peoples, but resistance met with immediate repression. The Chinese government demanded that Great Britain cede Hong Kong, Britain's small colony on China's southern coast. The British complied, handing the territory to the People's Republic in 1995. The Chinese government continued to insist that it was the only true China, threatening periodically the small Chinese Republic on the island of Taiwan. Claiming to be the legitimate heir to the Chinese Empire gave the Communists the stature of champions of the Chinese nation.

The post-Mao leaders redefined their foreign policy goals in those years to place national interests above world revolution. Their invitation to President Nixon to visit Beijing in 1972 signaled the beginning of normal diplomatic relations with the United States. By the end of the century, the United State had become the most important market for China's exports. Economic expansion through sales on the world market became Chinese government's primary concern. They were prepared to play by the rules of the international market economy, joining the World Trade Organization in 2001. Peaceful relations with their neighbors mattered as well. They ended their quarrel with the Soviet Union as well, though the two states never returned to the earlier alliance. Maoism was dead, and communist ideals, although not forgotten, did not get in the way of power politics. By the first years of the twenty-first century China was the major power in East Asia.

HIGHLIGHT: Revolution and Command Economies

When nationalist leaders took control of their new nation-states in Asia and Africa, they immediately searched for the policies that in the shortest possible time would give their countries a modern industrial economy. The market economies of the West offered one model, but left much initiative to private investors and give little assurance of rapid economic growth. The command economy of the Soviet Union was their other model. Stalin repeatedly proclaimed that his country was well on its way to the "shining future" of socialism. His prestige was at its peak in the years after the war. He and his supporters had no doubt that Soviet victory in war had come thanks to the socialist system that he and his party had imposed in the 1930s. History, they announced, was on their side. The argument made many converts among nationalists in former colonial lands who repudiated Western capitalism along with Western imperialism.

The great attraction of the Stalinist reforms lay in their apparent ability to insure rapid economic growth and their commitment to social justice and equality. In other words, they were both a means to industrial development and a socialist end in themselves. The term "command economy" best describes the Stalinist economic system, since the state possessed the powers to control all economic activities—in industry, commerce, and agriculture—and issued the commands that set production, price and wage targets. The goal was to maximize resources for economic development. When the communist regimes in China and Vietnam set out to bring economic revolution to their peoples, they recreated the institutions and policies of this command economy. Many nationalist regimes in Asian and African countries also introduced important aspects of this system. During the half-century after the Second World War, the economies of countries throughout the Third World resembled more closely that of the Soviet Union than Western capitalism.

Two characteristics of the command economy were particularly important in its operations. The first was the ownership and supervision by the state of all productive property within that state. The second was the control by the state of all trade with foreign countries. Taken together, these powers brought state administration into the economic affairs of the population to a far greater extent than existed in capitalist countries. Nationalization was an essential step in creating a command economy. In the Soviet Union, as later in communist China, the government issued decrees soon after the seizure of power dispossessing all the owners of industrial enterprises and commercial businesses. Even agricultural production came under the supervision of the state after collectivization of private farms.

The only private property left in the hands of individuals were their personal possessions and, in the countryside, the houses and surrounding plots of land where the peasants lived (and at times even these were taken away). Private production and profit making became illegal. The authorities denounced these institutions as vestiges of capitalist behavior. Illegal private trading never disappeared from the command economies, as their inefficient distribution system and endemic shortages created a ready market for scarce goods. But the state declared this private trade the work of criminals, to be punished by imprisonment and, in extreme cases, even death. The command economy of the communist regimes justified the repression of activities that in free market economies brought profit and praise.

All foreign economic operations also fell under the supervision of the state. Governmental agencies were responsible for the purchase of goods and services from foreign countries. Other agencies decided whether and what amounts of goods from its country should be sold abroad. The command economy permitted the state to isolate its people from the outside world more completely than Western countries had ever attempted, even during the 1930s depression. No international corporation or bank could make decisions that directly helped or hindered its plans for economic growth. The fluctuations of international prices could not block the import of items its leaders judged useful or desirable. At a time when Western economies were moving toward an interdependent global economy, communist regimes kept tight reins on all foreign transactions. They were protected from capitalist interference and were also cut off from the technological innovations of the Western economies. Most important, these controls assured the political leadership enormous power over the economies of their countries.

The socialist economies operated at the command of the state. In countries like the Soviet Union or the People's Republic of China, the state in turn was under the control of the Communist Party. Its political dictatorship extended into all areas of economic activity, in theory governed by the plans created by state planning agencies. The so-called science of command planning made fulfillment of the yearly plans the key measure of the success of economic activity. Managers of the state enterprises executed the orders of their ministries, while workers followed the orders of their factory bosses. No labor unions were permitted to hinder production by calling strikes, which were illegal.

The consumers whose living conditions depended upon this tightly controlled economy had to take what goods they could find, at prices fixed not by supply and demand but by state ministries. The socialist society guaranteed jobs to workers and (usually) a minimally adequate standard of living for all consumers. Choices were few, but everyone enjoyed a certain measure of security. Leaders like Mao Zedong altered important elements of the system, but never considered abandoning it. Socialism for them was unthinkable without maintaining the essential qualities of the command economy.

Yet it hid fundamental flaws so serious that by the 1990s, this system had vanished from almost all the countries where it had dominated economic life. These defects included the inability to assimilate effectively and rapidly technological innovations, the disregard for the choices of the population, a very low level of agricultural productivity, complete indifference to the environmental damage caused by economic projects, and incompetence of the officials who ran the system. In effect, the command economic system turned the entire economy of a country into one great corporation, whose board of directors consisted of the political leaders of state, whose employees worked in a vast bureaucratic network of ministries, and whose products enjoyed an absolute monopoly on the market.

Nowhere in the system did there exist any incentive to take risks, such as introducing more productive farming, experimenting with more productive methods of manufacturing, or offering new products for consumers. Beginning in the 1950s, Western economies undertook a vast retooling as electronic, telecommunication, and computer technologies brought revolutionary new methods of production and communication. Nothing comparable happened in the communist countries.

There, state ministries continued to prescribe gigantic economic undertakings that fulfilled the plans but wasted scarce resources. These projects were of little use to consumers, whose most effective means to acquire new products was the black market. They also did grave damage to the environment, for no organizations or laws forced the ministries to take account of environmental costs. But the flaw that ultimately undermined the entire system were the unfitness and corruption of the political and economic leaders. They held in their hands the wealth of their country, but had little interest and no training in how to use that wealth productively.

The all-powerful state bureaucracy was increasingly tempted to profit from its economic power and influence. These officials lived in seclusion in conditions immeasurably more comfortable than any ordinary citizen. Large numbers of officials took bribes in exchange for personal favors, extending even to illegal, black market operations. In the 1950s, one eastern European critic of the command economy called the communist bosses a "new class" who exploited their economies as ruthlessly as nineteenth-century capitalists. They failed to keep the promise of socialism and were incapable of achieving the economic performance of the capitalist countries. In economic terms, the command economy proved ultimately to be bankrupt.

WAR AND REVOLUTION IN INDOCHINA

On the southern edges of China, the land that the French had named Indochina passed from the French to the Japanese Empire in the early years of the Second World War. In the late nineteenth century, the French had created in the region one colony made of many peoples, among whom the Vietnamese and the Khmer were the two largest ethnic groups (and were bitter enemies). Indochina was also divided by religion, with many Buddhists but also an important Catholic community. Like China, its economy was based primarily on agriculture, with extensive large estates owned by a few wealthy landowners (many of them French) and worked by a poor peasant population. It resembled other colonial lands in the fact that, by the middle of the twentieth century, some of its people were prepared for nationalist revolt against colonial rule.

The French Colonial War

The colonial conflict in Indochina began in earnest at the end of the Second World War. The struggle was centered in the populous coastal region known as Vietnam. It provided the recruits for the Vietnamese Communist Party, whose founder and leader was Ho Chi Minh. He grew up and was educated in Vietnam, but left for Europe while a young man and did not return until 1940. For thirty years, he wandered through Europe and Asia. He spent several years in France, where he discovered communism and began his career as a revolutionary. He became an international agent in East Asia of Moscow's Communist International, helping the Chinese Communists and then creating in 1929 what he first called the Indochinese Communist Party. From that point on, his cause was independence and communist revolution for Vietnam. He, like Mao Zedong, firmly believed in the inevitability of global proletarian revolution, one chapter in which was the fight against imperialism. He honored the leadership and wisdom of the Soviet Communists, but, also like Mao, he and his party were an independent revolutionary party in the world communist movement.

The immediate objective of the Vietnamese Communists was the liberation of all Indochina from foreign rule. That struggle began with the war against Japan. In 1940, Ho organized and took charge of guerrilla war against the Japanese occupation forces. The jungles and mountains of Vietnam were the refuge of the guerrillas, while Japanese troops held onto the cities and coastal region. Before surrendering at war's end, the Japanese commander had, in a gesture of defiance toward the Allies, proclaimed Vietnam's independence. The withdrawal of his forces permitted the Vietnamese Communists, who were the principal anti-Japanese resistance force, to assume leadership of the Republic of Vietnam. Ho read in the course of the ceremony an independence statement that included passages from the American Declaration of Independence. He had no intention of following the American political path, but was keenly aware at the time of the need to convince the American forces in Asia of his reliability.

Prepared to negotiate with the postwar French government, Ho traveled to Paris in 1946. Had an agreement been reached there, Vietnam would very soon have become a communist state. While talking of eventual freedom for Indochina, French officials and military commanders there were adamantly opposed to granting power to the Vietnamese Communists. Resolved to restore some form of French colonial authority, in 1946 they attacked the communist-occupied areas in Vietnam and quickly moved their troops into the inland regions of Cambodia (land of the Khmers) and Laos. The Communists and their nationalist allies retreated to the countryside, where they, like their Chinese comrades to the north, resumed guerrilla war.

In its first years, it was a French colonial war. The war did not go well for French forces. They attempted to win the backing of nationalists there by creating in 1949 the independent states of Vietnam, Cambodia, and Laos. They still had to bear the principal burden of the bloody fighting. French generals promised quick victory against the communist guerrillas, but could not end the insurrection. Their army, made up of colonial forces as well as French soldiers, occupied key urban areas, but the countryside lay beyond their control.

In 1950, the conflict in Indochina entered the Cold War when the U.S. government intervened on the side of the French. It had previously judged the conflict to be a French effort to restore an outdated empire. The Cold War changed that view. By 1950, U.S. leaders had expanded the containment policy to include those colonial areas where communist insurrections were under way. In effect, they incorporated the Indochinese war into the global battle between the Free World and communism.

U.S. leaders concluded that Ho's victory in Indochina would constitute a triumph for global communist forces. That was a misguided and ultimately tragic judgment. Its origins lay partly in the growing influence of anticommunist political forces within the United States, outraged at what they considered the "loss" of China. They were so committed to organizing the combat against communism that they paid no attention to the human and material cost that intervention in a colonial region like Indochina would entail. In the background was the pervasive fear of Stalin's expansionism. North Korea's aggression appeared proof of this faulty theory. As a result, the French colonial forces found an ally in the U.S. government.

The United States began to provide France with military and economic aid for the war in Indochina. In return, it demanded of the French that they suppress the communist guerrillas. Not only was the French army unable to do so, but in the attempt it suffered a major military defeat. By 1953, its forces were overextended and weakened by its campaign to wipe out the communist insurrection. It could not protect its mountain fortress

of Dienbienphu, encircled that year by the Communists. The surrender of the fort and its ten thousand troops in early 1954 ended the French efforts to retain control of Indochina.

That year a new French government concluded that their military forces could not win the Indochina war. Their army had suffered one hundred thousand casualties in a conflict draining the wealth of the French economy for control of a distant country of no vital importance. The glories of colonial dominion in Asia no longer attracted them. Although the French army still occupied much of Indochina, the French government in 1954 agreed to negotiate with the Vietnamese Communists.

At that point the U.S. government expanded even further its involvement in Indochina. It was one of the participants at the Geneva conference that negotiated the end to the war. Representatives from the Vietnamese Communist Party, from the new Republic of Vietnam, and from France were there, as were delegates from China and the Soviet Union. Peace in Indochina was an international affair. The French and American negotiators sought a partitioned Vietnam, limiting the Communists to the northern half of the country where their centers of strength were located. Under the circumstances, they sought more than the territory the French actually controlled.

The Vietnamese Communists came to Geneva expecting a treaty granting them a unified Vietnam. But Ho's delegates found no support, even from the Soviet Union and China, for the formation of a single Vietnamese communist state. The Soviets and the Chinese, determined on a quick settlement to the war, promised Ho that he would soon attain his goal of national unification without further fighting. They assured him that his forces, still the only strong, organized political movement in northern and southern coastal areas of the country, would easily win all Vietnam in the elections that the peace negotiators planned to hold in 1956. Communists in other lands had proven adept, through intimidation and violence, at manipulating elections. Ho and his followers expected to do the same. National self-determination, the principle guiding this peace settlement, offered the Communists an apparently easy opportunity to take control of all Vietnam. Ho accepted the temporary partition of Vietnam, and in 1954 the French war in Indochina came to an end.

North and South Vietnam

The U.S. government was determined to prevent the Communists' seizure of the south. Although observers warned that South Vietnam had a slim chance to survive, the U.S. brought out of exile a nationalist leader, Ngo Dinh Diem, to become ruler of the new state. U.S. agents from the new international intelligence service, the Central Intelligence Agency (CIA), began to organize the hunt for Communists in the southern half of Vietnam. U.S. military advisers took over the task of forming a new Vietnamese army. U.S. economic and military aid poured into the country. By 1960, South Vietnam had received more than one billion dollars in American assistance. This was vital to the very functioning of its state and economy. The result was the emergence of a U.S. satellite state under client nationalist leaders who could not survive without American aid. In President Kennedy's words, South Vietnam was "our offspring."

That effort at creating a noncommunist Vietnamese state represented an audacious gamble, probably doomed from the start. In a land divided by political rivalries and with no strong institutions or outstanding noncommunist nationalist leader to guarantee the stability of a new political order, state-building was in the best of circumstances a daunting task. Nearly one million refugees had fled from communist rule in the north, most of them Catholics fearing Ho's political dictatorship and repression of their religion. Most of the south Vietnamese were poor peasants, reluctant to support either the Communists

or the Diem regime for fear of persecution by the other side. Diem's main interest lay in strengthening his personal power. Like Syngman Rhee in South Korea, he was persuaded that by building an authoritarian regime he could defeat the communist underground movement (called the Vietcong) in his infant country. With U.S. encouragement, he refused to hold the elections on Vietnam reunification scheduled for 1956. Instead, he built up his police and army, which were used primarily as instruments for internal repression. They proved effective in weakening the Communist Party in the south. By 1958, many of its members had moved to the north or were in prison.

Diem's plan for South Vietnam was a conservative government protecting landowners and business and receiving economic and military aid from the United States. A somewhat similar political formula had worked in South Korea at the end of the war there. But Diem had much less chance of making it work in his country. South Korea's leaders had in their favor their claim to be the rightful national heirs to the long history of a Korean state. Their regime had been independent since 1945. Diem lacked popular support among the Vietnamese and, more importantly, confronted a dynamic revolutionary movement determined to rid the country of what it called the "Western imperialists and their puppets."

After 1954, the North Vietnamese Communists quickly remade their country into a Soviet-style regime. They created a single-party state, eliminating all political opposition. With Chinese and Soviet socialism as their model, they forced the peasant farmers into collective farms. In doing so, they disrupted agricultural production and, by their own later admission, permitted the party and police officials to use brutal repressive measures against the rural population. Ho Chi Minh pursued his revolution from above with a fanaticism equal to that of Stalin and Mao.

In 1959, civil war came to South Vietnam. That year, Ho concluded that conquest of the south would come only by guerrilla war. Communist cadres returned south along the secret Ho Chi Minh trail, built on Cambodian territory. It brought military supplies and new directives to supporters to the south. The Communists' first targets were local rural officials, on whose shoulders rested the stability of Diem's rule in the countryside. Political assassination and intimidation destroyed the regime's control in many areas, where the communist underground established new bases of operations.

The weakness of the South Vietnamese state quickly became apparent. Peasants preferred submitting to the communist agents, who protected those who helped them. Diem's officials feared for their lives (twenty-five hundred were assassinated in 1960) and retreated into fortified camps. By the end of that year, the communist insurrection had spread widely, and U.S. officials were warning that Diem's state was in serious danger. U.S.-sponsored state-building had not succeeded.

The new insurrection, begun in 1959, gathered strength from the widening circle of South Vietnamese enemies of Diem and the United States, and from the readiness of North Vietnam to commit all its resources to the struggle. Supplies for the guerrillas came partly from captured government material, partly from North Vietnam. Central leadership and party cadres came south to aid and direct the southern Communists. Still a conflict among Vietnamese, the fighting was in 1960 essentially a civil war that the Communists were close to winning.

U.S. War in Vietnam

Then U.S. forces moved in. Opposition to communist China had become a central feature of U.S. Asian containment policy after the outbreak of war in Korea. U.S. leaders did not consider the fighting in Vietnam to be merely a local conflict. To them, it appeared another step in global communist aggression. If not stopped in Indochina,

they feared that other southeast Asian states would fall to communist insurrection "like a row of dominos." The new administration of President John Kennedy, elected in 1960, judged the South Vietnam civil war to be part of the Cold War struggle to prevent, in the words of one U.S. official, "China's swallowing up southeast Asia." Overly confident in the power of the United States, Kennedy and his advisers anticipated that greater military and economic assistance would assure Diem's victory. Increased military aid seemed the way to avoid direct U.S. involvement in the war while still insuring South Vietnam's victory.

U.S. intervention in the conflict proceeded in two stages. In the first four years (1961–65), it came in the form of very large amounts of military supplies to reequip the South Vietnamese army, which was responsible for the actual fighting. This policy permitted the doubling of the army's size by 1963. It was trained by fifteen thousand U.S. military advisers, not yet combatants but close to it. The political weakness of the South Vietnamese state was far more serious than the problems confronting the Vietnamese army. Increasing numbers of South Vietnamese were opposed to Diem's authoritarian rule. His political ambitions did not match the actual strength of his regime, and he appeared incapable of winning popular support and of reforming his corrupt state.

In 1963, the United States backed a military coup in a desperate attempt to find leaders capable of governing a viable South Vietnamese state. Vietnamese generals, with the tacit approval of U.S. officials, stepped into the internal political struggle. They seized control of the government and assassinated Diem (only a few days before President Kennedy's assassination in the United States). The U.S. officials in Vietnam hoped that the generals would restore order, end corruption, and strengthen the Vietnamese forces fighting the Vietcong.

Military rule only increased the internal disorder of the Vietnamese state. Within two years, ten

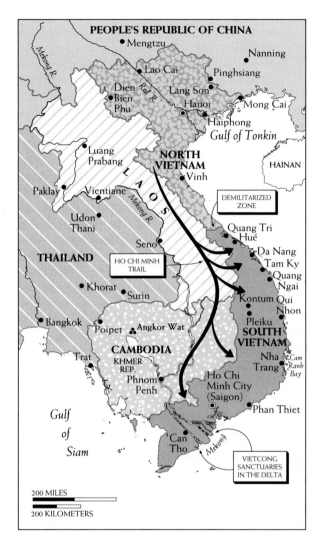

War in Vietnam

different generals had attempted to rule the country in a self-destructive struggle for political leadership. The most serious consequence was the inability of any of the generals to halt the expansion of communist-controlled areas, which extended over entire provinces by late 1964. Guerrillas had even encircled the capital, Saigon, while Communist Party cadres operated freely in the city. The South Vietnam government had lost its claim to Vietnamese national leadership.

Unless the United States itself took drastic action, within a few months the insurrection would succeed.

The prospect of "losing" South Vietnam was unacceptable to the U.S. government. President Kennedy's successor, Lyndon Johnson, won the 1964 elections primarily on a program of extensive domestic social and civil rights reform. Despite his commitment to what he called America's "Great Society," he had to turn his attention to

Vietnam. Faced with impending communist victory, he declared that he could not become the "first president to lose a war." U.S. leaders were motivated both by the belief that communist conquest of the land would be a serious defeat for the containment policy, and by the conviction that U.S. military might was invincible in a local war. This tragic overconfidence led one U.S. senator later to judge his government guilty of "arrogance of power."

Johnson's advisers guaranteed quick victory if U.S. land and air forces joined the war. Persuaded by their arguments, Johnson set about organizing direct U.S. military involvement in Vietnam. He expanded enormously the presidential war-making powers, permitting him to avoid any interference from the U.S. Congress. In early 1965, Johnson used those powers to order American combat forces into action in Vietnam. For the second time since the end of the Second World War, the United States entered a land war in Asia. The conflict did not resemble the Korean conflict, however. In guerrilla combat there existed no front lines. The enemy was everywhere, easily confused with the civilians. The only clear separation was that distinguishing Americans and Vietnamese. The Vietnam war posed problems the U.S. military had never confronted before.

The formula for victory included two separate military operations. The U.S. objective remained limited, as in the Korean conflict, to the defense of the territory not already part of the organized communist state to the north. U.S. land forces were responsible, in collaboration with South Vietnamese troops, for the "pacification" of the south, that is, for the suppression of Vietcong guerrilla operations. At the same time, the U.S. military began aerial bombardment of North Vietnam in the expectation that they could force its leaders to agree to end the communist insurrection in the south. The U.S. Air Force undertook the most intensive bombing campaign in its history.

The bombing failed to bring victory. North Vietnam, an agrarian economy, did not offer targets vital to its economic life, and its people were prepared to endure enormous suffering in that war of national liberation. At no time did the bombardment end the movement of supplies south to the guerrillas or force North Vietnam to seriously consider abandoning the war.

The land war in the south failed as well to achieve its main objective of suppressing the guerrilla forces. By 1968, the United States had more than five hundred thousand troops in South Vietnam, nearly as many as the South Vietnamese Army. Assisting infantry operations, the U.S. Air Force conducted intensive bombing attacks in rural areas of South Vietnam. The immediate result of massive U.S. military involvement was to prevent a Vietcong victory. The Communist guerrillas lacked the equipment and numbers to defeat the combined U.S.-South Vietnamese forces. They attempted in early 1968 one major offensive to seize urban areas in the south (the Tet offensive), only to suffer a crushing defeat. Their military strength dwindled by one third, from three hundred thousand to two hundred thousand, as a result of the bloody battles. North Vietnamese forces assumed the principal role in the fighting. The guerrillas dug hundreds of miles of underground tunnels, some thirty feet below ground, to escape the U.S. bombardments. Many soldiers died, but more took their place.

The diplomatic, political, economic, and human price of U.S. intervention in the Vietnam War grew to the point where it far exceeded the importance of victory to the United States. The most obvious result was heavy casualties among the South Vietnamese, helpless victims caught in the fighting between the two sides. As serious for Vietnam society was social disorder on a monumental scale. This was the direct consequence of the war. It brought the destruction of organized village life in many areas, a fall in agricultural production resulting from the bombing and the massive use of herbicides to defoliate forested regions, and the influx of four million refugees to the cities. The human suffering of the Vietnamese appeared out of all proportion to the limited war aims.

The cost to the United States, although it did not compare to Vietnam's hardship, was sufficient to cast grave doubt on the promised rewards of intervention. The total expense of air and ground fighting plus the aid granted the South Vietnamese government raised the price of war to more than $150 billion. Before war's end, the fighting left more than fifty thousand U.S. soldiers dead. Within the United States, bitter political conflict arose when predictions of quick victory proved wrong. Many Americans recoiled at the brutality of the war, revealed to them by instant television coverage. The diplomatic price of U.S. intervention proved high as well. The war deflected attention and resources from larger issues of great power relations, such as Soviet-American arms control and the worsening conflicts in the Middle East. The very continuation of the Vietnam War represented a defeat for the United States.

In 1968, the combination of these factors forced the U.S. government to rely again on South Vietnamese armed forces. The new Nixon administration began peace negotiations with the North Vietnamese government. The next year it began the withdrawal of U.S. troops. "Vietnamization" meant passing responsibility for the war to the South Vietnam government, more dependent than ever on U.S. military and economic aid.

The new policy also brought one final effort to end the flow from the north of supplies to the guerrillas. The Ho Chi Minh trail passed through the neighboring neutral state of Cambodia. Years of secret U.S. bombing had failed to prevent traffic, from bicycles to trucks, from moving along the jungle road. In 1970, American forces invaded Cambodia. The United States became the protector of an anticommunist military government there.

The only effect of this escalation was to widen the conflict. North Vietnamese supplies continued

to reach the south, for the jungle lay largely beyond the reach of U.S. infantry. Cambodian insurgents (Khmer Rouge) took over large areas of their country, with the military support of the North Vietnamese Communists. The effect of that invasion was to bring Cambodia directly in the war. The Khmer Rouge began their own war of liberation against the United States and its Cambodian allies. Still the U.S. withdrawal from Indochina continued, until by 1972 no combat troops remained in Vietnam or Cambodia.

The disappearance of U.S. forces doomed the South Vietnamese regime. The United States and North Vietnam did negotiate a compromise peace settlement in 1973, but it left the way open for a communist victory. The Vietnamese Communists accepted the existence of the U.S.-backed government in South Vietnam. In exchange, the U.S. negotiators agreed not to demand the withdrawal from the southern territory of all North Vietnamese troops. The continued presence of substantial North Vietnamese forces in South Vietnam gave them the bases from which to launch a new offensive when the right moment arrived.

The South Vietnamese leaders recognized the danger, refusing initially to sign the treaty. President Nixon overcame their opposition by secretly promising to send in U.S. military forces if North Vietnam did attack. The promise proved worthless, however, after Nixon's resignation from the presidency in 1974 in the Watergate scandal. The South Vietnamese leaders were no more successful than before in forming a strong nationalist regime. Nothing the United States did could ensure a strong, noncommunist nation-state in South Vietnam.

In 1975, the Communists were finally victorious throughout the lands once called Indochina. That year North Vietnamese troops launched their final offensive. They overwhelmed the southern forces in two months, and along with the army the South Vietnam state collapsed. Soon afterward the Communists joined South Vietnam to their People's Republic. At the same time, the

Khmer Rouge defeated the U.S.-backed military regime in Cambodia. Their revolution proved as brutal as any previous communist regime. In a three-year period, they imprisoned and executed millions of Cambodians. In the end, the revolutionary violence of the Khmer Rouge caused their downfall. In 1978, their troops invaded a border region of Vietnam that they claimed for Cambodia. This action provoked in return a Vietnamese military offensive, which easily overthrew the Khmer Rouge government. For a few years, the Vietnamese Communist Party ruled all Indochina.

In the end, the victory of the Vietnamese Communists did not prove the catastrophe for southeast Asia as predicated by the U.S. war party in the 1960s. Though it was a bitter humiliation for many Americans, U.S. diplomatic influence in Asia did not suffer. The major international event in East Asia in the early 1970s was the restoration of good relations between the U.S. and communist China. In global perspective, the Vietnam conflict turned out to be a sideshow.

Even the Vietnamese Communists' dream of bringing all Indochina under their rule collapsed in the face of anti-Vietnamese nationalism in Cambodia and the decay of Vietnam's command economy. Civil war in Cambodia continued for years between the new government, controlled by Vietnam, and a coalition of forces hostile to Vietnam. In 1990, Vietnam's forces finally abandoned in their turn that ruinous war. The government of Vietnam accepted to leave the country in the hands of a new Cambodian government.

In Vietnam, the failure of the command economy and the cost of military intervention in Cambodia produced an economic crisis that Vietnam's leaders could not blame on the decades of war. By the 1980s, the standard of living of the country had declined so severely that it ranked as one of the poorest societies in the world. In desperation, hundreds of thousands of Vietnamese fled the country, many by boat, in the hopes of finding refuge in the West. The communist revolution there was in human terms a calamity. The monuments erected in Vietnam and in the United States to the war dead marked the real price of the ruinous struggle for Indochina.

JAPAN'S RECOVERY FROM DEFEAT

In August 1945, the Japanese imperial government surrendered unconditionally to the Allies, accepting American military occupation and the imposition of peace terms decided by the Allies. The defeat was complete, both militarily and psychologically. The Japanese people heard their emperor in his first radio broadcast accept in his name the surrender and the loss of independence, a humiliation "unendurable" and "insufferable" but nonetheless inescapable. For another six years, American occupation authorities governed this defeated empire. Only the position of emperor reminded the people of Japan's imperial past. Like Germany, Japan was only a ghost of its former self.

U.S. Occupation of Japan

The treatment accorded the two defeated states was not identical, however. Japanese occupation was the sole responsibility of the United States. Its navy and air force had played the key role in the defeat of the Japanese Empire. American military forces alone occupied the country following the surrender. General Douglas MacArthur, U.S. Army commander-in-chief in the Pacific theater, became the supreme commander for the Allied Powers in Japan. He held absolute power in that country and was accountable only to the U.S. president. The territory he governed remained intact. The Soviet Union requested a separate occupation zone; MacArthur refused, and no Soviet occupation forces reached Japan. An Allied council had nominal authority to oversee MacArthur's work; in fact, it merely approved policies the supreme commander had already decided upon.

Ruins of Asian War: Hiroshima, December 1945 (*James Watkins Collection/Hoover Institution*)

Japanese occupation was a U.S., not an Allied, affair. Late in 1945, Stalin complained to the U.S. ambassador in Moscow that the Soviet general on the Allied council in Japan "was treated like a piece of extra furniture," but his protest was half-hearted. He accepted the fact that Japan was in the U.S. sphere of influence.

The fact that the United States exercised such extraordinary control over Japan led to a second important feature of Allied occupation. A central Japanese government carried out the orders of the supreme commander (in Germany no national government existed at any time during the occupation). The symbol of Japan's unity remained the emperor. Despite his purely titular political role, Japanese continued to treat him as a semidivine person.

When MacArthur assumed his post of supreme commander in late 1945, Emperor Hirohito made a brief ceremonial call, placing himself at the mercy of the victors. He informed General MacArthur that he wished to assume "sole responsibility for every political and military decision made and action taken by [his] people in the conduct of war" and to be judged for their conduct. Although the U.S. government was determined to punish Japanese war criminals, MacArthur decided not to hold Hirohito responsible. He preferred to obtain the emperor's backing for his occupation policies. His decision spared the Japanese people the humiliation of seeing their emperor tried like a common criminal. Hirohito's responsibility for the conduct of the war was left a state secret. Japan maintained its political unity and its imperial monarch, under American orders.

The country over which MacArthur assumed command was in ruins. Total Japanese casualties numbered nine million. All major Japanese cities had been destroyed—most by massive U.S. bombing raids, Hiroshima and Nagasaki by single atomic bombs—and millions of civilians were homeless. The merchant marine had lost almost all its ships. Most of the textile factories and coal mines had ceased to function, and food production had fallen by nearly one half its prewar level. To add to the miseries, more than six million Japanese who had lived in overseas imperial territories had fled to or were forced to return to Japan.

The destruction went much deeper than life and property. Respect for Japanese military leadership had vanished with the humiliating defeat. American ascendancy over the Japanese state and people undermined national pride and deference to the old elite. The Japanese empire-nation had lost its guiding code of behavior, leaving many of its people in a state of collective shock.

Their psychological response to surrender played an important part, albeit difficult to define, in the success of the American occupation. The most unusual aspect of the adaptation of the Japanese to the conquerors was their readiness to cooperate in the building of the new order imposed by the Americans. It reflected, in the opinion of a Japanese historian, a deep-seated hope that "something [could] be done" despite the terrible destruction, and a widespread conviction that Japan's "path to future greatness lay in absorbing America's technological civilization." The victors, in other words, held the key to recovery.

Reinforcing this attitude was the enormous respect General MacArthur enjoyed among the Japanese. His imperious manners, disliked by many Americans, embodied in the eyes of the vanquished Japanese the traditional authority of the warrior, displayed with remarkable American informality. Although he traveled daily in an open car to his headquarters, at no time in his six-year reign was he the target of an assassination attempt. The emperor had publicly accepted American rule and demonstrated his willingness to collaborate in the occupation. The Japanese people did the same.

During the years of occupation, U.S. authorities imposed a sweeping set of fundamental political reforms on the country. These included a new constitution, the introduction of universal suffrage, legal protection of women's rights, and the expansion of the entire educational system. More than two hundred thousand former officers and politicians were to be punished for wartime activities. Many individuals subject to purges vanished temporarily, however, only to reemerge in new positions of authority when the U.S. occupation ended. The purge included the trial and conviction of war criminals. Among the condemned was General Tojo, held guilty of launching the war, and the military commander of the Philippines. Many Japanese, unaware of the brutality of Japanese treatment of defeated peoples, found the principles applied in these trials to be a conqueror's justice. From a global perspective, the trials were a manifestation of Western confidence in an international code of law to govern war.

The new constitution was the principal political reform introduced during the occupation. MacArthur took direct responsibility for the constitutional reform. He presented the Japanese government with the document he expected them to approve. When translated into Japanese, its passages sounded to one Tokyo newspaper commentator "exotically like American English." MacArthur also insisted that it include an introduction stating that "never again shall we be visited with the horrors of war through the action of government." No other constitution in the world made pacifism a political principle. It was another clear indication of the extraordinary circumstances of U.S. military occupation. Despite its exotic aspects, the constitution fitted well the expectations and past democratic practices of Japanese citizens. It drew heavily on the British cabinet system and did not differ substantially from Japanese parliamentary democracy of the 1920s. A popularly elected parliament held sovereign power, choosing the cabinet headed by a prime minister. It became with relative ease the fundamental law of the land.

U.S. economic reforms were intended to restructure Japanese businesses and property holding. They touched agriculture, industry, and labor. The new laws on farming property produced the most important and enduring changes in economic life. The American occupation authorities ordered the massive redistribution of farmland. It was taken from absentee landlords who were paid a price so low that their land was, in reality, confiscated. Over one third of all Japanese arable land was transferred to five million farmers, previously tenants without their own land. The reform was so extensive that it resembled the initial land reforms in communist China and earned MacArthur the reputation of a radical. Some American critics called him a "socialist." As a result, the farmers became a major conservative political force in the country, supporting the new order that had given them their own farms.

U.S. efforts to encourage small business and labor proved much less successful. The spirit of these reforms resembled Franklin Roosevelt's New Deal reforms of the 1930s. This American version of free enterprise did not take hold among the Japanese business and political elite. An industrial reform broke up several of the giant economic firms, the *zaibatsu,* blamed by Americans for collaborating in the Japanese war effort. The U.S. occupation authorities passed laws intended to "tear down the concentration of economic power" in Japan. They promised that capitalist entrepreneurial opportunities would be "redistributed peacefully" among small enterprises. Conditions became more favorable for new business activities. Very large Japanese business firms, however, reemerged within a few years and soon dominated the country's industrial economy.

For a few years new laws protected and encouraged labor unions for factory workers and state employees. This led to a labor militancy unexpected by the reformers. Workers turned to socialist and communist union organizers and activists. Many unions came under the control of the Communist Party. Continued labor discontent, fed by shortages of basic goods and exploited by communist labor leaders, produced bitter strikes in 1946 and 1947. When the unions called in early 1948 for a nationwide strike, MacArthur used his exceptional powers as Supreme Allied Commander to forbid the strike.

By then the U.S. authorities in Japan had decided that economic reconstruction and social stability had to be their highest priority. They sided with Japanese management and withdrew their support for labor unions. This conservative social policy set the pattern for Japanese capitalism in the decades to come. The U.S. occupation authorities installed in Japan a type of democratic, free enterprise system that promoted political and economic practices closely resembling those in Japan of the 1920s.

The new Japanese political leadership, apparently subservient to the occupation authorities, in fact had an important role to play in the introduction of this new order. Japan had a strong socialist movement, though split into several parties, and the labor unions attracted millions of members on promises of fundamental social improvements. These groups proposed social reforms far more extensive than the measures backed by the U.S. occupation authorities. They had no real opportunity, though, to introduce their reform projects. In the 1947 elections the Socialist Party, with the largest vote, obtained only 25 percent of the total. It set up a coalition cabinet. U.S. occupation authorities' hostility to the Socialist Party was decisive in ending this first (and only) left-wing government in Japan's postwar history. They were very suspicious of any socialist reforms. As in Germany, they judged political conservatives best suited to Cold War policies. Political power shifted to the right, organized in the coalition of the Liberal and Democratic parties (soon to become one party). Their leader was Shigeru Yoshida.

Backed by the U.S. authorities, Yoshida became the dominant force in Japanese politics for the following decade. Dissension among the left-wing parties assured the Liberal-Democratic coalition control in parliament and leadership of the cabinet. The goals of the conservatives were to encourage Japanese business interests and to hasten the end of U.S. occupation. Rising Cold War tensions pushed the U.S. authorities to rely increasingly on Yoshida, prime minister after 1948, to assist them in their new containment policies.

In a major policy change (paralleling that in Germany), the U.S. government set out to hasten Japanese economic recovery by all possible means. The reform of Japanese economic and social institutions became a secondary consideration. MacArthur declared in 1948 that he wished to make Japan a "self-supporting nation" capable of resisting Soviet pressure from abroad and radical political agitation from within. In 1949 he used his occupation powers to force the Japanese government to drastically cut its expenses and to reduce the budget deficit to bring down inflation. This fiscal conservatism was essential to the country's economic growth under a free enterprise system.

Yoshida cooperated, for he welcomed the end to social reform policies. His collaboration had the strong backing of Japanese business and financial leaders, who were key supporters of his party. He also assisted in the creation of an anticommunist labor union movement and in the purge of Communists from administrative and union jobs. The new industrial unions cooperated with management, who held down wages and increased investments (a formula for recovery applied also in West Germany).

Yoshida's collaboration made him a valuable ally for the United States. It also advanced the political fortunes of his party and the conservative

program it supported. By 1950, the labor union movement had declined, torn by battles between Communists and noncommunists and weakened by conservative U.S. occupation policies. The primacy of business interests, the weakening of labor, and conservative political rule by Yoshida's Liberal-Democratic cabinet remained the dominant trends of Japanese internal politics in the decades ahead.

Japan in the Cold War

Once the enemy, Japan became a close ally of the United States in the Cold War years. The Korean War turned Japan into a major East Asian base for the U.S. military forces. Its geographical position on the eastern borders of the Soviet Union made it a desirable location for air bases for the U.S. Strategic Air Command, and its ports provided harbors to the U.S. Navy. The basic reforms had gone into effect, and Japanese political leadership was in the hands of conservatives. In 1951, the U.S. military ended their occupation of Japan, signing a peace treaty with the Japanese government. The peace treaty left Japan in possession of its Main Islands. It lost the Kuril Islands and Sakhalin to the Soviet Union. Taiwan was independent, and Okinawa was occupied by the United States. Japan began reparations payments to the countries conquered during the war (except communist China, with whom it had no diplomatic relations).

The Japanese government had little choice in devising its own foreign policy. Its margin of maneuver was small, for it was caught on the front lines of the Cold War and near the borders of the new People's Republic of China. Some Japanese nationalists hoped to restore Japan to a position of independent East Asian power, protected by its own army and navy and free to set its own course between the superpowers. Antimilitarists and pacifists, on the contrary, urged the neutralization of their country. They argued that Japan should take no part in the Cold War and should refuse the presence of any military forces, either its own or American, on its territory.

Prime Minister Yoshida chose a compromise between these two positions. In the U.S.-Japanese Security Treaty of 1952, he accepted a military alliance with the United States, permitting U.S. military bases in Japan and leaving his country (like West Germany) under the protection of the U.S. "nuclear umbrella." He agreed to comply with U.S. Cold War policies. Among Japanese the most controversial policy was non-recognition of communist China. It was a decision imposed by the United States. For another twenty years Japan had no official relations with its powerful neighbor. Yoshida refused, however, to give in to repeated requests from the U.S. government that Japan rearm beyond the minimum level of its self-defense forces. In those years his country was a disarmed state, relying on U.S. military protection and free to devote its energies and resources to economic growth.

The U.S. alliance aroused bitter controversy in Japan throughout the 1950s. The Security Treaty set the terms of this uneven union between the mightiest military power in the world, the United States, and its former Asian enemy. Opposition to its terms came principally from the Socialist Party and from a very strong pacifist movement. In 1959, when the treaty was being renegotiated, political opposition and street demonstrations grew so violent that the government was for a time paralyzed. This was the most serious crisis that Japan's parliamentary regime had confronted since the war. In the end, the Japanese public turned against the violent tactics of the opponents to the new treaty. It was ratified virtually by force in parliament that year. In return, the conservative prime minister resigned to quiet protests at his undemocratic handling of the crisis.

The "Economic Miracle"

Japan's phenomenal economic expansion began ten years after the war. First the country had to pass through a period of painful recovery from wartime destruction and the loss of colonial territories. Japanese businessmen remained in the postwar years reluctant to begin real reconstruction of the economy. They lacked foreign markets, had no domestic shipping industry, and feared the consequences of worker unrest and U.S.-imposed social reforms. By the early 1950s, these issues had been resolved to their satisfaction. The political conservatism of Yoshida and the ruling Democratic-Liberal coalition protected and reassured investors, and labor agitation subsided. Beginning in 1950, large U.S. purchases of goods for the troops in Korea gave a strong boost to the Japanese economy. The U.S. government permitted Japanese goods unrestricted entry into the American market. It began a major program of economic aid, the Dodge Plan (comparable to the Marshall Plan for Europe), encouraging the use of these funds for the modernization of the Japanese economy. Finally, it made U.S. modern technology accessible to Japanese entrepreneurs. Little did it expect the extraordinary success of these businesses in using that technology to build a great new industrial empire.

These favorable financial, commercial, and technological conditions laid the foundation for what became known as the Japanese "economic miracle." Per capita national income reached the prewar level in 1956. At about the same time food rationing finally came to an end. Japanese families still had to content themselves with a very modest standard of living. Surplus wealth went primarily into economic expansion. The Japanese people put into savings an average of 20 percent of their income (in the United States, savings averaged only 7 percent in the early 1960s). Industries went heavily into debt, using the savings of the Japanese people to invest in new products, new machinery, and the formation of commercial companies engaged in foreign trade. By the late 1950s, the economy was growing at the extraordinary rate of 10 percent a year; national income doubled every seven years. No Western capitalist country had ever matched that rate of expansion.

Foreign and Japanese observers debated the causes of this remarkable turnaround in the economic fortunes of the country. Some emphasized the superior educational level of the Japanese, highly trained and able to adapt easily to a new industrial era of complex electronic technology. Others underlined the favorable international conditions, including U.S. free trade and technology and the rising demand for products in Asia and the West. Everyone agreed that collaboration between government officials and leaders of industry had proven successful in their joint effort to expand Japan's share of the global industrial market. The conservative government committed financial resources, decreed legal protection, and created public agencies for the development of Japanese commerce and industry. The principal instrument of this free-enterprise planning system was the Ministry of International Trade and Industry (MITI). Its officials used their extensive authority over the country's financial and trading activities to oversee Japanese economic development.

The Japanese business and government elite put in place an economic system that came to be known as "guided capitalism." Bureaucrats in MITI gathered economic data to forecast international trends in technology and industry. With this information they recommended economic objectives for big business. The government used tariffs to create protectionist hurdles to foreign imports competing with Japanese goods. Businesses producing profitable exports received state subsidies in the form of low-interest loans. Guided capitalism cemented the alliance of conservative politicians, state officials, and business leaders. The Japanese respected democratic procedures, but behind the scenes real political power depended on what one Western observer termed Japan's "authoritarian institutions and techniques."

A quarter-century after its crushing defeat, Japan had emerged as one of the most productive, prosperous countries in the world. Its form of capitalism was studied and imitated by other Asian states. In the 1970s, the formula proved remarkably successful in South Korea, Taiwan, and Singapore, which together with Japan were labeled the "Four Dragons" of East Asia. Their economies boomed. With growth rates of nearly 10 percent a year, all four doubled their economic wealth every ten years. Many Asian leaders heralded guided capitalism as the "Asian way" to economic prosperity.

New industries sprang from the enterprise of Japanese businessmen. They proved remarkably capable at turning Western technology into reliable, inexpensive products. The story of some of these entrepreneurs reveals important characteristics of the Japanese "economic miracle." In the late 1940s, a young Japanese mechanic, Sochiro Honda, began to make motorcycles at a price far below Western imports. By the end of the 1950s his firm was the largest maker of motorcycles in the world, with markets throughout Asia and in the West. He enjoyed even greater success when his factories shifted to automobiles. When electronic inventions in the West opened up a new consumer market for television, a Japanese electronics engineer started a small firm in 1958 with $500 and seven workers to make some of these electronic items. His firm, Sony, became one of the principal world producers of television equipment. Recognition of new opportunities and quality work were important factors assuring the success of Japanese entrepreneurs offering new products for consumers in the expanding global economy.

Individual initiative combined in Japan with the old techniques of giant corporate management and government support. The major enterprises, called by the Japanese "business communities," brought banking, transportation, and sales operations into one firm, with branches extending into Asia and the West. Their employees and workers, grouped in company unions with guaranteed life-time employment and high wages, were the aristocracy of the labor force. They were far better off than those workers in small business, where labor was poorly paid and unemployment a constant threat.

Deprived of its overseas empire by defeat in war, the Japanese state made its economic might the foundation on which it built up a regional sphere of influence. The United States remained the major market for Japanese exports. Soon Japanese investors and exporters established important business connections in southeast Asia. Japanese-owned factories appeared throughout the region, assembling products made with inexpensive labor and Japanese technology. With the government's encouragement, Japanese businessmen invested in the new electronic industry. By the 1980s, Japan was a global center of computer manufacturing. Rapid expansion of the country's nuclear-power industry was another key decision of the Japanese government. In an era of Middle Eastern oil crises, it was determined to free the country from dependence on imported petroleum and coal. Until the 1990s, guided capitalism remained Japan's key to economic success.

By then, the U.S.-Japanese alliance had become an unusual, awkward partnership. U.S. diplomatic and military influence remained great, but Japanese financial and technological achievements gave its banks and industrial corporations an important role in the U.S. economy. Each year Japanese exports brought in tens of billions of dollars in foreign earnings. A part of these funds was reinvested in the U.S. financial and real estate markets. Each country depended upon the other. The Japanese economy was earning profits on a par with U.S. businesses. The Japanese population had reached a standard of living equal to that of Americans. Although Emperor Hirohito's death in 1989 briefly revived memories of the war and Japanese military defeat, by then it seemed part of a distant past.

SUMMARY

War and revolution had profoundly altered the history of East Asia. Japan no longer possessed either a great empire or a powerful military. Having occupied a vast area of East and southeast Asia, it had to abandon all its conquered territories. Its defeat opened the way to revolution and the emergence of new nation-states in that vast area.

The internal transformation of East Asian lands depended in large measure on forces unique to each country. The victory of the Chinese Communists transformed the political landscape of East Asia. Chinese nationalism fused with communist ideology to sustain a long revolutionary war. Although Mao's vision of utopian socialism brought the country two decades of political and social turmoil, the Communist Party dictatorship was unshakeable. The Chinese Statue of Democracy, erected by supporters of democratic reform on Tiananmen Square in 1989, fell that June when the tanks of the PLA crushed the protest movement. Ten years later, Japan's new Statue of Liberty (copied from the U.S. statue) was a tourist attraction as well as a symbol of Japan's postwar transformation. Japanese national pride suffered terribly in the aftermath of defeat, but the nation's ability to collaborate in the new economic endeavor brought Japan back among the great powers of the world.

Behind the diversity of historical experiences are apparent important similarities in the recent history of that region. This pattern repeats itself in different ways in other parts of Asia, the Middle East, and Africa. Movements for national independence became powerful political forces. The goal of economic development became an integral part of political action and of popular hopes. In China, unheroic but effective programs for economic growth replaced Mao's utopian campaigns of communist equality. The South Korean economy, guided by authoritarian leaders, managed to join the ranks of the new industrial nations by the 1980s. Only North Korea remained trapped in a Stalinist political and economic mold that left its people impoverished and oppressed. The over-riding goal everywhere else was to raise production and to improve the people's standard of living and well-being.

East Asia became more, not less, involved in global affairs after the fall of the great empires. The superpowers extended their rivalry into the region, and governments there looked to the West or to the Soviet Union for economic aid and for military support. Global markets lured manufacturers and governments to compete on an international scale. National independence and global interdependence constituted two inextricable facets of the postwar history of East Asia.

DATES WORTH REMEMBERING

1946–54 French war in Indochina

1950 Formation of Vietnam, Cambodia, and Laos

1950–53 Korean War

1950 Chinese conquest of Tibet

1954 French withdrawal from Indochina

1955 Creation of North and South Vietnam

1956 Beginning of Japanese economic boom

1957–71 Tibetan revolt

1959 Flight of Dalai Lama to India

1959 Communist insurrection in South Vietnam

1958–60 Great Leap Forward in China

1961 Beginning of massive U.S. military aid to South Vietnam

1965 U.S. military intervention in Vietnam

1966–75 Great Proletarian Cultural Revolution in China

1972 Withdrawal of U.S. troops from Vietnam

1975 Death of Mao Zedong

1975 Communist conquest of South Vietnam and Cambodia

1978 End of collective farming in China

1980 Introduction of "one child" policy in China

1989 Suppression of democratic movement in China

RECOMMENDED READING

Communist China

John Avedon (1988), *In Exile from the Land of Snows: The Dalai Lama and Tibet since the Chinese Conquest* (1984). A sympathetic history of contemporary Tibet and its leader.

Sergei Goncharov, John Lewis, Xue Litai, *Uncertain Partners: Stalin, Mao, and the Korean War* (1993). The best study to date of the murky origins of the North Korean invasion.

Jonathan Spence, *Mao Zedong* (1999). A short, critical reassessment of the life of this great revolutionary leader.

Postwar Japan

John Dower, *Embracing Defeat: Japan in the Wake of World War II* (1999). A thoughtful study of Japan's painful renewal following defeat.

Akira Iriyi, *The Cold War in Asia* (1974). An international history of East Asia that integrates Japan into the Cold War conflict.

*Edwin Reischauer, *The Japanese Today: Change and Continuity* (1995). A brief survey of recent Japanese social, cultural, and political history, by one of the senior historians in the field.

War in Indochina

William Duiker, *Ho Chi Minh* (2000). A lengthy critical biography of the communist leader.

George Herring, *America's Longest War: The United States and Vietnam, 1950–75* (2nd ed., 1986). A succinct discussion of America's failed experience in state-building and anticommunist war in Vietnam.

Memoirs, Novels, and Visual Aids

Orville Schell, *To Get Rich is Glorious: China in the Eighties* (1984). The perceptive observations of an old China hand watching with amazement the reemergence of capitalism in China.

Platoon. A brutal look through film (1986) at the Vietnam war seen from the perspective of the ordinary U.S. soldier.

Small Happiness (1980). A closeup documentary film, made by a team of Western anthropologists, of a Chinese village in the 1960s, paying particular attention to the new freedom enjoyed by women.

Chapter 4

New Nations in South Asia

Outline

The New Island Republics

Independence for India and Pakistan

India and Pakistan as Nation-States

Highlight

New Nations and Ethnic Strife

Spotlight

Sukarno

Within a few years of the end of the Second World War, the Western empires in South Asia had vanished. The Dutch left their colony in the East Indies, the United States gave full independence to the Philippines, and the British granted freedom to India, Burma, and Malaya. The political transition, coming in some cases after centuries of colonial rule, was abrupt. The move to independence was accompanied in some countries by civil war and ethnic conflict, leaving bitter memories and antagonism among the newly freed peoples. Although the Western states had ruled their colonies by force of arms, they also recruited and trained increasing numbers of their colonial subjects for military and administrative service. The languages in common use within their colonial borders gave ethnically diverse peoples a useful, and relatively noncontroversial means of communication. Their years of rule led to economic investment for the extraction of raw materials needed in Western industry, and to the construction of railroads and ports for the movement of goods. In these and other ways the centuries of imperial rule left their mark on economic and political life in the new states to follow.

Throughout South Asia, the anticolonial movements that took power made national unity the foundation of their plans for independence. It was a generous vision that held together leaders and supporters as long as the immediate aim was the expulsion of Western colonial rulers. It proved a difficult ideal to incorporate afterwards into the life of the new states. Leaders spoke of a nationalism that would transcend the deep internal social, religious, and cultural divisions within their countries, implying that they sought a nation-state of toleration and freedom for all. But they found that ethnic and religious bonds remained a powerful force among their peoples. Separatist movements often emerged whose goal was to defend the interests and integrity of their own community. Ethnic nationalism threatened the newly won unity of these states (see "Highlight," this chapter). Faced with abiding social disagreements and conflict, leaders often turned to authoritarian rule as a substitute for elusive national unity.

Freedom brought with it a very distinct sense of fundamental differences between the newly independent lands and the rest of the world. The broadest definition of this uniqueness came from the Indian leader Jawaharlal Nehru. Decolonization had, in his opinion, created the collective need for peace among the liberated peoples of the globe. He sought to distance his country from the international conflicts of the Cold War. Many other leaders shared his view and supported a policy of "nonalignment," refusing to ally with either the West or the Soviet bloc. Nehru described their place in the new world order as the "Third World," separate from the democratic "First World" and the communist "Second World."

The differences were not so great that these new nation-states could ignore the more industrialized countries. Their leaders confronted acute problems of poverty and economic backwardness that required outside help and aid. Their efforts to raise living conditions and to stimulate economic growth relied in some cases on the free-enterprise system of the West, in others on the central government controls resembling the command economy that Stalin's Soviet state had instituted. While often looking to foreign lands for aid and guidance, they adapted and altered these policies and institutions to suit their needs.

THE NEW ISLAND REPUBLICS

The history of the countries of southeast Asia in the quarter-century after the war followed a common pattern. The first years were a period of decolonization, that is, the elimination of political ties to Western states and the first stages of state-building. The new regimes set out to define a new international policy in their relations with East and West, gathering to discuss common problems and policies even when they were deeply divided on the most desirable course to take. Their political development in the following decade shifted toward authoritarian rule, with small groups of leaders controlling elections by means of political followers and clients. Everywhere, economic development was an increasing concern. Poverty remained an abiding presence among both urban and rural masses, while business and bureaucratic elites built up great wealth. Social and ethnic unrest erupted at times in spontaneous uprisings, giving support to guerrilla movements organized by revolutionary parties. State-building constituted a complex, often violent, process.

Philippine Independence

Liberation of the Philippines from Japanese rule came with the return in 1944 of General MacArthur and U.S. forces, two years after their defeat by the Japanese. Before the war, the U.S. government had granted the Philippines self-rule in a political system, copied from the American constitution, with an elected president and legislature. Dominating the political life of the islands were powerful families. Their power depended on their great wealth, which they used to sustain a political patronage system employing political "clients" to carry out their orders. They were the real rulers of the Philippines.

Japanese occupation only worsened the hardship of the peasant farmers, who made up the bulk of the population. They were forced to pay heavy taxes to their conquerors. A major peasant uprising erupted in 1943. The rebels attacked both the Japanese occupation forces and the great landowners, many of whom collaborated with the Japanese. This rural unrest, combined with ethnic conflicts among the peoples scattered across the archipelago, remained the major source of conflict in the postwar years.

In 1946, the United States formally granted independence to a new Philippine government. The first elected president had himself worked for a short period with the Japanese. His administration, like the preceding one, made no effort to punish collaborators. The transfer of political power to the Philippine people did not weaken the dominance of landowners and business elites. No revolutionary movement swept in new leaders or offered the peasant population a concrete plan for land reform. Independence came peaceably without upsetting the privileges and comforts of the Philippine upper classes.

Remnants of the colonial order continued to shape the country's economic and diplomatic relations with the United States. Reliance on U.S. leadership in world affairs was a guiding principle of the new Philippine regime. It joined the Western bloc in the Cold War, signing a military alliance with the United States that left in place American naval and air bases in the Philippine archipelago. In exchange, it received military and economic aid from the United States. It remained closely bound to the capitalist system brought by their American rulers, preserving the laws that protected its market economy.

The country's foreign trade was tied as tightly as before to the United States economy. Special trade agreements permitted Philippine goods to enter the United States without tariffs, and few restrictions stood in the way of Philippine families who wished to migrate to America. In return, U.S. investors received special financial incentives to found companies in the new republic. Close ties existed between Philippine traders and industrialists and U.S. bankers and manufacturers. The interests of the Philippine government and middle classes were closely bound to those of the U.S. government and economy. Socialist experiments had no place in the new order.

Despite social inequality and ethnic diversity, Philippine leaders were able in a few years to build the foundations of national unity. The greatest danger to the new government was the peasant uprising on the main island of Luzon. By the late 1940s, it had grown into a major rebellion with its own People's Liberation Army. It drew its support from landless farmers, who were bitter enemies of the large landowners. Beginning in 1950, Ramon Magsaysay, the dynamic and popular leader of the army, organized effective resistance to the guerrillas. Initially successful in taking control of large areas of the countryside, the insurgents lost support when his government finally passed reform laws to give land to tenant farmers. Most peasants abandoned the rebellion in exchange for ownership of their own land. Magsaysay proved a charismatic nationalist leader, very popular with the masses. His formula of reform and reconciliation successfully ended the insurrection by 1951. That year Philippine voters elected Magsaysay to the post of Philippine president, which he retained until his death in 1957. For a few years, the new Philippine nation-state enjoyed a period of peace, democratic government, and economic growth.

In the next decade, though, the republic's democratic constitution and representative government became subverted by a handful of powerful political bosses. Democracy turned into elite rule. The Philippine leader Benigno Aquino, writing in the late 1960s, lamented that his land was "consecrated to democracy but run by an entrenched plutocracy," and "dedicated to equality but mired in an archaic system of caste." One of these power-hungry politicians, Ferdinand Marcos, became for a decade dictator in all but name. The Philippines became a land of political intrigue, increasingly torn by civil rebellion.

Elected president in 1965, Marcos manipulated his legal position to expand enormously his presidential powers. His real backing came from his informal network of supporters that he had created through the system of political patronage. Marcos justified his increasingly authoritarian rule by the pointing to the social disorder and ethnic conflicts that continued to mark the country's political life. Muslim groups in the southern Philippines had rebelled against the central government and the presence of Catholics and the Catholic Church on their islands. In northern islands, communist-led guerrilla movements reappeared among the poor peasantry. But Marcos's brutal methods and corrupt regime failed to halt the disorder. Rather than allow new elections, Marcos proclaimed a regime of martial law in 1972. With the backing of the army, he arrested his political opponents and ended the constitutional guarantees of political and civil liberties.

His dictatorship did not resolve any of the major problems confronting his country. His regime was never capable of repressing the communist and Muslim uprisings. It was unable to improve economic conditions in the cities and in the countryside, despite vast amounts of U.S. military and economic aid. He used his authoritarian powers to amass enormous wealth for his family (some estimates after his fall placed his total wealth at more than one billion dollars) and to bribe and enrich his cronies and his powerful political machine. Power brought enormous benefits to him and to his followers. By the early 1980s, his corruption and political repression had aroused outrage throughout the country. Even the Catholic Church joined the call for his removal from power. In 1986, he had to flee the country when army leaders turned against him. By then the political opposition had reached the proportions of a mass uprising.

His successor as president was Corazon Aquino. She was the widow of a prominent opponent of the regime, Benigno Aquino, whom Marcos had ordered assassinated in 1983. She promised to restore democratic rule and reunite the country, but the heritage of decades of economic decay and authoritarian rule posed enormous problems. The country had preserved its national unity and restored democratic government. But it could not end the revolt among the Muslim populations on the southern islands. Nationalists could claim victory in their efforts to end the presence of U.S. military bases on the archipelago. In 1994, they rejoiced at the closure of the last U.S. naval base, whose buildings Philippino investors converted into headquarters for start-up computer and Internet companies. The global economy had replaced the Cold War as the Philippine's major link to the outside world.

Sukarno and Indonesia

In the East Indies, years of colonial war between Indonesian nationalists and Dutch forces followed liberation from Japan. Before withdrawing from the East Indies in August 1945, the Japanese occupation authorities had allowed nationalist collaborators to proclaim the independence of their country. No Allied troops reached the East Indies until weeks later. In the interval, nationalists created a government for a state that they baptized "Indonesia." Their leader was Sukarno. For the previous twenty years, he had campaigned against Dutch rule, preaching a semireligious message of Indonesian nationalist revival. But his creed proved less important in the independence movement than his charismatic hold over the Indonesian peoples. They found inspiration in his promise of Indonesian rebirth following independence.

When in late 1945 Dutch armed forces reached the islands, they ended this first brief moment of independence. The leaders of the Netherlands had desperate need of their vast colony, whose valuable resources, especially petroleum, were vital for the reconstruction of their war-torn homeland. But years of colonial war failed to reestablish by force of arms their control over the vast East Indian archipelago. U.S. opposition to their colonial war and their failure to end the insurrection brought the conflict to an end in 1949 (see Chapter 2). The Netherlands abandoned the colonial empire in Asia. Sukarno and his nationalist followers had won.

That year they proclaimed the victory of the independent Republic of Indonesia. Its borders were those put in place by the Dutch colonial rulers, and its state language was the Malay dialect that had become the common language among the subject peoples within the colony. Its new constitution promised parliamentary democracy to the eighty million people of the vast archipelago, whose islands stretched across three thousand miles. The peoples were divided by great inequalities of wealth, different cultures and languages, and an age-old distrust of peoples of neighboring islands. Most of the population practiced the Muslim religion; within Indonesia's borders lived the single largest Muslim community of any state in the postcolonial world. Buddhism continued to exert a strong influence among peoples in the central islands of Java and Bali, and large Christian communities had emerged in regions where Catholic and Protestant missionaries had been active. Political parties representing the various islands and peoples feuded among themselves, weakening their authority in a state unified only by its leader and by the nationalist liberation movement.

Sukarno was the national hero and became the first president of the republic. His stature rested not only on constitutional power and his nationalist ideology, but also on his vast following among Indonesians. Many virtually worshiped him. He was the guarantor of Indonesian national unity. The legislature, which still was a parliamentary democracy, was increasingly the scene of bitter political quarrels. Politicians from areas where Islam was powerful demanded that the state enforce Muslim religious laws among the population. Regional rivalries opposed the leaders of the various islands, many of whose peoples were deeply attached to their local culture. The army was the only effective national institution, whose presence ensured the unity of the new state.

Sukarno needed the backing of the army, just as its commanders needed the national legitimacy that he embodied. In the mid-1950s, the alliance between the two became the foundation for authoritarian rule. Like many other leaders of Third World countries, Sukarno was persuaded that the welfare of his new state depended upon his personal leadership. In 1956, he declared to Indonesians that he had dreamed of "burying" the old constitutional order and of giving his people

what he called a "Guided Democracy" and a "Guided Economy." In 1957, he took command of the state. His dream, when put in practice, translated into political dictatorship, a nationalized economy under state planning controls, and diplomatic nonalignment in the Cold War. Authoritarian rule replaced parliamentary democracy in Indonesia for the next forty years.

The leadership provided by Sukarno relied more on personal inspiration and favoritism than on coherent policies. His government seized all Dutch and other foreign businesses and estates, nationalizing the great oil fields of Royal Dutch-Shell. It lacked the trained personnel to run these state enterprises, however. As a result of this hasty nationalization, the country's economy passed through several years of painful recession. Sukarno accepted the economic assistance of Western and communist states, as both sides were competing for good relations with his country. To win the backing of the many political factions in his country he offered their leaders positions in the largest cabinet of any country in the world. His one hundred ministers worked largely for their own benefit, and that of their followers. Cronyism led to useless projects in the state-run businesses that enriched a handful of corrupt politicans backed by Sukarno. Meanwhile, the country went deeper and deeper into debt, and foreign trade declined for lack of funds to pay for imports.

Sukarno's dictatorship brought with it his own personality cult and nationalist ideology. He received the grand titles of "Permanent President" and "Great Leader of the Revolution." Boasting that his country was "living dangerously," Sukarno declared war on "neocolonialism" (shortened to NEKOLIM in his speeches) in all its forms. He blamed it for the economic hardship that his ineffective and corrupt regime had created. He encouraged the Indonesian army to seize islands on the borders of Indonesia, claiming them for his nation. Unity remained a fragile, contested creation. Sukarno and his army kept the island

National Heros and Imperialist Devils: Indonesian Government Poster Entitled "The Five Pillars [of Indonesian National Liberation] Crush All Forms of Imperialism," Approximately 1960 (*Howard Jones Collection/Hoover Institution*)

republic together, but the price was growing hostility of minority peoples toward Indonesian rule.

Sukarno's nationalist ideology and flamboyant leadership hid serious political weaknesses undermining his state. He himself realized that his personal powers were inadequate to maintain national unity. His solution was to search for a mass movement on which he and his regime could rely. He came to believe that the Indonesian Communist Party, the largest political organization in the country, would provide him with that disciplined popular support. He hoped that their backing would win him the diplomatic and military support of the People's Republic of China, at

a time when his government had few foreign allies. His rhetorical sparring with the West and expansionist foreign policy rested on a grandiose (and illusory) vision of Indonesia as a great power in south Asia.

The encouragement that he gave the Communists proved to be his downfall. By encouraging them, he became the center of a violent struggle for power. The Indonesian Communist Party and the army were bitter rivals for leadership in the country. The communist leaders seem to have believed that they had Sukarno's backing to seize power. In 1965, they secretly organized an armed uprising, beginning with the capture and execution of several of Indonesia's top military leaders. But their uprising failed, for the surviving generals, led by General Suharto, mobilized their troops to stop the insurrection. At the same time, they appealed to the population to join in resisting the Communists, whom they damned as "godless enemies" of the nation. Political revolt provoked mob executions.

Throughout the islands crowds, often led by military units or militant Muslim groups, attacked Communist Party centers throughout the country. Political and ethnic animosity within Indonesia, stirred up by pressures of nation-building, suddenly erupted in terrible violence. It produced a terrible butchering of Communists and their supporters, many of whom were drawn from the country's large Chinese community. Chinese migrants had moved to the East Indies during the centuries of Dutch rule. Many had become prosperous through trading and commerce. In a time of economic hardship, they became an easy target for the discontented, of whom there were many in Indonesia in the mid-1960s. Ethnic discord and political rivalries produced, there as elsewhere among the new nations, the seeds of mass violence. No one knows how many people died in the 1965 massacres. Conservative estimates point to a half-million dead.

In the turmoil Sukarno's regime fell from power. He was no longer trusted by his generals. The head of the army, General Suharto, took over control of the state. Indonesia remained a neutral, nonaligned country, taking foreign aid from East and West. General Suharto and the army leaders made national unity on the archipelago their highest priority, holding in check the ethnic unrest and denying the political opposition any public forum. Their second priority was economic development. They took apart Sukarno's half-hearted command economy, ending state planning. They sold nationalized enterprises (often to their own cronies), and opened the country to foreign investors (who often had to pay enormous bribes to set up operations). A small group of Indonesian bankers and investors received special favors from Suharto's government. In return, they secretly opened special bank accounts for politically influential individuals, among whom Suharto and his family were the most favored. Military dictatorship bred "crony capitalism" throughout the islands.

Gradually the Indonesian economy began to grow. By the 1980s, its abundant natural resources had become the cornerstone of an economic boom. Asian timber companies moved into the forested regions of Sumatra and Borneo, removing the valuable hardwood trees, burning the remaining forests, and leaving the land for plantation farming (see "Highlight," Chapter 8). By the 1990s, this Indonesian version of the "Asian way" of capitalism had turned the economy into one of the "newly emerging markets" of Asia.

SPOTLIGHT: Sukarno

In the early twentieth century, most of the peoples who inhabited the main islands of the Dutch colony of the East Indies still lived in isolation from one another and treated inhabitants from other islands as foreigners. The father of Sukarno (1901–70) was from the island of Java, but because he was one of the Dutch's few well-educated subjects he found work as a schoolteacher on the island of Bali. There he married a Balinese woman, whose parents were so outraged at her choice of an "outsider" from Java for husband that they banished her from her family. A half-century later, her son became the supreme leader of the new nation-state of Indonesia. It gathered within its borders all the islands of the vast archipelago of some seventeen thousand islands that the Dutch had gradually conquered over the previous two hundred years in forming their East Indian colony. It was an improbable dream of national unity that Sukarno and his followers made happen in the face of enormous obstacles.

Sukarno acquired his nationalist convictions while a student in the schools that the Dutch had founded to provide the colony with loyal native officials. His father was, as most Indonesians, a Muslim, but preferred to give his son a nonreligious education. Sukarno's university training pulled him away from the narrow, insular identity of an islander from Java, for it gave him the tools to imagine a unique Indonesian nation. As a boy he spoke both Javanese and Balinese. His schooling gave him fluency in Dutch (and later French and English), which opened up before him the literature of European nationalism. There he learned of the glory of national cultures, the dignity of independent, self-governing nations, and the injustice of empires and monarchs. His friendship with the first generation of Indonesian nationalists brought him within the circle of political parties already proclaiming their vision of a free Indonesia, and fighting the Dutch rulers to make their dream come true. Sukarno communicated most often in the language of his imperial rulers (just as Indian nationalists relied on English), but increasingly he made use of the Malay dialect that was becoming the common tongue among East Indies subjects, including the traders who moved among the islands and the native officials helping the Dutch. Sukarno's nationalism was shaped indirectly by the very Dutch imperialists whom he and his followers considered their worst enemies.

His revolutionary activities took shape within the Indonesian National Party, which he founded but whose idea of a nation termed "Indonesia" was a creation of predecessors in the Indonesian nationalist movement. He fought the Dutch through his writings and speeches, and for that suffered through years of imprisonment and exile. He proved himself an extraordinarily successful public figure, attracting a following through the force of his personality as much as through his message of national liberation. Over the years, he gradually codified his own nationalist ideology, which he termed the "Five Principles" of Indonesian unity. These were: nationalism (directed against insular hostility among the islanders), internationalism (acknowledging the rights of other nations), democracy (to him referring to a consensus, not majority rule), social well-being (care for the peoples of the nation), and belief in one supreme God (toleration for all religions). Like other twentieth-century revolutionaries, he believed in the power of ideas to produce a radical, progressive change in the way of life of the masses of the population. His was a creed of civic nationalism, adapted to the peculiar conditions of the East Indies (see "Highlight," this chapter). Like the creed that Gandhi formulated for India, it promised the new nation peace and prosperity on condition the peoples there overcome their ethnic, religious, and social conflicts. In these terms, it appeared a utopian vision. For him, it had the force of a religious faith, for which he sacrificed the security and comfort of ordinary life.

Sukarno struggled throughout his years in power to make that dream come true. In the course of the Second World War, he welcomed the help of those Japanese occupiers ready to encourage anti-Western nationalists. In return, he spoke publicly in support of the Japanese requests for Indonesian laborers needed to assist their war construction projects (virtually forced labor). By the end of the war, he was the undisputed leader of the Indonesian liberation movement. With the defeat of Japan in August 1945 he proclaimed the independence of Indonesia. He was the founder of a new nation-state.

In the years after the defeat of the Dutch in 1949, he found that his Five Principles were a poor substitute for effective rule, for which he had little taste. In 1957 he gave in to the temptation to

Sukarno in World War II: Cover to Japanese Pamphlet, 1944, Recruiting Indonesian Labor Brigades for War Effort (*Hoover Institution*)

assume dictatorial powers in what he termed a "Guided Democracy." Behind him the Indonesian army stood as the guarantor of his leadership, and of the unity of his nation-state. His leadership consisted principally in speeches condemning global imperialism and capitalism for his country's ills. His feeble answer to Indonesia's economic decline and ethnic conflicts was to praise the Indonesian Communist Party's proposals for a single-party state and a command economy similar to that of the People's Republic of China. His awareness of his own inadequacy as leader is the best explanation why in 1965 he encouraged the communist plot to eliminate their military rivals for power. It was a fatal choice. The victorious generals forced him to resign the presidency, keeping him under house arrest for his few remaining years. His dream of an Indonesian nation-state had come true, but its continued existence depended on a military dictatorship.

Singapore and the Global Economy

The political fate of the island of Singapore depended on its neighboring states, all former
colonies of the British Empire. In the territories
of Burma and Malaya, the experience of the war
years had given nationalist leaders the confidence to demand national independence after
1945. The British government offered no opposition to their request. The British Labor Party, in
power after 1945, readily agreed to organize
the transfer of power. Nationalists there welcomed the aid of British troops in defeating
communist-led uprisings in their lands. In 1948,
Burma became an independent state; a decade
later, the Malay colonies became the nation-state
of Malaysia.

The city of Singapore remained a British
crown colony. Its economic and strategic importance far outweighed its minute size. It lay on the
maritime path to East Asia and possessed the
finest naval port in southeast Asia. Its largely
Chinese population had been instrumental in
making it the commercial and financial capital of
the region. It was the exception to anticolonialism
(like Hong Kong), a prosperous remnant of an
empire surrounded by independent states.

The British government had no wish, or the
financial means, to maintain for long even this
minute imperial presence in the area. In 1963, it
ended its rule over the city, convincing Singapore's
leaders to join the Malaysian state in a federation.
This new state was a fragile creation, made up of
a multiethnic collection of disparate regions. The
Muslim Malay peoples, largely peasant and lacking the commercial skills of the Chinese, resented
the prosperity of Singapore. Their Muslim religious practices and communal organization constituted a vital part of their lives. Many feared that
their way of life would suffer if they were ruled
by Chinese politicians. The intensity of ethnic
antagonism between the two groups led to riots
by minority Malay in the city of Singapore and
political quarrels within the federal government

between the Chinese leaders of Singapore and
Malay politicians. Malay leaders, fearing that the
ethnic conflict would destroy their young state,
decided to expel the city from the federation. In
1965, Singapore was forced to form its own
independent state, an island of only two million
people.

Its isolation proved a blessing. Its leaders were
able to create the conditions for an economic
boom that rivaled that of Japan. The island-state
evolved into an authoritarian regime committed
to state-supported economic development. In free
elections, a majority of its population approved
the program of the People's Action Party. Once in
power, its leaders moved immediately to enforce
public discipline and rapid economic growth.
They virtually eliminated opposition political parties, independent trade unions, and any separatist
ethnic movements among the city's Chinese,
Malay, and Indian inhabitants. They severely punished all crimes, with small offenses punished by
whipping with a birch rod (introduced first by the
British). They instructed families to have more
children when Singapore's birth rate fell too low.
They turned their tiny state into a model of social
order, economic productivity, and authoritarian
rule. The head of the People's Action Party and
longtime prime minister, Lee Kuan Yew, promised
Singapore's citizens an "orderly, organized, sensi-
ble, rational society."

This authoritarian regime settled down to
guide its tiny state on its path to social order and
economic wealth. Its unstated bargain with the
population called for their submission to authoritarianism, which it claimed was rooted in Confucianism, in exchange for economic prosperity. It
invited foreign investors to develop oil refining
and textile and electronic manufacturing, staffed
by the island's industrious, educated work force.
It opened the door of the city-state to international
banks and welcomed global commercial firms to
use its port. On a small scale, it introduced to its
island the "guided capitalism" that had succeeded
so well in Japan. Not surprisingly, Lee Kuan Yew

championed the cause of the special "Asian way" of orderly capitalist countries.

Singapore founded its prosperity on global economic expansion and on its internal political stability. In economic terms, it succeeded beyond its wildest dreams, becoming one of the four East Asian lands termed the "Four Dragons" for their booming growth rates. The city's rate of yearly economic growth rose to above 10 percent by the 1970s, remaining at that level for the next twenty years. Soon the population's standard of living was second only to that of Japan among Asian countries. Economic conditions on the island were the envy of surrounding states. Militarily insignificant, its security depended on its vital role in the economic activity of South Asia. It, too, was a nonaligned country, seeking good relations with all countries, communist and noncommunist, conducting financial and commercial affairs with whoever had the means to pay. Although it resembled in size a city-state of Renaissance Italy, it contained within its borders all the dynamic economic forces propelling the global boom of the late twentieth century.

INDEPENDENCE FOR INDIA AND PAKISTAN

The legacy of the Second World War in India differed from that of other countries in south Asia in one vital respect. Japanese armies had never penetrated deeply into Indian territory. The British viceroy, the Indian civil service, and the Indian army remained the vital forces in the united provinces, while the six hundred princes who had accepted British rule continued to govern their principalities. Only those Indian soldiers who had been taken prisoner by the Japanese in 1942 and who had agreed to join the Indian National Army became collaborators against the British. Their welcome as heroes on their return to India in 1945 proved that opposition to the British overrode all other issues confronting Indians in the postwar years.

The End of British Rule

The National Congress leaders had vowed from the time they began their struggle for independence to preserve the unity that the British had given the subcontinent. They desired national independence and a democratically elected government that respected the rights of the entire population, regardless of religion or social rank. For Mohandas Gandhi, Congress's inspirational leader, special privileges for any religious community were a betrayal of his deepest belief in civic equality for all citizens ("secularism") within a free Indian nation-state. This vision was threatened by the social antagonism (termed "communalism") that divided the Muslim and Hindu communities, and by the political program of the Muslim League. Indian unity and independence were inextricable goals for the National Congress, but only indpendence proved attainable.

The half-century before 1945 had witnessed a rising number of violent incidents and riots pitting Hindus against Muslims. Every province mingled the two communities, though overall Hindus were the large majority. No single territory was exclusively Hindu or Muslim. The population of Calcutta, largest and most industrial of India's cities and the capital of the province of Bengal, was almost equally divided between these two groups. Their very proximity was a cause of friction and political rivalry, because self-rule raised the specter of one community losing power to the other. Individual rights appeared to many Indians less important that communal solidarity. National independence threatened to tear India apart.

The Muslim League preferred the partition of the subcontinent between Muslim and Hindu territories to one unified nation-state. If a unified Indian state, ruled democratically, placed government in the hands of the National Congress, the League feared that the new rulers would deprive the minority Muslims of civil and political rights, regardless of the promises of Congress leaders. What to liberal idealists appeared democratic

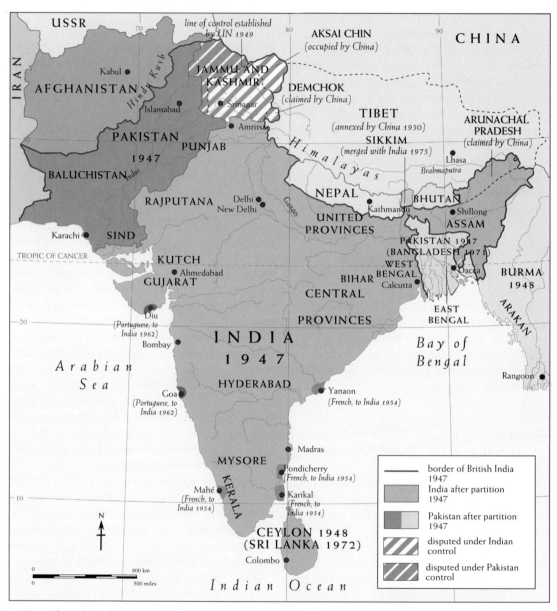

Postcolonial South Asia

safeguards of individual freedom seemed to the League a threat of minority persecution. In the postwar years, it made the achievement of a separate Muslim state of Pakistan its immediate objective. Its leaders did not seek a religious (theocratic) regime, for they considered the label of Muslim to be an ethnic marker of social and cultural identity. Their plan was a tremendous gamble, for no such nation-state, organized around Muslim religious loyalty, had ever existed. Still, the followers of the Muslim League were prepared after war's end to resort to communal violence to prevent Indian national unification and to achieve their goal of Pakistan.

Preparing for Indian independence was the first priority for British and Indian leaders. The British Labor government supported freedom for the peoples of the subcontinent as strongly as they did the empire's other Asian colonies. Its postwar financial crisis dictated rapid liberation for India, whose rule placed a heavy burden on the impoverished British treasury. Mass demonstrations and violence were a constant threat. The British proposed new elections to select an Indian leadership ready and able to negotiate the terms of independence.

When those elections were held in 1946, National Congress candidates won a majority in nearly all the provinces. Yet the Muslim League received the support of most Muslim voters. Who then spoke for India? Congress and the League both agreed to negotiations with the British, but each on its own terms. Mohammed Ali Jinnah, head of the Muslim League, demanded that Muslim representatives be granted an equal voice in negotiations alongside the Congress. But Jawaharlal Nehru and the other influential leaders of Congress refused to recognize the right of the League to represent the Muslim community, fearing that to do so would represent a fatal concession to partition. In July 1946, Jinnah concluded that his party could not become the sole negotiator for India's Muslims by legal means. He called on his Muslim supporters to prove forcefully to the British and to Congress their hold over the Muslim population.

The League's Day of Direct Action in August 1946 was the real turning point in the history of postwar India. Jinnah proclaimed that "the only solution to India's problem is Pakistan," that is, partition of the Indian subcontinent into what he referred to as "Hindustan" and his Muslim state.

To make clear that civil war was the alternative, he demanded of Muslims throughout India that they join in "direct action," including strikes, meetings, and demonstrations. He and the other League leaders must have known that rioting would accompany the demonstrations and that communal conflict would inevitably result. He accepted the possibility, saying: "We also have a pistol." The Muslim League's agitation did lead to Muslim-Hindu riots throughout the country. Ethnic hostility and fear deepened as the tragic process of partition began.

Bengal was the scene of the greatest bloodshed. Its capital city, Calcutta, was the scene of such violence that observers later called the events of those terrible days the "Great Calcutta Killing." Perhaps six thousand people died in that city alone, most of them innocent Hindus or Muslims attacked by mobs from both sides. British forces moved into the centers of rioting, gradually restoring order. Gandhi, horrified at the violence, set out on a personal pilgrimage through Muslim as well as Hindu areas of Bengal to restore peace and tolerance by his own personal example and teaching. Although he risked death at the hands of a fanatic, he helped calm the population, but only temporarily.

It was tempting to blame partition on the League. Nehru himself, without any deep religious feeling and cosmopolitan in his political ideology, hated the League and all it embodied. He considered the Muslim religious solidarity that the League cultivated to be "medieval," a dangerous anachronism in a "rapidly changing world of industrialism, science, and nuclear power." He repeated over and over his conviction that other religious groups "have nothing to fear from the Hindus." After his visit that August to riot-torn areas of the northern province of Punjab, he expressed despair and "shame" that Indians should have betrayed the "great ideals that [Gandhi] has placed before us." That year he and the other Congress leaders persisted in working for a free and united India. But the country was too deeply and bitterly divided. The Muslim League had inflamed, but not created, that bitterness and hostility. Its fault lay in condoning and leading the mob action. Ultimately, religious and social divisions, not political manipulation by the League, decided the fate of India.

Frustrated and baffled by the impasse in negotiations, the British cabinet in February 1947 proclaimed that Great Britain would pull out of India within a year. It was prepared to leave even if it failed to bring agreement among the Indian negotiators on a constitution and the means for the peaceful transfer of power. The statement was a declaration of defeat in the form of an ultimatum. The British government refused to take responsibility any longer for the escalating violence. One British official called the country's ethnic riots to be the "natural, if ghastly, process tending in its own way to the solution of the Indian problem." Jinnah had made his point. That spring the British government appointed a new viceroy, Lord Mountbatten, to make one last effort to achieve a negotiated settlement. He concluded that partition presented the only solution. The Muslim League, he reported, was ready to "resort to arms if Pakistan in some form were not conceded."

Partition of the Indian Colony

This outcome was impossible without the agreement of the National Congress. It spoke for the majority of India's population. Partition did not have the support of Gandhi, whose entire life and moral preaching had been dedicated to fellowship and toleration. He had pursued national independence because he believed it to be the path to Indian spiritual rebirth. Acceptance of Pakistan meant recognizing communalism and the victory of religious separatism. He considered the partition to be destructive and evil. But he did not impede the settlement. He allowed Nehru to assume leadership of the National Congress and to take on his shoulders responsibility for Indian independence. That spring Nehru concluded that par-

tition was inevitable. In June 1947, Mountbatten announced to India and the world that the subcontinent would receive independence not as one but as two states.

Partition cut through the fabric of Indian political, economic, and social life. The provinces with a substantial Muslim population would go to Pakistan, the rest to India. The populations of two key provinces, Bengal and Punjab, were divided among religious groups. The Punjab contained within its borders the Sikh religious community as well as Muslims (as numerous as the Sikhs), and a smaller group of Hindus. Provincial leaders reluctantly agreed to the partition of their two regions. A British official secretly rewrote the map of India to draw the boundaries separating the two states. The partition left the Indus River valley in the west and part of Bengal in the east in the new Pakistan state, itself divided into two separate territories. Three fourths of the subcontinent's population went into India, under Congress leadership.

The partition required the division of land, communities, economic systems, and the institutions of state administration and army. East Bengal's economy, dependent on the export of jute, lost its principal port and center of industry, Calcutta, which went to India. The vast irrigation system in the province of Punjab was disrupted because the frontier cut across its river and canal systems. The Sikh community there was split in two, with its holy city of Amritsar in India and its capital of Lahore in Pakistan. Millions of Hindus remained in Pakistan, and one third of all Muslims were still in India. August 15 was set as the day of independence.

Nehru spoke to the Indian people on Independence Day. He exulted in the newly won freedom from empire. "We are a free and sovereign people and we have rid ourselves of the burden of the past." Despite Jinnah's objections, his state kept the name of India. Even with partition, it remained one of the most populous countries in the world. The removal of the "burden of foreign domination" was in his eyes a great historic event; it was part of the liberation of colonial peoples in their move to equality with the western nations. He had ambitious plans for dealing with the "great economic problems of the masses of the people," including industrial development, redistribution of wealth, irrigation, and hydroelectric projects. First, however, the country had to "put an end to all the internal strife and violence."

In the capital of Pakistan, Jinnah spoke to his people. He prayed that "God Almighty give us strength to make Pakistan truly a great nation among all the nations of the world." He urged that Pakistani Muslims respect the rights of his country's Hindu population. That day the exact boundaries of India and Pakistan were made public, revealing the true dimensions of partition.

Centuries of British rule had created a legacy that helped shape the new states. British administrators had formed the Indian civil service, whose authority extended into the rural districts to the level of village life. British officers had trained an Indian army in Western military skills. After independence, Indian administrative and military personnel immediately began to serve in the new regimes, replacing the departing British officials. English had been the language by which many educated Indians communicated among themselves and acquired direct access to Western learning. It became the first official language in both states.

The constitutional origins of self-government lay in the Government of India Act that Great Britain had promulgated in 1935. It had created a federal state that allotted separate legislative powers to the provinces. It had proclaimed the principle of legislative control over the executive in a cabinet form of rule, modeled on the British parliamentary system. This constitution provided the basis of government for both Pakistan and India in their first years of existence. The era of British colonial domination also passed on a valuable economic inheritance. The enormous Indian railroad network and the ocean ports, sinews of an industrial economy, became the property of the new

states, as did the irrigation system and hydroelectric dams. The formal transfer of power from Great Britain to India and Pakistan occurred remarkably easily, and the new leaders imagined that their populations would heed their calls for peace and accept the partition as the necessary price for their freedom.

Independence and War

Neither the British nor the nationalist leaders understood the intensity of communal fears and antagonism among Muslims, Hindus, and Sikhs. As a result, they could not foresee the outpouring of anger and panic provoked by the announcement of the new boundaries on August 15. Westernized leaders such as Nehru and Jinnah had built up a vast following among the masses, yet were separated from them by class and education. They did not heed the warning from Sikh leaders in the Punjab that "our swords shall decide if the Muslims shall rule," or note the rising numbers of Sikh men joining armed bands in anticipation of conflict with Muslims. Only Gandhi sensed the tremendous human tragedy that partition had precipitated.

The two partitioned provinces, Bengal in the east and Punjab in the west, were the regions where greatest violence was likely to occur. Calcutta, capital of Bengal, had been the scene of the worst rioting in 1946. At the urging of Lord Mountbatten and with the backing of the leader of the city's Muslims, Gandhi agreed to go there. He was prepared to place his own life in jeopardy to prevent blood from flowing again in the city. He went to live in the worst slums of the city, proclaiming a fast to death unless the leaders of the religious communities there agreed to collaborate in keeping their peoples from rioting. So great was his moral authority that, almost single-handedly, he maintained peace in Bengal that month.

In the Punjab, however, violence erupted immediately. Refugees began to move across the border, becoming easy targets for mobs. Rumors of atrocities on both sides of the boundaries set Hindus and Sikhs against Muslims in Indian Punjab, while in Pakistan Muslim bands attacked Sikhs and Hindus. The fifty thousand troops that Mountbatten had at his disposal could do little to stop the rioting. The number of refugees swelled to a torrent as terrified families and entire villages set out on foot or in trains to find sanctuary, the Muslims to Pakistan, the Hindus and Sikhs to India. They became victims of roving bands of killers and robbers. The violence spread to the Indian capital of Delhi, where Hindu refugees from Pakistan spread stories of massacre, mass rape of Hindu women, and widespread looting by Muslims. In retaliation, Hindus attacked the city's large Muslim population. Mountbatten and Nehru, collaborating closely to prevent chaos from engulfing the country, had to call out the army to keep order there.

In the vast countryside, order was restored much more slowly. Perhaps a half-million Indians and Pakistanis died that year as a result of the hardship of flight or of mob violence. By mid-1948, an estimated five million refugees had arrived in India and perhaps an equal number in west Pakistan. Independence brought the worst civil strife in Indian history and left in its wake intense animosity between the peoples of the two countries. Nehru attacked the Muslim League as "fascist" and vowed never to let such religious fanaticism destroy the democratic and nonviolent principles of the Congress movement. Two years later he recalled in a sort of self-confession the anguish of those terrible months, when Indian leaders became "slaves of the events that inexorably unroll[ed] themselves before our eyes" and succumbed to "fear and hatred." He shared with his people the anger aroused by mob violence.

Gandhi himself came to Delhi late in the year to continue his crusade for peace and understanding. His efforts were directed toward the leaders of the two states as well as toward their peoples.

He attacked fanaticism no matter who preached intolerance, Hindu or Muslim. He received all who wished to talk with him despite rumors of plots against his life. On January 20, 1948, a Hindu political extremist, outraged at Gandhi's message of peace and conciliation, shot him as he was going to prayer. Gandhi died a martyr's death, another victim of the partition.

Most of the territories ruled still by Indian princes went peacefully, with some strong persuasion by British advisers, to the state in which the principalities were located. But the prince of Kashmir refused to make a firm commitment, causing a major, and long-lasting crisis. In late 1947, the Indian government decided to use military force to bring this land into their state. Although the prince was Hindu, the majority of his population was Muslim. Among them were strong supporters of unification with Pakistan. They had begun violent demonstrations to force their prince to agree to join the new Muslim state. Pakistani troops moved over the border to bring additional pressure on him. But Nehru, whose family was from Kashmir, was determined to keep the mountainous region in his state. That October Indian troops stopped the Muslim invasion and occupied most of the province. Nehru denied that his state was an aggressor nation and claimed that the Pakistani attack represented "aggression of a brutal and unforgivable kind, aggression against the people of Kashmir and against the Indian Union." In fact, both sides were guilty of aggression, turning to their armed forces for control of the vital Himalayan area.

The conflict over Kashmir escalated into open war between Pakistan and India. Pakistani troops attempted to expel the Indian forces from Kashmir. After several months of fighting, both sides agreed to an armistice, with the front lines close to their original location. The war had succeeded only in partitioning Kashmir by force. The failure to settle this issue left behind a poisonous legacy of Muslim-Hindu hostility in the mountainous province. The final consequence of partition was to turn Pakistan and India into out-right enemies. Their conflict endured for the next fifty years, and erupted twice in new wars. Pakistan, the weaker state, sought military alliance and foreign aid from the United States; India accepted military aid from the Soviet Union. In the early 1980s, both states secretly developed nuclear weapons for possible use against their neighbor. The division of Kashmir turned that front-line territory, once so beautiful it may have been the source of the myth of "Shangri-la," into a war zone. Partition was a tragedy for the population of the subcontinent and a terrible burden for the two new states.

HIGHLIGHT: New Nations and Ethnic Strife

The new states that emerged in the late twentieth century where empires once ruled all presented in one form or another the image of the nation-state. Flags, ceremonies, and heroes (real or mythical) commemorated and celebrated the historical achievements and prestige of a particular national community, united in one state. Leaders claimed that their government embodied special qualities of the people over whom they ruled. This was true in Latin America following the collapse of Spanish and Portuguese empires in the early nineteenth century. It was true in Asia and Africa after the Western empires withdrew from those continents in the decades after 1945. In their early years, these states were weak. Their governments had not, in most cases, had the chance to establish a solid foundation of authority and often were plagued by internal rivalries among ambitious individuals and political movements eager for power. The ideology of nationalism promised the new leaders a firm pledge of loyalty from their population. First, however, they had to convince the population of their own national legitimacy.

The creed of nationalism could be a trap for new states if politicians misused it. Its crucial shortcoming was the confusion surrounding the idea of a national community itself. The term could refer to all the people within the boundaries of that state, which derived from them a unique civic calling that distinguished it from other nation-states. This ideal of the nation is termed "civic nationalism." On the stroke of midnight, August 15, 1947, the Indian prime minister, Nehru, welcomed the freeing of "the soul of a nation" given at that moment its independence. He, like Gandhi, believed freedom and tolerance were by themselves bonds that would maintain the unity of the Indian people and their leaders.

But nation also could refer to peoples united by their collective sense of ethnic identity, which supposed a common ancestry and usually a common language. Civic ideals constituted a vague moral appeal by contrast with the belief in ancestral nationhood, characterized by one historian as "blood and belonging." This national ideal is termed "ethnic nationalism." When this form of national loyalty prevailed, the new states confronted the potential of serious internal divisions. All the new states contained within their borders more than one, and often many, separate groups with strong ethnic ties. Ethnic loyalty became especially meaningful in the lives of the population after independence from colonial rule. It offered the people within a particular community the reassurance of a shared collective identity, the social solidarity needed at moments of political unrest, and the bonds of mutual assistance invaluable in hard times.

These bonds of ethnic unity originated in many sources. Language formed the most prevalent and meaningful marker of ethnic identity. Among the population of India were fifteen separate major languages. After Indian independence, leaders of some of these peoples demanded a territory of their own within the Indian federation, even though other peoples shared that area. Religious practice was another powerful social bond. It was the foundation of the Muslim League's demand for a state of Muslim people to be carved out of the Indian colony. A belief in common ancestry was yet another ethnic link. Leaders of major and even small tribal groups claimed a special place in independent Nigeria because they believed their own people's uniqueness deserved special territorial recognition. Each time these claims for ethnic recognition appeared, they implied that civic nationalism was less important to some people than their own ethnic identity. That demand, in turn, raised the possibility that the very borders of the new state had to be redrawn, or even that the state should not exist as such.

Strife among ethnic groups in one state emerged out of the heritage of colonial experience, postcolonial politics, and economic hardship. The newly freed states frequently inherited from their colonial past a policy of favored treatment for one particular people. Often the imperial administration had recruited soldiers or subordinate officials to serve their colonial needs. Animosities built up over the colonial decades spilled out in ethnic conflict once independence had lifted imperial control.

This historical experience was only the prelude to the real difficulties created by independence. The new nation-states followed in their first years the democratic principle of popular elections to select their new leaders. Electoral competition created the possibility for political parties to emerge claiming to defend the needs of a particular people. In South Africa, the Inkatha Party spoke for the Zulu people alone, and denied the African National Congress's claim to be the true voice of all African peoples there. Voters often preferred candidates from their own people. Voting on the basis of ethnic loyalty insured that the candidates from the party backed by the largest ethnic group had the best chance of gaining power. Since the winners could use their position to distribute jobs and other rewards only to followers from their people, minority peoples could find themselves outcasts as a result of democratic rule. When the Ibo people of Nigeria believed themselves in this situation in the late 1960s, they rebelled against the central government. The resulting civil war, which lasted three years, nearly destroyed Nigeria.

The danger of conflict became particularly great when ethnic groups demanded the creation of a separate independent state for themselves. Ethnic nationalism rested on the belief in a "native land" that belonged by "right" to a particular people. The assertion was based usually on a people's historical claim of having lived there over many generations. It was even made, though, for lands where a people had not lived for centuries. The Zionist movement affirmed that Palestine was the real homeland for the Jewish people, though the Romans had expelled almost all the Jews from there almost two thousand years before. Nowhere did the inhabitants in a particular area all belong to one ethnic group, nor were all those identifying with that group located within one compact territory. The demand to govern one's "own" land meant necessarily that the other peoples there did not enjoy a comparable right. By its very nature, the claim to a native land created ethnic minorities. If these peoples responded by making a claim to the same land, no peaceful resolution could satisfy both sides. The fifty-year struggle between Palestinian Arabs and Israeli Jews emerged out of that dispute.

The search for a way to reconcile civic and ethnic national loyalties led political leaders to promise legal protection of ethnic differences. In many Third World countries, constitutions spelled out minority rights, the most important of which was usually language rights. Often fundamental laws created a federal political system to divide state powers between the center, whose representatives spoke for all the peoples, and regions where particular ethnic groups obtained their own leadership and local rights. This system became the legal foundation of ethnically diverse countries such as India, Nigeria, and, late in the century, the Russian Federation.

It was a fragile compromise, since in theory it denied to the majority people the right to create a nation-state in its image, and by necessity refused to a minority people the right to their own nation-state. When peaceful compromise failed to satisfy ethnic nationalist demands, the result was civil disorder, political repression, and civil war. These conflicts first appeared very early in the postimperial era in Asia and Africa. They continued to erupt, and with increased intensity, later in the century. One reason was the spreading struggle for a livelihood among impoverished masses in the Third World. The temptation for them was strong to blame their poverty on other peoples, accused of denying them access to economic benefits. In times of economic hardship in the 1960s and late 1990s, the Chinese minority of Indonesia, largely urban and engaged in commerce and finance, became a target for other peoples in that republic envious of their well-being.

Civil wars within the new nation-states emerged, in their early stages, from the conflict among ethnic groups. At times, the spark was the effort of minority peoples to secede and to achieve at any cost their own independent state. Many of these revolts were settled by military means. Though the Indian constitution and federal laws guaranteed respect for ethnic rights, the government turned to extra-legal powers of repression when violent nationalist movements among the Sikhs, then the Kashmir population, threatened secession and the breakup of India. The Nigerian government triumphed over the Ibo in a brutal civil war that resulted in the death of millions of civilians, most from starvation resulting from the economic blockade of the region.

Occasionally free elections brought the ethnic conflicts to an end, usually leading to peaceful secession. In 1993, the Eritrean People's Front, after decades of guerrilla war, forced the Ethiopian government to hold an election on independence for the people of the province of Eritrea. Its popular backing was overwhelming, and the new nation-state of Eritrea appeared in Africa. This was a compromise, and Ethiopian leaders, determined to reunite their state, launched a new war six years later to retake this land. Only Eritrean armed might saved the new state.

The collapse of multiethnic communist states in eastern Europe produced some of the worst ethnic conflict in recent times. These states, the most important of which were the Soviet Union and Yugoslavia, had repressed ethnic unrest among their peoples by creating "national republics" for the largest groups, but ultimately they relied on forceful methods resembling those of colonial empires. When the Communists lost power, these animosities quickly reemerged. The worst violence occurred in the Balkan state of Yugoslavia. It had created within its federation separate republics for its peoples, among whom the Croat and Serb peoples were the most numerous. Nationalism among these peoples erupted in civil war when the Yugoslav state collapsed in 1991. Hostility toward minorities was so great that some nationalists were prepared to forcibly expel or murder thousands of innocent civilians living in "their land" who did not belong to their nation. This cruel practice, called "ethnic cleansing," revealed how inhuman ethnic conflict could become.

In the 1990s, the problem of restraining ethnic conflicts became the principal issue facing the international community. Verbal protests from outside states and the United Nations could not halt bitter ethnic struggles such as the Yugoslav civil war, or the 1994 violence in the African state of Rwanda. The intervention of foreign troops could for a while restrain the mob rioting and killings. Some observers argued for the moral obligation of outside intervention to end the bloodshed. At times it seemed that, only when the fighting had created a human wasteland, did exhaustion end the violence. In these places, nationalism had replaced epidemics as the great killer of humanity.

INDIA AND PAKISTAN AS NATION-STATES

As a result of British withdrawal from the sub-continent of India, it appeared on world maps as a land divided into first two, then three large countries. Their leaders claimed, in their own terms, to govern nation-states. Complicating state-building was the painful task of healing the wounds caused by the partition of British India between Pakistan and India, then again of west and east Pakistan in 1971. Within India, small but violent nationalist movements among some of its peoples led to civil disorder and military repression. The promise of peace and civic nationalism that the leaders had originally promised proved beyond their ability to fulfill.

Nehru and the New India

A new Indian state took form under Nehru's leadership. In the first violent months, he and the head of the National Congress, V. Patel, ruled virtually as a military government. Yet the Indian government put together the elements of a democratic state. The first step consisted of completing the incorporation of the princely states into Indian provinces. In exchange for generous allowances, almost all princes renounced their power peacefully. Only the Muslim prince of Hyderabad resisted, until finally Indian troops occupied his land in 1948 to "restore order" in what was officially called a "police action." The removal of the princes from power amounted to a sort of national revolution, achieved almost without force. Only the unresolved fate of Kashmir continued to remind Indians of the complexity and potential tragic consequences of nation-building in one of the oldest civilizations in the world.

The creation of a new administration and army proved relatively painless. Despite Congress's earlier criticism of Indians working for the British civil service and army, the new government accepted willingly their assimilation into the new Indian state. It preferred the stability and efficiency provided by trained administrators and experienced military forces to the dangers of forming a state apparatus from scratch. This personnel proved its worth in those first chaotic months of independence, serving the new state as loyally as they had their former British rulers.

Enormous responsibility for the shape of the new state rested in Nehru's hands. His political authority was virtually unlimited, for he enjoyed immense popularity as father of his country. His political ideal, as he told an American audience in 1949, was to find "some balance between the centralized authority of the state and the assurance of freedom and opportunity to each individual." The National Congress had from the start gathered together diverse groups defending a variety of interests and creeds. The new state had to reconcile these divergent objectives. Nehru valued this diversity, accepting the compromises it forced upon him.

Agreement on basic political goals did unite all factions of the National Congress. Key to their plans was the creation of a liberal democracy in India. In all of Asia, only Japan had successfully adapted Western democratic institutions to its public life. It had the advantage of small size, a homogeneous population, and historical unity. Democratic government in India represented in practice an audacious gamble. It appeared to Congress leaders the best guarantee of toleration and equal rights to all Indians regardless of religion, language, or caste. To political and civil liberties Congress added social welfare and state-sponsored economic development, both intended to protect and enhance the well-being of India's impoverished masses. Three objectives—democracy, toleration, and socialism—pointed toward the transformation of one of the oldest civilized societies in the world. The task of the Indian leaders was formidable, and the very democratic institutions and diversity that they wished to protect severely restricted their means of action.

Jawaharlal Nehru (*Embassy of India, Washington, D.C.*)

The Indian constitution went into effect in 1950. It preserved and extended the federal structure first introduced by the British in 1935. The provincial states and the federal government were all ruled by ministries, dependent on majorities in their legislatures to retain power. The position of greatest importance was that of prime minister of the federal cabinet, empowered even to dissolve provincial governments (that is, to violate the principle of federalism) if there existed a threat to the unity of India. Nehru occupied that office until his death in 1964. Political and civil liberties were guaranteed to all citizens. Voting was by universal suffrage. The first elections for regular legislative positions took place in 1951. More than 170 million citizens had the right to vote, over half of whom were illiterate. This enormous electorate made India, as Nehru later remarked, the "largest functioning democracy in the world."

Nehru's political stature within India was so great that it might have undermined the very foundations of the free democracy that National Congress defended. Many years earlier he had written for an Indian journal an anonymous portrait of himself, warning that "in this revolutionary epoch Caesarism [i.e., dictatorial rule like that of the Roman general Julius Caesar] is always at the door, and is it not possible that Jawaharlal [Nehru] might fancy himself a Caesar? Therein lies the danger for Jawaharlal and India." He might have added that the danger existed in all the newly independent Asian and African countries. Sukarno of Indonesia did succumb to the temptation of Caesarism. Nehru's personal commitment to liberty was a key ingredient of Indian democracy.

Democratic Socialism in India

India's path to democratic socialism supposed fundamental social and economic reforms. Nehru's ideal was "a socialist pattern of society which is classless, casteless." His principal concern was the misery of much of the Indian population. One-half of his people were estimated in 1950 to live in abject poverty, lacking adequate food for an active life. He did not attempt a campaign of expropriation of private property, such as occurred in China. Peaceful reform and tolerance of diversity forbade that path of reform. Instead, he conceived of an economy divided into public and private sectors, with the state exercising substantial regulatory controls over both. India's established industries remained in private hands, as did its farms and commerce.

For the next forty years, the Indian state played a central role in the country's economic development. It claimed ownership of major industrial projects such as steel mills (built with state funds and foreign aid), of public utilities (gas and electricity), and of new irrigation projects. A National Planning Commission guided the development of India's "mixed economy" (part capitalist, part socialist). Its administrative personnel was responsible for crucial decisions on state investments, agricultural development, transportation, and foreign trade.

The commission used state funds to guide economic development in a manner best suited (in theory) to improve the living conditions of the people. It relied on a combination of elements of the Soviet command economy, which Nehru admired, and the collaboration of India's capitalists and peasant farmers. Its most ambitious plan for rural development relied on the voluntary efforts of millions of villagers. The Village Development Program granted state funds to village committees for the construction of wells and schools, for minimum health care, and for other measures essential to fight poverty. Within a few years, 150 million Indians shared in the benefits of this program. It proved a remarkable success, all the more so as Indian socialism excluded the use of Maoist methods of compulsion and mass mobilization.

Economic planning worked well in those first years. India's agricultural production climbed 3 percent a year, almost twice as fast as population growth. The second Five-Year Plan, although not as successful as the first, did maintain a comparable level of economic expansion. Industrial production, the great hope of that plan, grew 6 percent annually, a rate that increased to 9 percent in the 1960s. But India's population explosion of almost 2 percent a year frustrated hopes of freeing India from dependence on industrial imports and of insuring adequate food for the country. The government, to avoid conflict with Muslim religious authorities, made no effort in those years to promote birth control. Improved medical care and social welfare contributed as well to the expansion of the population from 350 million at independence to more than seven hundred million in the mid-1970s. It was a crushing burden for the economy.

Feeding the population became a problem so critical that only Western help saved the country from famine in the mid-1960s. Western agronomists had developed new, high-yield strains of dwarf wheat and rice. They intended their discoveries particularly for poor agrarian lands. These crops were unknown in those areas and required complex farming techniques. Large amounts of chemical fertilizers were needed to sustain substantial harvests year after year. The governments

Third World India: Field Workers Winnowing Rice, South India (*Indian National Congress Collection, Hoover Institution*)

of both India and Pakistan were initially hostile to these exotic crops. In desperation, India's Minister of Agriculture, faced with a grave population crisis and stubborn opponents, planted his own garden in the capital Delhi with the new wheat to prove its value. His gardening experiment, plus one thousand "demonstration sites" around the country, proved his point. In 1967, the government agreed to distribute the wheat seeds throughout India. Indian grain production soared, and by the mid-1970s the country was producing harvests sufficient to meet the needs of the growing population. The use of these crops required extensive application of insecticides and fertilizers, produced at new factories (owned by multinational corporations) like that outside the city of Bhopal. Famine in India was averted, at least for a few decades.

The "Indian way" of economic development did not produce miracles, but its results were substantial as measured over the first thirty years of independence. Perhaps the best comparison was with China, where famine and economic stagnation followed the Great Leap Forward of the late 1950s. By contrast, India's moderate policies avoided social turmoil and maintained for the first decades a steady rate of economic growth, albeit at a snail's pace.

Improvements also came in health and education. Average life expectancy among Indians doubled between 1950 and 1990, rising from thirty-two to sixty years. It was a phenomenal achievement, resulting from both the relative success of public health and the improvement in the Indian standard of living. Indian efforts to spread education were much less successful. During those same decades literacy spread to one half of the population. The key skill that opened access to the modern economy remained unobtainable for hundreds of millions of Indians. The Indian government was determined not to let this obstacle get in the way of disseminating its news (and national ideals) among the population. To do so, it set up a national television network, launched a communications satellite, and provided villages with television sets (coming before schools in some cases).

Despite these improvements, poverty remained widespread. In the 1980s, over one third of the total population was still impoverished. Once hidden in the vast countryside of the subcontinent, the poor became far more visible when, in a desperate search for a livelihood, they moved to urban areas. In the 1980s places such as Calcutta were the goal of a thousand new immigrants each day. India's cities became focal points of human misery. A wasteland around a new pesticide factory near the city of Bhopal became a shantytown for hundreds of thousands of these poor migrants, until an explosion at the plant spread poisonous gases that killed thousands of the inhabitants in 1984. Urbanization in such conditions was a sign not of economic development but rather of the ongoing struggle to survive of hundreds of millions of Indians.

Ethnic Diversity and Secular Democracy

During the same period, the Indian government put into effect laws intended to insure equal rights for India's multiethnic, multireligious population. "Secularism" was the term used by the National Congress government to describe their program. It was intended to assure the protection of civil law and a common citizenship to the entire population. Customs and entrenched social and religious prejudice built up over many centuries stood in the path of these goals. But Nehru insisted that secularism be achieved "through our own volition, as a result of our own experience," not "through any kind of force or pressure." It was a noble dream.

The constitution itself abolished the social category of untouchables and declared caste restrictions to be illegal. It established the principle of social equality for all Indians regardless of religion, caste, or sex. To become effective, its principles had to be embodied in laws touching the personal lives of the population. It confronted the deeply rooted customs of marriage and property ownership, bastions of caste exclusiveness and of the subjugation of women. Caste prejudices continued to divide the population, and intolerance toward untouchables weakened very slowly despite the special laws intended to protect them.

At the heart of the secularist project was the commitment of the Indian leaders to keep their state neutral in all religious matters. All official discussions and policies had to avoid even the slightest implication of preference for one religion or another. This concern was most acute in the state's relations with the minority Muslim population. They remained apprehensive at any threat to their religious laws and customs. Although it was not originally intended to do so, secularism turned into a form of defense of Islam. The Muslim community retained its own customary laws governing marriage and divorce. In this domain, the civil laws of the state did not reach all the people.

The majority Hindu population did slowly receive legal protection as individual citizens. In the mid-1950s, the Indian state issued basic laws establishing civic equality of rights for Hindu women. The Hindu Marriage Act of 1955 and the Hindu Succession Act of 1956 established the legal basis for equality among Hindu Indians. The Succession Act gave women equal rights with men in inheritance and ownership of property. The Marriage Act declared polygamy and bigamy criminal offenses, permitted divorce, and made provision for alimony. Subsequently, marriage dowry was made illegal. In daily life, this equality of condition spread first among upper- and middle-class women in India. They increasingly shared in the new opportunities for education and work.

Among the remainder of the population, social custom and family restraints continued to hold women in inferior status. "Purdah" (female seclusion) was still widely practiced among Muslims. The Hindu custom of marriage dowries, though illegal, became the source of cruel demands from the husband's family for expensive gifts from the family of the bride. When these were refused, the wife risked beatings, even murder, at the hands of her husband and his relatives. Women's defense groups estimated that in the 1980s between ten thousand and fifteen thousand women died each year as a result of these dowry murders. Only by comparison with past conditions could one conclude with Nehru that India's secular reforms instituted "equality of status and opportunity" among Indians.

In its multireligious, multiethnic land the Indian government kept its peoples together with a mixture of concessions to ethnic communities, appeals to civic nationalism, and military repression of movements that appeared to threaten the unity of the country. Ethnic loyalties, based on religion and culture, constituted a powerful force in a country divided by a multitude of distinct languages and cultures. Leaders of ethnic groups organized campaigns for the redrawing of provincial borders to give their peoples their "native land." Their demands posed the threat of partition if they sought to secede from India. Gradually, the government submitted to these pressures. In 1956, several provincial states disappeared, and new provincial territories, each grouping in majority a distinct ethnic group with its own language, took their place. But these concessions opened the way for further agitation among other peoples. India's bond of unity remained fragile.

Still, Nehru's achievements were substantial. He had focused the attention of Indians on national problems and had given them a sense of national pride. He could not possibly have created out of the enormous Indian population one nation in the full sense of the word. Just how important he was to India became apparent after he died in 1964. With only brief interruptions, the National Congress and Indian voters preferred the leadership of his family in the next quarter-century. They first chose his daughter, Indira Gandhi, then his grandson, Rajiv

Gandhi, to be prime minister. Their domestic program differed from Nehru's principally in their gradual rejection of command economy policies that he had introduced. Indian nationalized industry proved to be inefficient and costly, and the so-called licence state tied up private enterprises in complicated and unending requirements for official documentation. The new leadership relied increasingly on Indian capitalists and foreign investors for economic development, new jobs, and technological innovation. Still, Nehru's personal charisma seemed for a time to have become a family heritage, endowing his descendants with the symbolic majesty of national unity.

Ethnic strife was never absent for long from Indian life. In 1989, Kashmir secessionists yet again rebelled against Indian rule. Backed this time by Pakistan, they demanded for the Muslim population of the province the right to form an independent state. They operated out of camps in Pakistan, where they planned military raids and terrorist attacks on the Indian half of Kashmir. The Indian army was again called upon to enforce Indian unity. Its forces set up a regime of military rule in Kashmir. Occasional border skirmishes with Pakistan troops in the 1990s maintained an unsettled condition resembling low-grade war in the region. By then, both states had acquired the military arsenal for nuclear war. The danger of devastating conflict between the two states was greater than ever before.

Elsewhere in India, basic political liberties and the rule of law were transforming the character of Indian society. The community of untouchables, the most persecuted of India's masses, was no longer excluded from public life. Thanks to the parliamentary system, they used their voting power to elect their own leaders to provincial government. Educated Indians found well-paying jobs in new centers of the electronics and computer industries, funded by foreign investors such as Microsoft and overseas Indians who had themselves become wealthy entrepreneurs in this "new economy." Despite periodic civil strife between

Muslims and Hindus, India retained its national unity and democratic freedoms.

War and Peace in South Asia

Nehru understood decolonization to mean the beginning of a new era of international peace and cooperation among new and old nation-states. He shared with Sukarno and other leaders of the newly independent states their opposition to Western political or economic domination, which they called "neocolonialism." He slowly worked out his new foreign policy in the years following independence. It sought peaceful change through cooperation, with its ultimate goal the equitable distribution of wealth and well-being among all the peoples of the world. Nehru hoped to make India a leader in bringing good relations among the world's states, whether communist or capitalist, former colonies or old empires. In a speech in 1949, Nehru stated that his country's objectives consisted of the pursuit of peace not by joining any major power or group of powers, but through an independent approach to each controversial or disputed issue. His version of internationalism, reminiscent of President Wilson's approach, rejected the methods of power politics and balance of power in international relations (see "Highlight," Chapter 1). He refused to take sides in the Cold War, preferring what he called "nonalignment" with either camp. His ideals were those of a visionary who dreamed of an era of peace to come with the liberation of subject peoples.

He counted on his prestige as Indian national leader and on the influence of his large state to bring together a group of nations committed to his principles. He defended his policies before an international audience at Bandung, Indonesia, in 1955. This Conference of Non-Aligned States, attended by delegates from countries in Africa, Asia, and Latin America, agreed that there should be "no domination in the future" by powerful Western countries in former colonial lands. But the conference participants were so deeply

divided already over the issues raised by the Cold War that they could not agree on Nehru's program. They merely adopted a vague "Declaration on World Peace and Cooperation."

His foreign policy for India confronted two immediate obstacles. One was the conflict between his country and Pakistan. The second arose from India's serious border dispute with China. The first conflict brought to South Asia the instruments of power politics—military alliances and nuclear weapons. The second dispute revealed, yet again, that war remained the instrument of last resort in revolving disputes of state security. It proved the undoing of Nehru's idealistic foreign policy.

The Chinese Communists supported the theory, but not the practice of internationalism. In the 1954 Sino-Indian treaty, India and China agreed on basic principles of coexistence, nonaggression, territorial respect, nonintervention. Nehru came away believing that the Chinese had accepted wholeheartedly his internationalist foreign policy. The Chinese negotiators considered the agreement an insignificant paper concession to the Indian leader's utopian ideals in return for India's recognition of their conquest of Tibet. Their government had concrete territorial demands along the long Chinese-Indian border, and expected the Indian government to agree. If not, they were prepared to rely on force of arms to settle the matter.

The issue was national security, as defined by the Chinese government. It claimed territories in Himalayan mountains separating Tibet from Chinese western territories (Xinjiang), where it planned to build a strategic highway to move troops between these areas of rebellious peoples. But the Indian government claimed to govern these regions, through which the British Empire had marked out a vaguely defined border with China the previous century. Nehru did not attempt to confirm the boundary either by military occupation or by negotiations with the Chinese. He chose to deal with the boundary dispute by ignoring it. In the meantime, the Chinese government began to build their road. How could peace be preserved between neighboring Asian states when they confronted intractable territorial conflicts? Nehru had no solution to that problem.

The unresolved border issue and Chinese annexation of Tibet became a source of growing hostility in the late 1950s. By then, the Chinese road between Xinjiang and Tibet was nearing completion. It passed through high mountainous regions (fourteen to fifteen thousand feet high) where India had no frontier troops. Then in 1959, the Indian government welcomed the Dalai Lama when he fled Tibet after Chinese troops had quelled a major Tibetan revolt (see "Spotlight," Chapter 3). The Chinese government accused India of "walking in the footsteps of the British imperialists and harboring expansionist ambitions toward Tibet." Chinese and Indian frontier forces moved closer along their long high-mountain border. Nehru acknowledged that China, a "world power or would-be world power" and India confronted a crisis so acute that "for the first time two major powers of Asia face each other on an armed border."

Neither side was prepared to compromise. China was isolated, but its army was well trained and equipped for mountain war. Nehru claimed that justice was on India's side, denouncing China's "unlawful" seizure of Indian territory. He would negotiate with the Chinese on the condition that they concede Indian possession of the disputed frontier regions. The Chinese government refused. In 1962 the Indian army finally began to move troops into the remote areas where the Chinese highway was located. War had become unavoidable. China would not abandon its vital road link, and India chose to back its claim to the frontier region with military force.

The Chinese knew that military superiority was on their side. Indian troops were still few in number and unprepared to fight at high altitude. In late October 1962, Chinese troops attacked Indian frontier positions. Everywhere Indian resistance collapsed. Within three weeks, Chinese forces had destroyed Indian frontier defenses and

were in a position in the east to invade the Indian lowlands. Nehru accused the Chinese government of violating "all principles which govern normal neighborly relations between sovereign governments" by a "deliberate cold-blooded decision" to invade India. Nonalignment offered no protection at a time of military defeat. Fearing a Chinese invasion of India, Nehru appealed for U.S. naval and air support. The United States agreed, moving ships from the U.S. Pacific fleet into the Bay of Bengal, close to one of the areas of fighting.

Then the Chinese troops withdrew. In the west, they had defeated Indian frontier forces and had established control over the territory along their Himalaya highway. Their commanders sought no more. In the east, they pulled back behind the original border and proclaimed a cease fire with a twenty-mile neutral zone to separate the opposing sides. The war was over. Although no negotiations followed the end of the fighting, China had settled the border dispute by force of arms. Its army had fought and won a limited war for a specific territorial objective, applying a centuries-old Western principle of using war as a continuation of diplomacy by other means. India was powerless to alter the settlement.

Nation and Islam in Pakistan

The history of Pakistan as a new nation-state differed in fundamental aspects from India's. Islam, not civic nationalism, defined its uniqueness. Dictatorship, not democracy, became its preferred form of government. Alliance with the United States, not nonalignment, determined its foreign policy. The first years after independence revealed the fundamental differences between the two countries. In both states, the colonial political reform of 1935 had provided the first elements of independent political life, creating a federal state and establishing the cabinet system of rule for India. But the Muslim League could not nurture the political conditions needed for democratic government in Pakistan. Its problems were enormous. Its support among the country's population was weak, for it had never succeeded, as National Congress had, in becoming a mass movement. Its leader, Jinnah, died in 1948. Deep internal social and ethnic differences among Pakistanis thwarted his successors' efforts at state-building.

Only the Muslim religion provided a fragile bond among the population. The constitution proclaimed Pakistan to be an Islamic Republic. It was the first state to lay down the principle that the Quran was the basic law of the land. Many Middle Eastern states with large Muslim populations imitated its example later. A shared Muslim identity was not sufficient, however, to overcome regional and ethnic rivalries. The greatest threat to the unity of the new state was its territorial disunity. Its leadership and strongest supporters were in West Pakistan. In East Pakistan, the Muslim League ruled as outsiders, for the people there were deeply attached to their own Bengali language and culture. After 1954, East Pakistani voters voted for their own Bengali parties and rejected the leadership of the Muslim League.

Pakistan's parliamentary government proved incompetent and unstable. Prime ministers succeeded one another in rapid succession, six in the first ten years of independence. That instability and the internal conflicts between East and West Pakistan discredited democratic rule. In 1958, parliamentary democracy in Pakistan ceased to exist when the army took power. The "Caesarism" of which Nehru had warned became a reality in the Muslim state. A general, Ayub Khan, seized power that year and promised to introduce order and to set up "Basic Democracy." The term masked a military dictatorship. He agreed to a military pact with the United States, for the alliance brought his poor country massive U.S. aid—$4 billion between the late 1950s and late 1980s. He accepted U.S. advisers to encourage individual enterprise and capitalist development. This market strategy stimulated economic growth, but enriched a handful of successful capitalists and further deepened the country's social inequalities.

Military rule proved no better able to insure political unity than civilian government. Opposition to rule from West Pakistan grew steadily in East Pakistan. Its leaders protested the government's inadequate aid for their people, who were considered by economists among the most impoverished in the world. By the late 1960s, the disagreements had become so bitter that East Pakistan came under military occupation by forces from West Pakistan. Bengali political leaders were placed under arrest.

In 1971 the dispute produced civil war. Bengalis demonstrated and rioted against Pakistan rule. Military repression forced millions of Bengalis to flee across the border into Indian Bengal. The Indian government, eager to weaken Pakistan, welcomed the refugees. The conflict was becoming an international crisis. Under pressure from its own Bengal population, the Indian government decided to support the rebellion. When Pakistani forces refused Indian demands to end their military occupation, the Indian army invaded East Pakistan. Once again, India and Pakistan were at war. The fighting ended quickly with Indian victory. The peace settlement required that Pakistan grant its Bengal territory independence. The rebel leaders proclaimed the independence of their land under the name of Bangladesh.

Pakistan itself retained less than half the population of the prewar state. Its economy depended more than ever on U.S. foreign aid. Poverty and disease were severe. Among the lower classes, many men migrated overseas in search of work. They remained away, some for years at a time, in Europe and the Middle East. The "remittances" that they sent back to their families came to represent a substantial part of Pakistan foreign earnings. England remained the greatest lure. Migrants settled there in large communities, bringing with them their religious practices and social customs.

The great hopes of the first years of independence faded for many Pakistanis. What was left was the ideal of a country uniquely Muslim, and the reality of continued internal ethnic quarrels and the threat of war with India. Quranic legal and social regulations became part of the constitutional basis of the state after 1978. Educated Pakistanis who objected to the strict Islamic laws of their country could move to England, for them a place of individual freedom and secular rights.

Poverty among a rapidly growing population combined with hostility to Western culture to encourage the spread of fundamentalist Muslim beliefs and support for Islamic movements elsewhere. Backed by the U.S. government, Pakistan provided secret support for the guerrilla uprising in neighboring Afghanistan after Soviet troops invaded in 1979 (see Chapter 7). The only immediate result was to increase the influence in Pakistan of militant Muslims, including many foreigners eager to join the Afghan "holy war." The Pakistan government chose the dangerous path of giving support to these fanatics (including a Saudi Arabian named Osama bin Laden), in the hopes of increasing its power and extending its influence into Afghanistan. Military rulers justified their domination by warning of the religious and ethnic strife that threatened to destroy the country. The Muslim religion remained a dubious symbol of national unity in a land founded on the idea of an Islamic nation.

SUMMARY

The disappearance of Western empires from south Asia left to nationalist leaders the responsibility to deal with the acute social and economic hardship of their peoples and to insure political stability in conditions of ethnic and religious conflict. Did independence improve the lives of these populations? On what grounds does one measure progress in the history of developing nations: national independence, political freedom, eco-

nomic growth, the lessening of social inequalities, ethnic and religious diversity safeguarded within a nation-state? All of these goals appeared to a greater or lesser extent in the policies of Third World governments and in the public aspirations of the peoples of those lands. None of them was fully achieved in the decades following independence. The disappointment and anger provoked by these failures led to a search for simple explanations.

Neocolonialism provided one easy answer. Sukarno blamed Indonesia's economic failures and international weakness on the colonial heritage. His search for Western culprits was not, in historical hindsight, convincing. The roots of Indonesia's problems under his rule lay in ethnic divisions, poverty, and the incompetence of his government. His fall from power was caused largely by his own short-sighted efforts to create national unity around his charismatic leadership in a one-party state. It opened the way for army generals to use military force to bring order to the vast territories of the state and to impose their own rule.

Colonialism left a complex heritage that the peoples of the former colonies chose to accept or reject in ways that the concept of neocolonialism does not help us to understand. To enhance their power and glory, European conquerors had created large colonies out of scattered islands and disparate peoples. The Philippines, Indonesia, and India came into existence as unified lands under colonial rule. Imperial methods of rule did not by themselves create ethnic conflict but did make such antagonism more likely to erupt when the empires collapsed.

In the last decades of British rule, Indian nationalists nurtured and enriched the idea of an Indian nation. In Gandhi's national creed it became a lofty ideal of human solidarity and moral equality. Responsibility for the tragic collapse of that dream, destroyed in the partition of the subcontinent, rests with the political leaders, imperial and national, and with the deep animosities that divided the Indian masses. There, as in other parts of the world, ethnic antagonism aroused latent fears of outsiders, from within as well as beyond the new state borders. Loyalties were never a simple matter of language, culture, religion, or ancestry. In the case of Pakistan, its nascent national unity drew primarily on Islamic solidarity. But the state's partition in 1971 revealed that the unique language and cultural traditions of East Pakistan's Bengal people were more powerful bonds than the Muslim faith that they shared with West Pakistan peoples. The new nation-states were fragile creations.

Authoritarianism was a tempting answer to instability. Generals from national armies came at times to believe themselves the saviors of the state, but invariably resorted to brutal methods of dictatorial rule to remain in power. Burma (renamed Myanmar), once a model new nation-state, became in the 1980s and 1990s a glaring example of brutal military dictatorship and economic decay. Its generals preferred to seal the country off from the outside world for fear that the free flow of goods and ideas would undermine their regime. National independence and social progress were goals for Asian countries whose means and capabilities could not possibly match their dream.

DATES WORTH REMEMBERING

1946 Philippine independence
1947 Indian partition; independence for Pakistan and India
1947 Nehru prime minister of India
1947–48 War between Pakistan and India
1950 Sukarno first president of Indonesian republic
1951 Indian federal constitution
1955 Bandung Conference of Non-Aligned States
1962 Sino-Indian War

1964 Death of Nehru
1965 Independence for Singapore
1966 General Suharto ruler of Indonesia
1967 "Green Revolution" crops accepted by India
1971 Indo-Pakistan war and independence of Bangladesh
1981–89 Pakistan aid to Afghan rebels
1982 Sikh rebellion against India
1989 Revolt of Kashmir Muslims against India

RECOMMENDED READING

Southeast Asia

Theodore Friend, *Indonesian Destinies* (2003). An interpretive history of Indonesia, focusing on the major political leaders Sukarno and Suharto.
*Stanley Karnow, *In Our Image: America's Empire in the Philippines* (1989). A history of the close relations between the United States and the Philippines before and after independence.
C. L. M. Pendus, *The Life and Times of Sukarno* (1974). A critical biography of Indonesia's national hero and deposed ruler.

India and Pakistan

*Larry Collins and Dominique Lapierre, *Freedom at Midnight* (1975). A dramatic history of the personalities and circumstances surrounding the liberation of Britain's greatest colony.
Patrick French, *Liberty or Death: India's Journey to Independence and Division* (1997). A balanced historical assessment of India's recent colonial past and the tragedy of partition.

Memoirs and Novels

*V. S. Naipaul, *Voyage among the Believers: An Islamic Journey* (1981). A personal voyage of discovery through Asian Muslim countries by a West Indian novelist and essayist.
Salman Rushdie, *Midnight's Children* (1981). A vivid novel about independent India, viewed through the eyes of an Indian born at the moment of independence.
*Khrushwant Singh, *Train to Pakistan* (1956). A moving fictional account of the tragedy of partition, from the perspective of the people of a tiny Punjab village.

Chapter 5

Africa and Latin America in the Third World

Africa and Latin America were distant continents that confronted a similar dilemma in the last decades of the twentieth century. Both regions were divided largely into small states with meager resources to care for the needs of their growing populations. The difficulties created by this situation provide an important clue to their history in the decades that followed the end of the Second World War.

The liberation from imperial rule occurred in Latin America 150 years before that of African colonies. Almost the entirety of Latin America won freedom from the Portugese and Spanish empires in the early nineteenth century. It came largely through colonial revolts, whose leaders appealed to the images and symbols of revolutionary democracy and national liberation to explain the justice of their cause. The story of the nation-in-arms became one of the key ingredients by which politicians there created a mythical birth for their new nation-states. The real process of state-building was slow, and political unrest erupted frequently in the next 150 years.

In Africa, imperial conquest began in earnest only in the late nineteenth century, and was not complete until the first decades of the twentieth century. European empires retained their territories there for another half-century. Suddenly, over a period of twenty years between the late 1950s and the 1970s they granted freedom to their African colonial peoples. The coming of independence was unexpected for both the colonial rulers and their peoples. It occurred in large part because small nationalist movements in these areas encountered little or no resistance from their empires. The governments of Great Britain and France, which held the largest imperial domain in Africa, had turned their attention to internal affairs after the Second World War. They were primarily concerned with their own economic and social reforms. Africa, in this sense, received freedom by default.

The major tasks confronting Africa's new leaders were similar to those of former colonies in Asia, namely, the creation of stable political regimes and the mobilization of the resources of their country to overcome the poverty that confronted their peoples. Important features of the command economy adopted by the Soviet Union and the People's Republic of China attracted these leaders, looking for a quick road to economic development. The political model that they all sought to incorporate was the nation-state. The ideal of national unity informed their political speeches. The ethnic diversity of their populations required, however, that they offer trustworthy guarantees of political pluralism. It was a requirement that few could satisfy. The alternative was civil strife so severe it undermined the very foundations of organized, normal life. Just who would take these monumental tasks in hand remained a constant issue throughout the vast area. South Africa was exceptional, both because the liberation was delayed by a system of colonial domination ("apartheid") that remained in place until its abandonment in the early 1990s, and because it remained economically dynamic afterward. Elsewhere, by the last decade of the century, the African continent's new states had achieved a minimum level of stability, but in conditions of economic decay and sporadic civil wars.

Political leadership passed quickly through the hands of those elected leadership who had first guided their peoples on the path of independence. They were displaced forcibly by ambitious officers from the new national armies. By the 1990s, outside states providing invaluable economic assistance to African states had begun to put pressure on these dictators to restore some measure of democracy, but the results were disappointing. The crisis of the new African states was especially apparent in the remorseless economic decline that occurred in large areas of the continent. No easy answer could explain the origins of the decay of agriculture and industry. The sad result was clear. Surveys revealed that the living conditions for much of Africa's population were worse at century's close than in the first decade of independence.

In Latin America, political life also involved a struggle for power between political leaders and army officers. There, the conflict had persisted ever since independence from Western empires in the nineteenth century, and continued into the late twentieth century. In the decades after 1945, civilian and military governments there, as in Africa, turned to state controls over trade and finance to stimulate economic growth. They set up new social welfare programs for basic improvements in the living conditions of the population. Their efforts proved more successful than those of the African leaders. Gradually the standard of living in most Latin American countries improved. In a few, such as Brazil and Mexico, economic growth increased so rapidly it seemed in its own way to be a "miracle."

The opposition to military rule in Latin America grew so strong that by the late 1980s these dictators had abandoned power. Unable to govern effectively and confronted by mass political opposition from democratic forces, they yielded power to elected civilian leadership. This political transfer occurred in the same years as governments gradually ended the system of state economic controls introduced at mid-century. This move followed the trend in Africa and Asia. The capacity of the free market to produce ongoing economic development proved everywhere more effective than the techniques of strict state planning, and opened up economic opportunities to large numbers of the population. Only Cuba retained the basic features of a command economy into the 1990s. Despite the failure of their Soviet-type regime to realize its goals, the Cuban revolutionary leadership refused to abandon their dream of socialism.

Social inequality remained a pervasive condition throughout the region. Toward the end of the century, migrants left in greater numbers than ever before for North America in the hopes of escaping the poverty of their homelands. Still, the spread of democracy in Latin America was an encouraging sign of the decline of the old system of elite rule. Free enterprise did not bring social justice, but it appeared more suitable than state socialism in extending to a large portion of the population the opportunity to construct a satisfactory life on their own terms.

AFRICA'S LIBERATION FROM COLONIALISM

Independence came quickly to the African colonies of Western empires in the late 1950s and 1960s. This dramatic disappearance of empires in Africa marked the end of Europe's overseas colonial dominion. In the late colonial period, the only independent states in sub-Saharan Africa had been the countries of Ethiopia (under Italian control for a few years in the 1930s), Liberia, which was a small state created as a refuge for liberated slaves in the nineteenth century, and South Africa, granted independence within the Commonwealth by the British in 1910. Suddenly the other peoples of Africa ceased living under Western imperial rule. Their new leaders spoke proudly of their new African nations, even though many different peoples lived in each state, and they promised a better life for their citizens, though these countries were still very poor.

The colonial past had left an indelible mark on the peoples of this vast continent. European rulers had, there as elsewhere in their vast empires, carved out new political borders to delimit their territories. Each colony acquired its capital city and centers of trading and, to a much lesser extent, manufacturing. Colonial officials encouraged trade where possible in cash crops such as cocoa, palm oil, and peanuts; African farmers were quick to adopt the new crops, which they hoped would increase their income. But in doing so they became dependent on the international economy, whose periods of recession depressed prices on these crops and caused them severe hardship.

The encounter with the outside world brought profound cultural and religious changes. The social and psychological stress of colonial rule opened the way to large-scale religious conversion to Islam as well as to Christianity. Muslim missionaries offered Africans a coherent religious dogma and a strong religious community. The Islamic faith spread rapidly in the twentieth century through Africa. By mid-century, in east Africa and south of the Sahara over half the population was Muslim. The imperial states for their part supported the work of Christian missionaries, who offered the Africans who came to their centers basic social services, medical care, and schooling, as well as instruction in the Christian faith. Conversion was intimately linked to the disruptive impact of colonial rule. Imperial conquest undermined the credibility of the old animistic beliefs and elevated the Christian faith to the status of conquer's religion. Conversion to Christianity provided social standing and cultural capital to those Africans eager to learn and to profit from new economic and political conditions.

Under the pressure of Western colonialism, the old bonds of tribal unity were gradually dissolving. But the cultural and social void was filled very slowly with new institutions and ideologies. Religion itself became a source of dissent. The high plains of Britain's west African colony of Nigeria became centers of Islam, while the peoples living in coastal regions were more likely to convert to Christianity. The very process of conversion provoked dissension within the African communities. The Nigerian writer Chinua Achebe, whose father had chosen Christianity during British colonial rule, remembered that as a child he and all those in his church called themselves "the people of the church" and referred to the non-Christians around them as "the heathen" or even "the people of nothing." The nationalist message of resistance to empire and solidarity among African people appeared an alluring solution in these conditions of social and cultural disruption.

Nationalism in Africa

After the end of the Second World War, the British government reorganized their African colonies to prepare them for independence. Its plan for the transition consisted of a long period of self-government, under imperial supervision. Even then, its most optimistic goals foresaw a slow process of liberation lasting several decades. But its timetable proved useless under pressure of movements for colonial liberation and of Europe's reluctance to enforce colonial rule. One British statesman called these forces a "wind of change" sweeping away all the colonial empires. For the first time in African history mass nationalist movements spread across the continent.

The emergence of African nationalist movements was a remarkable development. It took shape when educated Africans became familiar with the nationalist ideology of the West, and was nurtured within the colonial world by shared enemies and new economic ties. The peoples within the European colonies in Africa were divided by tribal loyalties, by religion, and by language. Agreement among nationalists came from their perception of a common, imperial enemy. The presence of European administrators and soldiers ruling the colonies was the tangible symbol of colonialism. The capital cities that flew the flags of the empire and housed the offices of the key colonial officials became sites of nationalist demonstrations and unrest. The struggle for the overthrow of imperial rule was a common bond uniting African nationalist leaders and their peoples.

The areas where effective movements against European rule first emerged were the British colony of the Gold Coast (later Ghana) in west Africa, and Kenya, located in east Africa. In the 1950s members of the dominant Kikuyu tribe in Kenya organized a violent struggle against white settlers on their land. They named their organization the Land Freedom Army, but Europeans scornfully called it the Mau Mau. Their nationalist leader, Jomo Kenyatta, united his followers

around a program for the end to foreign rule and for distribution of the lands seized by Western settlers among the Kikuyu. Their greatest weakness, one which was apparent in the nationalist movements of other African colonies as well, was the reluctance of other tribal groups to join the Kikuyu revolt.

The British needed four years to repress the violence. In the process, they mobilized other tribes in Kenya to fight the rebels and resettled many of their African subjects in fortified villages. They captured Kenyatta and sentenced him to seven years in prison. The Mau Mau uprising caused the death of over thirteen thousand among the blacks (both Mau Mau followers and British supporters) and ninety-five whites. But in the course of the fighting, the British decided that they had to speed up the introduction of self-government in Kenya. In the end, Kenyatta had succeeded in forcing the British government to begin its withdrawal from east Africa.

The first anticolonial campaign to reach its goal of independence took place in the Gold Coast (Ghana), located on the Atlantic coast of west Africa. The pattern of political activism, and the difficulties of mobilizing mass support there, reveal important characteristics of African independence movements elsewhere in later years. The Gold Coast nationalist leader was Kwame Nkrumah. He was a dynamic and skillful organizer, who used his Western education to formulate his own nationalist creed of liberation and freedom. He began to gather supporters against British rule in the late 1940s. By then a strong labor union movement had appeared among African workers in the colony's port cities, where cocoa beans, the principal Gold Coast cash crop, were exported to the West. The once-powerful Asanti tribes lived in inland areas where the crop was grown. Those commercial links between the coast and the hinterland of the Gold Coast created a bond of common interests and interaction among the ethnic communities. The regional market, suffering from price fluctuations passed on to growers and workers by the international corporations, became a major source of grievances against British rule.

In 1949, Nkrumah created his nationalist party, the Convention People's Party. It united activists from urban and rural populations from as far away as the Muslim north. He promised that freedom would put an end to the hardships of the Gold Coast peoples, and would bring them a new era of progress and opportunity. Using language drawn from the Bible, he told his followers: "Seek ye first the political kingdom and all else will follow." Coupled with these promises he launched a campaign of passive disobedience against colonial laws. He drew inspiration for his anti-colonial movement from the example of Gandhi and the Indian National Congress. His party honored those activists whom the British sentenced to prison as the party's "Prison Graduates." By the early 1950s, his movement had won such widespread support that the British government, unwilling to continue its costly and fruitless repression, granted the colony extensive self-rule. A British prisoner at the time, Nkrumah agreed to step into the interim position of the Gold Coast's first prime minister. Both sides preferred to avoid violence by agreeing to political compromise.

Nkrumah's goal was an independent nation-state. In other words, he refused to use ethnic loyalties of any people as the cement for his nationalist cause. But the Asanti tribal leaders in the north feared the rule of the southerners in a centralized government. In response to their concern, the British offered the country a constitution with a federal system made up of separate autonomous territories for the major tribal groups. Nkrumah reluctantly agreed to the new arrangement, though he had not abandoned his goal of creating a unified state. Independence came to the Gold Coast, renamed Ghana, in 1957. It was the first African country freed from colonial rule. Nkrumah was its first president and a hero for African nationalists everywhere.

Nationalist leaders such as he could mobilize widespread support against colonialism, but their coalition of forces relied for united action on hostility toward the British enemy. Once the British had withdrawn, these nationalists could no longer count on the continued backing of the peoples in their new state, for they did not have in hand a program for state-building that could satisfy the concerns and interests of their ethnically diverse population. Decolonization in Africa posed problems of state-building more acute than anywhere else in the colonial world.

In the late 1950s, both the British and French governments chose to end colonial rule in Africa as quickly as possible. International pressures played an influential role in accelerating the African decolonization. The leaders of the newly independent states of Asia made the freeing of African peoples an international crusade. Both the United States and the Soviet Union publicly backed freedom for colonial peoples. The United Nations became a public forum where anti-colonial speakers denounced Europe's outdated imperial system. The weakness of the British and French empires became cruelly apparent in their failure to regain control of the Suez Canal in the 1956 war (see Chapter 7). That loss deprived them of the single most strategic imperial possession, and demonstrated to them (and to the rest of the world) that they no longer possessed the power to defend their colonies at a time of global decolonization. This event proved decisive in pushing the two governments to grant independence to their African colonial territories. Imperialism was a lost cause.

Independence for African Colonies

Once an area governed by distant European empires, Africa suddenly was transformed into a continent divided into more than forty sovereign states. The process by which liberation came depended, in large measure, on the policies of the imperial states. Great Britain followed the procedure that it had used in Asia of negotiating with

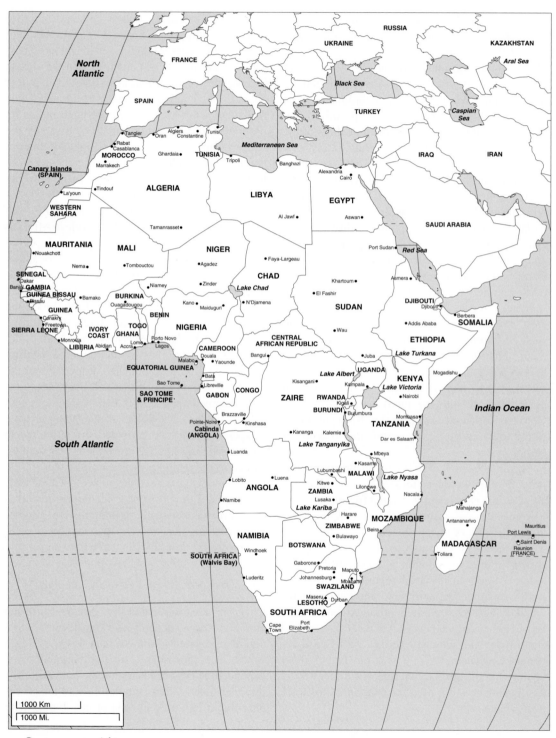

North
Atlantic

FRANCE

SPAIN

RUSSIA

UKRAINE

KAZAKHSTAN

Aral Sea

Black Sea

TURKEY

Caspian
Sea

Tangier
Rabat
Casablanca
Oran Algiers Constantine Tunis
Ghardaia
MOROCCO
Marrakech
TUNISIA
Tripoli
Mediterranean Sea
Banghazi

Alexandria
Cairo

IRAQ

IRAN

Canary Islands
(SPAIN)

La'youn
Tindouf

ALGERIA

LIBYA

EGYPT

Al Jawf

Aswan

SAUDI ARABIA

WESTERN
SAHARA

Tamanrasset

MAURITANIA
Nouakchott

MALI

Nema Tombouctou

NIGER

Agadez

Faya-Largeau

CHAD

Port Sudan

Red Sea

Niamey
Zinder
Lake Chad
Khartoum

Aqmera

DJIBOUTI

SENEGAL
Dakar
Banjul GAMBIA
GUINEA BISSAU
Bissau Bamako
GUINEA
Conakry
Freetown
SIERRA LEONE
Monrovia
LIBERIA Abidjan

BURKINA
Ouagadougou

Kano
Maidugun

N'Djamena

El Fashir

SUDAN

Wau

Addis Ababa

Berbera

SOMALIA

TOGO
GHANA
Accra Lome
Porto Novo
Lagos

BENIN

NIGERIA

CENTRAL
AFRICAN REPUBLIC

Juba

ETHIOPIA
Lake Turkana

IVORY
COAST

Mogadishu

CAMEROON
Douala
Malabo Yaounde
EQUATORIAL GUINEA

Bangui

Bata
SAO TOME
& PRINCIPE
Sao Tome
Libreville

Lake Albert
Kisangani

UGANDA
Kampala
Lake Victoria

KENYA

Nairobi

CONGO

GABON

ZAIRE

RWANDA
Kigali
BURUNDI
Bujumbura

Mombasa

Indian Ocean

Brazzaville
Pointe-Noire
Cabinda
(ANGOLA)
Kinshasa

Kananga

Kalemie

TANZANIA
Dar es Salaam

Lake Tanganyika
Mbeya

South Atlantic

Luanda

Lobito Luena

Kasama

ANGOLA

Lubumbashi

Kitwe
ZAMBIA
Lusaka

MALAWI
Lilongwe

Lake Nyasa

Nacala

Namibe

Lake Kariba

Harare

MOZAMBIQUE

Mahajanga

NAMIBIA

ZIMBABWE
Bulawayo

Beira

Antananarivo

Mauritius
Port Lewis

BOTSWANA

MADAGASCAR

Saint Denis
Reunion
(FRANCE)

Windhoek

Toliara

SOUTH AFRICA
(Walvis Bay)

Gaborone
Luderitz

Pretoria
Johannesburg
Maputo
Mbabane
SWAZILAND
Maseru
LESOTHO Durban

SOUTH AFRICA

Cape
Town
Port
Elizabeth

1000 Km
1000 Mi.

Contemporary Africa

nationalist leaders in each colony for the creation of constitutional, democratic government. After the Gold Coast, Nigeria became independent in 1960. There, the leaders of the major tribal groups agreed, as in Ghana, on a constitution guaranteeing federal government as the best means to protect ethnic diversity among its thirty-five million people while insuring the unity of the state. Then, in 1963, Kenya became an independent state under the leadership of Kenyatta, freed at last from British prison to move immediately to the presidency of the new government. The constitutional order of the new states resembled British parliamentary democracy. The British considered this Western import best for Africa. Many nationalist leaders thought of it as a temporary measure useful during the transition from colonialism to full independence. Despite the speed of decolonization, the British and African leaders managed to cooperate and to maintain peace among the population during the transfer of power.

French decolonization differed from the British method in one major respect. In 1958, the French government proposed a transition period of extensive self-government coupled with economic and military advisers and financial aid to all French African colonies. For this purpose, it reformed its colonial empire, called the French Union, to allow African subjects to vote on joining the Union. The alternative offered to Africans was independence outside the French organization and no French support at all. This policy was the creation of Charles de Gaulle, French wartime hero, who in 1958 once again became president of France. His offer of collaboration with African states through the French Union was an effort to maintain close ties between France and its former African colonies.

Most African leaders from France's empire accepted membership in the Union. They dismissed charges from opponents that his plan was a form of "neocolonialism." They believed it a helpful measure in holding onto power, for they faced daunting problems of state-building. They hoped

as well to obtain substantial French economic assistance, especially to fund expensive industrial investments and to sustain the value of their new currencies. In 1958, the colonies voted on joining the Union. In each territory, the voters adhered to the recommendation of their nationalist leaders.

All the French colonies in Africa save one became members of the French Union in 1958. They received economic aid, financial advisers and technicians, a monetary union with France, and permanent French garrisons located in strategic locations on call in the event of border conflicts or political unrest. In exchange, they safeguarded French investments in their country. Two years later, the French government took the final, inevitable step of recognizing the full independence of all these former African colonies, who became members of the new "French Community."

The moderate leaders of these new states were effective opponents of radical revolution. They knew it to be a danger to themselves as well as to France's economic interests. One African leader concluded later that "General de Gaulle is the greatest African of our time." His opinion revealed how highly he valued political stability, achieved at the cost of very little social reform. The aid that France provided did bring those countries substantial benefits. Among these, political stability in the early years of independence was the most important.

In the largest of all the African colonies, the Belgian Congo (later Zaire), decolonization became a nightmare of civil strife and bloodshed. The area experienced violent anti-Belgian demonstrations for the first time in early 1959. The protests were the work of a small nationalist movement supported largely by urban workers in the capital city, Kinshasa (formerly Stanleyville). This brief moment of political opposition was sufficient for the Belgian government to grant its colony independence immediately. In the previous decades it had made no effort to prepare the colony for self-rule. The nationalists themselves lacked a prominent leader supported by the peoples of that enormous country. Swept along by the "wind of change," in 1960 the Belgians freed their colony in the worst possible circumstances.

The results were tragic for the new state and for its population, both African and European. The colonial institutional structure quickly collapsed. The Congolese army mutinied and turned on the white settlers, who fled the country. Tribal groups fought among themselves. The only political leader with a substantial following, Patrice Lumumba, could not restore order in the army and refused any help from the Belgians. The disorders soon became outright civil war. The southern region of Katanga (later Shaba), which was rich in mineral resources and a center of mining operations owned by Western interests, seceded from the new state and created its own army.

The United Nations agreed to send troops from member states to keep the Congo from complete collapse and anarchy. In the course of the fighting, Lumumba himself was captured and executed by Katanga forces. After a long period of political disorder, a former sergeant of the colonial army, Joseph Mobutu, seized control of the government in 1965. By then the surviving white settlers had fled, the economy of most regions was in ruins, and many thousands of Congolese had died in the fighting and rioting. The Democratic Republic of Congo, renamed Zaire a few years later by Mobutu, had begun its slow decay into a failed state.

The Triumph of Democracy in South Africa

South Africa, the southernmost country of the African continent, had enjoyed self-rule since 1910. The full rights of citizenship were restricted, however, to the white population. A member of the British Commonwealth, South Africa had a privileged place in international trade because of its valuable natural resources. Like a European democracy, its government passed back and forth between conservative and liberal political parties competing to exercise the powers of the majority in the country's parliament. Its constitutional order was watched over by an autonomous judicial system, also modeled on British practices. But it excluded the non-European majority of the population from participation in this system, and subjected its African subjects to increasingly severe racial discrimination.

This restrictive democratic system opened the way for the country's Afrikaner people (formerly called Boers, the Dutch-speaking settlers) to insert racial intolerance into the constitutional order of the country. They numbered only four million, but their Protestant faith and their war with the British at the beginning of the century had made them a tight-knit community. Their three centuries of life as pioneers and farmers in South Africa had persuaded them that this was their native land. Their religious creed taught them that they were the "chosen people" and that the Africans were an inferior race. Their form of ethnic nationalism was racist at its very core. Their leaders were determined to hold onto this homeland by whatever means were necessary.

The economic wealth of the country, concentrated in gold and diamond mining, was in the hands of the English and other recent immigrants from Europe. Urban commerce was the special domain of Indian migrants, who had traveled there as subjects of the British Empire in search of work in the growing cities. Africans, for their part, had taken up labor in the country's vast mining industry. The Second World War had brought prosperity to the business interests of the country, dominated by the Anglo-American Corporation. Its holdings were extensive; one half of all the companies in the South African stock exchange were in its possession. Social inequality was not entirely a product of white domination. Most of the Afrikaners were farmers with relatively small plots of land, while some Indians and "Coloreds" (the term used to designate South African people of mixed ethnic ancestry) had prospered in trade. The poorest segment of the population consisted almost entirely of Africans. Still, by mid-century, an increasing number of nonwhites were entering the urban economy to meet the needs of commerce and industry. Some Africans had obtained an advanced education and had entered the middle class. Nelson Mandela, later head of the African resistance movement, was a trained lawyer. In those years, the social consequences of economic development were gradually undermining white segregation policies.

By then the government had enacted an increasing number of laws intended to exclude Africans, Asians, and Coloreds from contact with whites. In response, an increasing number of opponents of racial segregation had become supporters of the African National Congress (ANC). This organization emulated the methods and goals of the Indian National Congress. Formed in 1912, its members agitated peacefully for democratic freedoms and for an end to segregation in all forms. Its growing influence, and the support it received from liberal whites, presented Afrikaners with a serious threat to their domination.

The Afrikaner people had their own political party, called the Nationalist Party. In the late 1940s, the Nationalist Party triumphed in national elections in which the principal issue was the place of nonwhites in public life. The Nationalist program called for their complete exclusion. It won sufficient backing from the voters to take control of the cabinet. The new Nationalist government proceeded in the next ten years to put in place a policy of racial domination that it called "apartheid." It excluded nonwhites from all political rights, and curtailed their civil liberties. Africans did not even have the right to free choice of residence; they were forced to live in special settlements and permitted into urban areas to work solely as "guests" (the so-called pass system). Only the South African court system continued throughout the years of repression to honor (with major exceptions) the British principle of rule of law, even in trials of opponents of apartheid.

The Nationalists denied that the multiethnic, multiracial people of their country could possibly form one nation. Nationalism in their understanding existed only as ethnic loyalty. There was no place for the spirit of civic nationalism in their racist program. Their policies intentionally sought to strengthen the divisions among South Africa's African peoples, whom they referred to as tribes. They were responsible for creating a regime of white supremacy in the very years when the African peoples elsewhere in the continent were obtaining political independence.

The African National Congress was encouraged by the success in the 1950s and 1960s of nationalist movements elsewhere in Africa to intensify its fight against apartheid. In 1955, it approved a "Freedom Charter," which spelled out clearly its program for a multiethnic, democratic South Africa "belonging to all who live in it." Its Youth League attracted activists impatient with the placid methods of the older members. Young leaders such as Nelson Mandela came forward arguing that the ANC had to fight the increasingly harsh Nationalist racist laws with a new campaign of mass action. Nonviolence remained the basis of their tactics, but the repressive powers of the state were pushing them toward confrontation.

In 1960, the ANC organized large demonstrations against the restrictive pass system. At Sharpsville, an African settlement, South African police fired on the unarmed demonstrators, killing more than sixty. It was a massacre whose principal effect was to mobilize the ANC to directly confront the regime. More demonstrations followed. In response to massive arrests and brutal imprisonment, the ANC leaders agreed finally to a campaign of violent resistance to accompany its political action. Nonviolence was no longer sufficient. The Nationalists had created a political crisis of their own making.

Their response was to resort to still harsher measures of repression. They outlawed the African National Congress and arrested its leaders on charges of treason. For the next three decades their police hunted down all political opponents. The government pitilessly enforced the pass system and all the laws that maintained white supremacy. It created separate "homelands" for African tribes. Africans had no permanent legal residence outside these areas, located in poor regions of the country. The pass laws gave them temporary residence elsewhere in settlements, which became mass ghettos outside the country's major cities. The Nationalists' policies isolated South Africa from the outside world, caused its expulsion from the United Nations, and created a state of emergency in the country.

Resistance came from within and from outside South Africa. The African National Congress retained its mass following (although publicly silenced) and organized itself for survival as an underground organization. Violence within the country erupted frequently as protests were met with repression. In the 1980s, many Western countries joined in an international economic boycott of South Africa. By the late 1980s the government found itself in a grave crisis, facing social turmoil and a serious economic recession. The Nationalist leadership, under a new prime minister, F. W. de Klerk, finally conceded the hopelessness of apartheid. The very survival of South Africa depended upon instituting a new political and social order. The only solution had to be real democracy and racial toleration. De Klerk's government gradually dismantled the laws that had enforced segregation. Many Afrikaners protested, but they had no alternative program of their own to deal with the crisis.

In a desperate search for a solution, the reformers turned to the African National Congress. In 1990, they lifted all the legal restrictions that had denied the ANC the rights of a political party, and freed all its political prisoners. After a half-century of repression, the Nationalist Party recognized the African National Congress as its equal. The leaders of the ANC were prepared to cooperate. The Freedom Program had set out their conditions for negotiation. They had never abandoned their belief in the possibility of a peaceful multiethnic land of toleration and freedom. Their claim to speak for all Africans was challenged by a strong political movement among the Zulu people, the largest African tribal group in the country. This Inkatha party, like the Muslim League in India, had no hope of winning in national elections and demanded special recognition to protect the interests of its people. Reluctantly, the ANC agreed to collaborate with Inkatha.

In 1993, negotiations between the Nationalist government, the ANC, and Inkatha produced a new democratic constitution for South Africa. The next year free elections gave the ANC a majority of parliamentary representatives and the right to rule the country. The collaboration of the Nationalists, the ANC, and Inkatha ensured that, despite thirty years of violent confrontation, the transition of power occurred peacefully. This extraordinary, hopeful end to South Africa's political crisis owed much of its success to the remarkable leader of the African National Congress, Nelson Mandela.

SPOTLIGHT: Nelson Mandela

For most of his adult life, Nelson Mandela (1918–) was a political prisoner in South Africa. In 1994, he became president of that state. His decades of imprisonment and sudden rise to power were directly linked to the struggle against and ultimate defeat of the white supremacy regime in that country.

His childhood was spent within one of the African tribal groups living in South Africa. He was born to the ruling family of that tribe. The king sent him to an English-language Methodist secondary school to prepare him to be his heir and successor to the throne. But Mandela chose not to follow in the traditional path. He broke with the religion of his people, joining the Methodist

President Nelson Mandela (*Courtesy South African Consulate General, Los Angeles*)

church. After graduation, he left his tribal area to begin a new life in the booming cities of South Africa. He found work in a law office and ultimately earned his law degree.

In those years, the racial segregation imposed by the Nationalist Party touched him as much as other Africans and nonwhites of South Africa. He chose to make the fight against segregation his calling. When he was twenty-six, he joined the African National Congress, seeking the means to end tribal divisions and unite Africans, in his words, "as one people." He worked for many years with its Youth League to strengthen popular support for the ANC's program of racial equality and toleration. He was a dynamic, charismatic political organizer and forceful writer. He defended the ANC's program of democracy for all of South Africa's peoples. In his first years in the party, he backed the methods of nonviolent resistance to the racist laws of the Nationalist regime. For that work, he was arrested and accused of treason in 1955. "Because of my conscience," he wrote, "I was made a criminal."

His very life was at risk at the hands of the Nationalist government. The courts finally dismissed the charge of treason. When the Nationalist government in 1960 increased their repression against the ANC's political campaign, Mandela decided that the time had come to abandon nonviolent methods of resistance. South Africa had become, he wrote, a "land ruled by the gun." He saw no choice but to resort to the methods of intimidation and terror, principally attacks on state buildings and key economic installations. This became the special task of his new underground organization, the Spear of the Nation. He became a hunted man, able to speak freely in defense of his cause only during a brief trip to Europe in 1962. When he returned to South Africa, he was arrested, convicted of treason, and sentenced to life imprisonment.

Mandela's long years of prison were a time of moral and physical trial, of isolation and hardship. Yet his commitment to democracy for his country did not weaken, and his political stature grew stronger than ever. His determination not to give up in the face of the government's repression became an inspiration for ANC followers. In those years, he emerged as the real leader of the ANC. As the international campaign in opposition to apartheid grew stronger, his imprisonment became a measure of the cruelty of the Nationalist regime's racism. His loyalty to the ANC cause confirmed the inability of their police state to end democratic resistance. In 1980, the Security Council of the United Nations stated that Mandela's release from prison was the first step necessary to permit a "meaningful discussion of the future of the country."

The Nationalists themselves had to concede his prominence as political leader. Mandela had always accepted the principle of peaceful negotiations for the creation of a democratic state granting equal rights to all its citizens. His release from prison in 1990 came because the Nationalists realized that his active leadership of the ANC was their only real hope to end the country's political and economic crisis. He set the terms of freedom, accepting negotiations only after the government had released all South African political prisoners and had abolished its segregationist policies. In return, he made the peaceful transition of power possible. When the new South African parliament met in 1994 after the country's first free elections, the ANC held the absolute majority. Its representatives elected him to be South Africa's first African president. Mandela had achieved his goal, to which he had subscribed when he joined the ANC, of creating a country that belonged to "all who live in it, black and white." Like Nehru in India, he sought to be the leader of a multiethnic nation.

African State-Building and Failed States

During the 1960s the new African states proceeded slowly and painfully along the difficult path of state-building. The experiences of these countries varied greatly, but in the next decade two trends emerged. One was the appearance of authoritarian governments, most frequently under military rule, whose leaders replaced one another in forcible, sometimes bloody struggles for power. The other was economic stagnation and continued impoverishment among the rapidly growing rural and urban population.

Most African leaders quickly abandoned the democratic constitutions adopted at independence. Their peoples had been deprived of the experience of self-rule during the colonial years. After liberation, they valued political unification and economic development more than the creation of a fair multiparty system of government. Power soon passed into the hands of a political elite, consisting of civilian politicians and ambitious military leaders. One West African politician, whose state was among the best ruled on the continent, explained that "in young countries such as our own, we need a chief who is all-powerful for a certain period of time. If he makes mistakes,

we shall replace him later on." He offered his people political stability under strong central rule and believed this the best they could hope for. The experience of other African states suggested that he was right.

In Kenya, Jomo Kenyatta continued in power until his death in 1978. He had no serious political rivals, for his prestige and authority as father of his country was enormous. His political party dominated the government. Violence rarely disrupted public life, though one influential politician from a rival party was found assassinated and his murderers were never captured. Kenya experienced orderly rule and relative prosperity, with white settlers living alongside their former colonial subjects. The army remained small, and the press enjoyed the freedom to report critically on public events. In Kenyatta's lifetime, Kenya represented the best case of independence with a stable government protecting a peaceful society.

Other small African states passed successfully through the period of liberation from colonialism into independence. The key proved to be the collaboration between respected leaders and loyal citizens. The former British colony of Botswana, landlocked and largely desert, enjoyed a few decisive advantages in that transition. The British had left in place the tribal leadership of precolonial times, and independence in 1966 endowed those leaders with new legitimacy as national figures. The desert hid great reserves of diamonds, discovered first in 1969. Their exploitation remained a private business (though with a substantial share of the profits going to the state), which prevented unscrupulous politicians from using the lucrative operations to enrich themselves and their supporters. Democratic government continued to function effectively. By the 1990s, taxes from this industry provided elementary education for all the country's children and adequate health care for a population whose average life expectancy had reached seventy. Along with these benefits, Botswana's citizens enjoyed a standard of living comparable to that of emerging economies in Asia. Key to the country's well-being was effective democracy.

But in most new African states, authoritarian regimes brought only instability and misrule to their people. Ambitious politicians sought ever-greater power by manipulating parliaments, extorting state funds for their personal enrichment, and creating mass parties whose only purpose was to serve and to glorify themselves. Little or no political freedom existed, and enemies of the regime ended in jail, or assassinated. Events after independence in Ghana illustrate this trend. Nkrumah had promised an era of great reforms when he took power. He set about dismantling the free market system, introducing laws creating a type of command economy. Proclaimed by his party "Man of Destiny" and "Redeemer," he rewrote the constitution to make himself president for life. His greatest ambition was to be recognized leader of all the African nations. He helped to found the Organization of African Unity and spent vast sums of money entertaining visiting African heads of state.

His rule proved disastrous for his people. He lacked the skilled personnel and the personal ability to use effectively the resources at his state's disposal, including large grants of foreign aid. Economic conditions worsened, and the standard of living of the people declined. By 1966, nine years after independence, economic decay and political disorder had undermined his authority. That year his own military commanders forcibly removed him from power. The army, which was the only national institution with a semblance of legitimacy among the population, became the backbone of dictatorship; army generals took charge of the government. Ghanaians welcomed his departure, destroying the statues and photographs that had glorified his exalted leadership throughout the country.

The usual pattern in many African countries became government by force of arms. During the 1960s, a total of forty successful insurrections took place among African states. They were the work of small groups of leaders and armed followers. In no African state did a new government come to power in those years in an orderly manner through democratic elections. One African observer sadly concluded: "We will never be at peace again." In the midst of such political unrest, people turned for protection to their tribal leaders. Tribal power frequently determined the winners in the struggle for control of the state; the resulting conflict among tribes became a cause of bitter civil war.

The bloodiest of these wars was the conflict in Nigeria. It began when northern, Muslim peoples suspected (without substantial reason) that the Ibo people in the south had acquired a commanding role in the government of the Nigerian federation. They were fearful that their own well-being and security would suffer if Ibo people obtained special favors. The rumors were sufficient to set off bloody riots. Ibo settlers were attacked by mobs in areas where they lived among other tribal groups. The federal government appeared incapable of protecting the Ibo, who fled to their homeland. Ethnic violence led, in a vicious spiral of rumors, riots, and death, to civil war in 1966. An Ibo general convinced his people to secede from Nigeria.

He counted on Ibo solidarity, which proved amazingly strong. For three years in the late 1960s the Ibo people fought to establish their own state, called Biafra. Outnumbered and besieged by the Nigerian army, the Ibo abandoned the struggle only after their land was largely devastated and famine had decimated the population. Even then, their leaders refused to admit defeat and demanded that the people fight to the death. The foreign support that they had counted on melted away when the extent of the suffering became known outside Biafra. Nigeria was reunited, but at a terrible price. State-building in these conditions became a desperate effort to preserve, in the face of bitter ethnic rivalry, a country's meager remnants of civil order and political unity.

For the next two decades, authoritarian regimes headed usually by military officers governed most of Africa's new states. Their claim to power rested on the armed might at their disposal, not on any legitimate legal sanction. New leaders appeared usually after the violent overthrow of their predecessors in a turbulent struggle for power. When one strong ruler managed to remain in control for a lengthy period, the country was spared political turmoil. Invariably, though, the price was widespread corruption and persistent violations of civil liberties. At best, these leaders became aware of the urgent economic and social needs of the country. Their authoritarian practices made it fairly easy to end state economic controls and to allow a market economy to take root again. Ghana experienced a remarkable economic recovery in the 1980s after its military rulers abandoned the command economy that Nkrumah had put in place, and opened the way for free trade in farm produce and industrial goods.

At worst, these rulers ravaged the meager level of well-being of their peoples. In the decades after he seized power in 1965, President Mobutu of Zaire (formerly the Democratic Republic of Congo) accumulated enormous personal wealth while depriving the country's public services of desperately needed state financial support. His personal prestige as leader of the largest state in sub-Saharan Africa brought him the support of western states. Large amounts of foreign aid poured into his country. Most of the funds were wasted, going into his private bank accounts in Europe. He argued in television messages and public speeches that he was the guarantor of Zairian national dignity and solidarity. His message won him the support of those in his country who hoped Zaire's diverse peoples could be united under a just ruler in a multiethnic state. But he failed to satisfy their hopes.

His government nationalized the prosperous mining industry. Instead of reinvesting the profits, he appropriated its income for his own purposes. By the early 1990s, his mismanagement and the growing rebelliousness of his army had produced conditions in Zaire close to anarchy, that is, the absence of any organized state system and lawlessness. The country's administration fell apart for want of funds, the army lacked arms and air transport, road and river transport dwindled, airports ceased operations, and cities lacked police protection, sanitation, and schools. The borders of Zaire remained intact, at least on maps of Africa, and its flag still flew among the United Nations flags. In other respects, Zaire ceased to function as a real state. It had become a "failed state," among those places in the world where the population could no longer rely on their state for law and order and for the most elementary public services.

The Cold War penetrated the African region in the decades after decolonization. It came as a result of competition between the Soviet Union and the United States for allies among African states and for access to the valuable natural resources (including uranium) of the continent. The U.S. Central Intelligence Agency (CIA) established close ties with President Mobutu of Zaire, sending him secret military support and financial aid to help sustain his regime even after he proved to be a disastrous ruler. When in the 1970s civil war erupted in the former Portugese colony of Angola, the Cold War rivals took sides in an effort to influence the outcome of the conflict. Soviet advisers and Cuban military forces were able (temporarily) to help their Angolan ally gain the upper hand in that war. Their foreign assistance stopped with the end of the Cold War in the late 1980s. The Soviet Union and the United States had provided assistance to the African states for reasons of state interests, not because they had an abiding commitment to the well-being of African peoples. When that assistance dried up, Africans were left with meager resources to cope with widespread impoverishment and the spread of diseases, old and new.

Effective opposition to dictatorship emerged within African countries from small groups committed to the political and civil liberties promised in their countries' first constitutions. They were encouraged in their efforts by Western governments, whose economic aid was increasingly vital to the very survival of some African lands. In 1990, both France and Great Britain announced that their aid would go in the future only to African states that respected their peoples' civil liberties, that permitted voters in democratic elections to select their leaders, and that loosened the state's control over economic life. Many dictators did, in fact, make serious efforts to open political life to parties and permitted elections.

The results were disappointing, however. In Nigeria, the military rulers refused in 1993 to allow the newly elected president to assume office, arguing that they alone could keep the ethnic hostility of the country's peoples from erupting in a new civil war. Another six years passed before free elections finally brought a civilian president to power there, and then in conditions of worsening conflict among the land's many tribal groups. Elsewhere, elections became a moment of struggle among ethnic groups, some of whose political leaders played on the fears of their people to win their votes.

African countries remained deeply divided by religious and ethnic bonds that impeded the formation of strong ties of national loyalty. The writer Chinua Achebe condemned this "tribalism"

in his Nigerian homeland as a form of "discrimination against a citizen because of his place of birth." But his wish for the growth of civic nationalism in his country remained an optimistic vision of the future. Only a few African states had become fully independent and truly unified.

The Failure of Economic Development

Closely linked to political disorder was the failure of many African economies to grow sufficiently to support an adequate standard of living for their peoples. The population explosion in Africa was greater than in any other part of the world, with growth fluctuating between 2.5 and 3 percent a year in the last decades of the century. Food production fell behind the needs of the people. In some areas, farmers chose or were forced to plant crops for export in place of food crops. Many governments monopolized farm exports in an effort to increase state revenues by artificially lowering the purchase price of cash crops and pocketing the

"Sustainable Development" at the Grassroots Level: U.N. Sponsored Stove Technology, Tanzania, 1966 (*U.N. Photo 153352/Kay Muldoon*)

profits from foreign sales. In Ghana, the result of the price controls set up by Nkrumah and retained until the early 1980s by later military rulers was a drastic decline in cocoa production. Exports fell by almost one half, in turn cutting back funds available for needed imports. Elsewhere, these price controls kept down the cost of basic foods for the poor migrants flooding African cities, where food riots were a serious threat to the fragile stability of the government.

Social distress and economic impoverishment resulted from a combination of political, commercial, and environmental factors. Where civil wars broke out, the rural population had to flee for their lives, abandoning their villages and fields. In the 1970s and 1980s, the decline in the international price of agricultural products hit African countries especially hard, for it deprived the farmers of income and the states of desperately needed revenue. Environmental degradation of the land became a serious problem. It was a visible result of a growing rural population denied adequate state assistance. Soil erosion and soil depletion were twin markers of this decay. In countries just south of the Sahara desert, this process led directly to the expansion of the desert ("desertification"). The environmental crisis in its turn contributed to decline in agricultural yields and harvests. These political, demographic, and ecological difficulties produced a critical shortage of food throughout Africa. By the 1970s, the continent was harvesting substantially less food per inhabitant than in the previous decade. The situation worsened in the 1980s. By the end of the decade, overall food production had fallen 20 percent below its 1970 level.

Despite the fact that land had earlier been one of the sources of the continent's wealth, it could no longer adequately feed the population. Malnutrition was a fact of life for half of Africa's population. Economies declined, and families had to migrate to cities within or beyond the borders of their own country in hopes of finding work and food. Fearful of urban disorders, governments continued to keep food prices low to feed its urban masses. They relied in large part on foreign aid programs to supply this inexpensive food. It was all that stood in the way of serious famine.

The agricultural crisis hit even those countries such as Tanzania (formerly Tanganyika) where national liberation had produced stable political leadership. There, Julius Nyerere became president in the first free elections of the former British colony, and remained in that position until resigning twenty-four years later. He created a single-party state, banning any political movements except from his own. His prestige as founder of the Tanzanian nation assured him the backing of his people. In addition, his government put in place an array of welfare programs to improve the level of education, health, and nutrition of the people. He was proud of the relative social equality that his policies had achieved. To further this goal, he took up the cause of collectivized agriculture (rather like the Soviet collective farms). Villages became a part of state-run farms, and the villagers had to join work brigades on the farms whether they supported the reform or not. Farmers resisted the state's coercive controls, and erosion and soil exhaustion resulted from misguided state agricultural experiments. The result of his disastrous policy was a decline of food production in Tanzania by nearly one half its precollectivization level. In the 1990s, a new political leadership abandoned his unrealistic socialist policies, allowing farmers to cultivate their own land and sell their crops on the free market. Like China under Mao Zedong, the Tanzanian nation could be egalitarian only in conditions of economic decay.

The agricultural crisis was the key to the failure of economic development in Africa. This factor, more than any other, explains why in the decades after independence living conditions of the population scarcely improved, and in many regions actually worsened. The economic statistics tell a tragic tale of stagnation and decline. Until the 1980s the yearly rate of economic growth (domestic product per person) was less than 1 percent. The 1980s was a period of actual decline, averaging each year about 1 percent, in per capita wealth in Africa. One observer called that time the "lost decade" in the development of sub-Saharan African lands.

Economic aid officials in Western capitals concluded by the early 1990s that they had to cease subsidizing ineffective governments and to put severe conditions on financial assistance to African states. The French government curtailed its support for the currency used in the French Community of Africa. The resulting decline in the value of the member states' money forced their peoples to pay twice as much as before for imports. Officials from the World Bank, as a condition for loans, requested that African governments end their unsuccessful intervention in the economy and abolish policies of price and production controls. They insisted on policies to institute the basic features of a market economy with free enterprise, free prices, and balanced state budgets.

Private investors gradually returned to Africa in search of profitable enterprises. Outside investors were drawn especially by the mineral wealth of the continent. Zambia's great copper mines had once been one of the world's major producers, next only to those of Russia and the United States. Taken over by the government in the optimistic years of national liberation and command economies, mismanagement and neglect led to the collapse of production. In the late 1990s, the government was forced to sell the mines to a South African mining company. Years of repairs were needed before the mines could produce as before.

A few fortunate countries, especially Nigeria and Angola, possessed abundant petroleum reserves. These states opened their doors to international oil corporations, who in exchange for rights to oil export assured the central governments of a substantial share of the profits. These revenues created what observers called the "spigot economy" ("spigot" standing for both the export of oil and the control of "big men" over this financial bonanza). Political leaders paid off their clients with the funds, instead of looking for productive investments. The increase in state expenditures created inflation so severe that it made agricultural production unprofitable. In the worst cases, small-scale civil wars erupted when peoples in the area where oil was extracted protested the failure of the government to return to them their "fair" share of the profits. All these complications prevented the African economy from benefitting adequately from its natural resources. And though the presence of outsider investors and financial advisers was often deeply resented, African governments had no choice but to accept their presence.

For lack of adequate financial resources, state-run social services in African countries fell into decay in the late twentieth century. Education ceased to receive sufficient funds to train skilled labor. Medical care, which had dramatically improved life expectancy and infant care until the 1970s, became inadequate in the face of the population explosion and new epidemics. The most devastating of these was the spread of auto-immune deficiency syndrome (AIDS), carried by war and civil disorder into many African areas. In some countries health experts discovered in the 1990s that one-fifth of the population was infected with the human immunodeficiency virus (HIV) that caused AIDS. By the end of the century, health authorities estimated that about fourteen million Africans had died of the terrible disease. African migrants, desperate to sustain the well-being of their families, defied immigration laws to seek work in Europe and the United States. The African crisis was a global concern.

The tragic betrayal of the hopes raised by national independence had many causes. Responsibility lay most directly with incompetent and corrupt rulers, who manipulated their governments' resources in a destructive struggle for the spoils of rule. The sudden withdrawal of the European empires left a vacuum of power, which African peoples had little preparation to fill. They became the victims of their leaders' tragic misuse of political authority. The economic misery with which they struggled and the political insecurity of their lives pushed them to rely on clan and tribal ties and to mistrust leaders from beyond their ethnic group or of a different religion.

This "tribalism" produced ethnic conflict, the flight of refugees, and ugly massacres in country after country in the late 1980s and early 1990s. It had its roots in the failure of African national leadership. New forms of outside intervention appeared, in the shape of foreign troops sent on U.N. peacekeeping missions, of bankers advising governments on economic policy, and of diplomats suggesting the means of restoring democratic practices. No better alternative appeared capable of helping Africa out of its misery.

LATIN AMERICA IN THE COLD WAR

The end of empire had come for almost all the peoples of Latin America in the early nineteenth century. Nationalist revolution swept the continent. The weak colonial forces of the Portuguese and Spanish empires were quickly defeated. European settlers had led the rebellions, and they became the rulers of the new states. Their understanding of nation was defined by the administrative borders of their former colonies, by the European languages implanted by the empires, and by the exclusive control over these nation-states of the population of European descent who had settled the New World. They made no place in their new national communities for the Native American peoples.

These "Indians" made a meager living in the countryside as farmers or farm laborers. The Europeans held in their hands the wealth of countries, in the form of great estates, mines, commerce and industry. In Brazil, many tribes in the Amazon basin remained isolated, some completely unknown, for a century or more. Only the Catholic Church, whose faith had spread among most of the population during the colonial period, had in some

measure succeeded in breaching the barrier between these communities. In these terms, Latin America's economic and cultural evolution had little in common with lands in Asia and Africa which had just achieved their own national liberation.

Its history of relations with the outside world was unique as well. Its states were diplomatically and militarily weak. In the early twentieth century, the northern regions of Latin America fell within the sphere of influence of the United States. Occasionally, the U.S. government sent military forces or political advisers to settle civil disorders or political quarrels in the small countries in the area of the Caribbean Sea and the Gulf of Mexico, and in Central America. Only Mexico escaped U.S. domination after its revolutionary upheaval of the 1910s. In the 1930s, President Franklin Roosevelt finally renounced this interventionist policy, promising "good neighbor" relations with Latin American countries.

In the middle of the twentieth century, the United States remained the dominant power in the region. It was the principal source of investments and the major market for the sale of Latin America's raw materials, still its major export and principal source of wealth. The U.S. government expected Latin American governments to recognize the importance its strategic interests. In the Second World War, many Latin American states joined in the alliance against the Axis powers. In the Cold War, the United States relied on them to oppose the Soviet Union and the international communist movement. Its diplomatic and economic influence in the region was pervasive, and at times oppressive.

Latin America fit well the category of "Third World" region. Observers used the term to suggest the social and economic gulf between the underdeveloped lands and the developed countries, capitalist or communist. Living conditions among much of the Latin American population were so poor that they resembled those in Africa and Asia. Political leaders devised new political and economic strategies to deal with these conditions of

Contemporary Central and South America

underdevelopment. Their hopes centered on state policies for economic development. In these terms too the area bore a strong resemblance to countries in Asia and Africa. European and North American corporations controlled major indus- tries, and their banks were an important source of investment funds. Real political and economic in- dependence remained an elusive ideal, and achieving it became the highest priority for many Latin American governments.

The Lure of Economic Independence

After the Second World War, a new generation of Latin American leaders came to power who for the first time took an active role in promoting economic development. The war itself had expanded the global demand for Latin American exports; it also opened markets for its manufactured products. These new opportunities for economic growth offered an escape from dependency of these countries on the United States. Latin American economists argued that this "import-substitution strategy" would raise their countries into the ranks of developed economies and improve the living conditions of the population. Political leaders promised as well extensive improvements of the states' social welfare programs for their peoples. It proved a winning electoral program. But achieving success in both areas proved difficult, at times impossible.

An important, and controversial innovation in foreign economic relations was the introduction, with U.S. backing, of new policies intended to encourage outside investments for economic development. These offered tax exemptions and cheap labor to international business investors, primarily from North America. U.S. corporations, protected by their state and by Latin American rulers, expanded their ownership of mines, plantations, and industrial enterprises throughout the continent. These investments did not grow as rapidly as expected, however. The disappointing results forced Latin American leaders to continue to rely their own economic resources to fulfill their promises to the people.

The "import-substitution" plans for development called for active involvement by state agencies in the economic affairs of their country. Officials, working under government supervision, assumed special power over markets to bolster domestic industries whose products would replace foreign imports. State funding made subsidies available for the opening of desirable new industries, such as aviation and automobile. State tariffs and other regulations hindered foreign imports that might weaken these infant industries. The success of these plans depended on wise leadership, difficult to achieve in poor countries torn by political rivalries and confronting rapidly growing populations. The lure of increased independence and economic prosperity was all the greater. Conservative in their social policies, many Latin American governments were prepared to experiment with a limited type of a command economy.

The success of these programs depended, as in most Third World countries, on outside financial assistance. Latin American economies looked to Western banks for loans to stimulate industrial growth. Governments also needed loans and foreign aid to pay for basic public services needed to raise the people's standard of living. But economic boom times when exports brought plentiful state revenues, and abundant, inexpensive loans were followed by harsh times of international recession and domestic government deficits. Wild inflation resulted from continued financial payments on popular projects. Too often, governments found that as a result of their bad planning and reckless commitments they lacked even the means to repay their foreign debts.

Populist political movements defended the social and economic needs of the people, accusing their rivals of collaborating with foreign business interests (a common practice) and demanding increased state welfare policies for the poor (for which funds usually were insufficient). Leaders who refused these demands ran the risk of provoking mass protests. Those who supported the populist program bought popularity at the expense of financial chaos. Political strife, economic dependency, and international weakness kept Latin America in a tenacious grip in mid-century.

Populism in Argentina, Brazil, and Chile

The political and civil liberties promised in the nineteenth-century nationalist constitutions of Latin America had little chance to be enforced in the midst of the bitter quarrels among political parties and between civilian government and the military. The 1950s was a time when powerful leaders supported by populist coalitions dominated Latin American politics. Their moment of glory was cut short by army insurrections followed by a return to military dictatorship.

This was the political fate of Argentina, Brazil, and Chile, which were the dominant states of South America. In 1946, Juan Peron was elected president of Argentina. He had promised the voters an end to rule by the country's wealthy elite and a massive program of social welfare. With the strong backing of the labor unions, he formed a populist coalition of followers eager to see the country's oligarchy finally dethroned. Argentina was rich in raw materials and agricultural resources. President Peron used his presidential powers and political influence to make sure special welfare benefits went to the laboring population.

The political price of his policies was high. When his government had to curtail spending and cut back social programs, labor unrest grew. In desperation, Peron mobilized his supporters in a campaign against the Catholic Church, which he accused of excessive wealth and support for his political enemies. It was a dangerous move in a country with a strongly Catholic population. Argentina's social elite, fearful of Peron's populist program and outraged at his attack on the Church, encouraged ambitious generals to intervene in the political crisis. In 1955, their wish was fulfilled when Argentine military leaders overthrew Peron's regime. Argentina passed rapidly from populist democracy to military dictatorship.

This authoritarian regime remained in power, with brief interruptions, until the 1980s. The generals, claiming to defend the "Western and Christian world," proved to be oppressive and incompetent rulers. Staying in power was their main objective. They were little concerned with using the natural abundance that their country possessed to improve the well-being of the people. The country's opportunity for economic development slipped away and popular discontent grew. In the 1970s revolutionary groups fought the regime with bombings, kidnaping, and murder. They, too, were unconcerned with immediate economic issues, for violent revolution in Argentina appeared to them to be their country's salvation.

The military dictatorship responded with a ruthless campaign of mass arrests and executions. Tens of thousands of alleged subversives simply disappeared, their very names erased from the official records. When they left behind small children, the infants were officially classified as orphans and made available for adoption. But repression failed to quell social and political unrest. In the hopes of winning patriotic backing, the generals attempted in 1982 to seize the Falkland Islands in the south Atlantic, occupied by Great Britain in the nineteenth century. They lost the war against British forces. This humiliating failure thoroughly discredited their leadership and doomed their regime. Shortly afterwards, they withdrew from politics, leaving Argentina, once a prosperous land, economically impoverished and politically unstable.

Like Argentina, Brazil was rich in natural resources but plagued by political conflict and extreme social inequality. Its social elite lived in a world far removed from the poor population in the country's coastal cities and interior jungles. Brazilian politics posed specially challenging problems to its government, since the country was the largest and most populous of all Latin America. Its coastal regions were centers of modern urban life, while its enormous interior (especially the rain forests of the Amazon basin) remained largely untouched by modern industry and agriculture.

In the 1940s Getulia Vargas, a dynamic and charismatic political leader, took up the task of reviving Brazil's economy and improving the living conditions of its people. He mobilized a broad coalition from the middle and working classes to support his ambitious program of economic growth and social welfare. He sought above all the expansion of Brazil's industrial economy. His government used the powers and revenues of the state to subsidize private companies and to create nationalized enterprises in key sectors such as oil exploration, armaments manufacturing, and automobile production. His program produced substantial benefits, and his economic policies set the model for future governments.

After his death in 1954, his political heirs proclaimed their commitment to his vision of a "new Brazil." They made the enormous interior regions, still undeveloped, the object of the greatest colonization drive since the nineteenth-century occupation of the North American Great Plains. The state constructed more than eleven thousand miles of new roads that penetrated deep into jungle areas where Indians had once lived in absolute isolation. The roads brought settlers who carved out land for ranching and farming from the great rain forest. The Brazilian government spent enormous sums constructing for their "new Brazil" a new capital, Brasilia, in the middle of the wilderness. Intended to be "the capital that [would] unite the whole nation," it was inaugurated in 1960.

The cost of these immense development projects was far beyond the financial resources of the Brazilian government. To pay for them, it had to turn to Western banks, contracting enormous foreign loans whose repayment put a great burden on its budget. As in Argentina, power-hungry generals were the only ones to benefit from the social unrest and political conflict caused by the resulting financial crisis. With the backing of the conservative Brazilian elite, they overthrew the democratic government in 1964, beginning a twenty-year military dictatorship. The prevalence of the military in Latin American political life in the 1960s and 1970s constituted a depressing return to an old form of rule.

The Cold War was a distant event for Latin American countries. Yet the pervasive influence of the United States and the emergence of revolutionary movements inspired by Chinese and Soviet communism brought this global conflict into the political life of the region. The Cold War made its disruptive effects felt most visibly in the Pacific coast country of Chile. Unexpectedly it found itself the center of ideological and political crisis in the early 1970s.

Once a model of liberal democracy, Chile's political parties were split between radical and conservative forces by bitter ideological issues of social reform. With the backing of workers and peasants, a reform government, led by the socialist Salvador Allende, took office in 1970. His political strength depended on a coalition of socialist and communist parties. They had agreed on a radical populist program, including sweeping nationalization of domestic and foreign-owned industries. Their goals resembled those of socialist governments in Asia and Africa. While looking to Third World reformers, they were tempted in particular by the example of Fidel Castro's Cuba to break away from U.S. international leadership. Theirs was a vision of revolutionary socialist change. That spirit spread to the countryside where peasants began to seize large estates, and to the factory workers who repeatedly went on strike to demand wage increases. Opposition to this program came from business groups, from conservative parties and the military, and from the United States government. The country was gripped by bitter political and social conflict.

Determined to restore order, Chilean military leaders led by General Augusto Pinochet plotted to seize power in 1973. They and their followers were persuaded that the country faced a communist revolution. That fear was shared by the U.S. government, determined to crush any communist threat in Latin America. Its CIA agents began secret operations in Chile that year, helping to organize opposition to the Allende government with funds and promises of U.S. backing. The threat of communist insurgency there was a myth, but one that shaped the U.S. global containment policy in those years. Supported by Chile's middle classes and with the encouragement of the CIA, General

Pinochet successfully ended Chile's experiment in socialist government. In the course of his insurrection, his army ended Allende's life in their siege of his presidential palace. Arrests of supporters of Allende's regime swept across the country; the army and police executed without trial an unknown number of prisoners. For nearly two decades Chile was ruled by Pinochet's military dictatorship.

Military rule in Chile differed from that in Argentina and Brazil in one important respect. The Chilean generals, in their effort to promote economic development and social stability, opted for the capitalist strategy. In the decade after the insurrection, they invited American economists to be key advisers in implementing free-market policies. They pulled the Chilean government out of economic activities and cut back social welfare for the poor. All Allende's reforms disappeared, at the price of serious hardship to the working population and in conditions of prolonged recession. But by the early 1980s, the formula slowly produced substantial benefits to the population when the country began a period of rapid economic growth.

Central America Under U.S. Domination

In the 1950s, the U.S. government found its most faithful allies in Central America to be military dictators. Diplomatically, it sought to bring all the countries in the entire region, including the Caribbean islands, within its sphere of influence. The small states there had to adhere closely to U.S. anticommunist and procapitalist policies in their domestic and foreign affairs. The U.S. took its Central American allies where it could find them.

One of these was the head of Nicaragua, General Anastasio Somoza. He had seized power in his country in the early 1930s, capturing and executing his principal rival, the nationalist leader Augusto Sandino. Somoza's rule brought his family great wealth. At the same time, it guaranteed the landowning elite the protection of its comfortable living, and insured the United States a loyal ally in the Cold War. Rulers such as Somoza were in effect client politicians in their relations with the United States. They faithfully adhered to its diplomatic guidelines and protected American business interests. In exchange, they obtained economic and military aid from the American government, and an export market in the United States for their raw materials.

Cuban politics in the 1950s duplicated this pattern of rule. The dominant figure was Fulgencio Batista, dictator in the 1930s and then president after he himself introduced a democratic constitution in 1940. Keenly aware of U.S. political and economic interests in Cuba, he bent with the political winds from Washington. In the war years, he heeded the U.S. call for the renewal of democracy. In 1944, he withdrew (temporarily) from politics. The era of democratic government lasted only eight years. In the early 1950s, Batista realized that the United States once again tolerated dictators within its Caribbean sphere of influence, on condition that they back Cold War policies. His appetite for power was as strong as ever. With the support of the Cuban army, he seized control of the government in 1952. Elections scheduled for that year were not held. He banned the Communist Party and ended diplomatic relations with the Soviet Union. The United States asked for no more.

Batista's understanding of U.S. priorities was correct. Like Somoza of Nicaragua, he received generous U.S. military assistance to arm and train his small army. His state kept closely in step with U.S. foreign policy and cooperated with U.S. investors. Sugar, the country's major crop that was sold principally to the United States, epitomized Cuba's continued economic and political dependence on the United States.

Cuba's military dictatorship lasted until 1959. Its economy expanded in those years, for sugar sold well in the United States and foreign tourists flooded the country. Impressed by Cuba's flourishing gambling casinos, one American gambler exclaimed: "The future looks fabulous!" Many middle-class Cubans benefitted substantially during those prosperous years. The Cuban standard of living was among the highest of any Latin American country. Economic prosperity was not sufficient to safeguard Batista's rule, however. He proved to be an incompetent and unpopular ruler. Cuban nationalists condemned the commanding role of the United States in the Cuban economy, and accused Batista of neocolonialist subservience to the Yankees. His repression of political opposition served only to provoke more resistance, though he relied on his army to eliminate his enemies. He had exaggerated confidence in his military forces, and in U.S. backing. He was wrong on both counts.

The man responsible for the fall of the Cuban dictator was a remarkable revolutionary leader, Fidel Castro. Son of a successful sugar plantation owner, Castro grew up in comfortable conditions. He was sheltered from the effects of the depression as a child and given the benefits of an education reserved for well-to-do Cuban youth. But his political convictions were those of a radical nationalist. Trained as a lawyer, he entered Cuban politics in the late 1940s on a program of independence from the United States and social reform. In those years, a period in his life Castro later called his "bourgeois thralldom," he was no different from many other aspiring young Cuban politicians. National legislative elections were scheduled to be held in 1952, and he prepared to campaign for office. But Batista's military coup disrupted these plans. Among the most bitterly disappointed candidates for office was Fidel Castro. Batista's dictatorship transformed him from party politician into a revolutionary leader.

By early 1953 Castro had gathered a group of 150 followers, mostly young factory and farm workers, united in support of what they loosely termed the "Revolution." They pledged themselves to the restoration of the 1940 constitution,

to "complete and definitive social justice based on economic and industrial advancement," and to liberation from "any links to foreign nations," that is, to the United States. The emphasis on social reform and opposition to U.S. imperialism constituted the core of Castro's political ideology. It was a romantic mixture of revolutionary fervor, defiance of Yankee domination, and concern for the needs of Cuba's poor. It later became the heart of his revolution. His confidence in his political genius far exceeded his means of action, though. In mid-1953, he led his small band of followers on a reckless assault on Batista's regime. He was convinced that justice was on his side and that Cubans were prepared to rise up under his leadership. He was wrong. His uprising was easily quelled by the army, and he was captured and sentenced to a long jail term.

Castro's determination to overthrow his country's military dictatorship was undaunted. Amnestied by government in 1955, he fled to Mexico to organize a guerrilla force for a second attempt at overthrowing Batista. His revolutionary group, called the July 26th Movement (the date of his first insurrection), sought support among anti-Batista forces prepared to take up arms. A new rebellion was a risky undertaking, as Batista appeared firmly in control of Cuba. In other Third World countries guerrilla forces had attempted to seize power from authoritarian regimes, and a few had even succeeded. Nowhere in Latin America did a comparable movement exist, and the United States might prove a serious enemy.

Castro's Revolution

In late 1956, Castro and eighty comrades returned to Cuba to begin once more their attempt to overthrow the Batista regime. This time, he succeeded in establishing a guerrilla base in the mountains of eastern Cuba. Opposition to the dictator had grown by then to include political rivals, labor unions, and many farm workers. Within a year Castro had built his tiny army into an organized band of three hundred fighters supported by an underground political movement in most Cuban cities. He had alongside him his brother Raoul, a member of the Cuban Communist Party who had become his loyal aide and most effective political organizer. With him also was a young Argentine doctor named Ernesto (Che) Guevara, an experienced, longtime revolutionary. They proved dynamic and forceful rebel leaders, and found among the Cuban population many supporters repelled by Batista's brutal methods of rule. The guerrilla movement provided Castro with the instrument to seize power. Those who fought with him there became the leaders of revolutionary Cuba later.

The U.S. government, suspicious of Castro's revolutionary and anti-imperialist program, hoped that Cubans would find another solution to the growing political crisis. In 1958 it ended its military aid to Batista's regime, clearly a losing cause. It anticipated that a new government would emerge uniting a broad coalition of Cuban parties. But it did not publicly condemn Castro's movement. Its silence helped Castro win the backing of Cubans prepared for the sake of ending the dictatorship to ignore his radical reform ideas. The U.S. policy of nonintervention in the Cuban conflict left to Cubans the choice of political leadership. The consequences proved not at all what U.S. leaders had expected.

In 1958, Batista's hold on the government was rapidly slipping away. Castro had by then organized a broad coalition under his leadership. That fall, small groups of his Rebel Army operated in all areas of the country. In the cities, an urban guerrilla force, the Civic Resistance, fought police and army units. In December, guerrillas under the command of Che Guevara moved out of the countryside to attack the capital, Havana. Batista's army melted away, and his generals fled for their lives. Batista found no one to defend his discredited regime. On January 1, 1959, he abandoned power and fled the country. On his heels came Guevara's Rebel Army. Castro arrived a week later, having traveled across the length of Cuba and received a hero's welcome from hundreds of thousands of Cubans. Castro, at age thirty-two, was leader of his country.

A political revolution began in Cuba that was unlike any that had ever occurred in Latin America. An armed insurrection led by a small rural guerrilla army totaling at most two thousand fighters had ended the rule of a military dictator. Its political leadership, the July 26th Movement, possessed only the outlines of a reform program and exercised little control over its political allies. In a country of seven million, Castro's own forces were few in number. Supporting them was a collection of liberal and socialist organizations and movements. Castro's most valuable ally was the Communist Party, with about fifteen thousand members and a centralized leadership modeled on the Soviet Communists. It shared Castro's opposition to American domination and brought him cadres experienced in organizing mass movements. The coalition of groups that participated in the insurrection shared no common goal. Real unity came from Castro's own leadership. The new regime's ruling cadres came from the Rebel Army. This was the case in 1959, and it remained so in the years that followed.

The revolution that Cuba experienced bore some resemblance to other revolutions that had occurred in Third World countries in the postwar decades. But the consequences in Cuba were unique and unexpected. Within three years after Batista's fall the Cuban economy was run under a system of command economy identical to that of the Soviet Union. The country was governed by a one-party state supported by and dependent on the Soviet Union. Most significant of all, Cuba suddenly found itself on the front lines of the Cold War. Castro's decision to rely on the Soviet Union for economic aid and military protection weakened the U.S. sphere of influence in the Caribbean, and led to the most serious international crisis since the end of the Second World War.

From the first year of his revolution, Castro was the central figure in Cuban politics. Consolidation of political power was his first objective. His second was radical reform to improve the living conditions of Cuba's lower classes. His third was the withdrawal of Cuba from the U.S. sphere of influence. His aims resembled in many ways those of other Latin American populist movements. His program appealed to many Cubans, especially the poor peasant farmers and urban working classes. For them, he was their undisputed national leader. He was determined to maintain political control of the new state. He arrived in Havana in early January of 1959, warning that he would not allow the new leadership to behave "like the many revolutionaries of the past [who] roamed around fighting each other." He understood that task to mean the exclusion from power of any groups that might challenge his own leadership.

Within two months he assumed the formal powers of prime minister. Gradually all the important government positions passed to his colleagues in the July 26th Movement. Free elections were never held. In 1961, Castro formally dissolved the constitution of 1940, claiming it was "already too outdated and old for us." In fact, Castro refused to permit free elections and civil liberties to weaken his political domination of the country.

A Soviet-type centralized dictatorship began to take shape. Castro and those around him intentionally modeled their new regime on communist one-party states. Leadership of labor unions, once controlled by Batista's supporters, passed into the hands of Communists. Political opponents were prosecuted by a new security police acting in the name of the "revolution." The state took control of Cuba's press, radio and television, all placed under strict censorship. Castro called his rule "direct government by the people." Power actually belonged to the former guerrilla leaders.

Cult of Fidel Castro: "Cuban Solidarity" (*Poster Collection, Hoover Institution*)

The conflict between Cuba and the United States began shortly after the revolution. It originated in Castro's early efforts in 1959 to make tangible the ideals, as he understood them, of social equality and economic justice. To aid the urban poor, he had housing rents lowered by 50 percent and electric power rates cut by as much. In May, the new regime ordered the expropriation of all landed estates of more than one thousand acres, including all large sugar plantations owned mainly by foreign companies. Part of the land went to poor and landless farmers, while the largest plantations became collective farms under state control. Nationalization of foreign businesses continued through the rest of the year despite objections from the U.S. government.

The Cuban revolutionaries were determined to liberate their country from domination by the "Yankee imperialists." Castro announced in 1959 that Cuba would adopt a new foreign policy of nonalignment. He condemned U.S. Cold War policies and capitalist exploitation of Cuba's resources. The new Cuban leaders were searching for a way to escape the U.S. sphere of influence. But they realized that their country depended as much as before on sugar exports. These sales brought the income essential to finance their expensive reform program. The U.S. government had for decades supported the Cuban economy (and the state) through regular, massive purchases of sugar at a guaranteed price. In strictly commercial terms, Cuba was a dependency of the United States.

Castro decided to present the U.S. government with a daring, remarkable demand for indirect assistance. His proposal took the form of a request that the United States double its procurement of the sugar and agree to a 20 percent increase in the price. His demand represented a public claim on the wealth of the Yankee imperialists. It was a reckless move, in contradiction with his denunciation of U.S. foreign policy and typical of his revolutionary zeal to transform Cuba. Unable to believe that the Cuban revolutionaries were

beyond control, the Eisenhower administration refused to renegotiate the sugar agreement and demanded that U.S. businesses receive proper compensation from Cuba for their property losses.

Rather than retreat, the Cuban revolutionaries pushed ahead in their efforts to escape United States domination. They turned to communist countries with a request for the economic and diplomatic support denied by the United States. They were successful, for the Soviet leaders welcomed the opportunity to carry their new Third World policy of aid to "bourgeois nationalist" leaders opposed to western alliances into Latin America (see Chapter 7). In February 1960, the Soviet Union signed an agreement to buy Cuban sugar on a regular basis and to provide Cuba with a major loan to permit Cuban purchase of Soviet machinery, petroleum, and military armaments. Castro considered the treaty a victory for Cuban nationalism. The Soviet petroleum had to be refined in Cuba, and Castro ordered the U.S.-owned refineries to cooperate. After consulting with Washington, the oil companies refused to process this "Red oil." In June 1960, Castro seized their property.

His decision proved the breaking point in U.S.-Cuban relations. The U.S. government halted all purchases of Cuban sugar, and later that year declared a complete embargo on trade with Cuba. It had, in effect, begun economic war. Castro responded by seizing all U.S. property. He added to this list all the remaining privately owned industries, banks, and transportation in his country. By the end of 1960, trade and banking, most of industry and transportation, and one third of the agricultural land belonged to the state.

By then the Cuban leaders had decided to take control of the entire Cuban economy. They viewed the Soviet Union as their model, copying the Soviet command economy system. They introduced laws enforcing command planning, organized collective farming through the countryside, and used state revenues to develop nationalized industry. Their decision was made hastily, and they lacked the skilled personnel and the revenues for this mammoth task. They borrowed heavily from the Soviet Union and welcomed Soviet economic advisers to help in constructing a socialist economy on their island. In doing so, they made their country dependent on the Soviet Union both diplomatically and economically.

The U.S. government had already begun plans to end this pro-Soviet state so close to its shores. President Dwight Eisenhower had authorized the CIA to organize anti-Castro Cubans for a possible invasion. In early 1961, John F. Kennedy, just elected president, publicly warned that Cuba was becoming "communism's first Caribbean base." His Cold War strategy remained the policy of containment, enlarged by then to include covert measures against states suspected of allying with the Soviet Union. He approved the CIA plan for a U.S.-supported rebel invasion of Cuba. He believed CIA assurances that Castro was unpopular and that a mass uprising among Cubans would reinforce the small rebel force attacking the island.

Events proved them wrong. The fourteen hundred Cubans who disembarked from U.S. warships to invade Cuba at the Bay of Pigs in April, 1961, were stopped at the landing beaches. The new Cuban army quickly defeated the invaders. In the interior, Cuban police immediately arrested suspected rebel sympathizers. The invasion proved a disastrous, futile undertaking. Victory brought the Cuban revolutionaries greater popularity than ever before. They had defeated forces of the "Yankee imperialists."

Still, their new regime remained terribly weak in the face of their mighty neighbor. They had to anticipate another U.S. invasion, certainly more concerted and massive than the first. That reason alone may have incited Castro to seek a military alliance with the communist states. His understanding of global revolutionary forces had evolved as well. He believed that his country had joined the Third World's crusade against capital-

ism and imperialism. The enemy in this confrontation was the United States. Castro concluded that his country belonged both in the Third World and in the communist camp. He made this clear in December 1961, when he announced, "I am a Marxist-Leninist and shall remain a Marxist-Leninist until the day I die." It was an affirmation of faith that contained a direct appeal to the Soviet Union for protection.

The Soviet leaders proposed to him only part of what he sought. He hoped for a Soviet military alliance. Neither the Soviet Union nor the Warsaw Pact (the military alliance of communist states) were ready for this risky move. Instead, in the spring of 1962, the Soviet government proposed to place intermediate-range ballistic missiles in Cuba. These were to be installed and controlled by Russians. Castro agreed, believing that his country was obtaining military protection in the fight against world imperialism. The missiles, accompanied by Soviet technical personnel and anti-aircraft units, began to arrive in great secrecy early that fall. Then U.S. military surveillance penetrated the secret. The U.S. demanded the immediate removal of the missiles, and threatened to invade Cuba if necessary. The Cuban missile crisis began (see Chapter 7).

To end the crisis, the Soviet government agreed to withdraw its military equipment and personnel from the island. It did obtain from President Kennedy a commitment not to organize any future military operations, either with U.S. forces or anti-Cuban groups, to overthrow Castro's regime. The world at large welcomed the compromise agreement, for it avoided nuclear war. Castro did not share in the satisfaction at the settlement. His government received only a U.S. promise of nonintervention. It did not obtain military protection from the Soviet Union. Worst of all, Castro had no voice in the resolution of the crisis. Soviet missiles vanished from Cuba without his approval. From a frontline position in the world struggle against imperialism, his island was reduced to a sideshow.

HIGHLIGHT: The Third World

The term "Third World" appeared in the 1950s to identify a new part of the globe. It was the invention of a journalist who could not have imagined how successful his expression would become. It seemed to him an effective description of the newly independent countries like India and Indonesia whose situation was unlike either the democratic West or the communist East. Its use quickly spread. Leaders of these new nation-states used it to emphasize their prominence in the postcolonial world. Radical politicians and intellectuals went further still by using the expression to identify all those areas of the globe, once colonial or semicolonial, which revolutions had liberated or would soon completely liberate from Western, "neocolonial" exploitation. In other words, this term became useful in the ideological debates about the future of the peoples of Asia, Africa, and Latin America after the collapse of Western empires.

Its most meaningful and least controversial message in the decades that followed identified the great disparity in economic and social well-being between industrialized and nonindustrialized lands. In the postcolonial world, the peoples in many countries were miserably poor, while a few areas enjoyed relative prosperity. At a time when governments in democratic and communists camps (the "First" and "Second" worlds) each argued that their own social and political ideologies were the best guides to human progress, the Third World urged both sides to look to the crying needs of their peoples.

These needs were defined in a variety of ways. Evidence suggested that about one third to one half of the peoples in countries of Africa and Asia lived in absolute poverty, that is, lacked sufficient food to meet their basic needs for subsistence. Inadequate medical care for mothers and newborn children meant that one fourth to one third of infants in areas of poverty did not live to be one year old. In human terms, conditions of life in these lands truly appeared to belong to another, "third" world.

Economists based their analysis of "underdevelopment" on the obstacles in these countries standing in the way of economic growth and well-being. They emphasized the inadequacy of basic facilities for industrialization such as electricity and roads and the lack of technically trained personnel prepared to maintain public services. They stressed the extremely low productivity of agricultural land, on which most of the peoples in Africa, Asia, and Latin American depended for their livelihood. They warned that countries that relied largely on the export of raw materials, true for most Third World economies in the 1960s, lacked funds to pay for needed imports of industrial goods and new technology. They stressed as well the inadequacy of education in most Third World countries, where at most 50 to 60 percent of the population possessed minimal skills of literacy. These figures painted a picture of countries whose population faced a future of misery and disease identical to that of their ancestors. Outside help appeared the only possible way to break this infernal cycle.

That need became the basis for economic aid programs in part because of the formation of the Organization on Non-Aligned States. It first met in the city of Bandung, Indonesia, in 1955. India's president Nehru rejected the argument of "some great countries" (referring to the United States and the Soviet Union) that "their quarrels are the world's quarrels and that the world must submit to them." In his opinion, the former colonial lands should not be "aligned" with either side. They had their own needs, the most urgent of which was aid from developed countries, communist or capitalist, for economic development. The United Nations became another forum for political appeals from Third World states. Their numbers grew until they constituted a majority of the membership in the U.N. General Assembly. At their urging, the United Nations launched programs called "Decades for Development." The first of these extended through the 1960s. It invited wealthy countries to contribute at least 1 percent of the value of their yearly national income to economic programs for developing areas. Nothing comparable had ever been attempted.

These calls for help incited a large number of governments to begin programs for aid. They did so partly out of humanitarian concerns, partly in response to Cold War competition for allies among the new states. Western governments made the largest contributions in the 1960s. The U.S. program for Latin America, called the "Alliance for Progress," brought billions of dollars in aid to that region. It came in large measure in response to the Cuban revolution and Fidel Castro's appeal for revolution in Central and South America. The Soviet Union's aid often went to great construction projects, helping to construct a mammoth dam for the Egyptian government on the Nile river at Aswan. Competition among donors occasionally produced unusual results. India obtained at about the same time three separate steel mills, one built by the United States, one by Great Britain, and one by the Soviet Union.

Economic assistance to the Third World grew rapidly through the 1960s and 1970s. The French government's program of economic assistance was directed especially to its former colonies whose new leaders had chosen to join the French Community. The World Bank made major loans at low interest and for long periods to governments who proposed specific projects, such as road building or the construction of hydroelectric dams. In the 1970s, the oil-producing countries of the Middle East became major donors when rising oil prices increased their revenues. Economic aid in the form of grants or loans to Third World countries became a long-term commitment by international organizations and industrialized states.

The efforts by Third World governments and by foreign aid programs to break the cycle of poverty and economic underdevelopment proved in places a remarkable success, in others a sorry failure. We cannot easily attribute these achievements or disappointments solely to foreign aid, for local and private initiatives played a major role. Economic development and public health programs were at times very effective. One example was the work of Western agronomists, notably Norman Borlaug, to create new, highly productive varieties of wheat, rice, and other crops. The success of their research brought an increase in yields so great that observers called the results a "Green Revolution." India's farmers increased their wheat yield by over 500 percent in the two decades that followed introduction of the new crops in the 1960s, and did so without putting new land under cultivation. Borlaug warned that, unless India's population explosion was halted, these "miracle crops" would provide that country with sufficient food for no more than three decades. But for the time being, famine was held in check.

Other countries experienced remarkable improvements in industry and commerce. The most amazing transformation took place in small countries in eastern and southeast Asia. Once poor areas largely devoted to peasant farming, South Korea and Taiwan became by the 1980s important industrial centers selling complex electronic products on the global market. Their growth rates were as high as Japan, whose economic example they seemed to follow. They could not longer fit by any measure the model of Third World countries.

Serious obstacles stood in the way of economic development elsewhere. One was the reluctance of the industrialized countries to sustain massive aid programs, since few ever reached the level of yearly aid at or above 1 percent of their national income. A second was the worsening of the terms of trade between industrialized and nonindustrialized countries. Between the 1960s and 1980s, international prices on raw materials fell drastically, sometimes by as much as 50 percent, as poor countries increased production to obtain a greater share of the market. A third barrier emerged when many of the Third World states, having accepted very large loans and grants, were unable to repay these loans. In the 1980s, interest rates on loans rose while prices on exports fell. Third World countries in Africa and Latin America were so deeply in debt to foreign creditors that they could afford only to make interest payments on their loans. In these desperate circumstances, they lacked funds for their own development programs.

A fourth obstacle proved to be the poor political leadership of many Third World states. Governments introduced risky economic reforms (often versions of command economies) that wasted the resources obtained through foreign aid on unproductive programs. Others were attracted to gigantic projects, such as Egypt's Aswan dam, that consumed tremendous funds that might have been used to cope with more pressing needs. Critics argued that simple technological innovations were in the long-run better suited to the population and to the resources of poor countries. "Small is beautiful" was the motto of one economist who favored modest improvements in technology. By the 1980s, it was clear that Third World governments could not produce miraculous economic development through state policies. Their efforts were better directed to achieving what came to be known as "sustainable" growth that brought steady, small improvements adapted to their economies and resources.

The most serious obstacle emerged from the very success of policies combating diseases in these countries. The campaigns to halt epidemics, eradicate disease-carrying insects, and improve health care quickly raised the life expectancy of the population throughout the Third World. The immediate result was a population explosion in these regions, doubling the world's population between 1950 and 1990 (from 2.5 to 5 billion). This increase ate up the slow rise in farm production and industrial manufacturing. It left countries such as India with scarcely more food per capita in 1990 than in 1950.

The Third World was changing in shape. Well-to-do, well-educated professional and entrepreneurial classes were making their presence felt within countries such as India. They were nearly as far removed from the poor masses as were the prosperous Westerners. The essential problem of a world deeply divided between wealth and poverty, developed and developing, the well fed and the hungry, endured to the end of the century. The Third World remained a dominating presence in global relations.

DEMOCRACY IN LATIN AMERICA

In the decades that followed the missile crisis, Latin America gradually evolved toward an economically developed region where democratic governments coped, more or less successfully, with the needs of their peoples. Politically ambitious generals proved so incompetent that they were forced to withdraw from power. Economic plans for industrial development set in motion a process for development that raised the standard of living of a large part of the population. Increased well-being led millions of families to have fewer children, thereby slowing dramatically the increase in population. By the early 1990s, the region as a whole no longer belonged alongside sub-Saharan Africa within the Third World.

From Dictatorship to Democracy in South America

In the 1960s, the pressures in Latin America for social reform and economic development came from three new developments peculiar to the region. The Cuban revolution and Castro's stature as revolutionary leader crystallized social opposition to Latin American oligarchies. Castro laid down in early 1962 his guidelines for Third World revolution in his Second Declaration of Havana. He placed Cuba in the forefront of the "upward march of history." Cuba was to be a key player in the forthcoming triumph of socialism, because "the Cuban Revolution shows that revolution is possible, that the people can do it." He held up his revolutionary state as the model for revolutionary insurrection and economic development in all Latin American countries. To counter his program, governments in Central and South America turned their attention more than ever to plans for improving living conditions among their people.

Another reason for expanded efforts at social and economic progress was the decision of the U.S. government, pushed by fears of revolution, to sponsor economic development and social reform in Latin America. President Kennedy's Alliance for Progress, intended to assist all non-communist states in the region, included a request that they create their own development plans. Governments that complied were assured of U.S. economic and financial assistance, which ultimately totaled $20 billion in the next ten-year period. U.S. advisers strongly encouraged the Latin American leaders to impose heavy taxes on the wealthy to help pay for these programs and to institute land reform to provide farms for the rural poor and landless workers. The U.S. government also increased its military aid, directed specifically at repressing guerrilla movements like the one that led Castro to power.

A final important factor behind the concern for coping with poverty and social inequality was the decision of the Catholic Church to play an influential role in social reform. Pope John XXIII, elected in 1958, had initiated what he called a "reawakening" of the church. The Second Vatican Council, meeting between 1962 and 1965, gave the church's approval to his daring proposals. Many reforms and policies approved there had particular significance for global problems of economic inequality. These addressed the so-called pastoral mission of Catholics to care for the needy and underprivileged. The council looked to the needs of "the whole of humanity," calling on the clergy and the faithful alike to take an active role in social and economic reform to help the poor and oppressed. It welcomed state welfare policies and suggested that the faithful should create special organizations to assist in this enormous task. The Catholic Church was firmly opposed to violent revolution. Its program was meant to be an alternative path to social progress.

The consequences of its call "to all people of goodwill" to work toward peace and social justice had a profound political impact among Catholic faithful, particularly in Latin America. The Catholic Church had for centuries been an integral part of the daily life of the peoples there. It had exercised a very conservative role, preaching obedience to the state and deference to the social elite. Pope John XXIII's "reawakening" changed all that. To implement the decisions made at the Second Vatican Council, all Latin American bishops met in 1968. In the presence of the pope, the delegates laid down the principles of social action by Catholic priests and laity. The goals were those fixed at the Vatican conference—the need for peace based on justice, human betterment through social action, and major social reforms.

The impact of these decisions was long-lasting, though they are not easily measured. Within a few years nearly a million Brazilian Catholics, mainly from the poor laboring classes, had joined religious associations (called "cebs") to undertake local reform measures. In the years of repressive military dictatorship in the 1970s they were the only mass political movement in the country. The effect among Catholic clergy was equally profound. Although upper-class bishops resisted the reform movement, other bishops and priests began to speak out openly against injustice, at times at the risk of their own lives. While Castro's supporters called for Marxist revolution, the Catholic Church proposed its own ideology of social reform.

The three decades following the Cuban Revolution were a period of political transition to democracy and economic growth in Latin America. Popular demands for better living conditions focused the attention of military and civilian leaders everywhere on the need for economic development. In the 1960s and 1970s, Latin American economies expanded rapidly, in large measure because prices on raw materials were high, and banks were generous in lending funds. The United States remained a very influential presence, pushing economic development and backing anticommunist foreign policies.

Rule by military dictatorship, typical of the 1960s and 1970s, proved to be short-lived. All the dictators had by the late 1980s vanished. Most were forced to resign as a result of popular opposition to their repressive policies and, often, as a consequence of their inability to cope with a growing financial and economic crisis. Interest rates rose and commodity prices fell in the early 1980s. The old formula of raw materials exports and foreign loans no longer worked. State subsidies dwindled and nationalized industries went deeply into debt. Many Latin American governments were so heavily indebted to foreign banks and international lending agencies that they had to default on payments. Their leaders could no longer count on new loans. Lacking outside aid, they had to introduce painful measures of financial and economic austerity. These unpopular measures were beyond the limited competence of the military rulers.

Chile proved the exception, principally because the military regime of General Pinochet had from start adopted austerity and free-market policies. These finally brought substantial economic rewards in the 1980s, the very years when other military regimes faced similar choices. Even in Chile the military regime came under growing popular pressure to return the country to parliamentary democracy. Faced with growing foreign and internal opposition to his dictatorship, in 1988 Pinochet finally allowed free elections to take place. The choice was between authoritarian rule and democratically chosen leadership. The voters chose democracy and civilian rule. By then the country enjoyed a level of economic well-being remarkable in a region in the throes of serious economic crisis.

The nature of the predicament appeared most clearly in the crisis that faced Brazil in that decade. The military revolt that ended Brazilian democratic rule in 1964 had come in response to the social unrest stirred up by civilian government's failure to carry out measures for the redistribution of wealth among the poor. The new military dictators dealt ruthlessly with the revolutionary opposition and cut back on social welfare. Inflation dwindled for a time and foreign debts were paid.

The Brazilian military regime did continue the policy of state-sponsored development launched in the 1940s. They offered financial subsidies to industrialists and ranchers and poured funds into state enterprises. They hoped to expand the economic opportunities for conservative Brazilian investors and business interests. They undertook a vast program for the development of the Amazon region, still largely a wilderness inhabited by Indians and a few settlers. In opening the Amazon basin, they anticipated that migrants from Brazil's poorest regions would flood into the area. Social unrest would dwindle, and the country's economy would prosper. Their ambitious plans for economic growth came at enormous cost. But they understood little and cared less about the economic and financial risks that their projects created. Their objectives were political. They hoped to increase the independence and international influence of their state. Their dream was visionary; it was also wildly unrealistic.

Their program did partially achieve its goals. By the mid-1980s, Brazil had developed into one of the major industrial powers in the world. The Amazon basin had attracted large numbers of settlers and ranchers. But the program of Amazonian development led to the uncontrolled destruction of large forested areas opened to colonization. The most powerful new settlers were ranchers eager to acquire vast tracts of open land. In that frontier world, they made the law, even ordering the assassination of outspoken opponents of their land grab. Small farmers came in their wake, ready to extract as rapidly and cheaply as possible what produce they could grow on land that was quickly depleted. The two groups together burned vast regions of the rainforest. The devastation represented a tragedy for the inhabitants of the Amazon basin, particularly the Indians, but also those whose livelihood depended on the forest, such as rubber tappers. Equally as serious was the fact that the disappearance of the rainforest threatened an ecological disaster to a unique and vital environment. By the mid-1980s the fires had grown so great that the smoke at times shrouded the entire Amazon region. Environmental movements, such as Greenpeace, launched an international campaign to stop further destruction of the rainforest.

The financial, ecological, and social price that the country had to pay for the general's reckless economic policies proved so high that the military regime was ultimately compelled to abandon power. The state went deeply into debt to cover the expenses that it lacked the means to pay for. By the mid-1980s the resulting budget deficit produced a disastrously high rate of inflation and financial instability. At the same time, Brazil had accumulated an international debt of nearly $100 billion, higher than that of any other Third World country. It could not meet its debts and its attempts at fiscal restraint only heightened popular opposition. The poor population had benefitted little from the country's prosperity. The Catholic Church began to speak out publicly in support of the needs of the poor and backed protest movements in defense of the Vatican Council's reform program. Other political movements also were increasingly active. In the face of this opposition, the military government decided in 1985 to withdraw from politics. It allowed free elections to take place.

A new democratically elected government took over power in Brazil in extremely difficult circumstances. Gradually, it set about dealing with the state's financial crisis and the economy's inadequate performance. Its solution was to allow a full market economy to reappear. Within a few years it abandoned the policies of state-sponsored development, gradually opening the country to foreign imports and privatizing (selling to private investors) nationalized industry. It promised to curtail destruction of the rainforest, and in 1992 sponsored the first United Nations Conference on Environment and Development. Social inequalities and political instability still remained a part of Brazilian life, but the crisis appeared at an end.

Mexico's New Democracy

Mexico followed the path of the other Latin American countries toward political democracy and a free-market economy. The authoritarian one-party regime of the Institutional Revolutionary Party (PRI) had been in existence since the 1920s. It had brought stability to the country following the revolutionary turmoil of the early century. The price was the loss of political freedom. One Mexican critic called its regime the "perfect dictatorship," because it "suppressed methodically by whatever means any criticism that threatened its hold on power." In appearance Mexico was a political democracy, with an elected president and parliament, but in reality each president came only with the approval of PRI. Newspapers received secret subsidies from the party, and in return published the "news" supplied by the authorities. On the surface, the state was stable and the country calm.

Beneath the surface, the PRI dictatorship, like the communist regime in the Soviet Union, was falling into decay. Corruption spread as powerful gangs smuggling drugs into the United States bribed police and party bosses. Bankers and industrialists found that their businesses could thrive only after bribes to powerful officials. The nationalist fervor that had animated the post-revolution generation of Mexican leaders faded, leaving behind a regime devoted primarily to keeping its monopoly on political power and enriching its supporters.

The Mexican government had followed the same path as other Latin American countries in making the state a key player in the economic life of the country. A state-owned company managed the country's enormous oil fields. In the 1960s and 1970s, foreign sales of petroleum bolstered the state budget and induced foreign bankers to make large loans. The government allocated generous subsidies to important industries and used tariffs and other measures to hinder foreign competition. The recession in the 1980s ended those good times, leaving the Mexican economy in crisis and the state unable to repay its foreign loans. The government's attempt at economic independence could not meet the needs of Mexico's rapidly growing population (nearly 90 million by the 1980s). Illegal and legal migration to the United States increased dramatically as Mexicans departed in search of a better life.

Among the PRI leaders were some who, like Soviet reform leaders of the late 1980s, concluded that the welfare of the country required radical political and economic reforms. They decided that a free-market economy and the expansion of international trade offered the best hope for Mexican economic recovery. The success of their daring program depended on improved trade and economic ties with the United States. In 1994, the Mexican government agreed to join with Canada and the United States in the North American Free

Trade Agreement (NAFTA). The reformers realized the next year how important these ties were when wealthy Mexicans and foreign investors suddenly "dumped" (sold) Mexican currency on the international market. The peso, which had already begun a slow decline, plummeted in value. The Mexican government's salvation from the ensuing financial crisis came from a massive U.S. government loan, saving the Mexican state from defaulting on all its foreign debts (see Chapter 8). In these conditions of growing financial and commercial interdependence, Mexico entered a new era of cooperation with its former enemy to the north.

The reformers came to the conclusion that they had to open Mexico's political system to free elections if they were to succeed in their program of economic recovery. Their reform program encountered the opposition of PRI officials who had enriched themselves by their easy access to public wealth. They anticipated that the entrenched PRI leaders would lose power when voters had a chance to vote for rival candidates. It was a painful, at times violent process. With the strong encouragement of the U.S. government, the Mexican leadership coupled free-market reforms with the restoration of democratic rights. PRI reform leaders formally renounced the party's monopoly of political power. In 1997, for the first time in nearly a century opposition parties won a majority of the seats to the Mexican parliament. Three years later, the winner of the presidential elections of 2000, Vincente Fox, came from a reform political party. PRI had given up its "perfect dictatorship" in what amounted to a peaceful revolution. By the late 1990s, democratic government and a free-market economy had taken hold in almost all Latin American countries.

Cuba, Central America, and the Yankees

Though Cuba remained under U.S. economic embargo after the 1962 missile crisis, the Cuban regime no longer faced the threat of a U.S.

military invasion. Castro was free to pursue his socialist reforms. His path was erratic and the results in the next decades disappointing. His country regularly received large amounts of Soviet foreign aid, including cheap petroleum and wheat vital to the Cuban economy. Soviet yearly assistance totaled nearly $5 billion in the 1980s. The Soviet military assisted Castro's army with arms and advisers. Castro was able to send armed forces to aid Marxist regimes in Africa, first to Angola in 1975 then to Ethiopia in 1978. These military adventures were his greatest international success, reassuring him that communist Cuba was still part of the "upward march of history."

The social and economic impact of Castro's reforms brought the people substantial social benefits, but left many dissatisfied with the dictatorship, and with the command economy. Their living conditions improved in the 1970s, and the country did not experience the extremes of wealth and poverty of societies such as Brazil. Women in Cuba enjoyed greater opportunities and rights than women in most other Latin American countries. A revealing sign of the social revolution in Cuba was the fall in the birth rate, lowest in all of Latin America. Women's liberation was not the whole explanation, however, for most women had to work to support their families in an economy plagued by shortages of consumer goods.

The lure of life in the capitalist United States remained great. Many families had relatives who had fled the country after Castro's revolution. Large numbers lived in nearby areas such as Florida; a large part of Miami became "little Havana" for its Cuban residents. When given the opportunity in 1979 to emigrate to the United States, hundreds of thousands more Cubans departed. Small groups continued illegally to flee in small boats, many of which sank in the stormy seas between Cuba and Florida. But Castro remained convinced of the virtues of Marxist-Leninist socialism, even after the collapse of communist regimes in Eastern Europe and the fall

of the Soviet Union in the early 1990s. A billboard slogan appeared in Cuba reading "Socialism or Death!"

In Central America, Catholics, reformers, and revolutionaries joined in opposition to the entrenched social and political elites. Each group chose a different path of opposition. Following the 1968 conference of Latin American bishops, the Catholic clergy took the lead in denouncing military rule and economic injustice. When conditions worsened some even spoke out in favor of insurrection as the only means left to attain freedom and justice. El Salvador's army, fighting revolutionary Marxists in the countryside, turned against these reformist clergy. In 1981 officers assassinated the country's archbishop, Oscar Romero, to silence their critics. In the face of political conservatism and military repression, there was little place for real social reform.

Cuban socialism provided a model for the revolutionary regime that emerged in Nicaragua in the 1980s. The Somoza dictatorship there faced in the late 1970s opposition from a coalition of resistance groups, radical and liberal, calling themselves the Sandinistas (Sandino, a political reformer, had been assassinated by Somoza). The Catholic Church joined forces with Marxist revolutionaries in 1979 to organize a popular insurrection that ended the Somoza rule. The radicals in the coalition refused to share power, however. Much like Castro in 1959, they set out to create socialist institutions under a single-party dictatorship. Their small country was incapable of meeting their Marxist expectations, however, and they faced the bitter opposition of the conservative U.S. government. The United States gave military supplies and training to an anti-Sandinista guerrilla force called the "Contras," and declared an economic embargo of the country. The revolution aroused widespread opposition from the population, whose living conditions rapidly worsened.

Confronted by a grave economic crisis and social unrest, in 1989 the Sandinistas allowed the people to choose their future leaders in free elections. A majority of the voters preferred the democratic opposition, and the Sandinistas left the government. Their socialist experiment was over, leaving an impoverished population as evidence that their reform program was not the key to social justice or prosperity.

Despite some signs of economic growth, at the end of the 1980s most countries of Central America and the Caribbean remained lands of political instability and economic poverty. The precariousness of their governments opened the way for political extremists and dictators whose actions only worsened economic conditions. Close to the United States, these lands remained subject to U.S. military intervention when American leaders judged their internal or foreign policies unacceptable to U.S. interests.

Twice in the 1980s, U.S. military forces occupied countries in the region. In 1983, they forcibly expelled from the island of Grenada the Marxist government trying to introduce a revolutionary regime there. In 1989, they removed from power Manuel Noriega, the military dictator of Panama. He was involved in international drug smuggling, and had recklessly proclaimed his intention to seize the Panama Canal, still U.S. territory. Close to the United States, these small states remained within the U.S. sphere of influence. In the same years, increasing numbers of migrants from these lands left their homes to settle in the United States. Some were refugees from political oppression, but most sought work and better conditions of life. These small countries on the very borders of the United States remained a part of the Third World.

SUMMARY

When the term Third World appeared in the 1950s, the areas of the globe it described seemed far removed from the West. The readiness of European states to grant independence to their African colonies arose in large part because their leaders and most of their population were prepared, even eager, to distance themselves from old imperial ambitions and to proceed with the urgent task of reconstruction from war. The fall of these empires created new states separated from and far removed from Europe's immediate concerns. The nationalist leaders of the African states were eager for independence and the freedom to set their countries' future course. The new postcolonial age in the Third World seemed an era of promise beyond the conflicts of the Cold War. The liberation of South Africa from white rule held the hope that there too a better life was open to all the people. In Latin America, nationalism was winning more converts to the idea that real independence from the United States was at last attainable. New leaders everywhere agreed that the path to this goal was economic development.

The obstacles proved to be far more serious than expected. The problems encountered in Africa and Latin America varied from country to country. The most common was incompetent leadership, often from military dictators, far more interested in personal power and wealth than in the welfare of their people. Obstacles also arose from a lack of resources and skills, leaving ambitious economic projects to fall into decay. There was no quick route to prosperity and well-being. The promise of Soviet leaders that their form of socialism was both just and productive proved hollow. The Cuban experience revealed that a small, agrarian country remained as dependent on outside powers when it was part of the communist world as when it was within the Western international economy. The experiments in state control over economic development that emerged in Africa and Latin America did initially contribute to short periods of prosperity. Their shortcomings appeared after the initial spurt of growth had ended, when inefficiency, corruption, and lack of productivity became a serious obstacle to continued development. In the end, the Western system of free-market production and distribution proved to be less wasteful and disruptive. The capitalist idea of social justice was confined within a system in which productivity and enterprise received the highest rewards.

In Latin America, the return to market economies gradually yielded results that were impressive and long-lasting. One measure of the impact of a rising standard of living was the dramatic fall in the birthrate in countries such as Brazil between the 1960s and 1990s. More and more families were persuaded that their own resources were sufficient for their old age, and that the survival of every one of their newborn children was, if not certain, at least probable. Their lives no longer depended on a desperate daily struggle for food and their future appeared secure. The continued high birth rates in many countries of Africa revealed, on the contrary, how unsuccessful the efforts there had been to cope with poverty. In most areas of Africa local economies were in serious decline. These grave problems brought in outsiders to take a hand in economic reforms there. Western intervention came again to parts of Africa where failed states and decaying economies worsened poverty. Increasing numbers of migrants left these areas to search for work in distant urban centers. Some traveled on to cities in the Western world. The Third World was by the 1990s more than ever a part of an interdependent world.

DATES WORTH REMEMBERING

Africa

1948 Introduction by Nationalist Party in South Africa of apartheid
1955 Approval of Freedom Charter by African National Congress
1957 Independence for Ghana (Gold Coast)
1960 French Community membership for former French African colonies
1960 Independence for Nigeria
1960 Independence for Belgian Congo (Zaire)

1960–63 Civil war in Zaire
1961–93 Imprisonment of Nelson Mandela by South African government
1965–96 Joseph Mobutu leader of Zaire
1967–70 Biafran civil war in Nigeria
1993 End of apartheid in South Africa
1994 Nelson Mandela president of South Africa

Latin America

1934 U.S. "Good Neighbor" policy in Latin America
1946–55 Juan Peron Argentine president
1955 Beginning of Brazilian plan to develop Amazon rainforest frontier
1959 Castro's revolution in Cuba
1960 Completion of construction of Brazil's new capital, Brasilia
1961 Cuban Bay of Pigs invasion
1962 Cuban missile crisis
1962–65 Second Vatican Council
1964–85 Military dictatorship in Brazil
1973–88 Military dictatorship in Chile
1985 Democratic government in Argentina
1985 End of military dictatorship in Brazil
1989 Democratic government in Chile
1992 First United Nations Conference on Environment and Development
1994 North American Free Trade Agreement among Mexico, Canada, and United States

RECOMMENDED READING

The "Third World"

Nigel Harris, *The End of the Third World: Newly Industrializing Countries and the Decline of an Ideology* (1986). An inquiry into the economic success of East Asian lands and its lessons for "Third Worldism."
Akie Hoogvelt, *The Third World in Global Development* (1982). A historical view of the difficulties of economic development in the Third World.

Independent Africa

Mary Benson, *Nelson Mandela: The Man and the Movement* (1986). A sympathetic biography and portrait of Mandela that relies in part on prison interviews.
*Frederick Cooper. *Africa since 1940* (2002). A thoughtful analysis of the evolution of the continent

as it passed from the last bastion of European colonialism to a land of nation-states.

Karl Maier. *This House Has Fallen: Midnight in Nigeria* (2000). A perceptive, grim picture of Nigeria's descent into a failed state.

Postwar Latin America

*Thomas Skidmore and Peter Smith, *Modern Latin America,* 5th ed. (2001). A brief survey of the history of Latin America with separate treatment of major countries.

Tad Szulc, *Fidel: A Critical Portrait* (1986). A detailed and critical biography of Castro as a personality and political leader.

Memoirs and Novels

*Chinua Achebe, *Anthills of the Savannah* (1985). A story of lost hopes by a Nigerian novelist whose stories chronicle Nigeria's colonial and post-colonial history.

Nelson Mandela, *Long Walk to Freedom: The Autobiography of Nelson Mandela* (1995). The moving personal reflections on a life that led the author from prison to presidency of South Africa.

*Alan Paton, *Cry, the Beloved Country* (1948). The powerful novel, by one of the country's finest writers, of South Africa's years of brutal racism.

Chapter 6

Nations at War in the Middle East

Outline

    Israel and the Middle East

    Nation-Building and Petroleum

    War, Peace, and Islam

Highlight

    Islam and Nation-States

Spotlight

    Golda Meir

The history of the Middle East after 1945 is dominated by wars, revolutions, and civil strife. More than any other region in the world, it became an arena of political conflict and war. No one state dominated the territories once ruled by the Ottoman Empire. Its collapse after the First World War marked the first step in the remaking of the Middle East.

In the 1920s Western governments took charge, in one manner or another, of drawing the borders of the successor states. The lands of Egypt and Iran were already well defined, with frontiers historically established and governments nominally independent. Elsewhere the borders and even the names of states existed only as remnants of Ottoman provinces (such as Syria and Palestine). The territorial outline of these areas became the basis on which the Western powers laid out the frontiers of the new states after the First World War. In that multiethnic, multireligious area, each country gathered peoples of diverse languages, cultures, and clan loyalties within its borders. Later observers called them "states without nations, nations without states."

Sectarian religious quarrels (principally between the Sunni and Shiite Muslims) and rivalries among ethnic groups presented serious obstacles to political unity. Conservative monarchs (like the rulers of Iran and Saudi Arabia) relied on traditional fidelity to their throne, but their legitimacy was threatened by pan-Arabism, by Muslim fundamentalism, and by social unrest. The vision of a great Arab nation offered one alternative ideology. Arab intellectuals drew their inspiration for this grandiose national community from the medieval Arab empires that had ruled the entire area. After 1945, Arab political leaders frequently called for the creation of a pan-Arab nation. Often, though, such appeals to Arab nationalism were based on the claim by one particular Arab ruler that his leadership was the only basis for Arab unity.

Authoritarian rule proved the most prevalent method of governance throughout the region. By the 1960s, military dictators had taken power in most Middle Eastern countries. They justified their rule by promoting social reform and, often, by claiming to be defenders of the Muslim faith practiced by most of their peoples. But all the economic indicators of development revealed that at century's end the Middle East remained sunk in poverty. Impoverishment and deep devotion to Islam combined to make an Islamic form of nationalism a powerful magnet to attract popular support. Disunity and the struggle for power among conservative monarchs, Muslim fundamentalists, and ambitious generals sustained conditions of disorder and instability in the political life of these lands.

The violent history of the region was also due to factors outside the Arab community. The Jewish settlers living among of Arab-speaking peoples in Palestine achieved the Zionist dream of a Jewish nation-state shortly after the Second World War. The inflexible opposition of Arab states to the very existence of Israel led to four separate wars between Israel and its Arab neighbors. Pan-Arab nationalism came to mean resistance to Western imperialism and also to Zionism, by which Arab leaders referred to the state of Israel. In later decades, Palestinians entered into the struggle against the Jewish state in an effort to forge their own nation-state. Nationalism was at the heart of the Middle East's turmoil in the last half of the century.

The recent history of the Middle East is also a story of oil. Its oil fields, concentrated in the area around the Persian Gulf, contained greater petroleum reserves of higher quality than anywhere else in the world. The dependence of the industrial countries on this vital resource brought the pressures of the Cold War to bear on the oil-rich countries. The Soviet Union and the United States kept close watch on the unstable governments there. Each intervened in the political life of these states, and used their global might to protect allied

countries. The governments of lands with large oil reserves nationalized their petroleum industry to get direct access to a share of the profits, and created an international cartel to set levels of production and prices for this increasingly valuable commodity. The fabulous wealth to be drawn from oil production became the cause of war when Iraq attempted to conquer oil-rich areas on its borders. Internal and international conflict remained the central feature of the postwar history of the Middle East.

ISRAEL AND THE MIDDLE EAST

The Middle East was the birthplace of three major religions—Judaism, Christianity, and Islam. For many millions of people, Jerusalem was the most holy place in the world. It remained a center of pilgrimage and worship for the faithful of all three religions in the twentieth century. It had also been for long the main city in the region known as Palestine. This was the area in which Zionists were determined to create a Jewish national homeland. Their goal appeared attainable after the defeat of the Ottoman Empire by the Allies in the First World War. Their determination to achieve this goal brought them into conflict with the British rulers of the League of Nation's mandated territory of Palestine, then, after the withdrawal of the British, with the neighboring Arab states and the Arab-speaking peoples of Palestine. The new nation-state of Israel extended its borders across a landscape where for centuries Muslim and Christian religious communities had dwelled under foreign rule and worshiped at their own holy sites. National and religious differences combined to make this one small region of the Middle East a cauldron of ethnic conflict and war.

The Struggle for Palestine

The end of the Second World War immediately brought out the long-standing antagonism between

Arabs and Jews in the British mandate of Palestine. By war's end the other mandated territories— Lebanon and Syria, Iraq and Jordan—had received their independence under constitutional monarchs (in the latter two) or elected parliamentary governments. No political movement or leader enjoyed comparable authority in Palestine, where six hundred thousand Jewish settlers lived among 1.2 million Arabs. Each community sought self-rule to the exclusion of the other. Arab opposition to British occupation and Jewish migration had erupted in a prolonged and bloody Arab revolt in the late 1930s. When British forces finally suppressed the insurrection, the British government had laid plans for the partition of the territory. While the Zionist movement had welcomed the prospect of a Jewish nation-state, even reduced in size, Arab leaders were united in opposition and vowed to resist any grant of territory to the Jews. The prewar deadlock in negotiations for Palestinian independence had raised, as in India, the prospect of civil war. The leaders of each community were resolved to control a territory that the other group considered its own.

The Second World War deepened the conflict over Palestine. It brought independence to Arab countries, united in their opposition to a Jewish state in Palestine. In those same years, the horrors of the Holocaust united Jewish peoples as never before in support of the creation of their own nation-state. The Zionist commitment to that cause became a crusade. The war temporarily ended all discussion of future Palestinian self-government, Jewish migration, and partition. The British made the preservation of order in Palestine their sole objective, virtually ending Jewish immigration. Yet those were the very years when Jewish persecution in Europe rendered the establishment of a Jewish homeland in Palestine a matter of life and death.

During the war, the British government hardened its political domination of the region. Fighting remained at a distance, but the Axis powers made themselves felt nonetheless. In Palestine, the Muslim religious leader, the grand mufti of Jerusalem, had publicly announced his support of Nazi Germany and had fled to Berlin. He made radio broadcasts to the Middle East calling for Arab revolt against the British. In Egypt and in Iraq, some nationalists appeared ready to welcome Rommel's German divisions when his offensive reached the borders of Egypt in 1942. The vital importance of the Suez Canal and of the region's petroleum gave the British government reason enough to use its forces to repress any signs of possible Arab collaboration with Germany. In Iraq and Egypt, they forcibly installed political leaders sympathetic to the Allies. Palestinian Jews for their part welcomed the opportunity to join in the war against Nazi Germany, sending thirty thousand men to serve in the British Army. They later became the core of the Israeli Army.

The Palestinian crisis erupted immediately following the war. The British government, caught between Palestinian Arabs and Jews and intent on keeping good relations with the Arab states, refused to open the country to more immigrants. Jewish refugees scattered across Europe looked to Palestine for a new home and were helped on the way by the Zionist organization. Desperate migrants sailed from Europe to the Holy Land in decrepit old boats such as the *Exodus*. Some ships sank before reaching their destination. Others were captured by the British, who placed the passengers in internment camps in Cyprus, prisoners again.

The Zionist movement acquired a valuable ally in 1945 when the U.S. government publicly supported their demand for renewed Jewish immigration to Palestine. American political leaders were sympathetic to the cause of a Jewish state, and were under strong pressure from American Jewish organizations to assist in the creation of a Jewish homeland. President Truman's announcement of the new U.S. policy brought the full weight of American international influence to bear on Britain's Palestine problem. It made the crisis an international affair.

The profound disagreement on political objectives and the ethnic strife among the peoples in Palestine made peaceful negotiations impossible. Palestinian Arab leaders all agreed that their land had to become one independent nation-state under the rule of the Arab majority. The Zionists demanded special territorial protection for their people, whom they feared would suffer persecution in an Arab-dominated state. Palestinian Jews began in 1945 a forceful resistance movement to force London to heed their demands for immigration and self-rule. Small terrorist organizations even launched attacks against British troops and colonial officials.

Unable to transfer power peacefully to a Palestinian state, the British government turned to outside help. In early 1947, the British government declared that it was placing the fate of its Palestine mandate in the hands of the United Nations. It had abandoned the hopeless effort to bring the two sides together and had resolved, as in India, to withdraw quickly. The U.N. had to determine whether Palestine should become one state or two. The United States played the key role in mobilizing the votes needed for approval of the creation of two states, one for the Arabs and the other for the Jews. Even the Soviet Union and its allies backed the plan, hoping in this way to prove their opposition to "British imperialism." In November of that year, a majority in the U.N. General Assembly voted in favor of the partition of Palestine, to be divided into Arab and Jewish states. As in India, the existence of two deeply antagonistic communities, each intent on defending its own national rights, had led to the creation of new borders around areas to become, somehow, nation-states. Each people had opted for an ethnoterritorial nationalist formula, and the U.N.'s decision meant international approval for this solution.

This action was unacceptable to the surrounding Arab countries. Opposition to a Jewish state had become a key test of loyalty to the cause of pan-Arab nationalism and to the Palestinian people. An additional factor behind their decision to intervene in Palestine was the competition among Arab leaders for political influence in the Middle East and for control of the Palestinian territory. The king of Jordan hoped to annex lands west of the Jordan River and feared expansionist Syrian plans for a Greater Syria encompassing all the land from Iraq to the Mediterranean. The Iraqi and Egyptian monarchs were rivals for leadership of the Arab countries. They agreed on only one point—the Middle East had to remain Arab. This objective brought them together in 1945 in a regional organization called the Arab League. They proclaimed its purpose to be "coordinating policies" and "strengthening relations" among its members (Syria, Lebanon, Jordan, Iraq, Saudi Arabia, and Egypt). Its immediate objective was to prevent the formation of a Jewish state in Palestine.

Egypt was the founder and leader of the League. It was the largest and most powerful Arab state. Its population had grown rapidly, rising from ten million in the early century to sixteen million. The standard of living of the urban and rural masses probably had stagnated in those years, creating the conditions for serious social disorder. Conditions of unrest and political corruption strengthened the role of the Muslim Brotherhood among the Egyptian masses (see "Highlight," this chapter). Its membership after the war increased to more than one million, and it (with considerable exaggeration) claimed to have a half-million Egyptians in its paramilitary force, the Phalanx. No political party possessed such mass support. It alone offered material help and spiritual guidance to the country's lower classes. Its Muslim fundamentalist program made the Islamic faith its guide to social reform, and the grounds for its unyielding resistance to a Jewish homeland in Palestine.

In the winter of 1947–48, Palestine was a land torn by civil war. Jewish and Palestinian military units fought each other for control of villages and towns as the British forces gradually withdrew to the coast. The Palestinians received arms from the Arab League, while the Jews had to take their weapons where they could find them. The day after the last British troops left Palestine in May 1948, Jewish leaders formally established the state of Israel. They had achieved their goal, but enemies on every border endangered their new state. Egypt, Iraq, Syria, and Jordan immediately declared war on Israel and ordered their armies to destroy the new state. The first Arab-Israeli war had begun.

Egypt took the lead. The Egyptian army marched off to fight its first war while volunteers from the Muslim Brotherhood's paramilitary forces joined the Palestinian Arabs. King Farouk ignored the warnings of his generals that his army was poorly prepared and equipped for war. He believed that Arab forces would quickly annihilate the outnumbered and ill-armed Jewish army. He, and most Arab leaders, underestimated the ability of the Jews to resist.

Surrounded on three sides by enemies, the Jewish forces fought for the survival of their new state and for their community. The Palestinians did not share the same nationalist fervor. Many Arabs, fearing for their lives and their religion under Jewish rule, fled the Jewish-controlled areas. Only a few Arab forces could match the fighting skill of the Jews. The Jordanian Arab Legion, led by English officers, seized part of the area on the right (western) bank of the Jordan River and the old city of Jerusalem. The ancient Jewish neighborhood was for months surrounded and under siege before Israeli troops had to withdraw outside the walls of the old city.

The other Arab forces fared poorly. Among the Egyptian officers, some, like Captain Gamal Nasser, fought bravely. Most officers in the army did not share his commitment to the war. The army was badly led, and badly supplied by the Egyptian government. The Egyptian attack on southern Palestine collapsed, and was followed by retreat from the entire Negev Desert. Lacking any coordinated strategy, the Arab forces conducted separate campaigns and could not prevent the Jews from seizing an area even larger than that granted by the U.N. partition plan.

The failure of the Egyptian offensive was the key to ending the war. In February 1949, the United Nations obtained agreement from all sides to an armistice. Israeli forces occupied the coastal region of Palestine, a part of the Jordan River valley, and the Negev Desert to the shores of the Red Sea. Jerusalem was divided. The armistice line marked a new partition of the Palestinian territory, which was now split between Israel and Jordan. The old city of Jerusalem and much the Jordan River valley stayed in the hands of the Jordanian forces. The armistice confirmed the victory of Israel, a small, oddly shaped state surrounded by enemies. The flight during the war of most Palestinian Arab inhabitants from Jewish controlled areas made Jewish settlers the majority of Israel's population. Palestinians found at war's end that they had no state of their own.

The new Israeli government began the process of constructing a Jewish nation-state. The new state was a parliamentary democracy. It welcomed Jews from any country and made Hebrew, the Biblical tongue not spoken for two millennia, the official language. It bore some resemblance to a theocracy, that is, a state whose inhabitants were inspired by a religious faith. Yet at the same time it was a modern nation-state whose laws protected political freedom and individual opportunity. It introduced social reforms inspired by the socialist movements of Europe. It supported the creation, begun earlier by the first Jewish settlers, of collective farms called "kibbutz." Members of these cooperatives shared the revenues from their crops as they struggled to make the desert fertile.

Though Israel guaranteed freedom of religion to its Christian and Muslim minorities, to many Arabs it was the object of abiding hatred. It had broken apart Palestine. Its legal and social order embodied Western secular values rejected by Muslim fundamentalists. Surrounded by enemies, the Israelis had to arm their nation in anticipation of another war.

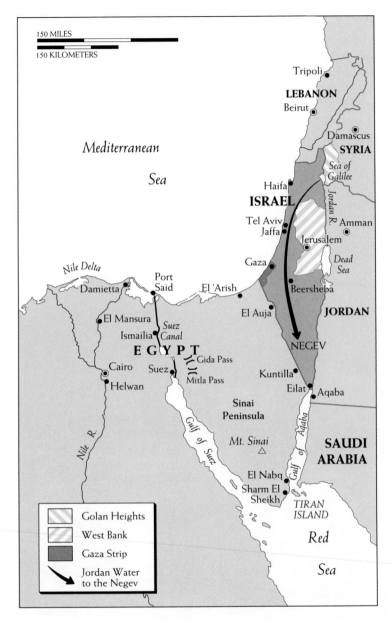

150 MILES

150 KILOMETERS

Tripoli

LEBANON

Beirut

Damascus

SYRIA

Mediterranean

Sea of Galilee

Sea

Haifa

ISRAEL

Jordan R.

Amman

Tel Aviv

Jaffa

Jerusalem

Gaza

Dead Sea

JORDAN

Nile Delta

Port Said

El 'Arish

Beersheba

Damietta

El Mansura

El Auja

Ismailia

Suez Canal

E G Y P T

NEGEV

Cairo

Gida Pass

Suez

Kuntilla

Mitla Pass

Helwan

Eilat

Aqaba

Sinai Peninsula

Nile R.

Gulf of Suez

Mt. Sinai △

Gulf of Aqaba

SAUDI ARABIA

El Nabq

Sharm El Sheikh

TIRAN ISLAND

Red

Golan Heights

West Bank

Gaza Strip

Jordan Water to the Negev

Sea

Israel and Its Neighbors

The defeat of the Arab League's forces was a public humiliation for the Arab countries. A constant reminder of the defeat was the presence of seven hundred fifty thousand Palestinian refugees, scattered throughout the Middle East but concentrated in refugee camps in Egyptian territory. The Palestinians received little help from the Arab states. A few were able to find a new home for themselves in other parts of the Middle East. Most remained in miserable refugee camps under U.N.

care, hoping for the day when Israel would no longer exist and they could return to their homeland. In all respects, the Israeli victory was a disaster for the Egyptian monarchy, unable to unite Arab forces and to organize and lead its army. The months of war proved a bitter lesson for Egyptian army officers. They returned to Egypt convinced that the corrupt political leadership of their country had betrayed them, the Egyptian nation, and the Arab cause.

SPOTLIGHT: Golda Meir

Golda Meir (1898–1978) devoted her life to the creation of a Jewish homeland in Palestine. Her family fled the Russian Empire when she was nine years old. By then she had experienced first-hand anti-Semitic hatred, widespread among the population where her family had lived. She had also begun to learn of a new movement called Zionism dedicated to the creation of a Jewish homeland in Palestine. Though she grew up in the United States, she decided when she was twenty years old to make that cause her own. The decision changed the course of her life.

Prime Minister Golda Meir Reviewing Israeli Soldiers, 1969 (*UPI/Bettmann*)

The lifelong service that she rendered to Zionism drew upon her remarkable personal qualities and her commitment to the goal of a Jewish homeland. With her husband, she moved to Palestine in the 1920s. "The Jews must have a land of their own again," she wrote, "and I must help to build it by living and working there." She became a pioneer on a Jewish farm (a "kibbutz") reclaiming desert land. The pioneers laid claim to a Palestinian homeland, in the midst of Arab-speaking Christians and Muslims, by making the land prosper once again. In her words, "only self-labor could make it possible for the Jews to earn a moral right, as well as a historical right," to that land.

Like the other Jewish migrants, she firmly believed that their claim to Palestine was morally and historically justified. The harsh life that she led for the next decades had as its goal the acquisition of a territory belonging to the Jewish people. That land was the birthplace of the Jewish religion, but she did not wish to make it a religious state. The Jews formed a community like other peoples who desired their own nation-state. She believed in toleration for all religions, hoping that the Arabs would "live with us in peace and equality as citizens of a Jewish homeland."

Her dream inevitably meant that those Arabs would have to become a minority nationality in a state of the Jews. Many Muslim Arabs rejected the idea that infidels should govern them and their holy places in Palestine. Their religious convictions excluded the possibility of the Jewish secular state for which Zionists such as Golda Meir struggled. Conflict between Arabs and Jews was unavoidable.

Her own personal life became consumed by her work for the Zionist cause. She admitted later that she had too little time for her marriage and children. She left her family for long trips to Europe and America to encourage Jewish immigration and to raise funds for Jewish settlements, then for the state of Israel. But her greatest contribution lay in political leadership. Along with a handful of other Zionists, she came to embody for many Jews the selfless dedication that had made the incredible dream of Israel come true. When she arrived in 1948 in Moscow to serve as first Israeli ambassador to the Soviet Union, crowds of Jews celebrated outside the Israeli embassy at the risk of arrest and imprisonment.

She also possessed the talents of a farsighted political leader. The Zionist movement had always regarded women as equal to men in its work, though bias against women in politics remained strong among some Israelis. Her government believed in and needed her abilities. In 1949, it offered her the position of Minister of Labor. She proceeded to lay the foundations of the social welfare policies of Israel. Her greatest challenge was to create a shared loyalty among the "flood of Jews from opposite ends of the earth who spoke different languages and who were ignorant of each other's traditions and customs." It was, she remembered, "the most satisfying and the happiest years of my life."

In a real sense, Israel absorbed her remaining years. She moved from her Labor post to become Minister of Foreign Affairs in 1956. Thirteen years later she reluctantly agreed to become the prime minister of her country. Why, she asked, should a "seventy-year-old grandmother head a twenty-year-old state?" The answer was that no one else could. Her commitment to a Jewish homeland had carried her as a young woman to Palestine. Her sense of duty to that land elevated her ultimately to the most powerful political position in her country. It was a career that few men could match.

Revolution in Egypt

The Egyptian monarchy was increasingly unpopular in the years after the war. Free elections in 1950 (the last multiparty elections until 1984) revealed to what extent parliamentary politics had become the affair of a small political elite. Few voters bothered to cast their ballots. The state was weakened still more by King Farouk's ambition to control the government. The new cabinet mobilized popular support for an anti-British campaign to oblige the British to withdraw their troops from the Suez Canal zone. These forces had stayed on by agreement with the Egyptian government after independence in 1924. The British refused to negotiate, and the movement grew increasingly violent. In early 1952, riots broke out in Cairo protesting the British presence along the Suez Canal. The king dismissed the cabinet, took over the government, and called in the army to repress the rioting. In doing so, he sealed his own fate.

Egypt's revolutionary officers chose that moment of political chaos to move into action. The leader of this secret opposition was Gamal Nasser. As a student before the Second World War, he had been active in the nationalist movement. For him, as for nationalists in other poor countries, the nation symbolized a new, just community in which "the weak and the humiliated Egyptian people [could] rise up again and live as free and independent men." The son of poor parents, he chose the career of an army officer. It was for him the means to improve his own life, and to advance the cause of Egyptian nationalism. In the first years, army life brought him no glory and little opportunity. It did form the bonds uniting Nasser and other officers, including Anwar Sadat (his successor as ruler of Egypt), who later set about remaking Egypt. His political career began after the Palestinian war. He and his colleagues realized, as he wrote later, that "our battle was taking place in Cairo. We knew that we had to liberate our country first, in order to be able to fight." Believing themselves betrayed by the monarch

and the parliamentary regime, they resolved to restore Egyptian power and influence on their own. Their military conspiracy pointed to a political revolution in Egypt.

The officers, under Nasser's leadership, organized a secret group calling itself the Free Officers. Founded in 1949, it grew to about one thousand members. When in the summer of 1952 King Farouk ordered the army into Cairo to end the rioting, its members set in motion their plans for a military "coup," that is, the overthrow of the monarchy by military force. They secretly took over command of the armed forces with the help of General Naguib, a senior officer who shared their opposition to the monarchy. Army units surrounded the royal palace and forced the king to abdicate. On leaving the country Farouk warned the victorious insurgents: "Your task will be difficult. It isn't easy, you know, to govern Egypt."

The process of remaking the Egyptian nation-state had only just begun. Few Egyptians regretted the departure of the Turkish king. Several contenders for power aspired to govern the republic. Liberal political parties hoped to preserve constitutional government, as well as to protect the interests of the financiers and landowners who supported them. The followers of the Muslim Brotherhood looked to an Islamic republic to bolster the Muslim religion and to wipe out the social and moral decay that they believed to be caused by Westernization.

The officers were not prepared to tolerate political diversity and dissent. Nasser later referred sarcastically to the "dispersed followers and contrasted remnants, chaos, dissensions, surrender, and idleness" that they encountered in the months after overthrowing the monarchy. It is unlikely that they ever seriously considered sharing the responsibilities and powers of rule. Their response to political rivalries was to eliminate their rivals and to end parliamentary rule. They dissolved parliament and the cabinet, replacing them with a Revolutionary Command Council (RCC). It consisted of the leaders in the Free

Officers conspiracy, under the chairmanship of Gamal Nasser. The council abolished the constitution and in early 1953 disbanded all political parties. Lacking a mass following, the liberal parties disappeared from public life. The small Communist Party became the target of outright repression and its leaders were thrown in jail. Nasser proclaimed that "the Communists are agents who believe neither in the liberty of their land nor in their nation but only do the bidding of outsiders." To the officers, Egyptian nationalism was the ideological inspiration for the resurgence of their country.

The Muslim Brotherhood presented the RCC with its most dangerous rival. The military leaders opposed the Brotherhood for two reasons. They did not share the Brotherhood's goal of Islamic revolution. They were Westernized officers, for whom the Quran fixed religious belief and practices, not state policy. In addition, the Brotherhood challenged their own political power. In January 1954, Muslim leaders began mass street demonstrations aimed at forcing the council to implement their plans for an Islamic revolution. The ruling officers seized the opportunity to arrest the Brotherhood leadership and to ban the organization. As in previous periods of repression, the Brotherhood went underground. In October 1954, one of its members attempted to assassinate Nasser. The police asserted—although without real proof—that the Brotherhood was plotting to overthrow the new regime. Police repression worsened, and prisons filled with political prisoners. The revolutionary officers had defeated all their rivals for power.

Their new regime immediately incorporated the objectives of pan-Arab nationalism into their foreign policy. They reiterated their determination to prepare for a new war with Israel. At the same time, they took steps to strengthen the national liberation movements underway in North Africa. This was the last area where Arabs lived under Western colonial rule. Arab nationalists from Tunisia, Morocco, and Algeria, still part of the French Empire, found refuge in Cairo after 1953. There they organized their resistance to French colonial forces and received financial assistance from the new government. Their leadership and popular unrest forced the reluctant French government to grant independence to Morocco and Tunisia in 1956.

Algerian nationalists faced determined opposition, however, from France. French forces had conquered Algeria over a century before and opened the country to colonists from southern Europe, all of whom received French citizenship. This settler colony had a special place in the French Empire. The one million European settlers of French culture and citizenship were deeply hostile to the Arabs and to the idea Algerian independence. The French government refused negotiations with the Algerian National Liberation Front, whose headquarters were in Cairo. In 1954, the Algerian nationalists called for an insurrection against the French. The French government sent in hundreds of thousands of troops, some just withdrawn from Indochina, to defeat the Arab nationalist revolt and to protect the European settlers.

This new French colonial war lasted until 1962. By then it had consumed thousands of lives and kindled terrorist movements on the part of both Europeans and Arabs. The French government, faced with an apparently endless guerrilla war, decided to grant Algeria its independence. More than one million Algerian Europeans and Arabs who had collaborated with the French fled to France. The last colonial war had ended. Western empires had disappeared from the Middle East.

NATION-BUILDING AND PETROLEUM

The new Egyptian regime's seizure of the Suez Canal marked in a spectacular manner the collapse of European power in the Middle East. The impact of the growing global economy, fueled increasingly by petroleum, lured Western private companies into the region. Access to petroleum brought great profits to oil corporations, and was a vital strategic interest to all developed economies. Governments of the Middle Eastern lands possessing large oil reserves were themselves eager to obtain revenues from oil sales in this global market. The age of nations took shape in the same years as the new states entered the interdependent global economy.

Nasser and the Egyptian Nation

The military leaders of Egypt had vague plans for social reform and leadership of the Arab countries. They had overthrown Egypt's monarchy, claiming that they alone could transform the country into a modern nation. They knew that their experiment was risky. Their country was poor, and their hopes to expand the power of the state and to improve the living conditions of the Egyptian population depended on new revenues. Still, they were convinced that they were the rightful national leaders, the "vanguard," as Nasser wrote in 1953, whose "mission had not ended."

They disagreed among themselves on basic issues of government. Some officers preferred to introduce a constitutional democracy, giving power back to the political parties. Nasser was determined to keep the military in charge of the country. In early 1954, the dispute ended with his victory. Proclaiming that their revolution was threatened by a return to the corrupt practices of the monarchy, he placed his followers in positions of control throughout the Egyptian government. The country's military regime consolidated its hold on the state, and Nasser emerged as the principal leader.

He set about creating a new sort of authoritarian state. In place of political parties, he and his fellow officers created their own mass party. Called at first the Liberation Rally, it changed names frequently in the decades to come. They stipulated that it alone enjoyed the right to propose candidates for election. They imposed censorship on radio and the press and deprived labor unions of the right to strike. In 1956, they introduced a new constitution that created a National Assembly, but it enjoyed no real legislative power. A secret police operated beyond the rule of law to pursue the enemies of the military rulers. A cabinet replaced the Revolutionary Command Council, but it consisted of the same officers who had led the country since 1952. Nasser held the title of president of the Republic. In fact, he was a benevolent military dictator committed to national revolution.

Nasser's most ambitious project was the damming of the waters of the Nile behind a new, giant dam at Aswan. It was to be a structure so huge it would dwarf the pyramids (and the new lake it created would drown precious relics of Egypt's pharonic past). Plans for its use foresaw both abundant water for irrigation (the arable land of Egypt was to increase by one-third) and hydroelectric power in a greater quantity than all the electricity then available. A great source of pride to Nasser, it embodied his hope for social betterment and his grandiose vision of a national revolution in Egypt. He called it Egypt's "pyramid for the living." Paying for the dam presented serious difficulties, however. The Egyptian state lacked the necessary financial means. Like India, it could not initiate important economic projects without outside help.

The most dramatic result of the military revolution was Egypt's defiance of the West. Following the example of Nehru of India, Nasser adopted a policy of nonalignment for his country. He refused to join the Baghdad military pact with Turkey, Iran, and Iraq. He called the treaty (in terms that echoed Nehru's judgment of SEATO) a "modern version of a protectorate" and condemned its members for collaborating with "western imperialism." His refusal seriously undermined his state's chances of substantial aid from the United States.

Egypt's conflict with Israel gave a warlike character to Nasser's new foreign policy. Egypt remained formally in a state of war with the Jewish state, and it forbad any shipping bound for Israel to pass through the Suez Canal. Yet the Egyptian army was still badly equipped and needed to import modern weapons. These could be paid for only by foreign loans. The United States hesitated, concerned that aid might fuel a new Arab-Israeli war. The Soviet Union was ready to help. The new post-Stalin leaders were prepared to support reformist governments in the Middle East and in Asia that were not members of western alliances. Their offers of arms and financial credits presented the Egyptian regime with a tempting source of assistance.

In late 1955, Nasser accepted the offer. He announced that the Egyptian government had signed an agreement with the Soviet Union to obtain a long-term loan, to be repaid in cotton and rice exports. The funds would allow Egypt to buy from communist countries fighter planes, tanks, arms, and naval vessels. He was acclaimed by nationalists throughout the Middle East for his action. He called the arms deal a policy of "positive neutrality." Cold War passions among Western leaders magnified out of all proportion the implications of both his aid to Arab rebels in French North Africa and his arms agreement. He appeared a dangerous revolutionary and potential communist ally.

The price of his arms deal with the communist countries became apparent in mid-1956. He had begun negotiations in 1955 with the World Bank, which was largely financed by the U.S. government, for a major loan to begin construction of the High Dam at Aswan. He staked the prestige of his regime and of his own leadership on the mammoth project. Negotiations dragged on until July 1956. Suddenly the United States announced its refusal to participate in the projected loan. Great Britain soon made the same decision. Their message was clear: Nasser's cooperation with communist states had cost his state Western financial assistance for the Aswan Dam. The decision represented a public humiliation of the Egyptian leader, and a serious diplomatic blunder by the United States.

The Suez Canal and the 1956 War

In 1956, the Suez Canal was still an economic enterprise run and owned by Europeans, a remnant of the age of Western imperialism. It was also a valuable piece of property bringing substantial income to its owners. The last British troops withdrew from the Suez zone early that year. The Suez Canal was a tempting prize to Egyptian nationalists such as Nasser. He was attracted both by the revenues that it would yield and by the prestige that its seizure would bring to his regime. In July 1956, he declared to an enormous crowd of Egyptians gathered in Cairo that his government had taken possession of the Canal. "Our pride, our determination, and our faith," he cried, had been challenged by the West. Nationalization of the canal proved that "this nation will not accept humiliation and degradation." If the "imperialists" did not approve of his action, they could "choke in their own rage." His defiance of the West brought him and his country into direct confrontation with European states. It was a move enthusiastically applauded by his people.

The Egyptian seizure of the Suez Canal incited the British and French governments to make one final effort to reassert their imperial power in the eastern Mediterranean. They viewed nationalization as a threat to their security. The canal remained a vital pathway for strategic goods, especially petroleum, to western Europe. They were deeply suspicious of Nasser's nationalist policies. Strategic and ideological reasons incited the two states to launch a reckless, ill-conceived invasion of the canal zone. They found a ready ally in the Israeli government. Israel's economy suffered from the Egyptian blockade of its shipping through the canal, and its leaders feared another Egyptian invasion. The three states attacked Egypt in late October 1956. Israeli tank units raced across the Sinai desert to the canal, while a British and French naval force and paratroopers seized the Suez ports and the entire canal zone. Militarily the operation was a complete success. Politically it failed. Nasser became a national hero for the Egyptian people. Diplomatically the invasion proved a disaster.

Opposition came from all sides. Almost the entire membership of the United Nations condemned the attack. The Soviet Union offered Nasser more military aid and warned Britain and France of its readiness to take "all measures" to protect Egypt. The U.S. government condemned the invasion, for it was outraged by military action and intent on keeping good relations with Third World countries. It made its opposition painfully real by reducing economic aid to Great Britain and France. It also refused to protect the British currency, which was losing value rapidly as panicky Britishers bought up dollars. Lacking U.S. support, the British and French were isolated and unable to continue the war. Faced with global diplomatic protests and a major financial crisis, the British convinced the French and Israelis to withdraw from the canal zone. President Eisenhower had used U.S. economic power and diplomatic influence to defeat their intervention.

The Suez crisis was Nasser's greatest triumph. He had defied the European powers and won. In the Middle East his action revived the popularity of pan-Arab nationalism. To Egyptians he became their undisputed national leader. His only achievement in the war had been to block the canal with sunken ships, closing it to navigation for another year. A serious economic recession swept Europe as a result of the sudden petroleum shortage. In the peace settlement, Nasser accepted a U.N. proposal for the stationing of an international peacekeeping force in Egypt. Its task was to patrol the Egyptian-Israeli frontier to prevent Arab terrorist attacks on Israel and to block a new Israeli invasion. The outcome of the Suez crisis gave Nasser the illusion of great power. His action made him, for a few years, the leader among Arab states and among nonaligned countries of the Third World.

Egypt and Pan-Arab Nationalism

The Suez war gave a sudden impetus to state control of the Egyptian economy. Nasser welcomed the development, calling it "Arab socialism." He implied that these reforms set a model for all Arab lands. Until 1956 the Egyptian economy had functioned along free-market lines, allowing private ownership of banking, industry, and agriculture and welcoming foreign investment. The war brought the state new economic powers. The government suddenly became, without any long-range plan, the owner of the Suez Canal Company and responsible for the operations of the canal. During the war Egypt took possession of foreign-owned and operated enterprises in any way connected with France and Great Britain. These included many banks, insurance companies, and industrial enterprises. The nationalized holdings gave the government an important role in the small Egyptian industrial economy.

The Suez crisis expanded the Free Officers' goal of "social justice" into a larger vision of socialism. It took a form somewhat like the Soviet command economy. The government turned to economic planning to provide the economic guidelines needed by the state to operate the nationalized businesses. It created in early 1957 a National Planning Committee and later that year approved a Five-Year Plan for economic development. Foreign aid came from the Soviet Union for construction of the Aswan Dam. The United States shipped food supplies to help feed Egypt's growing population. Nasser declared that the goal of the Egyptian revolution was "a cooperative, democratic, socialist society." Like India, Egypt became a mixed economy. Small commerce and farming stayed in private hands, while major enterprises were state owned.

For a few years, the Egyptian people benefitted substantially from the reforms. Throughout the

1960s, the economy grew steadily, though its growth slowed from 6 percent in the first years to 2 percent after the disastrous 1967 war. But economic development could not cope for long with the population explosion resulting from an annual increase of one million people. The state subsidized the sale of cheap food to Egypt's urban masses to avoid social unrest, for the city had become a place of welfare as well as work. Imported agricultural produce, provided in large measure by foreign aid, became the sole protection against famine.

The Aswan Dam was Nasser's great project for the transformation of Egypt. It was completed in 1970, forever ending the yearly flooding of the lower Nile region. The reservoir, named Lake Nasser, stretched more than three hundred miles upstream, impounding water used to generate hydroelectric power (ten billion kilowatt hours per year) and to irrigate agricultural land (one third more than before). Periodic great floods no longer devastated the Nile basin, and years of low rainfall in the Nile headwaters no longer meant drought for Egypt's farmers.

The dam was a technological marvel and the pride of Egyptians. The ecological price was high, for the irrigation water carried disease through the canals and left deposits of salt on the land, no longer cleansed by flooding. The Aswan Dam illustrated vividly the vision and limits of Nasser's socialism. Its planners could take pride in Egyptian economic growth, but in achieving this goal they permanently destroyed the balance between people and nature that had existed before.

Egypt in the years after the Suez war became the center of pan-Arab nationalism and supported socialist movements in other Middle Eastern countries. From Cairo, the Voice of Arabs Radio defended the cause of Arab unity and called for opposition to imperialism, feudalism (typified by Saudi Arabia), and Zionism (Israel). Nasser revived the vision of a great pan-Arab state to

Pyramid for the People: The Aswan Dam under Construction (*Hulton-Deutsch Collection/Corbis*)

unite all "progressive" Arab lands, that is, states not ruled by conservative monarchs.

He initiated a concrete step toward the pan-Arab dream when in 1958 he signed a treaty of union with the government of Syria. The Syrian government joined in proclaiming its faith in a pan-Arab state and backed Egyptian leadership, but its leaders had more practical reasons for joining Egypt. They needed Egyptian protection in the face of serious internal religious and political unrest and the threat of war with Iraq. What appeared to be a sign of pan-Arab nationalism was for them an affair of state.

This United Arab Republic (U.A.R.) became an extension of the Egyptian state. Nasser was its president and Egyptian officers assumed important posts in Syria. The U.A.R. proved a disappointment, though, to its Syrian supporters. The breaking point came in 1961 when Egypt imposed its socialist policies on the Syrian economy. Discontent with the U.A.R. brought the Syrian army and business community together. In September 1961, the army seized power and repudiated the agreement with Egypt. At first Nasser considered sending Egyptian troops to invade Syria, then abandoned the idea. He blamed the failure of his political union on capitalist and imperialist enemies. The real reason was the weakness of pan-Arab nationalism, which proved irrelevant to the needs and interests of the various countries.

In that divided region, the conflict with Israel posed the most serious threat of war. Nasser was first among Arab leaders in proclaiming his opposition to the state of Israel. Time and again he spoke out for "liquidating the Israeli aggression on a part of the Palestine land." His deeds in the ten years following the Suez war were not, however, warlike. He accepted until the mid-1960s the U.N. peacekeeping force along the Egyptian-Israeli frontier. Purely symbolic, its presence on the Egyptian side of the border absolved Egypt of the responsibility to undertake a dangerous new war. It was a conflict that the country could not afford and that Nasser's army could not win.

Petroleum and the Middle East

The political revolution in Egypt came just as the Middle East became the principal source of petroleum for the global economy. This was an economic revolution, bringing enormous revenues to a few Arab states and elevating questions of revolution and war in the Middle East to issues of vital strategic interest to major states around the world. The loss of access to the oil in that area posed the threat of economic collapse to developed countries. The 1956–57 recession in Europe had shown how devastating the interruption of oil shipments from the region could be. The Middle East acquired an international importance that overshadowed the political ambitions of leaders such as Nasser.

The boom in Middle Eastern oil production was the result of the discovery there of vast petroleum reserves. Geologists had detected major oil deposits first in the territory of Persia (Iran) early in the century. Oil fields equally vast were found elsewhere in the region bordering the Persian Gulf, and up the river valleys of the Tigris and Euphrates on the territory of Iraq. By the 1960s, these discoveries revealed that two thirds of the world's known oil reserves lay in that region. The deserts of impoverished countries like Saudi Arabia hid some of the highest quality petroleum in the world. The people of the tiny principality of Kuwait had previously had to rely mainly on pearl fishing for their livelihood. They soon became immensely wealthy after their ruler in 1946 turned the spigot to pump petroleum from his oil wells to ships in the gulf.

The global market for petroleum became a reality in mid-century. In the Second World War, the mobility of Allied forces depended on ready access to oil. U.S. leaders realized that their country would in the future be forced to rely increasingly on foreign oil as domestic demand grew and American oil fields dried up. The Middle East's oil-producing countries, especially Saudi Arabia, attracted particular attention. President

The Middle East and Inner Asia in 1990

Truman informed the Saudi king after the war that "no threat to your kingdom could occur which would not be a matter of immediate concern to the United States." Strategic interest in Iranian oil led the Western states to intervene secretly in a bitter political conflict that erupted in Iran in the early 1950s. They supported the monarch (the "shah") in his fight against his enemies, who appeared hostile to the West. National interests brought Western involvement in Middle Eastern politics with or without the agreement of the governments.

Until the 1950s, the international oil corporations operated without having to consider the interests of the Middle Eastern countries where their refineries and oil wells were located. Even a strong ally of the West such as the shah of Iran resented the power that they enjoyed over oil production and prices. The rulers of the oil-producing states received royalties based on the profits of these corporations from production. These companies defined their goals principally in terms of price stability and profits.

Sensitive to Western governments' need for oil, they also protected their own corporate interests. When need arose, they limited production and agreed on a single wholesale price for crude oil to avoid ruinous price wars. The postwar discovery of new oil fields continually put their efforts in jeopardy. An economic recession in the West in the late 1950s reduced demand so seriously that they agreed among themselves to lower the price of oil to below $2 a barrel in the hope of promoting sales. In doing so, they aroused the resentment of the Middle Eastern oil-producing states, including Iran and Saudi Arabia.

The rulers of these two countries shared common interests both in preserving their monarchies against internal political revolutions, and in establishing state control over their petroleum industry. They had begun expensive programs of economic development, paid for by the income from their oil royalties. These suddenly declined when the international oil companies cut prices on crude oil. The monarchs of the two states hoped that by acting together they could force the oil corporations to heed their financial needs.

In 1960, they obtained the agreement of all the major oil-producing states (except the United States and Mexico) to form a new international association, the Organization of Petroleum Exporting Countries (OPEC). The immediate objective was to stabilize oil prices and to coordinate petroleum policies to protect "our interests, individually and collectively." Behind this modest aim lay the audacious goal of fixing levels of oil production and prices. An international oil cartel was born.

While their organization had little immediate impact on oil production, the tremendous increase in Western demand for oil in the 1960s improved their economic situation substantially. By then, petroleum use had risen so rapidly that it provided over half the West's energy supplies. Industrialized economies could not function without it. In the late 1960s, oil prices began a slow increase, rising to more than $2 a barrel. Revenues going to the states of Iran and Saudi Arabia reached nearly $1 billion. Although their policies were conservative, the monarchs of these two states had lent their political weight to a radical shift in the global economic balance of power. In the world of international finance and economics, these revenues and the possession of great petroleum reserves gave the OPEC countries new power and influence.

WAR, PEACE, AND ISLAM

War and civil strife in the Middle East erupted several times in the last third of the twentieth century. Each conflict sent its reverberations echoing around the world, at times because Cold War competition intruded, at other times because the global economy had to confront serious oil shortages. A revolution in Iran made Islam a powerful political force after Muslim religious leaders seized control of the government. Their goals were a return to the principles of the Quran. Religious issues became deeply embedded in the Israeli-Arab confrontation. Committed Muslims and Jews reshaped the territorial dispute into a crusade of one religion against another. Calmer judgment among Israeli and Palestine leaders counseled compromise to permit the two peoples to live at peace with one another. The mid-1990s agreement on Palestinian self-rule offered hope for peace, but it faced strong opposition on both sides. War against Israel no longer dominated Middle Eastern politics, but the Palestinian problem remained unresolved.

HIGHLIGHT: Islam and Nation-States

In the mid-twentieth century Islam was the second-largest religion in the world. It was the dominant faith in lands stretching from northern Africa to Indonesia. The conquests of European colonial empires brought the peoples of these areas under Western rule. The defeat of the Ottoman Empire in the First World War brought down the last remaining empire governed by Muslim rulers. But Islam remained a vital force among Muslim peoples. Some of their religious leaders began to work for the renewal of the Islamic faith as the means to isolate Muslims from the corrupting influence of Western culture. Other public leaders believed that the bonds that united the Muslim community formed the basis for new political movements capable of resisting the West by incorporating certain modern institutions and values. Slowly Islam adapted its message and action to meet the challenge of Western domination.

The doctrinal unity of Islam, like Judaism and Christianity, is founded on a sacred text. The Quran (also spelled Koran) is believed by Muslims to be the revelation of God as received by his prophet Muhammed, who lived in the Arabian Peninsula in the seventh century. That divine message defined the essential faith for Muslims, for whom there could be no other God and no other source of religious truth. Wherever they lived and whatever their own culture and language, the Quran gave them their religious language (Arabic, for that was Muhammed's tongue) and prescribed their basic religious practices. Muslim scholars over the centuries had elaborated religious rules (the Shari`a) governing Muslim everyday life, including family law, marriage, inheritance, and much more. Customs varied from country to country. The requirement that women conceal their faces behind veils in public became increasingly common in many places. In these ways, the Islamic faith made itself a vital presence in the public and private affairs of many millions of Muslims.

The arrival of Western empires served in some ways to give greater scope and vigor to religious activities in the Muslim world. The growth of international and regional trade opened new markets in Asia and Africa. For many centuries, Muslim merchants had worked to make converts to Islam among the unbelievers (infidels) with whom they traded. This missionary work expanded along with commerce in the nineteenth and twentieth centuries, especially in colonial areas of sub-Saharan Africa. Christian missionaries there competed with Muslims, who had the advantage of preaching a faith that stood in opposition to the West.

The empires contributed, unwittingly, to the dramatic growth of pilgrimage to the Holy Places located in Saudi Arabia, on the Arabian peninsula. That deed, to be undertaken during the holy time called Ramadan, was one of the sacred duties of all Muslims. Steamship lines and railroads opened rapid and much safer routes for pilgrims from distant lands intent on reaching Mecca and Medina. A few Westerners traveled secretly to these places, and marveled at the devotion of so many Muslim pilgrims who came together from Asia, Africa, and the Middle East to fulfill the holiest of religious acts.

Despite these common traits, deep divisions had appeared within Islam in the millennium since Muhammed had preached the new faith. Like Christianity, Islam had splintered into religious movements, each claiming to be the only true carrier of Muhammed's teaching. The largest of these was the Sunni Muslim community. The next in size, though much smaller, was the Shi`a Muslim group, centered in Iran and southern Iraq. Between the two movements, disagreements led, at times, to violent conflict and religious persecution.

In the twentieth century these disputes mattered less to Muslim leaders than the challenge of the West. Western beliefs and practices were the inspiration for two widely debated programs for reform among Muslim peoples. One was usually referred to by writers and political leaders as modernism, the other secularism. Those who supported the modernist path to reform argued that certain characteristics of Western historical development were useful and constructive and had no damaging impact on religious faith. Muslim leaders included science and technology in particular under the label of modern, but some of them extended the list to public schooling in native languages and to practical science and mathematics. The most radical reformers even called for constitutional democracy.

The other major program was usually defined as secularism. Its supporters stressed the need, along with the other modernist reforms, for states to back the creation of a national community in which civil laws, not Islam, governed everyday life. To achieve this goal, they were prepared to introduce secular civil and criminal law codes (i.e., law not based on religious edicts) to replace, or to supplement, Muslim customary law. Secularism rejected the claim of Muslim authorities, guided by religious rules, to exercise complete legal judgment in the public affairs of the individual and the family (the secular sphere, as opposed to the religious sphere of worship). Marriage, property rights, and inheritance belonged to this secular sphere. Proponents of this reform program were equally opposed to reliance on Muslim law in deciding criminal punishments (for example, amputation of the hand of a convicted thief, and stoning to death to punish adultery).

These discussions emerged in many countries among Muslim scholars and public officials. The issues became particularly critical with the fall of the Western empires and the emergence of independent Muslim states. Were the leaders of these countries to place the needs of their national community above those of the broader community of Muslim believers (the "umma")? Some religious and political leaders argued against nationalism, emphasizing the priority to maintain international Muslim religious solidarity. At heart, they relied on the strength of a revived and renewed Islamic community to defeat Western cultural and economic temptations. They believed that the social duties called for in traditional Muslim law should become the foundation for new organizations of solidarity and defense of the faith. In the 1920s, the Muslim Brotherhood took on these duties in Egypt. Its example spread in later years to other Middle Eastern lands. They were confident that new, competent leaders would emerge from Islamic schools that taught the Muslim religious canon.

Most political leaders in postcolonial nation-states inhabited by Muslim peoples refused to trust such half-measures of religious reform. They placed their hopes on the emergence of nationalism among their peoples. It had to be based on a shared language and culture. They did not deny that religious allegiance among a country's Muslims belonged within this "national culture," but sought to place religious practices in the private, not public domain of everyday life. The leaders of the new nation-state of Turkey, created in 1920 on the ruins of the Ottoman Empire, made sure that defenders of Islam would not impede their state-building. Their most dramatic measure was the abolition of the position of caliph, who had been since the time of Muhammed the supreme religious authority among all Sunni Muslims. Their state was to be resolutely secularist.

Later, in both Indonesia and Pakistan the new leaders sought to create not an Islamic state but a secular nation-state. They recognized that their national community was deeply marked by

Muslim culture but conceived of their task in secular, nationalist terms. This meant that secular law, not Muslim law, was the set the guidelines for issues touching on everyday life. In Pakistan, the project was a failure. The country was split into hostile ethnic communities and lacked the means to cope with the misery of the masses of the population. In those conditions of disorder, Pakistani religious leaders forced the government to rely increasingly on religious law and practices to maintain the unity of their weak state.

The nation-building project in the Arab-speaking world drew from the work of Arab writers who believed that the Arab language brought distinctive cultural qualities useful for nationalism. They called their approach pan-Arabism. From these groups too came strong supporters of the secularist program, for they backed reforms modeled closely on what they believed were the essential qualities of western nation-states. Nasser of Egypt made the secularist and national program the basis of his regime after seizing power in 1952. The Muslim Brotherhood opposed his policies and called for a state based on Muslim law. Nasser had its leaders arrested, driving the movement underground. A decade later, the Baath ("Rebirth") parties in Syria and Iraq followed in Nasser's footsteps, seizing power in their countries to build secular nation-states. Their leaders restricted the public role of Islam and forced proponents of an Islamic state, either Sunni or Shi`a, into exile.

Literacy for Women: Adult Reading Classes in Yemen Arab Republic, 1983 (*U.N. Photo 153539/John Isaac*)

The Shah of Iran took up the same set of policies in the 1950s. He aroused ultimately such bitter opposition from the Shi`a religious leaders of his land that they organized a revolution in 1979 to overthrow his monarchy. They installed in its place an Islamic Republic ruled by Muslim clerics guided by the Quran and religious law. Neighboring Afghanistan experienced a similar upsurge of Muslim fundamentalism when Afghan Communists launched their radical secular revolution in 1976. Twenty years later, the most extreme of these religious movements, the Taliban party, seized power in an effort to impose on the Afghan people a Muslim theocracy (a state based entirely on religious precepts and led by religious leaders). They held power for four years before being overthrown by a coalition of Afghan guerrilla forces and U.S. armed forces in 2002 (see Chapter 8). Secular nationalism became a deeply divisive issue among Muslims.

In the late twentieth century, opposition to modernism and secularism in Muslim countries took the form of a powerful, often violent international movement. Conservative Muslim religious leaders were vehemently opposed to secularism, since they believed it a deadly threat to the survival of the Muslim community and its spiritual values. They often linked it with materialism, which they understood to be personal gratification through material possessions to the neglect of spiritual duties. The mode of resistance that they particularly encouraged took the form of political movements, such as that of the Taliban, dedicated to seizing state power. Observers called them "fundamentalist" Islamic groups (since they claimed to defend the fundamental tenets of Islam), or "Islamist" groups (since they made Islam the supreme cause that they espoused).

Committed to the dogmatic imposition of Muslim law and practice (as they understood them), some of these groups, such as Al Qaeda, used terrorist tactics of assassination and bombing. Others adopted the tactics of political parties, seeking to win elections to national parliaments. When successful, they proceeded to pass laws restricting civil and political liberties, reinforcing Muslim law, and banning women's political activities, public education, and paid work. Movements using state institutions to institute fundamentalist Islamic laws came into existence in several countries, including Sudan, and in the northern provinces of Nigeria. In all cases, their rigorous Islamic regulations aroused strong opposition both from people of other religions and from nationalists who defended the secularist program. Still, at the end of the twentieth century, the issues raised by modernist and secularist reform programs remained unresolved, producing a cultural and political crisis throughout the Muslim world.

The Six-Day War

The conflict between the Arab countries and Israel remained in the 1960s the greatest threat of war in the Middle East. Leaders of the Arab states refused to accept the presence of the Jewish state in their midst. In the 1960s, the Palestinian refugees organized their own resistance movement to take back the territory they considered their homeland. They were scattered throughout the Middle East, but their major refugee camps were located in Egypt and Jordan. There they

gradually formed new social organizations to help rebuild their lives. In the early years, they received financial aid from Arab leaders who sympathized with their cause.

The Palestinians themselves had to overcome internal quarrels before Arab states took heed of their demands. Finally in 1964 several Palestinian movements agreed to form a unified coalition that they called the Palestine Liberation Organization (PLO). The founders of the PLO set their goal to be "Palestinian self-determination following the liberation of our country," that is, the destruction of the state of Israel. Arab League backing was still half-hearted. Other issues appeared more pressing to most League members. They hoped to exercise some moderating control over the Palestinians. No Arab leader dared call for a peace settlement, though, since to do so would require recognizing the state of Israel. The king of Jordan maintained secret contacts with his Israeli neighbor, but feared assassination if he openly negotiated with Israel. Arab supporters of the PLO were hostile toward the very existence of a Jewish state in Arab land and hoped to avenge the defeats of 1948 and 1956. As a result of PLO efforts, Arab leaders increasingly talked of a new war on Israel.

The talk led to action in 1966, when new leaders in Syria from the Baath party called for a "revolutionary war" to defeat Israel and to "liberate Palestine." The Syrian regime followed Nasser's example in promising their people a special Arab form of socialism. They condemned conservative Arab monarchs like the king of Saudi Arabia who adhered closely to tribal ways and traditional Muslim practices. Leaders of other Arab states suspected the Syrians of wishing to spread the political influence of their own state in the area of the Fertile Crescent, from Lebanon to the Persian Gulf. These internal divisions were hidden behind public statements in support of the Palestinian cause.

As Nasser had done a decade earlier, the Syrian government turned to the Soviet Union for military and economic aid. The Soviet leaders were eager to enlarge their network of allied states to include Syria. They praised the Baath Party's socialist policies, which they viewed as a politically progressive step and a promising sign of solidarity with Soviet interests. Nasser's Egypt had shown the way for Soviet ties in the Middle East. In 1966, Syria became Moscow's second ally there. Soviet aid went to the Syrian government. It secretly went as well to the PLO, some of whose soldiers traveled to eastern Europe to receive training from Soviet agents. PLO guerrilla fighters were encouraged by the Syrians to launch raids from their territory on Israeli settlements. The Middle East was becoming an arena of Cold War conflict between supporters of the Soviet Union and of the United States.

U.S. leaders recognized that the strategic interests of the Western alliance required good relations with oil-rich countries, especially Saudi Arabia and Iran. The West's dependence on oil from Arab lands demanded no less. Yet, the U.S. government was sympathetic to the Israeli national cause. It embodied the hope of Jewish peoples for a haven from persecution. This tiny state respected human rights better than any other regime in the Middle East. Israel functioned as a democratic state, promising civil liberties to their 2.5 million Jews and three hundred thousand Arabs. It protected the religious practices of the Muslims and Christians. Its Arab citizens remained a suspect people, though, and were excluded from full political participation in public affairs. They enjoyed fewer rights than the Jews but were protected under the constitution from persecution. No other state there could claim to do as much for its minorities.

The Israeli leaders relied for the defense of their country primarily on their own military forces. The U.S. commitment to Israel took the form of a public promise to protect the "right to exist" of the state of Israel. It was a message directed to Arab countries. The U.S. government had defined its goal in the Middle East to be peace and political stability. Its promises to Arab oil countries and to Israeli created a dilemma, for strategic interests collided with its readiness to defend Israel. As the likelihood of war with Syria grew, Israeli generals laid their own plans for war. Fearing a concerted offensive by the surrounding Arab countries, they conceived the desperate strategy of striking first. Secretly, they prepared to launch an attack on Egypt, Jordan, and Syria in turn, attacking each country separately in the hope of ultimately defeating all.

The PLO campaign against Israel remained the immediate grounds for war. Israeli generals decided to destroy the bases in Jordan and Syria from which PLO guerrillas were penetrating their country. Raids on these camps provoked a public outcry in Arab countries. The Syrian government demanded that Egypt immediately prepare to join the fight against Israel. The danger of a new Arab-Israeli conflict was growing. Nasser could not refuse his support, for he had spoken out too long and too fervently for the "liquidation of Israeli aggression." Of what use was Egyptian talk of Arab solidarity, the Syrian leaders asked publicly, if Egypt kept the U.N. peacekeeping forces between its army and Israel?

In 1967, Nasser abandoned his cautious policy. In May of that year, he ordered the U.N. forces to leave Egypt. At the same moment, he closed the Gulf of Aqaba, on Egypt's eastern border, to shipping bound for Israel from the Indian Ocean. In the tense atmosphere of that spring, these steps signaled preparation for war against Israel. No evidence suggests that he had in fact ordered the Egyptian military to make ready for an invasion. The most likely explanation for his reckless action was his ambition to be leader of "progressive" Arab countries. It was a role he could not sustain except by placing Egypt at the forefront of the impending war against Israel. Nasser's action constituted the fatal step in the outbreak of another Middle Eastern war.

Fearing concerted Arab attack, the Israeli government approved the risky plans of its military for a preventive war on its Arab neighbors. Two decades after the first Arab-Israeli conflict, the same enemies met once again in June 1967. The Arab states proved as poorly prepared as before, and the Israeli army and air force functioned with extraordinary skill and deadly precision. Their "Six-Day" War was a resounding triumph for Israel. It turned into a military disaster for Egypt. That state was Israel's principal enemy, since it possessed the largest Arab armed force. In the first hours of war, Israeli planes destroyed the entire Egyptian air force. In the next three days, Israel's armored columns

occupied the whole Sinai peninsula to the Suez Canal. Its army then attacked and defeated Jordanian forces on the west bank of the Jordan River and in the city of Jerusalem. Finally, it forced Syrian troops out of the mountainous border area known as the Golan Heights. It achieved these victories in six days. The defeated Arab states accepted a U.N. truce, leaving Israeli troops in possession of all the territory occupied during the war.

Egypt, Palestine, and Peace with Israel

That war proved a turning point in the recent history of the Middle East. It made clear to Arabs and Jews alike the rewards that Israeli political unity and military skill had brought. In the words of an Arab historian, Arabs understood that "a small state had displayed their historical inadequacy, had seized massive chunks of land, and had devastated the armies whose weapons and machismo had been displayed with great pride."[1] Victory in the Six-Day War brought the Jewish state all Palestine, the ancestral lands of the Jews. Conquest of the Gaza Strip on the Mediterranean Sea and of Jordanian Jerusalem and the West Bank territory gave Israel rule more than one million Palestinians, some in refugee camps but most living in their own communities. To whom should the land of Palestine belong? The question became an urgent political and religious issue for the Israeli government, for the Israeli people, and for the Palestinian Arab population.

In the next two decades, the Israeli answer in policy and everyday practice was that the occupied territories would be integrated into the life of their state. Disregarding the United Nation's resolutions calling for withdrawal from these lands, conservative Israeli leaders offered incentives and protection for new Jewish settlements in the West Bank area. These settlers took possession

1.   Fouad Ajami, *The Arab Predicament: Arab Political Thought and Practice since 1967* (New York, 1981), p. 12.

by the late 1980s of nearly one-third of the entire land, and most of the precious water rights. Palestinians had to make room for the settlers, paying for the defeat in loss of their water and their land. They found work as laborers in Israeli enterprises, often traveling regularly across the "green line" that still separated Israel from the occupied lands.

Politically that line was very real. Palestinians in these areas remained a disenfranchised people, ruled by the Israeli state and under military occupation. In the opinion of one Israeli observer, Israel's three million Jews exercised by choice or by necessity in the mid-1980s a sort of "majority tyranny" over the 2.5 million Palestinian Arabs. To him, the process of economic integration of the peoples of Israel-Palestine appeared irreversible, yet political unification seemed unattainable. An additional source of conflict came from the religious aspirations of fundamentalist Jewish groups to settle all the ancient territory of the Jewish tribes, in the process displacing the Palestinian Arab inhabitants. Israeli leaders clung to their vision of an enlarged Jewish land and the Palestine Liberation Organization (PLO) continued to demand an Arab state in all Palestine.

For two decades after the war, the PLO attempted to achieve this goal by force of arms. It created military camps for its militia forces. Its troops seized the southern part of Lebanon in the early 1970s after being expelled from Jordan. The PLO clashed with Lebanon's government over the seizure of the southern region. In 1975, a civil war began that tore the tiny country apart. Both Syrian and Israeli armed forces intervened in the fighting, each seizing strategic territory along their borders. Lacking a strong military and unified political leadership, the Lebanese state disintegrated into a collection of warring private armies defending the territory of their Christian and Muslim communities. The PLO's militia failed to advance the struggle against Israel, however. They were incapable even of defending PLO camps from Israeli army attack.

In those same years, the PLO undertook a campaign of international terrorism to pursue "war by other means" on Israel. Their terrorist acts used the time-tried methods of assassination and destruction to publicize their cause and to intimidate Israel. The PLO launched terrorist attacks on targets associated, even remotely, with Israel. It began the campaign in 1969 with the hijacking and destruction of three airplanes belonging to U.S. airlines. Even Israeli Olympic athletes became their victims when terrorists attacked the Munich Olympic Village in 1972. Many innocent lives were lost in that struggle. A secret war went on for years between the Israeli secret service and international terrorist organizations supporting the PLO. But terrorism proved as unsuccessful in weakening Israel as the PLO's military operations against Israel.

The most effective form of Palestinian political protest against Israel proved to be the mass uprising (called in Arabic the "Intifada") in Israel's occupied lands. It began in late 1987, when thousands of Palestinians in towns and refugee camps spontaneously joined mass demonstrations against Israeli troops. Their only arms were stones, against which Israeli occupation authorities deployed their military and police forces. They had no plan of action, for the PLO had no part in organizing the Intifada. It surprised its leaders (in exile) as much as it did the Israeli government. At the start, leadership for the demonstrations came from within the Palestinian community. The Intifada extended to strikes and economic boycotts against Israeli enterprises. The Israeli military discovered that force could disperse the demonstrators—with many wounded and some killed—but could not stop the uprising. This first Intifada continued sporadically until the early 1990s. The demonstrations were the first sign of substantial national unity among Palestinians and made clear their refusal to accept the integration of the occupied territories into Israel.

In Egypt, the defeat of 1967 set the Egyptian government on a new course in foreign and

Confronting the Palestinian Uprising: Israeli Troops in Bethlehem, 1988 (*United Nations Relief and Works Agency*)

domestic policy. Nasser himself died in 1971. His successor, Anwar Sadat, was also a former member of the Free Officers of 1952. He rejected Nasser's policy of state socialism for Egypt and launched a secularist program (including laws to protect the rights of Egyptian women). He did not believe that Nasser's determination to make Egypt the leader of the struggle against Israel was in the country's interests. Sadat did seek to recover from Israel the Egyptian territory beyond the Suez Canal lost in the Six-Day War. He was determined, once this goal was achieved, to remove his state from the interminable conflict draining the resources of his country.

His daring project supposed first of all that he restore Egypt's international standing after its

crushing defeat in the 1967 war. He had the backing for another war from the other Arab states, including Saudi Arabia. The Saudi king's influence rested on his country's role as exporter of oil. Demand for petroleum in the early 1970s had risen so rapidly that it had become a product in short supply. Oil-producing countries had by then won from the petroleum companies the legal right to control their oil production. They were in a new position of power. With Saudi backing, Sadat decided to risk another war with Israel.

In late 1973, his armies launched a surprise attack across the Suez Canal (the Yom Kippur War). The initial fighting went in their favor. Israeli forces retreated from the canal. Both the United States and the Soviet Union intervened to back their respective allies, and the war turned into a major international crisis. The Soviet Union sent arms to Egypt. The United States rushed military aid to Israel. When the Israeli army succeeded in turn in pushing Egyptian forces back beyond the canal and Soviet leaders threatened to intervene militarily, the U.S. government declared a "stage 3" nuclear alert, readying its forces for possible nuclear war. To support Egypt, the Arab oil-producing countries declared an embargo (that is, a ban) on oil shipments to the United States, and curtailed oil production. The price of petroleum shot up to $14 per barrel, oil rationing began in the United States, and an international recession set in as a result of the oil shortages. The nuclear confrontation combined with the oil embargo put enormous pressure on both sides to negotiate a settlement. A truce ended the war, leaving Egyptian forces in control of a strip of territory on the eastern side of the Suez Canal. Sadat now was in a strong position to negotiate with Israel.

He proceeded in the next years to implement the second stage in his new policy. He turned to Israel with an offer of peace, breaking ranks with the other Arab states, and abruptly ended Egypt's alliance with the Soviet Union. He appealed to the U.S. government to become Egypt's ally and principal source of economic and military aid. He was successful in both endeavors. Egypt and Israel signed a peace treaty in 1979. Egypt, first of any Arab state, formally recognized the existence of the state of Israel. The Israeli government, in turn, restored all Egyptian lands seized in 1967. The U.S. government began shipping military equipment to Egypt and increased its shipments of food, needed to feed the impoverished Egyptian masses. It was more deeply involved than ever in the Middle East, providing aid to both Israel and Egypt.

The danger of a new Arab-Israeli war dwindled, but Sadat's daring moves cost him his life. He had formally recognized that the Jewish state belonged within the Middle Eastern polity. Muslim fundamentalist groups condemned his policies of peace with Israel and his social reforms

(including greater rights for women). He was assassinated in 1981 by a group of Egyptian army officers and soldiers, members of a Islamist terrorist group. This brutal action, motivated by their conviction that Egypt's leader had joined the enemies of Islam, was a sign of the rising importance of Muslim fundamentalism in Middle Eastern life.

Despite continued terrorist violence, the Egyptian government stayed faithful to Sadat's political course. It directed its efforts to helping an impoverished population that had grown to 55 million by 1990. It ended the severe restrictions on free enterprise, promoting Egyptian economic development by a combination of state aid and private employment. Egypt became a land of relative freedom among repressive Arab states. Its most serious enemy remained the Muslim Brotherhood. Its supporters began a campaign of terrorism in the 1980s, directed against Egyptian intellectuals such as the Nobel Prize winning novelist Naguib Mafouz, accused of the sin of modernism (abandonment of Islam), against the Coptic Christian church, and even against foreign tourists. Muslim fundamentalism was a powerful force in Egypt, sustained by religious fanaticism and widespread poverty that the state appeared incapable of ending.

For fifteen years, Sadat's peace initiative remained without sequel. The PLO refused the offer of autonomy for the occupied territories included in the 1978 peace agreement. Its followers clung to their hope of taking back all of Palestine. The leaders of Syria and Iraq competed in their warlike threats against Israel. Israel remained in a state of war with its other neighboring Arab states.

Conditions changed dramatically in the early 1990s. The changes were partly the result of new Israeli political leadership that took power in 1993. The ongoing Palestinian Intifada made clear that the occupied territories could not remain under Israeli rule. For the first time, the Israeli government declared its readiness to negotiate a compromise settlement with the PLO. Prospects for peace improved also because of the decline in power of the radical, anti-Israeli Arab states. Iraq had become the leader of these states in the 1980s. But its defeat in the Gulf War of 1991 ended its regional influence and dashed the hopes of the PLO for Iraqi backing for a new war against Israel. Palestinian radicals had lost their last patron.

The PLO leader, Yasir Arafat, took a step as daring in its own way as Sadat's peace initiative two decades before. In 1993, he agreed to recognize the state of Israel and discuss a peace accord with the new Israeli government. Arafat was prepared to admit publicly that endless bloodshed could not bring to life the dream of a Palestinian state, and that Israel had itself to be party to the creation of a country for the Palestinians. That year the PLO and Israel reached a peace agreement (the Oslo Agreement). It opened the way for a Palestinian state, to be created in slow stages out of the occupied territories, and recognized officially the state of Israel. The PLO ordered a stop to terrorist attacks, and brought to an end (temporarily) the Palestinian uprising. The next year, the king of Jordan signed a peace treaty with Israel. The period of Arab-Israeli wars had finally come to an end, almost five decades after the creation of the state of Israel.

For a few years, Arafat's authority was sufficient to keep anti-Israeli Arabs from street violence and terrorism. The Palestine-Israel agreement promised Palestinian self-rule in the occupied territories (Gaza, the west bank of the Jordan river). Just what territory (and what part of Jerusalem) should go to the "Palestine Authority" remained to be negotiated. The Israeli government had somehow to curtail the expansionist plans of Jewish settlers whose communities were located in the midst of the lands to go under Palestinian rule. These issues were complex and aroused passionate resistance from extremists on both sides.

In 2000, with these issues still unresolved, Arab militants took to the streets again to attack Israeli troops and settlers in the occupied territories. This "second Intifada" differed from the first principally by its level of violence. This time Palestinian insurgents used rifles and machine guns to attack Israeli forces. In addition, Muslim terrorist groups resorted to suicide bombings in Israel itself, killing hundreds and wounding thousands of bystanders. The Israeli army responded with attacks on suspected terrorist centers in Palestinian territories by helicopter gunships and tanks. The Israeli government began construction on a gigantic wall to separate Palestinian areas from Israel and Israeli settlements. Within a few years, Palestinian casualties were numbered in the thousands. Palestinian workers, once employed in Israel, were without work. War, not peace, remained the dominant state of affairs in the Holy Land.

Iran and the Islamic Republic

Like other Middle Eastern lands, Iran's population was made up of peoples of different languages and cultures. Almost all were followers of the Shi`ite branch of the Muslim religion. In the middle of the twentieth century, its monarch claimed the title of "shah," that is, emperor, but the land had long since lost all ties with the great Persian emperors of antiquity. After the Second World War, Iran's ruler, Reza Shah Pahlevi, chose to cooperate with the western powers. He continued the policy of granting the monopoly on Iran's oil production to the corporation British Petroleum. He placed his country firmly on the side of the West in the Cold War years.

A nationalist alternative to the shah's pro-Western policies briefly emerged in Iran in the years after the Second World War. A coalition of political groups called the National Front, headed by a dynamic political leader, Dr. Mohammed Mossadeq, promised political and economic independence from the West. Iran's religious leaders proclaimed their backing for the movement, which they hoped would protect their "Islamic nation" from the West and modernism. Mossadeq's program included nationalization of British Petroleum's oil properties and neutrality for Iran in the conflict between East and West. With strong backing from voters among Iran's lower classes, Mossadeq's coalition won parliamentary elections in 1951. He became prime minister of Iran. One of his first acts was to order the nationalization of the country's oil wells and refineries. The worsening political struggle within Iran led Mossadeq to denounce the rule of the shah. Violent demonstrations in support of his government forced the shah to flee the country. Without any coherent plan, Mossadeq had set in motion forces leading the country toward political revolution.

This Iranian affair, which began as a dispute over nationalization of the country's petroleum industry, appeared to the U.S. government a Cold War conflict. In 1953, the Eisenhower administration extended the policy of containment to include opposition to anti-Western regimes in strategic areas around the Soviet Union. The presence of Communists in Mossadeq's political coalition was proof to the U.S. government that his government was a pawn of the Soviet Union. The U.S. Central Intelligence Agency sent covert aid to the shah's supporters in the country. Mossadeq was unable to hold together his National Front coalition. Popular demonstrations against Mossadeq and opposition to his rule by army leaders, secretly encouraged and financed by U.S. agents, forced the prime minister to resign in mid-1953. This U.S.-backed political revolt placed the shah back on his throne. His dependence on the West was greater than ever.

To cope with the country's political and social unrest, the shah laid out three new policies. The first was to bolster his political power. He purged his country of all political revolutionaries and expanded his police force to repress opposition from Muslim clerics. He tolerated parliamentary politics but remained the power behind the government. Although not a dictator in the full sense of the word, his rule remained authoritarian.

His second objective was to restore cooperation with the Western states. He brought Iran into the Middle Eastern military alliance, the Baghdad Pact, alongside Great Britain, Turkey, and Iraq. He signaled his desire for good relations with the United States by signing a separate defense treaty with the United States. In return, the U.S. government provided his state with large amounts of economic and military aid, more than to any other state outside the NATO alliance. U.S. advisers helped train his military forces and provided assistance in bolstering his new police force. In global power politics, the shah aligned Iran on the side of the West.

His third objective consisted in the modernization of Iran's society and economy. He called his plan a "White Revolution," combining political order (symbolized by the monarchical color white) and social reform. His objective, he explained, was to make Iran the equal to "the most developed countries in the world." With funds from the sale of oil, his government invested heavily in modern industry and urban services. Seizing the extensive land holdings of Muslim religious societies, it redistributed land to peasant farmers.

In social and cultural matters, the shah's goal was a secular society. He looked to the example of Kemal Ataturk's reforms in Turkey as the model for his own modernist program. Islam was to be excluded from public affairs and restricted to the private sphere of worship and morality. Civil law, not Quranic law, set marriage and property relations. The shah's government discouraged Muslim traditional practices, such as veiling of women, and demoted the prominence of Islam in accounts of Iran's past glories as a great empire. In the shah's opinion, Iranian history began long before Islam reached the country in the eighth century.

Challenging the Muslim religious leaders placed the shah in opposition to clerics such as the Ayatollah Khomeini. Their overriding concern remained the defense of the "Islamic nation." Khomeini, the most forceful of these religious figures, championed a fundamentalist program of strict adherence to Islamic practices and laws. His deepest convictions, like those of the Muslim Brotherhood in Egypt, turned him against modernism and secularism. For speaking out against the shah's reforms, he was expelled from Iran in 1963.

The obstacles in the way of the shah's ambitious plans were great. He confronted serious opposition to his regime from groups demanding political liberty—mostly students and educated professionals—and from religious leaders and their followers, principally the poor urban classes. To achieve his economic goals he exhausted his state's revenues. His income from petroleum sales proved inadequate for his grandiose projects. Social unrest worsened as a result of wild inflation and hardship caused by rapid economic growth.

The core of opposition to his regime came from the Muslim clerics. He had given the vote to women, made civil law the foundation of marriage, family, and inheritance, and stripped Muslim religious institutions of their vast land holdings. His reforms placed Iran on the same path to modernity that Ataturk had chosen for Turkey. For this, the Muslim leaders judged him unfit to rule. In the mid-1970s they organized their supporters to bring down his "godless" regime. Forces opposing the shah grew rapidly. The Muslim clerics proved remarkably effective revolutionaries. In a few years, they brought together a broad coalition of anti-shah groups. In 1979, they orchestrated a mass revolution that ended the shah's reign. Demonstrators took control of the streets of the cities, and workers went on strike, paralyzing production in the oil industry. The army was overwhelmed by this revolutionary upsurge. Its troops mutinied, refusing to shoot the demonstrators. Lacking popular support and the means to repress the uprising, the shah was forced to flee his country.

The victor was Ayatollah Khomeini. He was the inspirational leader of the revolutionaries, and became the principal architect of the theocratic Islamic state that came into existence in 1980. His strict reading of the Quran inspired his radical reform program. He was convinced that by following its precepts, he could create an Iranian Islamic Republic. Its religious purity, in his utopian view, would recreate Muhammed's original state. Symbolic of the renewal of Islamic practices was his order that women must once again hide behind traditional veils in conformity with Muslim traditions.

This Islamic Republic looked toward the restoration of Muslim law and faith throughout the Muslim world. Its religious leaders held the reins of power in the Iranian government and in the courts, and commanded a vigilante militia charged with punishing Iranians who failed to obey Muslim practices. They denounced the corrupting influence of wealth and the pursuit of individual pleasure. They called on Muslims everywhere to return to the strict guidelines of the Quran and of Muslim law. Their message found supporters among Sunni as well Shi`a Muslims in the years following the revolution. They became a major force behind the upsurge throughout the Muslim world of Muslim fundamentalism in the 1980s. They condemned rulers whose secular reforms weakened Muslim rules and practices. They promised reforms inspired by the Quran's social concern to alleviate the misery of urban masses. Their vision was of a renewed and united community of Muslim faithful.

By word and deed the leaders of the Islamic Republic spread far beyond Iran's borders their militant program. Public figures in any sphere, cultural, social or political, were targets of their religious wrath. In 1988, Ayatollah Khomeini ordered the execution of the Indian writer Salman Rushdie for having published the novel, *The Satanic Verses,* judged sacrilegious and blasphemous to the Muslim faith. Forced to flee his home, Rushdie went into hiding for several years; two translators (in Japan and Norway) of his novel were murdered, presumably by Khomeini followers. The Iranian government gave its support, including generous subsidies, to terrorist movements in lands where they believed the Muslim faith was threatened. They called on Iraqi Muslims to overthrow Saddam Hussein's regime. When Iraq invaded Iran in 1980, they urged Iranian troops to destroy Saddam's forces. But their holy war was a failure there. The Ayatollah's Muslim fundamentalism found few Iraqi sympathizers, and fewer still ready to risk their lives for his religious cause. The Iranian army was able to force Iraq forces back to the border, but could not advance further in the face of Iraq's modern armaments (including deadly chemical weapons). The war ended in 1988 with an armistice, leaving millions of Iranian war dead.

Gradually in the 1990s, Iran's Islamic Republic weakened its rigorous Quranic laws imposed on the population. In private and out of sight of the "vice police," many people sought simple pleasures such as dancing to Western music and watching Western television. In 1996, voters chose a reform president. His powers remained feeble, however. Muslim clerics, still the power behind the state, clung to their dream of a theocratic land leading the entire Muslim world toward the righteous life.

Their message found a sympathetic hearing in many Muslim countries. The Muslim Brotherhood had for decades fought against secularism and modernism in Egypt; there, small terrorist organizations carried on the battle, attacking Christians and foreign tourists. Supporters were especially numerous in Muslim lands where governments proved incapable of coping with the impoverishment of the masses. By the early 1990s, several other governments in the Middle East, northern Africa, and Asia had made Muslim law the legal foundation of their states. This rise of fundamentalism was a disturbing trend to those who believed that religious toleration and civil liberties offered the best guarantee of individual integrity. The fundamentalists' defense of their religious faith and practices brought with it the persecution of religious minorities and the rejection of civil liberties protecting individual citizens no matter what their faith. The Iranian revolution revealed that western liberal ideals and secular reforms had aroused a deep and determined opposition grounded in Muslim religious values and practices.

The Oil Wars of Iraq

By the 1980s, almost all Middle Eastern states, except Israel, had fallen under the control of au-

thoritarian regimes. None of the states functioned as democracies with free elections and with effective guarantees of civil liberty for their peoples. One reason for the emergence of strong leaders was the existence everywhere of antagonistic social, ethnic, and religious communities. No general agreement on majority rule and minority rights was possible where each community feared the others. The lack of a democratic consensus created conditions of disorder and conflict which were seized upon by authoritarian leaders to justify their rule. Military and political leaders, who often relied on particular clans or tribes to find loyal followers, competed in a brutal struggle for power. Although the victors claimed to speak for their nation, for all Arabs, or for Islam, they directed their efforts principally to protecting and preserving the wealth and privileges brought them by political power.

The history of Iraq in the last half of the century followed closely this pattern of authoritarian rule. The country's territory centered around the river valleys of the Tigris and Euphrates. Once called Mesopotamia, it was inhabited by a diverse population that included most major ethnic and religious groups of the Middle East. The bulk of the inhabitants (nearly two thirds) belonged to the Shi`a Muslim faith, Sunni Muslims were numerous as well. Small communities of Christians were scattered across the country. The Muslims were mostly Arabic-speaking, but the northern, mountainous area was inhabited by a large population of Kurdish people, with their own language and culture.

Independence from the British in 1940 left the country under the rule of a monarch, King Faisal I, put on the throne in 1921 when the League mandated state came into existence. He enjoyed meager support among the population. He in turn had a low opinion of his subjects, who he judged "devoid of any patriotic idea, imbued with religious prejudices, and riotous." In 1959, an ambitious general overthrew the monarchy and tried to govern by military might. In the next decade, political strife among the military brought only confusion and disorder to the land. Finally in 1969, a progressive secular movement calling itself the "Rebirth" (Baath) party seized power in a bloody insurrection. Among its leaders was a young Iraqi named Saddam Hussein. He had made a political career as a member of this political party. Its policies borrowed heavily from the socialist, secularist, and pan-Arab program first promoted in Egypt by Gamal Nasser in the 1950s. Saddam Hussein became one of the party's leaders by dint of his organizing skills during the years of underground struggle before the 1969 revolt.

During the early years in power, Saddam Hussein and his colleagues proceeded with their agenda of internal reform. The first step was taking over the prosperous oil industry. The boom in oil prices after the 1973 Israeli war brought enormous revenues to their government. Throughout the 1970s, they used this wealth to invest in new industrial development, to introduce an extensive program of social welfare, including health care and old age pensions, and to expand the country's education system. They encouraged women to seek professional careers such as educators, doctors, and lawyers. To bolster the ethnic unity of the state, the Baath leaders encouraged resettlement of the Arab-speaking population throughout the country where other ethnic groups were concentrated. They forcibly removed Kurds from key northern cities and installed Arab migrants from the south. Finally, they strengthened their military forces, spending large sums to create a modern air force and to mechanize the army (largely with purchases from the Soviet Union). Kurdish nationalists retreated to the mountains to continue their fight for independence, but with little success. By the end of the decade Iraq had emerged as one of the strongest states in the Middle East.

During those years Saddam Hussein gradually built up his control of the Baath party, and through it of the Iraqi state. He used his influence as chief of the secret police, in that one-party state, to eliminate his rivals as well as to keep down opposition from Muslim fundamentalists and Kurdish nationalists. The government's leadership was gathered in the Revolutionary Command Council (in imitation of Nasser's Egypt), where he could govern without reliance on the Baath party. In 1979, he eliminated his last rival for power. He openly acknowledged his admiration for Joseph Stalin's style of leadership. He became "President, Leader, Struggler"—his official titles—by "climbing over the bodies of his enemies," as Russians had said of Stalin. By 1979 he had become Iraqi dictator.

On close examination, his methods of rule bore a strong likeness to European fascism. The socialism that he professed served in part as an ideological bond to hold together the peoples of his divided country. Iraq was a "state without a nation," that is, it lacked one predominant ethnic population. In place of that unity he substituted authoritarian rule. Nationalism became the preferred ideology and propaganda tool in that system. Like fascist leaders of Europe earlier, he used it to claim to speak for and rule over the Iraqi population, and like them, he glorified warriors and war. He sought leadership of all Arab countries (like Nasser before him). To do so, he was prepared to promote the anti-Israeli crusade. His army was a key instrument in this cause. He began a secret program to develop nuclear weapons, but it was brought to an abrupt halt when Israeli warplanes destroyed Iraq's nuclear reactor in 1981. Like the Italian fascist dictator Mussolini, he turned the human and economic resources of country to military conquest.

His first target was Iran. Its rich oil fields lay on the borders of Iraq. In 1980, it was in the throes of its Islamic revolution, whose Muslim leaders had issued the call for the overthrow of his "godless" regime. That year, he ordered his armies to invade Iran to put to an end, he claimed, this militant Islamist regime. His principal objective was seizure of the Iranian oil fields near the Persian Gulf, which he expected to conquer without

Kurdish Warlord, 1965 (*William Carter Collection/
Hoover Institution*)

difficulty. After initial success, his forces had to retreat in the face of Iran's "holy war." To push back the Iranian army, he deployed all his army's weaponry, including chemical weapons. He obtained outside financial and military assistance from neighboring states fearful of Iranian Muslim zealotry. Even the United States sold military equipment to Iraq on the time-tried balance-of-power principle that "the enemy of my enemy is my friend."

The Iraq-Iran war dragged on for eight years until the two states, exhausted by the fighting, declared an armistice. The armies withdrew to the original borders. Saddam's dream of glorious victory left his country with a half-a-million war casualties and $80 billion in foreign debt. Only by the wildest stretch of the imagination could anyone believe that the 1988 cease-fire was an Iraqi victory. He held in public to this fantastic tale, though, and no one in Iraq dared openly dispute his fantasy.

The heroic vision was embodied in Saddam Hussein's enormous Victory Arch, which he had built in the center of his capital city, Baghdad. It consisted of two giant crossed swords, planted in the ground and held by huge bronze fists modeled after Saddam's own hand. Around the base of the fists were gathered five thousand helmets of Iranian soldiers captured during the eight years of war. In his speeches, Saddam compared his rule with that of ancient Mesopotamian kings, at other times with Saladin (a medieval Muslim prince and victor over the Christian crusaders), or simply with Nasser of Egypt.

The reality was that he had squandered Iraq's resources on a futile war of aggression that left his state deeply in debt to other Arab states. Among these was the tiny principality of Kuwait, located on the very borders of Iraq. Its tremendous oil reserves (judged fourth largest in the world) were tempting booty, and it was defenseless against his large army. Saddam decided for the second time to wage war for petroleum. If victorious, his state would dominate the Middle East.

His troops crossed the borders of Kuwait in the summer of 1990. He expected no effective international opposition to Iraqi seizure of the tiny, neighboring state. The Soviet government, on which his state had once depended for most of its arms, was in the midst of a serious political crisis caused by Gorbachev's reforms. Its advisers in Iraq had lost all influence over his foreign policies. The United States had failed several times in previous years to use its military force effectively in the Middle East. It had been unable to free its embassy hostages in Iran in a military operation in 1980, and it had proven incapable of ending the civil war in Lebanon in the early 1980s. International peacekeeping appeared to him an unlikely occurrence. Iraqi troops met almost no resistance from the tiny Kuwait army, and Saddam Hussein immediately declared Kuwait to be a province of Iraq.

Instead of easy victory, within a few weeks Saddam confronted the largest military coalition since the Second World War fighting under the flag of the United Nations. Iraq's conquest of Kuwait revealed to leaders around the world two important realities about global relations after the Cold War. The first was the simple fact that, without outside protection, any small state was vulnerable to an aggressive neighbor. The United Nations guaranteed in principle the inviolability of states' borders, but only concerted action of its powerful members could make that promise effective.

Equally important was the fact that the globe's economic growth depended upon a steady supply of Middle East oil. Its price decided prosperity or recession in distant lands. Iraqi seizure of Kuwait's oil fields would permit Saddam to dominate the world market. Middle Eastern states around Iraq such as Turkey, Syria, Egypt, and Saudi Arabia, previously divided, discovered in Iraq a common enemy who threatened them all. Governments in areas as distant as Japan and Argentina realized that they shared a common interest in demonstrating their commitment to the protection of states without strong military forces. The leaders of the Soviet Union and the United States, once bitter enemies, found in opposition to the Iraqi invasion a common cause to unite them.

The head of the coalition was the United States. Its government had for forty years argued that U.S. strategic interest required access to oil from the Middle East. It had publicly extended its protection to Saudi Arabia and to Israel. Saddam Hussein's sudden victory in Kuwait put in question the security of both lands. His forces could easily move beyond Kuwait into Saudi territory. His support for anti-Israeli groups, notably the PLO, raised the specter of another Arab-Israeli war. The U.S. government turned to the United Nations to condemn Iraqi aggression. Citing the U.N. Charter, the Security Council unanimously opposed the conquest of Kuwait and called for Iraqi withdrawal. This declaration became the basis for the coalition of states, soon numbering more than thirty, that gathered around the United States. While proposing negotiations, the coalition prepared for war.

The strategy for defeating Iraq proceeded through two stages. First, an international economic blockade cut off trade to and from Iraq. It was incomplete, though, since the neighboring states of Iran and Jordan did not support the coalition and allowed goods to Iraq to cross their borders. Saddam Hussein refused to take seriously the demand for withdrawal. To end this stalemate, the coalition began military operations. It launched a massive aerial bombardment of Iraq, destroying Iraq's air force. This was followed in February 1991 by a sudden ground offensive in Kuwait, led by American, British, and French armored divisions employing new electronic weapons against the Iraqi army. These forces surrendered virtually without resistance, though large numbers of Iraqi military and civilians died under air attack while attempting to flee Kuwait. The U.N. invading force stopped in southern Iraq, however, before reaching the capital Baghdad. Arab members of the coalition preferred limited victory to the collapse of Iraq, and U.S. military leaders were eager to keep casualties low among their troops. After a month of fighting, Saddam Hussein surrendered and signed a cease-fire agreement.

The war was over, but the coalition's military victory was incomplete. The principal goal of freeing Kuwait was achieved with the withdrawal of all Iraqi forces from Kuwait. Before doing so, Iraqi agents exploded all the country's 800 oil wells. Enormous oil fires fouled the atmosphere of the region for nearly a year before being completely extinguished. Saddam Hussein remained in power, but the United Nations took severe measures to limit his regime's power. The Iraqi government had to dismantle its nuclear weapons and destroy its stock of chemical and biological weapons. It had to allow U.N. inspectors access to their entire country to ensure compliance with these demands.

The U.N.'s most unprecedented action was the creation of a protected zone in northern Iraq for the Kurdish minority. Of the total twenty million

Fires in the Desert: Kuwait Oil Fields, 1991 (*Reuters/Archive Photos*)

Kurds living scattered across the northern Middle East, more than three million lived in Iraq. Their periodic uprisings aimed at freeing themselves from Iraqi rule had ended each time in defeat and the destruction of many Kurdish villages. Kurdish guerrilla forces joined in the 1991 war, risking death at the hands of Saddam's army. To prevent another ethnic massacre, the U.N. demanded that the Iraqi government withdraw its forces from the Kurdish territory. The Kurds were to govern their own area. Allied fighter planes flew regular patrol missions over northern Iraq to keep Iraqi warplanes and troops out of this region. Never before had the United Nations used its powers to divide up the territory of a state that threatened the lives of an ethnic minority. Kurdish leaders posted on the borders of their Iraqi territory a sign reading "Kurdistan."

An unstable peace returned to the Middle East. Saddam's attempt to dominate the region had collapsed. To ensure that he would not be tempted again to send his military into another war, U.S. naval forces remained near the Persian Gulf, and a small number of U.S. air and ground units were stationed in Saudi Arabia. The economic blockade of Iraq continued, though it was increasingly ineffective. Petroleum from Iraq's enormous oil fields reappeared in small quantities on the world market as allowed by the U.N. for purchases of civilian goods. Iraq still possessed the world's third-greatest reserves of petroleum, a natural resource indispensable to the global economy. Saddam's regime relied on that reality in its hopes for future political power. Humbled in the eyes of the world, Saddam remained dictator ruling over an impoverished people forced to live among the ruins of wars for which he bore the responsibility.

SUMMARY

The political life of the Middle East appeared in the years after decolonization to be an ongoing saga of civil strife and authoritarian leadership.

Only Israel and, to a lesser extent, Egypt enjoyed a consensus among their populations on national unity and political participation. Palestinians living in Israel were excluded from full citizenship by the Israeli government. Most Middle Eastern lands were deeply divided by generations-old animosity among religious and ethnic communities. The fervor with which many peoples clung to communal bonds arose from their distrust of repressive political leaders. These rulers talked of national unity but governed by favoring their own political followers, ethnic communities, and clans. Ethnic loyalties were so pervasive that observers called the trend a new form of "tribalism," that is, exclusive ethnic solidarity.

State-building was a mockery in times of civil war among these warring groups. In the case of Lebanon the conflict tore the country apart for an entire decade. Authoritarian rule by military dictators kept divided lands together by force. It also produced corrupt regimes incapable of healing ethnic distrust or of pushing for economic development to alleviate the poverty of their populations. Sales of petroleum on the international market sustained the incomes of those countries, such as Iraq and Iran, fortunate enough to possess large oil reserves. Other countries experienced prolonged economic decline.

The continued importance of religious issues marked the Middle East more than any other part of the postwar world. In Muslim lands and in Israel, fundamentalist movements sustained public concern for religious purity in thought and action and fought secularist and feminist reforms. Misery and the insecurity of everyday life among the impoverished masses led many Muslims to seek support and reassurance in their faith. They were encouraged to do so by religious leaders dreaming of a renewal of spiritual values. The struggle to sustain that faith in the midst of technological wonders and images of Western modernity was at the root of crises in private lives and public affairs throughout the Middle East.

DATES WORTH REMEMBERING

1939 Start of Saudi Arabian oil production
1945 Formation of Arab League
1948 Independence of Israel
1948–49 First Arab-Israeli War
1952 Nasser in power
1955–63 French war in Algeria
1956 Suez crisis
1960 Creation of Organization of Petroleum Exporting Countries (OPEC)
1963 Independence for Algeria
1965 Creation of Palestine Liberation Organization (PLO)
1967 Israeli-Arab Six-Day War
1967 Golda Meir named prime minister of Israel
1973 Israeli-Arab War
1975–81 Civil war in Lebanon
1979 Egyptian-Israeli Peace Treaty
1979 Iranian Islamic Revolution
1980 World population estimated 5 billion
1980–88 Iraq-Iran war
1988 Palestinian uprising in Israeli-occupied lands
1990 Iraq invasion of Kuwait
1991 Gulf war
1993 Oslo peace agreement between PLO and Israel
1994 Israeli-Jordanian Peace Treaty

RECOMMENDED READING

Postwar Middle East

Samir Khalil, *Republic of Fear: The Inside Story of Saddam's Iraq* (1992). A history of the rise of Saddam Hussein by an Iraqi refugee.

Efraim Karsh and Inari Rautsi, *Saddam Hussein: A Political Biography* (1991). Still the best biography of the Iraqi dictator and his politics of violence.

*Bernard Lewis, *History: Remembered, Recovered, Invented* (1975). A study of the recent creation of nationalist myths in Iran and Israel.

Roy Mottahedeh, *The Mantle of the Prophet: Religion and Politics in Iran* (1985). A thoughtful inquiry into the influential role of the Muslim clerics in Iran in the twentieth century and the rise of the Islamic Republic.

*Daniel Yergin, *The Prize: The Epic Quest for Oil, Money, and Power* (1991). A very thoughtful analysis of the role of oil in the history of the West and the Middle East.

Israel and Its Wars

Michael Cohen, *Palestine and the Great Powers, 1945–48* (1982). A balanced evaluation of the role of the Great Powers in the partition of Palestine and the formation of Israel.

*Larry Collins and Dominique Lapierre, *O Jerusalem!* (1980). A dramatic account of the struggle for Israeli independence.

Charles Smith, *Palestine and the Arab-Israeli Conflict* (1988). A clearly presented history of the wars between the Arab states and Israel.

Islam in the Middle East

Fred Halliday, *Nation and Religion in the Middle East* (2000). A valuable study of the modern politics of Islam, focused on the issue of nationalism and Islam in the Middle East.

Nikki Keddie and Beth Baron, eds., *Women in Middle Eastern History: Shifting Boundaries in Sex and Gender* (1991). Articles on a range of topics on women's roles and Islam in Middle Eastern countries.

Memoirs and Novels

*Thomas Friedman, *From Beirut to Jerusalem* (1989). Gripping memoirs by a *New York Times* correspondent in the Middle East during the 1980s.

*Naguib Mahfouz, *Midaq Ally* (1966). An intimate glimpse of Cairo families at the end of the Second World War, written by the Egyptian Nobel Prize author (and target of Muslim fundamentalist attacks).

Golda Meir, *My Life* (1975). The personal memoirs of an extraordinary life from Russian ghetto to head of the state of Israel.

Chapter 7

The Cold War and the Fall of the Soviet Empire, 1953–1991

Outline

European Nations and European Union

The Soviet Union and the Cold War

The Fall of the Soviet Empire

Highlight

The Cold War in Outer Space

Spotlight

Andrei Sakharov

The Cold War dominated global relations in the decades that followed Stalin's death. The Soviet leadership was determined to keep in place the essential institutions of Stalinism, held up by what appeared to be an invincible dictatorship. The competition between the superpowers spread beyond Europe and East Asia to other parts of the world. Its effects were felt even in Cuba, where the Cuban missile crisis brought the world to within a few hours of nuclear war. The dictator's disappearance did make possible an easing of Soviet–U.S. tensions. The two governments signed important treaties to limit armaments development and to stabilize East-West relations in Germany. Both sides realized that nuclear war would be a global catastrophe. Despite repeated Cold War disputes, these decades turned out the longest period of peace in the twentieth century.

The reconstruction of Europe outside the communist countries was an uncertain and contested undertaking in the early postwar years. The future was unknown. The promise of democratic socialism held the greatest attraction for the war-weary peoples. Functioning democratic institutions and public consensus on liberal political goals gradually became a part of daily life. The process, despite its complexity, proceeded remarkably well. By the 1960s, recovery was complete. Twenty years later, the major debates of public life dealt with the shortcomings of the postwar reforms and with the integration of Europe's nation-states into the European Union.

While Western nations improved the quality of life for their people with amazing speed, the entire communist system in the East endured with little change until the late 1980s. Then it suddenly collapsed. The fall of communism occurred with extraordinary swiftness. Weaknesses within the Soviet Union, hidden for decades from outside view, forced the leaders there to undertake risky reforms. The blind faith of some Soviet political and military leaders in the Stalinist system incited them to attempt to overthrow the reform government. They failed miserably, and their defeat discredited the old system so thoroughly that the Soviet Union fell apart in 1991. The Cold War disappeared along with the Stalinists and their state, leaving in its wake tens of thousands of useless but lethal nuclear weapons.

In eastern Europe, popular opposition to communism proved so massive that the entire satellite system vanished within a few months in 1989. The crucial first step came when the reformist leaders in the Soviet Union openly condemned the Stalinist system, which was still in place in the satellite countries. The profound desire among peoples in these countries to be freed from Soviet domination and communist rule quickly assumed the proportions of a popular uprising. The collapse of these regimes was revolutionary in its speed, and the scope of reform was breathtaking. New leaders introduced a democratic and capitalist order. The process bore little resemblance to earlier revolutions, for it occurred almost without violence. In a sense, it represented a return to the past, for the new central Europe resembled the nation-states put in place in 1919 by the Paris peace negotiators.

The Stalinist period left bitter memories of hardship and a legacy of political repression and destruction of natural resources. The term "totalitarianism" became popular there to condemn that hated past. Lenin, Stalin, and their followers had proclaimed that their communist system was a model for humanity. The liberal reformers wanted the world of the 1990s to know that communism was a bankrupt social experiment and a human tragedy.

EUROPEAN NATIONS AND EUROPEAN UNION

The peoples of western Europe had, first of any region of the world, acquired a strong awareness of their national identities. Their nation-states, and the nationalism that glorified these states and their peoples, became a model for other peoples in the twentieth century, for good and ill. Both the promise and the defects of nationalism had entered the fabric of European life. The solidarity that emerged within these national communities created enduring bonds of loyalty. The terrible world wars that had pitted nation against nation left no doubt how destructive nationalist fanaticism could be. These nations had created vast colonial empires, which to many Europeans had embodied the superiority of their civilization (and to some, on the contrary, demonstrated the arrogance of Western racism).

The end of the Second World War proved the turning point in their histories. They abandoned their empires to focus their energies on their countries' reconstruction and renewal. Their leaders agreed to cooperate in supranational institutions for the sake of economic development and, most important, to create indissoluble ties among previously warring states. Europe's governments sacrificed the principle of the absolute independence of their nation-states to overcome nationalist enmity. Their European Union was the outstanding achievement of Europe's postcolonial age.

Reconstruction and Welfare States

The destruction of Western Europe had appeared so serious and its consequences so threatening to the political stability of the West that the United States government had promised massive economic assistance for reconstruction in 1947 (see Chapter 2). The Marshall Plan was an extraordinary event, not only in the foreign relations of the United States, but in the relations of the European

Europe 1992

states among themselves and with their former wartime ally.

European governments had agreed to collaborate in making crucial decisions about how vast sums of aid were to be spent. The U.S. government set strict conditions on granting European states billions of dollars of aid (ultimately more than $13 billion). Most controversial was its requirement that all participating governments make public their economic needs and their financial condition. A European-wide committee, called the Commission on European Economic Cooperation (CEEC), united representatives of all the western European countries in administering the Marshall Plan aid. It decided on the priorities in recommending where U.S. aid was to go.

European integration was an alluring dream in those years. The Marshall Plan's approach to unification came with an immediate payoff.

The aid proved effective beyond the highest hopes of its planners. It proved vital both to the region's economic recovery, and to governments' ability to introduce sweeping social welfare reforms. By 1952 industrial production in western Europe, even in West Germany, had surpassed the prewar level. The ruins of war gradually disappeared, and food rationing finally came to an end. The future direction of Europe's economy was clearly marked out as well. The postwar international economy possessed effective mechanisms for trade and financial transactions. The Bretton Woods system (see Chapter 1) had created a set of institutions to insure that countries within the global free market could count on international assistance to keep trade flowing and to encourage them to work to lower trade barriers. The dollar became the principal currency of international exchange, backed by the strength of the U.S. economy.

The collaboration between the United States and western Europe insured that these countries would restore their market economies. European governments became more deeply involved in economic affairs, principally through nationalization of private companies and state forecast planning for economic development. But their economic and financial powers never extended to the elimination of the market economy. Its key criterion of success was productivity (the efficient use of resources as measured by output and price). That measure remained a fundamental reality in the economic reconstruction and development of Europe. Ultimately, the failure of nationalized industries to meet that test caused European governments to sell off completely or reduce drastically their nationalized enterprises in the 1980s.

European consumers found more and more goods available as production increased and wages rose. Employment remained at a very high level during the three decades after the war, and personal income increased rapidly along with the standard of living. By the 1960s, leisure became a reality in long weekends and yearly four-week paid vacations. Families traveled to inexpensive vacation resorts such as those created by the new "Club Mediterranee" company. The automobile became a purchase accessible to a majority of the population. The first "dream" car was a Cadillac, but later the German Mercedes-Benz cars claimed that honor. By the 1970s, living conditions in western Europe had improved so dramatically that they approached those in the United States, whose prosperity had been the envy earlier of all Europe. The hardships of depression and of wartime destruction became distant memories.

The social and economic reforms introduced in the postwar years succeeded remarkably well in overcoming divisions and in uniting the peoples of western Europe. The details of the reforms varied substantially from country to country, but at their core was the goal of guaranteeing to all the people a substantial measure of social welfare and security. Postwar socialist movements promised that state ownership would ensure employment and good wages. They, and other reform movements, came to believe deeply in the responsibility of the state to contribute to their people's basic social needs. These including inexpensive or free medical care, free and accessible higher education, and decent housing. They proposed to pay for these expensive programs by high taxes on the well-to-do and on private enterprises. Extremes of wealth and poverty among the population appeared to them a social injustice. In this sense, all hoped to promote some type of "social democracy" among their people.

These reforms became imbedded in European life. From Italy to Sweden, from Great Britain to West Germany, social welfare and direct state involvement in crucial economic activities was a major concern of all governments, whether conservative or liberal. By the 1980s, the most important political issues in western European countries focused on correcting shortcomings in the welfare state. No one seriously proposed abolishing the entire system and returning to conditions of the early century.

Weaknesses in the socialist system did lead to calls for remedies. These problems included a high rate of inflation fueled by labor union pressure for yearly wage increases, inefficient nationalized enterprises that required state subsidies to remain in operation, and serious budget deficits (which contributed to inflation) and high taxes caused by the growing cost of paying for extensive welfare programs. The solutions adopted in European countries varied widely, but in every case they entailed restrictions of the scope of state support for social services and the sale (privatization) of state-owned enterprises to private owners. The poor and laboring populations lost some of their benefits, but even sizeable numbers of workers voted for parties that proposed reducing the responsibilities of the welfare state. The "father-state," as the Germans called it, no longer appeared the sole or supreme guarantor of the country's welfare.

The most severe cutbacks to the welfare system and to nationalization occurred in Great Britain. There the Labor Party's postwar reforms had gone furthest toward curtailing the market economy and extending generous financial assistance to working people. In 1979, the Conservative Party under the leadership of Margaret Thatcher decisively defeated the Labor Party in elections whose major issue was the welfare state. Thatcher's program constituted a comprehensive rejection of state management of economic affairs and a wholesale reduction of welfare programs. What came to be known as "Thatcherism" entailed the privatization of almost all nationalized enterprises, the reduction by one half of state payments for various social welfare programs, and the lowering of taxes. Thatcher's principal goal was a productive economy. Welfare was a secondary consideration.

In these terms, the program was a success. By the early 1990s, the economy was booming, inflation ended, unemployment drastically reduced, and the standard of living rose. But even the "Iron Lady," as Thatcher came to be known among friends and enemies, could not eliminate the welfare programs entirely. When she suggested ending free public health care, the popular opposition was so great she had to abandon her plans. The postwar vision of a safety net insuring the basic needs of the population had become a permanent part of the people's expectations in all European states.

The United States joined in the move toward comprehensive welfare programs and greater state supervision of economic affairs in the 1960s. The election in 1960 of John F. Kennedy to the U.S. presidency began a period of extensive social and political reforms, carried on by Lyndon Johnson after Kennedy's assassination in 1963. The "Great Society," as Johnson named his 1964 reform platform, included new laws to protect the civil and political rights of all citizens. The goal was an end to the century-long segregation and oppression of blacks. Reforms also brought new welfare policies for a "war on poverty," in spirit and intent resembling the social welfare measures introduced in Europe after the Second World War. No private enterprises were nationalized. Still, the government's yearly budget, and the controls over banking and interest rates exercised by a federal agency (the Federal Reserve Board) guided the country's economy in a manner inspired by the ideas of John Maynard Keynes. Later, conservative political leaders, echoing arguments in Europe, questioned the high rate of taxes and expensive social welfare programs. In the United States, as in Great Britain, a majority of the voters in the 1980s appeared more concerned with the success of a productive market economy than with state promises of social justice and less economic inequality.

Western Europe's Recovery

The division of Germany was the last great unresolved problem left by the war. The decision of the Western Allies to proceed with the reconstruction of their zones of West Germany had confirmed the partition of Germany between communist and noncommunist regions. It set the western part on a path of recovery that ultimately integrated Germany into the European community. German voters in this Federal Republic of Germany voted in the two decades after independence for the conservative Christian Democratic Party, under the leadership of Konrad Adenauer. His priorities lay in erasing the poverty in which Germans lived at war's end through intensive reconstruction of the country's industrial economy. His formula for recovery proved successful.

By the 1960s, the country's industrial economy was the most prosperous of Europe. Its population, swollen by the influx of more than ten million refugees from eastern Europe, was still not able to meet the economy's need for workers. Migrants arrived to fill these jobs from poor lands in southern Europe, especially Yugoslavia, and from Turkey. Like migrants to Europe's other prosperous countries, they lived as second-class citizens. They enjoyed economic and social benefits, including access to the welfare system, but were excluded from active political participation (in Germany, they were denied the right to citizenship). Countries like West Germany were becoming multi-ethnic and multi-religious, for their prosperity was bringing Third World peoples within their borders.

Adenauer refused to accept the division of Germany between the communist east (the German Democratic Republic) and the democratic west. He remained committed to the reunification of his country. This could come only with the collapse of the communist dictatorship in East Germany. West Germany's democratic regime and its flourishing economy diverged increasingly from the drab conditions in the east. West Berlin, built up as a beacon of prosperity under continued Allied military occupation, turned into a magnet drawing easterners. Young East Germans took advantage of the open border between East and West Berlin to migrate to West Germany. There they were welcomed as refugees and helped to create

new lives in the Federal Republic. Their migration soon became a flood; by 1961, more than three million refugees had abandoned the communist East to make a new life in West Germany.

The Adenauer government had no way of ending the partition, however. It was a helpless observer in 1961 when the East German government, backed by Soviet tanks, constructed a wall around West Berlin. The refugee flow was cut off, except for the handful of daring individuals who attempted to break through the barrier. Most were shot down by communist border guards. West German television broadcasts kept alive enticing images in the east of western prosperity and the hope among viewers that their lives might somehow, sometime, change for the better.

In 1969, a new West German government decided to recognize the partition. It was headed by the Social Democratic Party, which had once been a strong defender of Marxist socialism. German prosperity and its electoral weakness forced it to renounce this program. Its new goals emphasized expanded social welfare policies, and improved relations with the communist countries. The Social Democratic government put this "eastern policy" in motion immediately. It signed a treaty recognizing East Germany and another with Poland renouncing any claim to the German lands annexed after World War II by Poland. Through a number of separate agreements a kind of informal German peace treaty emerged, confirming the division of the German nation into two states. The former Allies regarded the partition of Germany and Berlin as a permanent part of the new European international system. They foresaw no alternative for peaceful relations between East and West. Eastern Europe remained within the Soviet empire, its peoples ruled by communist dictatorships.

On the southern fringes of the continent, however, authoritarian rule gave way in Greece, Spain, and Portugal to democratic political systems in the 1970s. Political upheavals in each land brought about the abrupt transition. All three were countries where many people and clandestine political movements had kept faith in human rights through the years of repression. They found in western Europe's successful democratic experience the justification for their liberal faith. In material terms, democratic government appeared to assure the people substantial benefits. This was evident to Greek, Spanish, and Portuguese migrants who went in increasing numbers seeking work in the booming northern economies.

In Spain, the political transition occurred with remarkable speed. In 1975, General Franco, dictator since his victory in 1939 in the Spanish Civil War, died and was replaced at his request by the heir to the former Spanish monarchy. Faced with widespread opposition to continued dictatorship, King Juan Carlos immediately ordered elections to prepare a new constitution. In 1977, he ceded his executive power to the newly elected government. Spain became a constitutional, parliamentary monarchy. Despite protest from a handful of Franco's supporters, the new regime established effective rule in the country within a few years. Similar pressures from the people and from European states brought the end to the dictatorships in Greece and Portugal in those same years. Only the eastern European countries remained frozen in their Soviet-imposed and enforced communist regimes.

Western European Unification

In those years of recovery and renewal, Europe's leaders agreed to begin the process of European unification. To do so, they had to curtail the scope of national sovereignty on which their nation-states had been founded. One hundred years earlier the region had been the heartland of nationalism. The agonies of two wars had revealed just how destructive were the hatred and intolerance incited by extreme nationalism. Europeans searching for a stable peace realized that bonds had to be forged among nation-states and that a federation of European states might undo the

damage that ethnic and nationalist conflict had caused. They realized that political unification had to overcome the deeply felt sense of national loyalty among European peoples. The most serious hurdle was the abiding hatred for Germans still shared by many Europeans.

The experience of collaborating in the distribution of Marshall Plan aid demonstrated that economic cooperation was feasible. The first serious proposal for unification came from the French leader Jean Monnet. A former banker, he made his mark in postwar France as the head of the state's economic planning commission. He grasped the simple truth that a unified Europe could be reached only by stages. He concluded that economic unification was the first practical step in that direction. He proposed in 1950 the formation among Europe's democratic lands of a tariff-free "common market" for iron, steel, and coal. It required that western European states agree to abolish all tariffs among themselves on trade in those products. They would create a supranational commission, that is, a governing body whose policies no member state could veto, to coordinate production and wage plans among the enterprises in these key economic sectors.

The European Coal and Steel Community (ECSC) became a reality in 1952. Six states in Western Europe—Italy, West Germany, France, and the Benelux countries of Belgium, the Netherlands, and Luxembourg—signed the treaty creating the ECSC. This unprecedented agreement emerged out of discussions among the political leaders of Italy, Germany, and France, all of whom belonged to Christian Democratic parties. Their commitment to a Christian concept of peace and humanitarian values created a shared ideal for reconciliation among nations and, in particular, for the reintegration of Germany within Europe. The specific agreement that they reached was a practical, not an ideological undertaking. It sought new ways to speed the recovery of their economies. The Labor government of Great Britain refused to join, clinging to the dream of

British "splendid isolation" and suspicious of the important role that business interests would play in the Community. Although political unification remained a distant dream, the Coal and Steel Community was a historic event in the relations among European nations. It was a first step toward integrating Germany into an association of western countries.

In the next years, its success was measured by pragmatic decisions of the ECSC commission to implement the treaty. Tariffs on coal and steel shipments among the member states quickly disappeared. Managers of nationalized and private mines and factories agreed, sometimes very reluctantly, to its orders for levels of production. It even closed unproductive mines. This was a very unpopular move but came along with assurances to the unemployed miners of long-term retraining benefits. The ECSC proved that economic integration was possible.

Then Monnet proposed a far more radical reform to create an economic union of western Europe. He proposed that a "common market" unite the member states in free trade for all industrial, commercial, and agricultural transactions. Thanks to the success of the ECSC, agreement came quickly. In the mid-1950s, the six governments in the Coal and Steel Community, led by France and West Germany, accepted his plan for a European Economic Community (EEC). It began operations in 1958. The shift to a free-trade area was complex, for it entailed the dismantling of tariffs on trade among these states, the coordination of subsidies to disadvantaged manufacturers and aid to the unemployed, and the formation of a unified financial market. It represented a momentous step toward Monnet's dream of a politically united Europe.

The barriers on commerce declined dramatically and far more quickly than the treaty signers had expected. By the mid-1960s, western Europe had begun a new era of economic collaboration. The Common Market operated on the basis of market competition, whether conducted by private or state-owned enterprises, by small farmers or agribusiness. All the political parties (except the communists) in western Europe agreed on the desirability of economic unification. Nationalism remained a potent political force, especially when Charles de Gaulle became President of France. He did not reject the EEC, but looked to a "Europe of Nations" (led by himself), not to a "United States of Europe." Still, he was the exception; once he had withdrawn from French politics, his country became a cooperative member once again, ending its opposition to Great Britain's entry into the Common Market. Common interests, and a shared vision of future collaboration insured that the participating states never again would claim full sovereign powers in the area of trade. The Common Market was truly supranational.

The prosperity of the EEC countries guaranteed that its influence would grow. The U.S. government acknowledged its new role in the global economy. In 1963, it signed with the EEC a comprehensive treaty lowering tariffs. Freer trade between Europe and America benefitted businesses on both continents. It also reinforced the economic and financial ties among the western democratic nations. The economic integration of Europe accelerated with the addition in the 1970s and 1980s of important members including Spain, Denmark, Greece, Great Britain, and Ireland. By the late 1980s, the total population of the EEC countries reached 300 million. At the time, it was the single most populous free-trade region in the world.

The vision among Europeans of closer unification led to renewed efforts to strengthen their economic ties in the early 1990s. A new treaty of unification, put into effect in 1994, renamed the group of states the European Union (EU). Its most ambitious objective was the creation of a single currency for the entire region. To achieve this, governments had to lower inflation rates and balance their budgets, possible only if they curtailed expenditures on social welfare. This new Europe did not attempt to eliminate social inequality, though it did redistribute financial resources from wealthier to poorer member states.

Not all European Union countries agreed immediately to the monetary union. Great Britain, clinging still to shreds of its traditional splendid isolation, refused to join, as did other smaller states. Pushed by German leaders, the major continental states proceeded to meet all the conditions for a common currency. For them, financial unity was worth abandoning their own currencies and coordinating fiscal policies. On January 1, 1999, a single European Union currency, called the euro, went into use.

The vision of a politically united Europe remained unfulfilled. Institutions for political collaboration were in place, including an elected European parliament, but they possessed no sovereign powers. Still, the Union exerted a powerful attraction on surrounding peoples, including the communist countries and even the Muslim land of Turkey. The momentum toward integration was slow, but irreversible.

The borders of this new Europe stopped at the Iron Curtain. The Cold War's division of the continent menaced European recovery, keeping alive fears of another world war in which Europe would be at the center. In an effort to establish principles for a stable peace between East and West, Western states invited representatives of the communist lands to Helsinki, Finland, in 1975. The negotiators from the East were eager for agreement on the permanence of the new borders of European states, especially those of the Soviet Union and Poland. The western diplomats hoped in exchange for acknowledgment from the communist countries that human rights (civil and political liberties) constituted the only stable and just basis for government.

The communist regimes had never recognized individual freedom to be a necessary or desirable objective. But for the sake of assurance of permanent state borders, they allowed this cornerstone of democracy to be included in the final Helsinki Agreement. The signers agreed to renounce the

"threat or use of force" to settle international disputes, and committed their states to respect "fundamental freedoms, including the freedom of thought, conscience, religion, and belief." It seemed at the time an illusory promise that the eastern governments would disregard.

In the next decade, the human rights provisions remained a dead letter in the Soviet-dominated countries. But when the communist regimes vanished at the end of the 1980s, the Agreement laid out the basic conditions on which eastern Europe could be reintegrated politically into the rest of the Continent. And in the background was the prosperous European Union. What the last Soviet leader, Mikhail Gorbachev, called the "common house of Europe" had found a new, firm basis for a peaceful future.

THE SOVIET UNION AND THE COLD WAR

The Cold War began in the late 1940s. It ended forty years later. Its origins lay in the expansion of the Soviet Union into central Europe at the close of the Second World War, and in Western fears of Stalinism. It disappeared when the communist regimes of Europe and the Soviet Union collapsed. Its focal point had been the city of Berlin, divided into Soviet and Western zones of occupation. It combined power politics and profound ideological differences. This potent blend made compromise and agreement extremely difficult. It posed the gravest threat to civilization in the history of modern states.

The nuclear arms race between the Soviet Union and the United States kept alive the likelihood of nuclear war on a global scale. Each side came to recognize the terrible consequences that use of these weapons would have on their peoples, yet continued to perfect ever more deadly weapons in the expectation that failure to do so would jeopardize its security. The Soviet and Western troops stationed in their separate zones of Berlin were hostages to the war plans devised by each superpower to prepare for an unthinkable nuclear war.

The Soviet Empire

Stalin's death in 1953 ended his brutal rule, but not the communist dictatorship that he had put in place in the Soviet Union and in eastern Europe. His heirs, a handful of men in the Communist Party's Politburo (then called the Presidium), reverted to the methods of collective party rule that Lenin had created. They vied among themselves for leadership of the country until, in 1955, Nikita Khrushchev managed to take control of the party and state.

For the next decade, Soviet foreign and domestic policies were shaped by the policies and institutions in place since the 1920s, and by the personality and aims of the new Soviet leader. Born in a poor peasant family, Khrushchev rose through the ranks of the Communist Party in Stalin's years to become a member of the leadership group around the dictator. He, like his colleagues in the Presidium, never doubted the fundamental truths of Marxism-Leninism, namely, the historical superiority of their command economy and egalitarian social system, the inevitable collapse of capitalism and the global triumph of Soviet socialism, and the necessity for communist dictatorship. Their attitudes and methods of rule were formed in the harsh world of Stalin's personal dictatorship. This political culture nurtured in them a suspicious, antagonistic view of the West. It sustained their dogmatic conviction that they knew what was best for the Soviet people and for the "socialist camp" of satellite countries.

They broke with the Stalinist system on one crucial issue. The entire party leadership understood that they had to end Stalin's terrorist methods of rule. The enormous power of the secret police threatened their own political dominance and violated the Leninist system of single-party rule. They proceeded to remove from office and to execute for "crimes against the people" the head of the secret police, Lavrenti Beria. The laws authorizing terror were abolished, and thousands of Stalin's victims were released from jail or prison camps. This quiet "destalinization" did not proceed fast enough for Khrushchev. In early 1956, he publicly denounced Stalin's crimes and the "cult of the personality" that had surrounded the dictator with an aura of infallibility. Soviet citizens opposed to all forms of Stalinism took heart when they heard of his speech. Peoples in eastern Europe looked forward to an end of the Stalinist sphere of domination over their lands.

In fact, the Soviet leaders had not renounced the use of repressive measures when needed to protect their system. They kept the secret police, now called the Committee of State Security, or KGB, to suppress political dissent and religious practices. They still authorized the state censorship committee to enforce the monopoly on truth of Marxism-Leninism. They were determined to keep intact the "socialist camp," by force if necessary.

Khrushchev himself remained in power only as long as the collective party leadership was in fundamental agreement with his policies. He undertook a series of economic and social reforms to improve the poor living conditions of the Soviet people. In 1961, he even promised them that they would live in conditions of abundance within a few years. His vision of "communism in our generation" took the shape of a grandiose welfare state, offering its inhabitants free housing, schooling, transportation, and health care. To him, a communist society (the highest stage of history, according to Marx) meant egalitarian living conditions for all guaranteed by state programs in support of collective consumption. The Western individualistic consumer society of private cars, stereos, blue jeans, and rock-and-roll music embodied the evils of corrupt capitalism. He was equally opposed to the privileges that the communist elite of his country had come to enjoy. He blamed officials in the state and even in his own

Nikita Khrushchev, 1960 (*Patty Ratliff Collection/Hoover Institution*)

party for the corruption spreading through the country. He dreamed of reviving the revolutionary zealotry of Lenin's years. In a real sense he was the last communist dreamer of the Soviet regime. But when he attempted to end their comfortable, secure positions of power, they turned against him.

His colleagues were not prepared to let him undermine the privileges that they enjoyed or the stability of their one-party dictatorship. Khrushchev failed in his efforts to end the abuses of bureaucratism. He could not understand that bureaucratic institutions constituted the essential mechanism by which the party retained its strict controls over political power, productive property, and public culture and information. Critics called this system "USSR Inc." Even his own colleagues in the Presidium finally turned against him, voting

in 1964 to send him into early retirement. They undid many of his reforms and ended public denunciations of Stalin's crimes. Dogmatic in their ideological views and fearful of reform, they kept tight control over the population, the vast state-run economy, and the Soviet empire. This modified Stalinist system remained in place for another twenty years until, too late, another party reformer attempted to remedy its grave defects.

In those years, the Soviet leadership's confidence in this system was bolstered by its popularity in other parts of the world. Khrushchev and his successors looked upon the Third World as an arena where capitalism and socialism contended for dominance. Their Marxist-Leninist convictions assured them that their side would win. In the short term they were prepared (as Stalin had not been) to provide economic assistance to non-communist regimes in Asia, Africa, and Latin America that were sympathetic to their socialist ideals. They did require that these countries be "non-aligned" in the Cold War conflict, that is, not become allies of the United States.

They found a sympathetic audience among Third World leaders around the world. In late 1959 Cuba's new revolutionary leader, Fidel Castro, found a warm welcome when he appealed to Moscow to help his new government construct socialism in Cuba. In Africa, socialist-led regimes in Angola in the west, and Ethiopia in the east, obtained in the 1970s not only Soviet aid but assistance from Cuban armed forces in defeating their internal enemies (who themselves received help from the U.S. and its allies). When, in 1977, a group of Afghan Communists seized power in their country, Soviet economic assistance came immediately.

The balance of power was in those years as much a concern of Soviet as of U.S. leaders. Their new global policy sought to swing the world's balance in their favor. Soviet intermediate-range missiles reached Cuba in 1962, primarily because Khrushchev judged Soviet strategic interests would benefit. The arms race occupied an important place in this new Soviet world policy. Power politics had become more than ever a part of the Cold War.

Unrest in the Soviet Empire

Khrushchev and his successors were resolved to keep the communist regimes of eastern Europe in power. They recognized the urgency of ending the terrorist system of rule and the policies of economic exploitation that Stalin had put in place there. They altered the terms of trade between the Soviet Union and the satellite countries to allow improvements in the peoples' miserable living conditions. They made concessions to the deep-seated longing of these peoples (as well as Soviet peoples) to develop the cultural and historical traditions of their nations. But they were prepared to use military force to prevent these countries from freeing themselves from Soviet domination.

In 1956, Soviet leaders acted quickly and forcefully to quell revolution in Hungary. Late that year illegal demonstrations by Hungarian students and workers, protesting political and economic oppression, quickly turned into a mass uprising against Stalinism. Hungarian reformers, supported by the entire population, announced their intent to end the communist dictatorship and break their military ties with the Soviet Union. They took their inspiration from Khrushchev's denunciation of Stalin, who had imposed Soviet rule in their land. The Hungarian army joined the protesters and reform Communists took over the government. Destruction of a giant forty-foot statue of Stalin in the middle of the capital Budapest revealed the depths of hatred toward the Soviet dictator and his satellite system. The uprising was successful in bringing to power an independent government. It introduced reforms to restore civil and political liberties, and declared their intention to make Hungary a free, neutral state.

Its plans clashed with Soviet insistence on military control in eastern Europe and on the preservation of communist dictatorship. Khrushchev did not permit desertion from the "socialist camp." A week after the uprising began, Soviet troops invaded the country. They crushed the rebellion and put in power Communists loyal to the Soviet Union. Hungarians lost their chance for national independence, but not their hostility to communist rule.

Europe's most dangerous and visible border divided the communist and noncommunist countries into two enemy camps. That line ran through the middle of Germany. To the east, fifteen million Germans in the German Democratic Republic were under communist rule. The discontent of East Germans at their political and economic plight was evident in the flight of hundreds of thousands of refugees to West Germany each year. The drain on the economy of the Soviet satellite was so damaging that Soviet leaders had to take forceful action or see the East German population literally slip away. Their ultimate objective was the withdrawal of the Western powers from West Berlin, which would fall under East German control. But the West refused to make any concessions.

In 1961, Khrushchev took the risk of a major international crisis and possibly war by allowing the East German regime to build an impenetrable physical barrier around West Berlin. Suddenly that August, East German workers protected by Soviet troops encircled West Berlin with concrete walls topped by barbed wire and guarded by East German border troops. The "Iron Curtain" had descended on the last small opening between east and west. The U.S. government preferred not to challenge the Soviet action for fear of provoking a military confrontation. Europe remained divided between Soviet and Western military alliances, between communist and democratic states. The Berlin Wall became, to many Europeans, the symbol of the failure of postwar peacemaking.

In the two decades that followed, Soviet leaders sent their armed forces twice more to countries where popular resistance threatened the power of communist governments. In Czechoslovakia, the Communist Party was in 1968 powerless to stem a popular movement, led by labor unions, intellectuals, and reform Communists, opposed to the Soviet-style dictatorship and command economy. Czech reformers hoped for Soviet acceptance of their reforms. They promised continued allegiance to the Soviet military alliance. But the Soviet leaders feared that their eastern European empire was a risk if communist rule disappeared there. In August of that year, their military forces occupied the country and forced upon the Czechs a compliant government of Moscow's own choosing. Shortly afterward, the Soviet leader, Leonid Brezhnev, defended in principle what Red Army troops had already put into practice. His "Brezhnev Doctrine" asserted the right of the Soviet Union to intervene in the affairs of any allied state in the "socialist camp" in need of assistance to maintain communist rule.

In 1979, Brezhnev applied the doctrine once again when he ordered Soviet troops into Afghanistan to support the feeble new communist regime. Afghan Communists, in control of the government for only two years, had already antagonized the peoples of that Inner Asian land with their radical reforms. The population was deeply attached to tribal ways and Muslim traditions. Guerrilla forces, called "mujahaddin," found vital help from neighboring Pakistan. Resistance to the communist regime quickly threatened to overwhelm its meager forces. The Soviet government refused to let the new state collapse. It sent nearly 100,000 troops to fight the Afghan rebels. The latter obtained potent military assistance from the United States, where the government feared (incorrectly, as we now know) that the Soviet Union sought to turn Afghanistan into a strategic base for expansion into South Asia. Once a remote Asian borderland, Afghanistan became a hot spot in the Cold War.

The weakness of communist satellite governments was most apparent in Poland. Opposition to the Polish Communist Party came from intellectuals, workers, and the powerful Catholic Church. Polish national unity had emerged out of centuries of foreign domination. The state of Poland had vanished during the war years of Nazi occupation. Liberation by the Soviet Red Army in 1944 had restored the nation-state, but it had fallen immediately under communist rule. The Polish people were as hostile as other eastern European nations to Soviet-dominated regime. Their Catholicism remained the core of their nationalist solidarity. Its influence grew when, in 1978, a Polish priest was elected to the highest position in the Catholic Church, taking the name of Pope John Paul II. His voice added international backing to Polish resistance to communism.

In 1980, underground opposition came into the open when Polish workers throughout the country

Soviet Poster Attacking Afghan Anti-Communist Guerillas and U.S., 1985 (*Poster Collection/ Hoover Institution*)

joined a general strike to protest their lack of freedom and harsh living conditions. The Pope publicly applauded their massive, peaceful rebellion. They created a nationwide free labor movement, called Solidarity. The Polish Communist Party lost all authority. Solidarity commanded the respect of the people. The Soviet Union's leaders threatened military intervention to end Solidarity's rule. They found allies in Polish generals, who were fearful of a Soviet invasion and were prepared to use their own troops to end that brief moment of political freedom. General Jaruzelski, in command of the army, declared martial law, outlawed Solidarity, arrested many of its supporters, and ruled the country as a military dictator.

Soviet control of the eastern European states remained intact until the late 1980s. Moscow's orders were executed by obedient leaders, whose rule rested in last resort on the menace of Soviet repression. Eastern Europe appeared firmly within the Soviet empire.

The Cold War and the Arms Race

After the Second World War, Soviet domination of the satellite countries and Stalinist dictatorship had provoked among Western governments and their peoples a widespread fear of Soviet expansionism (see Chapter 2). Gradually, U.S. containment policies had shifted toward military alliances throughout the world. The most important of these was the North Atlantic Treaty Organization (NATO), uniting North America and western Europe. To containment the U.S. government added a policy of nuclear deterrence, that is, the development of armaments so devastating that Soviet leaders would never consider launching an offensive war against the West. U.S. military forces possessed by the mid-1950s both atomic and hydrogen bombs. Technological advances gave them ever more effective and expensive means of destroying the Soviet Union.

By the end of the 1950s the U.S. armed forces commanders had put in operation their key strategic weapons. They relied on three methods of launching nuclear bombs on Soviet targets, one from supersonic bombers stationed on airfields around the globe; a second from nuclear-powered submarines, equipped with ballistic missiles, that patrolled the Soviet coastlines; and a third from land-based intercontinental ballistic missiles (ICBM) in the United States capable of striking any region of the Soviet Union. Their "triad" of armaments was crucial to their policy of deterring a Soviet attack in Europe or Asia. Seeking to maintain military superiority over their enemy, their strategy was a spur to the escalating arms race.

After Stalin's death, Soviet leaders continued his development of modern armaments. Their nuclear scientists and engineers proved as capable as U.S. specialists in mastering the skills needed to produce the most powerful bombs ever created. They too realized that these weapons were so devastating that nuclear war was inconceivable. Still, they were convinced that their country's security and influence in the world depended upon matching the military might of the United States. Khrushchev announced in 1956 that, contrary to Stalin's grim forecast, war with the capitalist states was not inevitable. His (relative) optimism was based on the argument, identical to that of U.S. leaders, that his country's military advances held in check the Cold War rival.

His claim to strength included a recognition of the terrible consequences of modern war. In 1953 Soviet scientists had exploded their first hydrogen (thermonuclear) bomb. In 1957, they launched into space the first satellite, which they called "Sputnik" (meaning "little traveler"). The exploit dramatically confirmed Soviet technological skill. It also demonstrated that their military scientists had developed long-range ballistic missiles (rockets capable of carrying nuclear weapons at distances

of several thousand miles). In the mid-1960s, the Soviet military forces expanded still further to include for the first time a multi-ocean navy. It possessed nuclear submarines capable of launching ballistic missiles on distant targets. The United States and the Soviet Union by then each had the awesome capacity to destroy the other country many times over.

Each in their own way, Soviet and U.S. leaders understood that the nuclear arms race had no winners, only losers. The cost of the weapons buildup was terribly high, especially for the Soviet economy. The U.S. spent 5 percent of its yearly national income on defense expenditures, while the Soviet economy, less than half as wealthy as the United States, had to commit 20 to 25 percent of its output to its military program. Secret cities in the Soviet Union were entirely devoted to weapons development. This financial burden, and the realization that the arms rivalry worsened relations and heightened the risk of war, gradually made leaders on both sides look to some means of finding limits to the arms race.

Before that happened, however, they confronted for a few critical days the likelihood of nuclear war. The Cuban missile crisis of 1962 had its roots in Castro's revolution and U. S. opposition to Cuban communism (see Chapter 5). Castro's pleas to Soviet leaders for military protection brought help, though not in the shape of a military alliance. In the spring of 1962, Khrushchev proposed stationing a complete Soviet missile division on Cuban soil. It would be so close to the United States that its intermediate-range ballistic missiles could strike any part of the United States. The reasons for his reckless offer are still not clear. His own commander of rocket forces opposed the action. The most likely explanation is that he anticipated from this move an enormous boost to Soviet global power and influence. He did not allow the Cubans to control the nuclear weapons on their soil. This foreign initiative was strictly a Soviet undertaking.

When the U.S. government discovered the missile installations in Cuba that fall, it demanded

The Arms Race on Parade: November 7th Celebration in Red Square, Moscow, Approximately 1965 (*Patty Ratliff Collection/Hoover Institution*)

their immediate withdrawal. President Kennedy and his advisers all agreed (as did the U.S. allies in Europe) that this Soviet move would represent a devastating diplomatic and political defeat for the West. The Cold War had its own peculiar logic of victory and defeat, measured by the relative diplomatic and military power of each side. Kennedy's advisers disagreed on the proper response. Decisive action was vital, and some U.S. military and political leaders argued that it had to begin with the invasion of Cuba. If the Soviet forces responded with nuclear weapons, or Soviet troops invaded West Berlin in retaliation, war was a certainty. Kennedy put off the invasion, preferring to use a naval blockade of Cuba to stop

further Soviet ships reaching Cuba while leaving the opportunity for negotiation open for a few days. His caution was rewarded.

With only a day left before the U.S. invasion of Cuba was to begin, Khrushchev accepted the compromise solution worked out in secret between U.S. and Soviet leaders. He agreed to withdraw his missiles from Cuba in exchange for a public commitment by the U.S. president not to authorize an invasion of the island. As important to the compromise was Kennedy's secret agreement to withdraw U.S. intermediate-range ballistic missiles from Turkey. Both leaders spoke in private of their overriding resolve to avoid nuclear war. In the language of the time, nuclear

End of the Cuban Missile Crisis: U.S. Destroyer Inspecting Soviet Freighter Carrying Soviet Missiles Back to USSR, November 10, 1962 (*UPI/Corbis-Bettmann*)

deterrence pushed both sides to settle the conflict peacefully.

That dangerous encounter demonstrated the urgency to find some common grounds for negotiations to rein in the nuclear arms race. The nuclear arsenals of both superpowers were in the service of their foreign policies, which they defined in terms of both national interests and political ideals. The achievement of international arms controls required that each side put aside their ideological differences to confront directly essential strategic issues. President Nixon's security adviser (later secretary of state) Henry Kissinger made this clear when in 1969 he affirmed that "we have no permanent enemies. We will judge other countries, including communist countries, on the basis of their actions and not on the basis of their domestic ideology."

The readiness of both sides to view their conflicts around the world more from the perspective of state interests and less in ideological terms made possible negotiations to separate arms issues from Cold War rivalries. In this perspective, global competition did not require the endless development of ever more powerful weapons of war. These understandings came after each side accepted the necessary, but illogical idea that these weapons were of use solely to prevent the other side from beginning, or threatening to begin, a war.

In conditions of mutual suspicion and competition, this elementary truth was the only possible basis for agreement. The two superpowers acknowledged that each state needed sufficient offensive nuclear weapons to deter an attack, that is, to be able to defend itself by destroying the aggressor. Each side could guarantee its acceptance of the policy of deterrence by agreeing not to build defensive nuclear weapons (in other words, leaving its people defenseless against the other side's weapons). In the conditions of the Cold War, this became the fundamental definition of peace, appropriately labeled by one American leader "MAD" (Mutually Assured Destruction). It was the key to the success of the first major Soviet-American nuclear arms treaty.

The first Strategic Arms Limitation Treaty (SALT I) was signed in 1972. In it, the Soviet and American governments agreed not to develop or deploy defensive (anti-ballistic missile) systems. Those defensive missiles that they had begun to install had to be destroyed. Inspection of each side's fulfillment of the treaty was insured by the use of U.S. and Soviet military surveillance satellites, constantly stationed over the other country. The agreement ended one part of the nuclear arms race. Deterrence became the cornerstone of peaceful relations between the Soviet Union and the United States.

The treaty remained incomplete, however. It failed to restrict the development of new offensive nuclear weapons. Scientists on both sides were, in the peculiar language of the arms race, constantly "modernizing" their country's nuclear arsenals. Their work in itself helped to sustain the arms race. To slow this dangerous process, Soviet and U.S. negotiators finally signed in 1979 another arms treaty (SALT II). It limited the numbers of certain offensive weapons, principally intercontinental ballistic missiles and submarine-launched missiles. The arms race had not stopped, but the leaders of the superpowers had at least been able to place certain limits on their nuclear arsenals. In doing so they recognized that their awesome military power could at best maintain between their two states what one American official called "an enduring strategic stalemate."

Good relations between the Soviet Union and the United States remained dangerously vulnerable to local conflicts, new armaments, and political rivalries. In 1981, the new U.S. president, Ronald Reagan, launched an armaments program more extensive (and vastly more expensive) than the programs begun in the early 1950s. The United States introduced a deadly new generation of missiles that could strike a target a few yards square at a distance of hundreds of miles. It deployed as well another type of missile, equipped with a secret global positioning radar system, that permitted it to hug the curvature of the terrain and to avoid Soviet radar defenses. In a search for the ultimate defense (and potentially in violation of SALT I), President Reagan authorized a program to create a supposedly impenetrable shield in outer space over the United States. It was to be made of defensive space weapons, including giant laser beams, against incoming (Soviet) ballistic missiles. The United States poured billions of dollars into the so-called Star Wars program. Reagan's armaments initiative undermined the armaments treaties and led the Soviet government in turn to accelerate development of its own missile weapons. The arms race was a tragic reminder of the superpowers' failure to bring peace to the postwar world.

HIGHLIGHT: The Cold War in Outer Space

The dream of exploring space first inspired novelists and visionary scientists. At the time when explorers were completing the mapping of the last unknown regions of the world, the French novelist Jules Verne laid out in his 1865 story *From the Earth to the Moon* a fantastic tale of human space travel and exploration of the moon. One hundred years later, this dream was reality. It was the product of the competition between the Soviet Union and the United States for military might and global prestige. The Cold War penetrated even outer space.

It reached that far initially when rockets became a reliable means to transport nuclear weapons to any point in the globe. Military rockets had first appeared in the German arsenal during the last months of the Second World War. The threat that this weapon posed at the time was not great, since the German research into nuclear weapons had led nowhere and Allied armies were rapidly advancing on Germany. The U.S. and the Soviet governments were both aware of the enormous military potential of this German technology.

U.S. Army forces, the first to reach the German rocket center, seized all the German V-2 rockets. The German space scientists had fled, but soon surrendered to U.S. authorities. Brought back to the United States, this live "war booty" became the founders of the new U.S. rocket program. Extremely expensive, it proceeded slowly for the next ten years. Air Force visionaries were more interested in experimenting with manned flights by rocket-powered aircraft (the "X" series) capable of attaining speeds that would carry them into space, and ultimately would permit them to orbit the earth.

Soviet rocket developments in the late 1950s altered the U.S. space program's pace and direction. The Soviet military had an urgent need for missiles to carry their nuclear weapons, since they lacked adequate long-range bombers like those in the U.S. Strategic Air Command. Stalin himself had given the Soviet program highest priority at war's end. He had personally ordered the release of the country's outstanding rocket engineer, Sergei Korolev, from the prison laboratory where he had been serving a twenty-five-year sentence for "counterrevolutionary activities." Working in absolute secrecy, Korolev proved one of the most inventive and successful scientists working for the Soviet military. His achievements were comparable only to those of physicist Andrei Sakharov, who was responsible for developing the Soviet hydrogen bomb (see "Spotlight," this chapter). By the mid-1950s, Korolev and his research team had tested long-range liquid-fuel rockets capable of carrying a cargo into space. If that cargo were a nuclear weapon, it could attain any region in the United States in the space of an hour. The intercontinental ballistic missile was a devastatingly effective new weapon of war.

It appeared to Nikita Khrushchev a dramatic means to demonstrate the great accomplishments of the Soviet socialist system to the whole world. At his orders, the first public demonstration of Korolev's rockets came in the form of a small metal ball, containing a tiny radio. In the fall of 1957, Korolev used his new rocket to launch into orbit around the earth the very first artificial satellite, named "Sputnik." It attracted enormous attention, all to the benefit of the Soviet Union. It marked the real beginning of the Space Age. It also set the Cold War on a whole new direction.

The U.S. military program for missiles had also developed powerful rockets. It still had nothing that could rival Korolev's inventions. Accused in 1957 by members of Congress and the press of "losing the Cold War in space," the U.S. government immediately set out on a crash program to launch its own space satellites. The first, hasty efforts produced the predictable fiascos. Observers baptized the failed U.S. launchings later that year "Kaputniks." Urgency grew as Soviet rockets successfully carried still heavier payloads into space. The "Chief Designer," as Korolev was known in the West (his name remained secret until after his death), seemed capable of miracles. If his rockets were so effective, then they could even carry a human cargo into space orbit. The fact that the United States did put reliable rockets into operation and in 1958 placed in orbit satellites that made notable scientific discoveries only accelerated the momentum of the "Space Race."

That race took four important, distinct directions. In the early years, the most visible public achievements came from the determination of both Soviet and American political leaders to accomplish space exploits to enhance the global standing of their political systems. This propaganda competition hid the very important, and largely secret, military use of space. Then governments and industrial enterprises found in communications and navigational satellites an invaluable, and economically profitable use of space in the electronics age. Finally, the pursuit of scientific knowledge remained an important part of space developments. It produced an enormous array of new discoveries made by manned space stations and voyages, and by unmanned probes of outer space.

Aroused by the first satellite launchings, public expectations and political priorities in both the United States and the U.S.S.R. quickly centered on placing a human cargo in orbit. Beyond that was the enticing prospect of sending that cargo to the moon and back. The Soviet "Chief Designer" flaunted the competence of his rocket team when a space capsule containing the first "cosmonaut," Yuri Gagarin, circled the earth in early 1961. Within a year, several other Soviet cosmonauts, including a woman, had proven the capacity of humans to survive the rigors of brief space travel.

At an early moment in this series of Soviet victories, the U.S. president, John Kennedy, concluded that the United States could no longer be "second best" in space. He promised that the United States would "land a man on the moon" by the end of the decade. The new National Air and Space Administration (NASA) found itself suddenly with a yearly budget of several billions of dollars to carry out this plan. It faced a public and government demanding that it produce immediate results. The first U.S. "astronaut," Alan Shepard, was launched into space late in 1961. His capsule returned immediately to earth, rising beyond the earth's atmosphere and then rapidly descending like a human cannonball. NASA had an enormous and complex task before it.

Its success in the moon project represented an extraordinary engineering achievement. The secret Soviet program to land a cosmonaut on the moon was a failure. Korolev died in 1965, and his research team was unable to create the reliable rocket and guidance systems necessary for the daring space voyage. In those years, U.S. space engineers designed a giant rocket (the Saturn), thirty-six stories high. It had sufficient capacity to send a space ship with three astronauts into orbit around the moon, plus a landing craft. The first moon landing took place in 1969. The "first steps for mankind," announced by Neil Armstrong when he set foot on the moon, brought the United States its greatest space triumph. His companion Edwin Aldrin followed him out of the craft to plant a U.S. flag in the moon's soil. NASA won the race to the moon.

That achievement was the high point of manned space probes. The United States in those years confronted serious domestic and international problems, and the government had made major financial commitments to expand social welfare programs for the American people. The disillusionment that some Americans felt at the space program appeared on a placard, held later that year by a demonstrator in front of the White House in Washington, which read "You Promised Us Food, but You Gave Us the Moon." Funds to NASA dwindled, and the final lunar landing occurred in 1972.

The military use of space proceeded with great speed. The possibilities for surveillance of earth from space created the alluring prospect of uncovering military secrets, such as rocket installations, weapons, and troop movements, without complex spy projects or risky high-altitude flights. The U.S. military's previous efforts at air reconnaissance of the Soviet Union from jet planes had provoked a serious international incident. A Soviet ground-to-air missile had in 1959 shot down a U-2 spy plane flying ten miles above Russia. The Soviet government put the U.S.

Winners of the Race to the Moon: Astronaut Nelson Aldrin and U.S. Flag, Moon, 1969 (*NASA*)

pilot on public trial after he parachuted to earth and was taken captive. His confession broadcast one of the secrets of the Cold War to the entire world.

Satellites performed far more effectively than any pilot. Placed in orbits passing repeatedly over enormous areas of the globe, their highly accurate cameras made even objects ten feet square clearly visible on the photos sent back to earth. Both the Soviet and United States military had by the late 1960s achieved marvels of technological perfection in their spy satellites. The nuclear arms limitation treaties (SALT I and SALT II) were trustworthy documents because each side possessed all the photographic evidence needed to confirm any violations, not because they believed the other's promises to respect its provisions. Ironically, the space race produced the means for more effective peacemaking between the superpowers than could ever have been imagined when the Cold War began.

Still, military leaders continued to look upon space as an arena of war. Ballistic missiles acquired extraordinary accuracy by the 1980s. The technology and engineering skills necessary for building ballistic missiles became sufficiently easy to master so that other governments whose military acquired nuclear weapons had their own rockets for use in the event of a possible nuclear war. Space appeared to some U.S. scientists and to President Ronald Reagan the place for the ultimate defense against ballistic missile attacks. The "Star Wars" program wasted enormous funds in the vain expectation that satellites equipped with powerful laser beams could destroy all incoming missiles before they ever reached the United States. The plan was expensive and unrealistic. An impenetrable space shield covering the United States proved unattainable, since precision space targeting on such a vast scale was impossible to achieve. Research on the program continued in the 1990s, but on a very reduced scale.

The Soviet Sputnik satellite had transmitted signals from a tiny radio solely to let everyone on earth know that it was flying overhead. The lesson was not lost on governments and businesses involved in communications. Suddenly possibilities opened up for instantaneous radio and television signals to reach the remotest parts of the earth. Microwave signals, containing words, numbers, music, or voices, could travel out to satellites in fixed position relative to the earth (approximately twenty-two thousand miles high) and return to waiting receivers ("satellite dishes") so small and inexpensive by the 1980s that consumers could afford them. Industries that relied on the new electronics technology viewed space as a new frontier for economic expansion and profits.

Global television networks appeared, such as the American CNN and the British Star networks, that broadcast commercial programs around the world twenty-four hours a day. People in countries where state censorship severely restricted television programming, such as China, began buying their own satellite dishes to watch uncensored entertainment and news. Businesses engaged in international financial transactions were able to communicate with branches and conduct their affairs instantaneously throughout the world. Satellite communication made the earth a much smaller place.

Governments, especially in the Third World, that relied on radio and television to spread among their peoples their message of national loyalty and solidarity understood as well the benefit of satellites. By the 1980s, the Indian and Indonesian states possessed their own communication satellites that permitted the state-run radio and television networks to transmit their programs throughout their vast countries. The U.S. Global Positioning System (GPS) used navigation satellites to give exact longitude and latitude positions to ground stations. Used at first solely for the military, it soon served the needs of shipping companies and sailors seeking reliable information on the position of their boats. Using a small electronic navigation device. GPS became an essential piece of equipment for navigators, whether on giant supertankers and small sailboats. Useful knowledge, financial investments, and national propaganda all moved through these satellites. By the 1990s, they numbered about five hundred (with the debris of another one thousand still in space). What appeared shooting stars in the night skies was often their reflected light.

Scientific discoveries accumulated as a sidelight to the propaganda and military exploits. After the frantic space race that ended with the moon landings, the scientific programs of both states became more prominent and received more attention. In many ways they were linked still to Cold War competition. Scientists obtained financing in part for the potential military benefits that might emerge from their research. The Soviet government directed its resources toward the creation of a permanent space station, where their cosmonauts discovered the possibilities and limits of human life in outer space. These Soviet space stations first appeared in the early 1970s. They expanded in size and complexity in the next decades. They were maintained constantly even through the period when the Soviet Union ceased to exist and the Soviet space center in Central Asia suddenly became the property of a newly independent country (Kazakhstan). Cosmonauts remained on board for seven and eight months at a time. Space for them became a temporary home.

At Home in Space: Soviet Orbital Station Saliut-7, 1985 (*Hoover Institution*)

The U.S. scientific space efforts moved in two directions. Its space probes increasingly relied on unmanned satellites filled with equipment that automatically recorded scientific observations. This information brought to light geophysical conditions not only on earth, revealed through space photographs, but also on the moon and planets of the solar system. Satellites reached Mars and Venus in the early 1960s, and ten years later they circled Jupiter. The first U.S. satellite to touch the soil of another planet was the Mars landing of 1975. The most ambitious astronomic experiment was the launching in 1990 of the Hubble Space Telescope. It was a giant precision instrument capable of viewing and photographing distant galaxies with a clarity many times greater than the best earth-bound telescope. It revealed no military secrets, and only later, after serious technical problems were corrected, did it prove its capacity to uncover hidden secrets of the universe. Its achievements belonged strictly to a world beyond the Cold War.

Space shuttles were the second new area of U.S. space developments. The old Air Force dream of a plane capable of going into orbit and returning to land on earth was partially realized when NASA launched the first Challenger shuttle in 1981. These spacecraft were sent up "piggyback" on enormous rockets and kept in space for several days before returning to land like an airplane. The shuttles became orbiting laboratories in which astronauts carried out missions to test materials, to take photographs of earth, to repair other satellites.

Each launching and landing of U.S. space shuttles attracted a large audience. Space continued to hold some of the mysterious attraction that Jules Verne's novel had created among its readers. The success of the missions became the guarantee of NASA's continued funding. When in 1986 one of the shuttles exploded shortly after launching, killing the astronauts on board, NASA was blamed for haste.

After the fall of the Soviet Union, NASA joined in the new international era by collaborating with the Russian space agency. U.S. space shuttles linked up with Russian space stations. In 2000, the International Space Station became the first multi-state endeavor to permanently sustain human activity in space. Construction of the station itself drew on Russian experience. U.S. space shuttles brought the equipment for the Station and provided regular transportation from and back to earth for astronauts and cosmonauts. The Space Station embodied a post–Cold War view of space exploration. The urgency that the Cold War had given to space exploration declined, yet the public interest in and scientific rewards from space probes remained. Viewed from space, the earth appeared a colorful, but very finite and tiny object floating in an incredibly vast universe. The ultimate moral lesson from space exploration was humility.

THE FALL OF THE SOVIET EMPIRE

By the 1980s, the communist system of the Soviet Union was incapable of maintaining the country's role as superpower. The elderly Stalinist leaders clung to the illusion of global might, partly out of dogmatic conviction, partly out of ignorance of the decay of their empire and of their own state and society. A few among them realized the extent of the crisis. By then a group of younger Communists were even beginning to put forward daring plans for reform. But as long as the Stalinists remained in power, nothing could be done.

The End of Soviet Communism

The Stalinists finally lost their control of the Soviet government and the Soviet Communist Party in 1985. The generation of Communists old enough to remember and to revere the Stalin revolution of the 1930s was disappearing. Their successors could no longer continue to hide the country's economic crisis and spreading political corruption. The system inherited from Stalin had failed in key areas to meet the needs of the country. It was too inflexible to adopt the technological innovations revolutionizing Western industry, its bureaucratic command system nurtured incompetence and inefficiency, its rigid, centralized controls ignored the needs and wishes of consumers, and its military forces, absorbing nearly one fourth of the country's yearly national income, could not match the electronic wizardry of U.S. weapons.

Popular discontent was a real factor as well. Food and shelter adequate to the people's basic needs were available, though signs of a crisis in health care were already apparent (especially in the declining life expectancy). The population's standard of living stagnated and the economy virtually ceased growing. Only the export of raw materials, especially oil and natural gas, permitted major investments to continue. An illegal black-market economy offered scarce goods to those people with the means to pay its high prices. In exchange for special favors, corrupt officials protected the illegal operations by halting efforts to enforce the laws against these "speculators." People referred to this alliance of black-marketeers and communist officials as the Soviet "Mafia." Russian economists likened (privately) their country's economic condition to that of a state in the Third World.

The single-party communist dictatorship, in theory responsible for the economic well-being of the Soviet Union, was critically weakened by corruption and special privileges. Party bureaucrats held power virtually for life, and many turned their positions into a source of personal wealth. They lived far better than the average Soviet citizen thanks to bribes and influence peddling. It was in their interest to ignore both the real needs of the population and the damage to the environment caused by their economic plans. Claiming to have put their Leninist talents in the service of socialism, these party officials were trapped in their own delusions of power. The entire country suffered as a result. With some variations, a similar political and economic crisis existed in all the communist countries.

Some high party officials, aided by the head of the secret police (KGB), had attempted a few modest reforms even before the last Stalinist leader died in 1985. Their earlier failures made them even more determined to build a reform movement within the new leadership. Their alliance was crucial when the time came to select a new General Secretary of the Communist Party of the Soviet Union. As in the past, the highest Communist Party committee (Politburo) was the body empowered to make the choice. Under pressure from reformers, its members elected in 1985 their youngest colleague, Mikhail Gorbachev, to the position of General Secretary. They realized that reforms were

necessary, both to sustain their country's might and to meet basic needs of the Soviet people. They expected that the result would be an improved socialist system and revived Soviet empire. Their single-party dictatorship would, they imagined, remain the core of the Soviet system and the pillar of world socialism. They were wrong on both counts.

Gorbachev proved an extraordinarily skillful party leader and a dynamic reformer. He quickly became aware that corrupt and incompetent party officials were deeply entrenched throughout the Communist Party apparatus. They relied on censorship and secrecy to protect their power and privileges. In 1986, they attempted to cover up the terrible accident at the Chernobyl nuclear power complex in Ukraine. Within a few days, detectors of radioactive fallout located across northern Europe relayed the news of an enormous explosion there and of atmospheric radioactive fallout that proved ten times greater than the Hiroshima atomic bomb. Gorbachev was outraged at his officials' arrogance, disregard for human safety, and clumsy efforts to hide the accident from public scrutiny. He resolved on the daring move to open up debate in all the public media (a policy termed "glasnost" in Russian). No longer could they hide behind a curtain of secrecy.

Very soon the flood of information overwhelmed the state organs of censorship. For the first time since the 1917 revolution, access to all the news became a public right. Television, radio, and the press seized the possibility to criticize the old order. Old-time Stalinists were outraged, but Gorbachev proved a master of the instruments of power and a daring architect of a new Soviet regime.

He sought political allies wherever he could find them. He released all political prisoners from jail. He authorized religious toleration, allowing churches, synagogues, and mosques to open, permitting religious texts to be published, and joining with Christian leaders in 1987 to celebrate the one-thousandth anniversary of the conversion of Russia to Orthodox Christianity. His most radical measure was the call in 1988 for free elections to the Supreme Soviet (the national parliament). For the first time since 1917, voters were given the opportunity to choose among several candidates for legislative positions. With some hesitation, reform Communists ran for office against conservative Communists.

Gorbachev gambled that the voters would reject the Stalinist party officials, and he was right. The elections, held in 1989, revealed that Russians in key urban areas of the country had turned against their old party bosses. As Gorbachev had hoped, the communist old guard lost to reform candidates, and suffered public humiliation in the process. The dictatorship of the vanguard party, instituted by Lenin in 1917, was beginning to give way to democracy in some Soviet republics.

Gorbachev's reform policies opened the way to the collapse of the communist regimes in eastern Europe. He recognized that the crisis of his country was so grave that renewal could occur only with the collaboration of Western states and investors. Freedom for the peoples of the Soviet satellite countries was the fundamental condition to lasting good relations with the West. To achieve that he was prepared to abandon the Soviet empire in Europe and Asia. He publicly renounced the Brezhnev Doctrine of intervention in defense of communist regimes threatened by internal opposition. To prove his resolve to stand by the new policy, he ordered the withdrawal of all Soviet troops from Afghanistan; the last troops returned to the Soviet Union in 1989. He secretly informed the communist leaders in eastern Europe that Soviet forces no longer stood behind their feeble regimes. In doing so, he gave the peoples of eastern Europe the freedom to choose their own political systems. He realized that these east Europeans would insist on what his minister of foreign affairs termed "the liquidation of those imposed, alien, and totalitarian regimes." But no one anticipated the speed with which the communist governments would disappear.

The Polish Communist Party was the first to lose power. The years of Polish military dictatorship after 1981 had forced the Solidarity labor movement to exist as an illegal, underground organization. But its hold on the population, like that of the Catholic Church, remained an insurmountable barrier to the restoration of communist rule. The crisis of the Polish command economy remained unresolved. General Jaruzelski was aware of his inability to deal with these problems in the face of general hostility of the population. After Gorbachev initiated the policy of political pluralism in 1988, the Polish leader ordered that free parliamentary elections be held in Poland in 1989. He did so in the certain knowledge that Solidarity would win. What neither he nor the Polish Communists expected was that opponents of the Communists won every single elected seat in parliament. They accepted the results, though, and that summer Poland was governed for the first time since 1939 by a freely chosen, noncommunist government. It began the painful process of dismantling the command economy. The new Poland was to be a democratic nation-state with a free market economy.

Sweeping reforms came rapidly also in Hungary and Czechoslovakia. In both countries they ended with the formation of democratic governments committed to a free-market economy. The Czechoslovak Stalinist leadership, imposed by Soviet troops in 1968, had refused any reforms since then. In late 1989, popular demonstrations led by students quickly assumed massive proportions throughout the country. The police were overwhelmed and the state paralyzed. Without the backing of Soviet troops, Czech communist leaders had to resign.

The leading political opponent of the regime was the playwright Vaclav Havel, who had spent years in prison for his outspoken defense of freedom. At popular demand, he became president of the new Czech democracy. At the end of that year, he thanked the young people for their "love of freedom and civic courage" in fighting the old regime. He promised to help build a new country "with economic prosperity and also social justice, a humane republic that serves the people." His appeal for understanding, toleration, and forgiveness sought to revive national pride and respect for other peoples in a Europe of democratic nation-states.

The bonds of national loyalty and the desire for a restored, unified Germany were so strong in East Germany (the German Democratic Republic) that they undermined the very foundations of the communist state. The people's hostility to the regime was augmented by their resentment at being denied the freedom and prosperity enjoyed by the Germans living in the Federal Republic to the West. Although the postwar partition of the country had been accepted by the West, it was not acceptable to them. The Berlin Wall was the most visible and repugnant sign of the Communists' refusal to allow their subjects any personal liberty. West German television had for years broadcast its programs to East Germans, spreading vivid images of the West's way of life. The appeal was overwhelming. In the summer of 1989, Germans from the East by the thousands began to flee to the West through Hungary, whose government permitted them to escape to West Germany. That fall the flight had reached the proportions of a mass exodus. Demonstrations began in East German cities against the regime, with anticommunist banners proclaiming that "We Are the People!"

The collapse of German communism began with the regime's desperate decision to grant freedom of travel to East Germans. On the night of November 9, the gates through the Berlin Wall were opened to all inhabitants of East Berlin. The western section of the city became the center of an enormous celebration by East and West Berliners. Some of them climbed the wall itself to celebrate. So great was the attraction to East Germans of the way of life and institutions of West Germany that the German Democratic Republic quickly disintegrated. Free elections in 1990 brought to power political parties that promised the quickest possible unification with the Federal Republic. In mid-1990, the West German financial system incorporated the eastern territory. In October, the country was united, and plans began to make Berlin once again the capital of a united Germany.

The restoration of national independence, political democracy, and capitalism in eastern Europe in 1989–90 was a direct consequence of the reform policies of the new leadership in the Soviet Union. Without their refusal to intervene, communist regimes would have clung to power. But the real initiators of the move to liberal democracy were the populations of those countries. By means of demonstrations and strikes, and under the guidance of oppositional groups, they moved quickly to take control of their countries' governments. Only in Romania did the communist regime fight back, capitulating after a week of street battles. Elsewhere the transition of power occurred remarkably peacefully. Disagreements on the future of the countries appeared as soon as freedom was achieved. Still, agreement was unanimous everywhere that communism had to be removed completely.

SPOTLIGHT: Andrei Sakharov

Modern science created wonders for the betterment of human life; in the service of the state, it also produced an array of weapons more destructive than ever in human history. Andrei Sakharov (1921–89) knew and participated in both realms of scientific endeavor. Called upon as a young man in 1948 by the Soviet state to participate in the nuclear weapons program, he became the country's preeminent nuclear physicist, recognized and honored as the creator of the Soviet hydrogen bomb. Trained as a theoretical physicist, he demonstrated extraordinary powers of conceptual creativity in the most complex, innovative spheres of modern physics. He had every

Andrei Sakharov (*Scientists for Sakharov/Hoover Institution*)

reason to trust in his rational powers of analysis and understanding. When he applied these skills to criticizing the Soviet system, he became an outspoken opponent of communism and defender of human rights and democracy. For that, he fell from the glorious status of "Hero of Socialist Labor" into the persecuted ranks of dissident. All this because of his powers of reason.

His patriotism convinced him in 1948 that his participation in the Soviet nuclear weapons program was necessary. He and his colleagues at the secret atomic research city of Arzamas called themselves "soldiers in the new scientific war." They believed that U.S. nuclear weapons were a deadly threat to their country. The U.S. had made the name Los Alamos, where the first atomic bomb was developed, a watchword for nuclear weapon research; the Soviet scientists followed closely U.S. research (thanks in part to the skillful work of Soviet spies), and nicknamed their city "Los Arzamas." Sakharov took on the task before him as a challenge to his intellectual powers. His remarkable genius made him the driving force behind the research needed to explode a thermonuclear device, whose destructive power was one thousand times that of an atomic bomb. In 1953, he witnessed the successful test on the steppes of Kazakhstan. At the celebration following the explosion, his toast went to the continued success of the explosions of these "devices," "but always over test sites and never over cities." The tone displeased the Soviet generals in charge. Sakharov had for the first time fallen out of step with the Soviet regime.

He followed that path out of the absolute conviction in the correctness of his reasoning. His decisive break with the regime came slowly, and followed directly from his work on the bomb. Over the next decade, Soviet nuclear tests detonated ever more powerful devices, culminating in 1962 in the explosion of a giant thermonuclear bomb of fifty megatons (the equivalent of fifty million tons of TNT). Sakharov was increasingly concerned at the death and disease caused by the tests themselves, whose radioactive fallout spread over thousands of square miles. That year, his knowledge of the research convinced him that the cost in human lives far outweighed any further gains from testing. To continue, he informed his superiors (including Nikita Khrushchev) was "pointless and criminal." His appeal earned him the suspicion of the communist leaders, and its failure caused him "bitterness, shame, and humiliation." He had become, as a matter of conscience and reason, an outsider in the Soviet system.

In the years that followed, he became an outspoken critic of injustice. He did so knowing that his acts could bring punishment to him and his family from the secret police. His conviction in the rightness of his cause drove him on. Opposed to the award of scientific honors to a mediocre scholar noted only for his collaboration with the party authorities, he openly condemned the individual for "pseudoscientific views, degradation of learning, and for the defamation, firing, arrest, even death of many genuine scientists." He was successful, for his prestige among Soviet scholars was enormous. But his public protest could do nothing when in 1964 two writers were imprisoned for having published abroad stories critical of Soviet communism. Other protests at persecution of intellectuals followed this one, all predicated on his conviction that freedom of speech in all realms of public inquiry was a fundamental human right. In 1968, he made public his political views in a pamphlet entitled "Progress, Coexistence, and Intellectual Freedom." Sakharov had never been a Communist; now he had become an outspoken defender of human rights. He gradually worked out a program for the fundamental reform of the Soviet system, to be replaced by a liberal democracy, a market economy, and a multinational federal state with true autonomy for all the peoples of the Soviet Union. His writings, all circulated in typewritten form (Soviet censorship had complete control of all printing presses) made him an international celebrity, and an enemy of the regime.

Only his fame in the western world and his past record as "father" of the Soviet hydrogen bomb saved him from imprisonment or exile to a Siberian prison camp. In 1975, he received the Nobel Prize for Peace, and sent to Sweden a message defending the absolute need for an "open society" to maintain real peace in the nuclear age. The Soviet regime was closing in around him, using all the arbitrary powers at its disposal to make his life an ordeal. His final act of defiance was to protest in 1979 the Soviet invasion of Afghanistan. At that point the secret police made him a prisoner in all but name. He was sentenced to exile in a "closed" city (forbidden to foreigners) far from Moscow and was constantly harassed by police. His only remaining means of protest were hunger strikes, which brought him brutal hospitalization and forced feeding to prevent death. His health worsened. His fate appeared to be that of yet another victim of the Soviet dictatorship.

Then in 1985 reform leadership set out to remake the Soviet system. Gorbachev's ideas were radical, by comparison with the neo-Stalinism of his predecessors. Sakharov, whose program was even more extreme, was now politically useful. His call for a multiparty, democratic system made Gorbachev appear a moderate, and his freedom would signal to the world the readiness of the reform leaders to break with the past. Gorbachev personally freed him from exile, welcomed him back to Moscow, and permitted his public appeals for the end to communist dictatorship.

Despite his persecution of the previous 20 years, Sakharov was prepared to collaborate. When the new Soviet legislature met in 1989, he was one of the freely elected deputies. He spoke eloquently there against the old-line Communists and Russian nationalists, and for peaceful reform. He was an international celebrity, and a hero for millions of Soviet citizens. Appeals for his help came from all sides, and the strain upon him was enormous. Suddenly at the end of the year, he died of a heart attack. His funeral was a day of national mourning. He had lived to witness the end of communism and the birth of an open society in Russia.

The End of the Cold War

In his first years of power, Gorbachev did not grasp the gravity of his country's economic crisis. He lost precious time before finally accepting the advice of economists to abandon the command economy. His slogan of radical reform (the Russian term was "perestroika") came to mean the introduction of a limited free market in all sectors of the Soviet economy. The structural and social obstacles to such changes were far greater than those he encountered in introducing political and civil liberties. The public had for decades enjoyed low-priced, state-subsidized consumer goods and services (generally of poor quality and in short supply). They continued to rely on these state goods to meet their basic needs. Managers and workers had become accustomed to inefficient methods of work. A popular Russian judgment of this system was the simple comment: "They pretend to pay us, and we pretend to work." The country's industrial and agricultural equipment was obsolete, and the state lacked the resources for the massive investments needed for reconversion and technical modernization. All these problems were the result of wasteful and shortsighted state economic management and the price of the communist leaders' determination to make their country a global superpower.

The economic difficulties worsened the tense relations between the non-Russian nationalities and the Soviet state. Lenin's attempt to create a "community of socialist nations" in the Union of Soviet Socialist Republics had failed. Newly elected reform leaders in some national republics publicly likened the Soviet Union to the nineteenth-century tsarist empire, whose regime also kept its peoples under authoritarian rule. The Soviet Union was, in historical terms, the last empire. Decolonization had swept away all European empires except that of the Soviet Union. The eastern European states had shown the way out of the empire. Soviet republics quickly followed their example.

By 1990, almost all of the fifteen national republics that made up the union had officially proclaimed their "sovereignty" (a formal action with no immediate legal consequences). Even the Russian Soviet Republic, largest of all, took this step of protest against the Soviet constitution and communist rule. Nationalism, long forced underground by Soviet repression, suddenly emerged to become a powerful movement among Soviet peoples. National bonds of loyalty were far more influential than Soviet patriotism or the Marxist-Leninist ideology.

In the western republics of the U.S.S.R., free elections became the path to independence. The Polish example of national liberation in 1989 inspired nationalists in bordering Soviet regions to attempt the same. National parties in the Baltic area (Lithuanian, Latvian, and Estonian Soviet Republics) swept regional elections in 1990. They made public the secret Hitler-Stalin agreement of 1939 to partition eastern Europe and to allow the annexation of their small states by the Soviet Union. Their leaders immediately called for an end to this unlawful loss of their countries' independence. Their goal was secession from the Soviet Union. The country was beginning to fall apart.

In this growing crisis, influential old guard Communists in Moscow demanded that Gorbachev use the Red Army and secret police to quell the nationalist unrest. He resisted, fearing the end of his reform campaign and a new era of hostile relations with the West. In desperation, Stalinist leaders in the party, the army, and secret police organized in August 1991 a conspiracy to overthrow Gorbachev and reinstate the old dictatorship and save the Soviet Union. They were Gorbachev's one-time colleagues whom he had trusted and relied upon to obey his orders. He never suspected them of betrayal. Their attempted uprising proved an abject failure, however.

Mass opposition to the conspiracy revealed that millions of people in Russia had repudiated com-munism and welcomed democratic reforms. Their leader was a dynamic anticommunist reformer, Boris Yeltsin. He had once belonged to the Communist Party, but in 1988 had resigned in disgust at its corruption and conservatism. He had joined the democratic movement. He set out to take the lead of the reform movement in the Russian Soviet Republic. In the spring of 1991, he campaigned in the first popular election ever held for president of the Russian Soviet Republic. His program was democracy, a free-market economy, and Russian nationalism. His electoral victory was overwhelming. With this popular backing, he led the resistance to the Stalinist conspiracy that August. Explaining to Red Army generals that he was the legitimately chosen leader of Russia, he won the army to his side. Hundreds of thousands of Russians took to the streets of the major cities to stand in the way of the forces of the conspirators. The Stalinists backed down, leaving the Communist Party discredited and the Soviet Union in disarray.

Yeltsin and Russian nationalism were triumphant. He outlawed the Communist Party, and

Hero of Russian Democracy: Boris Yeltsin, Moscow, August 1991 (*Hoover Institution*)

moved ahead with his own reform program for Russia. The Baltic republics had already seceded from the Soviet Union. Gorbachev's defeat of the August conspiracy and Yeltsin's triumph established Russia as independent in all but legal terms. That fall, the Ukrainian Soviet Republic held an election to decide whether to remain in a reformed Soviet state; Ukrainians overwhelming voted for independence. Gorbachev and the Soviet government were powerless to stop the disintegration of the union. Quickly the leaders of the other fourteen republics of the Soviet Union followed suit, proclaiming the independence of their republics late in 1991. Communism was gone, and so, on December 25, 1991, was the Soviet Union. Overnight Gorbachev became an ordinary Russian citizen, and the red flag, with the hammer and sickle, vanished from the flagpole atop the Kremlin walls in Moscow.

The disappearance of communist regimes and the collapse of the Soviet Union brought the Cold War to an end. In the late 1940s, George Kennan had foreseen the day when the Soviet empire would decline and negotiations would resolve the basic security issues dividing the United States and the Soviet Union. That time came forty years later. The Warsaw Pact, the military alliance of the eastern European countries under Soviet domination, disappeared. Subsequently, its member countries (except Russia) all sought to join the Western military alliance (NATO). Among the countries seeking admission in the 1990s to the European Union were all the eastern European states freed from Soviet domination. The U.S. leaders signed new arms agreements with Gorbachev, then with Russia's president, Yeltsin. These treaties provided for the actual reduction of nuclear armaments. Intermediate-range and short-range missiles were to be completely destroyed, and intercontinental missiles drastically reduced in numbers. Armies saw their numbers cut throughout the former communist countries and in the West. Defense industries suddenly lost their booming market for weapons.

The dream of turning "swords into ploughshares" was only partially realized. Nuclear weapons remained in the possession of other states around the world besides Russia and the United States. China, India, and Pakistan all had such weapons, as did France, Great Britain, and Israel. Still, the terrible threat of nuclear war ceased to dominate global relations. Europe was no longer divided in two. The U.S. government extended economic aid to Russia. Soviet athletes in search of high pay joined Western professional sports teams, and Russian students appeared in Western business schools. The walls had fallen.

SUMMARY

For almost fifty years the Cold War had divided Europe and the world into two antagonistic alliances and competing political and social systems. In the first decades after the Second World War, the future of European lands appeared to depend on outside forces. The United States and the Soviet Union, great victors in the war, had the decisive hand in postwar global relations. The European border separating the two camps was baptized the Iron Curtain. Berlin itself brought together these opposing forces in one tiny spot on Europe's map, where pessimistic observers forecast the Third World War would begin. West German leaders welcomed the "nuclear umbrella" extended over their country by U.S. armed forces. It was preferable to being defenseless in the face of the forces of East Germany and the Soviet Union. West Berlin was reconstructed to be a Western beacon and a refuge.

Peoples in the communist countries had no choice but to submit to Soviet domination. If they had been allowed to express their preference, they would immediately have claimed their national independence and made the West, not the Soviet Union, their source of cultural, political, and social values. In these terms, there could be no moral equivalence in the Cold War between East and West, or between Soviet and U.S. foreign policies. The tenacity of Cold War tensions rested on that fundamental reality.

The pressures that brought down the communist system came in part from this abiding hostility of the peoples of the east toward communism. But theirs was, in Vaclav Havel's term, only the "power of the powerless" to refuse to collaborate. The real force that ended the Soviet Union and Soviet domination in eastern Europe lay within the Soviet Union itself, and most especially in the expectations and plans of the new reform leadership that came to power in 1985. No popular protest forced Gorbachev to launch his radical plans. The Soviet political elite enjoyed the fruits of their privileges and powers within the land. But the incapacity of that system to sustain an effective economy, a great-power military force, and a dynamic leadership appeared so grave that Gorbachev and his supporters were prepared to take great risks to remake it. They could not overcome the nationalist loyalties of the peoples of their vast empire, or efface the memories of the cruelties that the Stalinist regime had inflicted on these peoples. That tenacious nationalism, more than any other factor, crushed their hopes for reform and destroyed the Soviet Union.

At the end of the twentieth century, nationalism in Europe was not what it had been one hundred years before. In many respects, western Europe set the model for reform in the former communist countries. Liberal democracy flourished among European countries. Economic activity lay increasingly in the hands of private interests. European governments chose to return most of their nationalized industries to private ownership, keeping only indirect controls over finances and production. Most of the countries freed from communist rule sought membership in the European Union to obtain access to markets and investments. No ideological program dominated the lives of the population of Europe or promised an end to social inequality. People directed their energies to making a better life for themselves, counting on the social welfare policies put in place after the war to help in time of need.

The Soviet Union, the last colonial empire, had vanished. Europe's map was again divided into independent nation-states. Ethnic and national antagonism resurfaced when national liberation permitted ethnic groups to organize in eastern Europe, and when migrants from Third World countries appeared throughout Europe. But the age of nationalist wars and communist revolutions was a thing of the past. The success and popularity in the east of the European Union suggested that Europeans from east and west were prepared to look ahead to a postnational era.

DATES WORTH REMEMBERING

1952 Formation of European Coal and Steel Community (ECSC)
1952 First test of hydrogen bomb by United States
1953 First test of hydrogen bomb by Soviet Union
1955 Khrushchev new Soviet leader
1956 Soviet repression of Hungarian revolution
1958 Soviet launching of Sputnik satellite
1958 Formation of European Economic Community (Common Market)
1961 Construction by East Germany of Berlin wall
1962 Cuban missile crisis
1969 Moon landing by American astronauts
1972 Nuclear arms treaty banning defensive missiles (SALT I)
1975 First Soviet space station
1975 Helsinki Agreement on European borders and human rights
1977 Constitutional monarchy in Spain, replacing Franco regime
1979 Soviet invasion of Afghanistan
1980–82 Solidarity movement in power in Poland

1985–91 Gorbachev Soviet leader
1989 Soviet troops withdrawn from Afghanistan
1989 Collapse of communist regimes in Eastern Europe
1989 First free elections in Soviet Union
1990 Reunification of Germany
1991 Election of Boris Yeltsin as President of Russia
1991 Collapse of Soviet Union
1993 Treaty on European Union

RECOMMENDED READING

The Recovery of Western Europe

Derek Unwin, *The Community of Europe: A History of European Integration since 1945* (1994). A careful study of the process leading from the Coal and Steel Community to the European Union. Also, *Western Europe since 1945* (3rd ed., 1981). A balanced survey of the remarkable postwar recovery of Europe.

The United States, the Soviet Union, and the Cold War

Aleksandr Fursenko and Timothy Naftali, *"One Hell of a Gamble": Khrushchev, Castro, and Kennedy, 1958–64* (1997). A revealing history of the Cuban missile crisis using newly opened Soviet archival materials.

Richard Lourie, *Sakharov: A Biography* (2002). A careful, admiring portrait of a scientific genius and courageous opponent of communism.

*Alex Nove, *An Economic History of the USSR* (3rd ed., 1992). The best account of the rise and fall of the Soviet command economy.

William Walter, *Space Age* (1992). A beautifully illustrated history of space exploration, focusing on the civilian aspects.

*Tom Wolfe, *The Right Stuff* (1979). An ironic view of the space frenzy that possessed the United States when it confronted the first Soviet space exploits.

The End of the Soviet Empire

Jonathan Steele, *Eternal Russia: Yeltsin, Gorbachev and the Mirage of Democracy* (1994). The best analysis, and eyewitness account, of the fall of the Soviet Union, by a English journalist stationed in Moscow in those years.

*Gail Stokes, *The Walls Came Tumbling Down: The Collapse of Communism in Eastern Europe* (1994). The dramatic story of the sudden disappearance of communist regime in the late 1980s.

Memoirs, Novels, and Visual Aids

*Robert Kennedy, *The Thirteen Days* (1968). Memoirs of one of the key participants in the Cuban missile crisis; also film version (2001) with the same title.

Jack Matlock, *Autopsy on an Empire: The American Ambassador's Account of the Collapse of the Soviet Union* (1995). An American's inside view of the dramatic events of the Gorbachev years.

People Power: The End of Soviet-Style Communism. An outstanding PBS documentary (in the series "People's Century"), using documentary footage and interviews with participants to trace the fall of the communist regimes.

Chapter 8

Local Wars, Global Economy:
The World after the Cold War

Outline

Highlight

Spotlight

Colonial empires had vanished from the world by the 1990s. The term "overseas" referred to distant nation-states, not to territories where a Western empire governed subject peoples. The emergence of hundreds of new nation-states in the place of the fallen empires was the most spectacular and enduring global political upheaval brought by the twentieth century.

New economic bonds replaced the old ties that empires had maintained. The term "global economy" referred both to the spread of industrial and technological innovations to countries around the world and to the growing interdependence of the economies of all the regions of the globe. The new nation-states possessed sovereign rights and flew their flags among the member states at the United Nations headquarters in New York. Their economies depended, however, on international economic relations whose centers were usually far beyond their borders. Western governments, responding to pressure from business interests, encouraged developing states to integrate their countries in the global economy, especially by lowering their tariffs on imports from manufacturers and farmers in the developed world. Currency speculators paid no heed to the economic needs of the new states in their search for rewarding short-term investments. Prosperity or recession was a global process which smaller countries were powerless to influence.

The most prosperous regions included not only North America and western Europe, but also countries around the eastern shores of the Pacific Ocean. Japan had become the first newly industrialized state in the area, followed by lands as small as Singapore and as large as China. Their increasingly important place in the global economy gave their leaders a voice in international affairs that bore little relation to the size of their national armies or to their military alliances. The process of national liberation from empires had divided the political map of the world into hundreds of nation-states. But the regional and global economic relations that they were drawn into created a new map of interdependence that disregarded these state borders. Claims to national independence and outbursts of nationalist rivalry disrupted these bonds, but could not destroy them.

By the end of the century, international economic relations had come to resemble a global free market. The old trade and regulatory barriers put up during the depression by governments had dwindled significantly. In former communist countries, the collapse of the command economies ended their isolation from the outside world. Their new leaders welcomed foreign investors and their new, privately owned industrial enterprises struggled to compete on the international market. On a global scale, the big economic forces were the multinational corporations and major banks and financial institutions, whose investments and speculative operations moved trillions of dollars around the world in a single day. Profit set the measure of success or failure, even when the consequences were economic hardship in distant areas.

This process, called "globalization," included vastly increased movement of goods (such as petroleum), services (like finance and banking), and peoples (especially labor migration), and indirectly made itself felt in global problems of air pollution and the spread of epidemic diseases (especially AIDS). Few people shared any longer the naive faith of pre-1914 Westerners in the wonders of industry and technology and in the inevitability of human progress. The consumption of energy through the burning of fossil fuels, key to the entire Industrial Revolution, had created such atmospheric pollution that it was altering the world's climate.

The Second World War proved, at the end of the Cold War, to have been the last world war.

Following the collapse of the Soviet Union in 1991, the United States was the sole superpower in a world plagued by terrorist movements and by small-scale wars. Civil wars, that is, armed confrontations among hostile groups within a state's borders, wrought devastation in the Balkans, and in Afghanistan. Other conflicts were regional disputes. Of these, the most serious was the U.S. conquest of Iraq in 2003.

Poverty, ethnic hatred, and political rivalries all in one way or another contributed to the outbreak of violence. Peoples in countries where civil war became acute sought protection from outside forces, in the form of regional alliances or nearby states, or from the United Nations. Foreign help was the only effective means to bring some degree of peace to their people. Where no such forces appeared, these wars endured, often until economies had decayed, cities lay in ruins, and large numbers of the population had become homeless refugees. Nongovernmental humanitarian organizations came to these dangerous regions to offer health care and food to stop hunger and disease. Their efforts, however meager, were often all that stood in the way of famine and epidemics.

In the 1990s, the United Nations became more active than ever before in the affairs of its member nations. It was freed at last from the paralyzing Cold War quarrels between the Soviet Union and the United States. The Security Council received urgent pleas time and again to intervene in local and civil wars for which no easy solution existed. The 1990 seizure of the tiny state of Kuwait by Iraqi forces began the brief Gulf War. It ended with the triumph of a coalition of United Nations forces led by the United States and aided by, among others, the reform leaders of the Soviet Union. Hopes for a "new world order" rested on the promise of the United Nations to protect states, small and large, from aggression. But power politics, that is, the reliance on a state's military might, remained a viable alternative for major countries, as the

United States demonstrated in its conquest of Iraq in 2003. The dream of international peace remained remote in the early years of the twenty-first century.

THE EMERGENCE OF THE GLOBAL ECONOMY

The international economy that had emerged among the Western countries in the early twentieth century gradually expanded across the globe into Asian, Latin American, and African lands. It drew its strength in part from the economic expansion of the United States, and increasingly from the growing productivity of Europe and of new industrial regions in East Asia. The political boundaries of nation-states were of less importance than regional economic groupings, usually gathered around one particularly productive, wealthy country. Japan played that role in East Asia. Germany was similarly influential in central and eastern Europe.

Within these very productive economies, major corporations accumulated enormous wealth. The economic resources of companies such as Sony in Japan, Royal Dutch-Shell in the Netherlands, or Microsoft in the United States, overshadowed in wealth the total national income of many countries. The skyscrapers of cities as distant as Tokyo, Singapore, London, and New York were headquarters to most of the multinational corporations. They were the visible sign that these places counted among the world-class cities in the new global economy.

Global Interdependence

In the immediate postwar years, the United States played a crucial role in laying the foundation for the rapid global expansion of economic production and trade. The U.S. government had financed international institutions for trade and lending to spur recovery from the war. The enormous wealth of the U.S. economy made it the motor behind global economic growth. It was the principal trading partner for countries in Europe and Asia. Soon after the war the dollar became the principal international currency. It had a stable, fixed value. Until 1971, the U.S. government guaranteed the monetary value of one ounce of gold at $35, using the gold standard to sustain the dollar's stable value. U.S. foreign aid to European and Asian states accelerated economic growth. Japan and West Germany, once enemies of the United States, quickly became prosperous and productive centers of their regions and kept close economic ties with the United States.

Trading and investment were, as in the past, particularly vigorous between Europe and the United States. The new prosperity of Europe attracted major U.S. companies, such as General Motors and International Business Machines (IBM). Termed "multinational" because of their vast financial resources invested throughout the world, these firms set up new factories and opened new markets for their goods. Western Europe's rapid economic recovery made it the single most profitable market in the world for U.S. investors, whose total investments in Europe jumped from $2 billion in 1950 to $60 billion in the mid-1970s. In those decades, European banks and corporations utilized the U.S. dollar for their trade and financial exchanges. Europeans held dollars in such quantities that their holdings earned the name of "Eurodollars."

Gradually, the U.S. currency was joined by other strong currencies as money of exchange for the global economy. By the late 1960s, the U.S. economy no longer dominated the world's trade and industry. Too many U.S. dollars were flowing across the Atlantic to pay for an increasing amount of imported goods. Inflation in the United States began to reduce the dollar's value. At one ounce of gold for $35, the price of the dollar was too cheap. International investors and financial speculators turned increasingly to the stable currencies of Germany and Japan. Their sales of dollars were so great that the U.S. government and central bank could not longer hold the dollar at its fixed, low value. In 1971, the U.S. government had to abandon the gold standard. It allowed the value of the dollar to fluctuate according to market demand. Soon $300 were needed to buy one ounce of gold.

For the rest of the century, no currency could claim a stable, international value. The U.S. dollar remained the least risky currency in that unstable financial world. In countries suffering in the 1990s from high inflation such as Russia, consumers and producers alike preferred to make their transactions in dollars (preferably in $100 bills). Certain small South American states, unable to control inflation in their own currencies, adopted the dollar as the legal medium of exchange.

Monetary instability in the late century stimulated such global currency speculation that at times it created international financial crises. In 1997 and 1998, international investors, fearful of losing money on risky loans in east and south Asian economies, suddenly withdrew their loans and "dumped" (that is, suddenly sold) their monetary holdings in these currencies. Their massive, panicky selling devalued these monies, curtailing imports and raising interest rates to such an extent that it caused a severe regional recession in Asia. The crisis was soon over, but the lesson was clear. The world's financial markets, where trillions of dollars were traded every day, held enormous power over the fate of peoples and countries.

The global economic expansion of the late century drew increasingly on technological innovation. The electronics and computer industries became the most dynamic centers of development by the 1970s. Their managers set up production in developed and developing countries, wherever costs were lowest and profits highest. These fundamental new conditions of global interdependence made a return to the economic isolationism of the 1930s depression years unthinkable.

Beginning in the 1960s, countries of east and southeast Asia emerged as new centers of economic power and productivity. These areas included first Japan, then the countries called the "Four Dragons" (South Korea, Hong Kong, Taiwan, Singapore), and finally the most populous country in the world, China. The simplest measure of their remarkable boom in the late twentieth century was their rate of economic growth. Each of these East Asian lands managed to reach an annual growth rate of close to 10 percent. Japan attained this extraordinary level of growth in three decades from the 1950s, the "Four Dragons" in the 1970s and 1980s, and China beginning in the late 1980s. No other region in the world had generated such rapid economic growth. In real terms, these economies were able at that rate to double their annual income every ten years.

After Communism: China and Russia in the Global Economy

In the People's Republic of China, the economic reforms launched by Deng Xiaoping in 1978 gradually opened the country to a market economy. Twenty years later, his successors were firmly committed to collaborating in the global economy. They welcomed foreign investors, who poured billions of dollars into the country. Their economy acquired direct access to the wealth of Hong Kong, financial center of East Asia, when Great Britain returned the tiny territory to China in 1997. Years before, wealthy Hong Kong business interests had become the major investors in the People's Republic. The products of these new enterprises found markets in the global economy, especially in the United States. The U.S. had become the major trading partner of China.

The biggest problems faced by the Chinese economy resulted from rapid population growth. Millions of rural migrants left their villages to seek jobs in the coastal cities' booming economy.

An increasing number joined the flood of illegal migrants bound for Europe and the United States, going deeply into debt to smuggling gangs and risking death on the long trip in sealed trucks and ship containers. Those who stayed in China's cities found air and water contamination there as bad as the worst polluted urban areas in the world. Groundwater was in increasingly short supply in northern China as a result of wasteful industrial and agricultural use. Without severe restrictions on water usage, the Chinese Academy of Science warned that later in the twenty-first century large areas of the country would face severe, prolonged drought.

Rising demand for energy to power the booming economy persuaded the Chinese government to begin construction in 1995 on the Yangtze River of the single largest hydroelectric dam in the world. Its reservoir was so vast that five million people had to be displaced and millions of acres of productive land were lost. The communist government gambled that it could find work for the country's enormous population only by pursuing economic modernization, no matter what the cost. Though the Chinese state remained a single-party dictatorship where the communist ideology was in political speeches acknowledged to be the ultimate source of truth and happiness, the country no longer bore any resemblance to Maoist China.

The economic fortunes of Russia, heir to the ruins of the Soviet Union's attempt at state socialism, remained bleak through most of the 1990s. While the Chinese manner of ending the command economy released dynamic and productive forces, the Russian conversion to a market economy led to a serious economic depression. The breakup of the Soviet Union (see Chapter 7) threw up barriers to trade among the newly independent republics, which once had been tightly bound together by Soviet planning and investment. The sudden end of the Cold War brought to a virtual standstill the mammoth Russian defense industry. It lost its lucrative state purchaser and

lacked any experience in selling its sophisticated weapons on the international market. The most serious obstacle to Russian economic recovery was the dearth of people who knew how to make a capitalist economy function. Managers of the old state-owned industries had never learned about productivity and efficiency. Chairmen of the state-controlled collective farms had never worried about meeting the needs and tastes of Russian consumers.

The resulting economic depression lowered the country's industrial production by one half by 1995. The people's standard of living dropped and public services deteriorated. Factories stopped paying wages and other benefits. Millions of urban Russians were forced to acquire plots of farm land to grow their own food. Around the country's major cities appeared vast open-air markets where people scrambled to sell whatever goods came to hand to earn a petty income. It seemed in some areas that Russians had reverted to a barter, or even natural economy.

A few investors, who often were closely allied with political leaders, profited greatly by the purchase of formerly nationalized enterprises, especially those controlling valuable natural resources such as oil and aluminum. One observer called the rapid, chaotic sale of state enterprises "the sale of the century." Critics of the semilegal or illegal methods of these investors called it "gangster capitalism." These "new Russians," and a new middle class that emerged around them, were still a very small minority of the population.

The chaotic conditions extended to Russia's new democratic political institutions. Local government fell apart for lack of taxes, which most citizens and companies paid rarely or not at all. Police failed to control the growing number of criminal gangs, baptized the "Russian Mafia," and estimated to number about five hundred in the mid-1990s. These gangsters prospered by extorting contributions from frightened businessmen, who risked execution if they failed to pay. Soon they branched out into international drug smuggling and prostitution rackets.

The federal government proceeded slowly to put into place the legal framework for the rule of law and for a market economy. Until the late 1990s, the legislature was a bastion of nationalists lamenting the decline of their homeland and of former Communist Party bosses chosen by rural electors. A powerful "agro-industrial" lobby defended the obsolete collective and state farms. The clearest indication of their hostility to a free market was the parliament's refusal until 2000 to approve laws permitting the purchase and sale of collective farm land.

Gradually Russia moved from its communist past toward a partially democratic, somewhat capitalist order. Boris Yeltsin, the first president of the Russian Federation, remained in power until 2000. His reelection in 1996, in which his chief opponent was the head of the revived Communist Party, indicated that most voters had turned their backs on the old regime. In 1998, he attended the reburial in St. Petersburg's most historic cathedral of the remains of the last tsar, Nicholas II, and of his family, placed alongside the tombs of Russia's previous emperors. The ceremony was not intended to be an appeal to a return to a monarchy; it was an act of homage to all the victims of Soviet revolution and terror. Yeltsin used the moment to beg his countrymen to put behind them "a century of bloodshed" and join together in constructing a country of liberty and toleration. His ultimate, dramatic gesture was to suddenly resign his office on New Year's Day 2000. After an election campaign freer than any in the country's short history as a democracy, a large majority of electors voted for Yeltsin's heir apparent, Vladimir Putin.

Russia's democratic reforms had produced an authoritarian presidential regime, not a western parliamentary democracy. The skill of the new president at using the powers of the presidency gave the country a stable leadership dedicated to restoring the international influence of Russia.

His government respected and, with some lapses, maintained the political and civil liberties that the reformers had introduced earlier. The Russian army inherited most of the armaments of the Soviet Union's armed forces. They provided the Russian government with the weapons of a superpower. The vast natural resources of the country provided the wealth needed to launch the economic recovery, which was well under way by the early years of the new century. Yet the land was burdened with extensive environmental pollution, and a serious demographic decline. A grim sign of the social crisis that still gripped the country was the high death rate among Russian men (with a life expectancy of fifty-eight years, lowest of any Western country) and the declining rate of childbirth (also one of the lowest among developed countries). The collapse of Soviet communism had left a country in ruins, and the construction of a new Russia was only beginning.

In the entire world, only the state of North Korea remained frozen in the socialist institutions of Stalinism, copied from the Soviet Union in the late 1940s. The result by the 1990s was impoverishment and periodic famine for the population. The collective farm system was incapable of providing adequate food. Nationalized industry barely functioned, with only armaments factories receiving substantial state subsidies to keep operating at full capacity. No foreign investors, except a few South Korean banks and the South Korean state, were prepared to risk their funds in that bankrupt economy. Only massive foreign aid, consisting of food and petroleum from China, and food and financial contributions from South Korea, kept the country from collapse. That awful possibility, with the resulting massive exodus of refugees, made both governments unwilling supporters of North Korea's Stalinist leadership. Yet that government continued to parade well-armed troops through the central square of the capital to impress foreign dignitaries, and publicly proclaimed in

2003 that it had acquired the capacity to produce nuclear weapons. These, it claimed, were needed to defend the land from "U.S. aggression." Behind this facade of power, the country was a pathetic relic of the Soviet experiment in state socialism.

The New Industrial Revolution

Many of the twentieth century's major scientific discoveries found technological applications by the late century. The biological sciences yielded insight into the very nature of life and the operations of the human mind. Understanding of the chemistry and structure of genes revealed vital information on the processes of heredity. At the same time, it made possible the manipulation of genetic material to develop medicines to treat an increasingly large number of diseases. Good health and a relatively long life became a tangible goal for an increasing proportion of the population in most countries. Genetically modified food plants came in increasingly numbers from the research laboratories of major corporations. They found some farmers eager to increase profitability of crop yields but also encountered bitter resistance from environmental groups and the public at large, fearful of the impact of these crops on the animal and plant world.

The appearance of computers and telecommunication instruments brought the countries of the world into instant contact. Through the instantaneous transmission and analysis of information from almost all parts of the globe, this new electronics industry dissolved borders and opened potential access to a vast pool of knowledge. But political and cultural barriers remained in place. Shared knowledge was restricted, imperfect, and too often misunderstood. This modern technology was only as effective as its operators could make it. They used it primarily for the sake of the global economy.

Electronics and telecommunications did not exist as important industries until the 1950s. They

began to expand at a rapid rate in direct response to new discoveries. Technological innovations in this area combined the sophistication of rocketry and earth satellites, the extraordinary power of computers to analyze information, telecommunications equipment for instantaneous transmission of data around the world, and the television screen. The scientific and technological work that went into these inventions was complex and expensive. It was concentrated principally in the United States and Japan, where private companies and public institutions funded extensive research. Much of the new equipment served the needs of businesses, which brought it to other countries in their trading and investment operations. In many respects, these new sectors set in motion the new industrial revolution.

Television had the greatest direct impact on popular culture in developed and developing lands. It provided the channel of communication to enlarge people's awareness of social and political conditions through images as well as the spoken word. Invented before the war, it did not spread widely among Western countries until the 1950s. Almost immediately it began to appear in the newly independent nations of the Third World.

Broadcast companies, privately owned and operated in the United States, came under state control in most countries. The cost of television production required state financing. More important was control over the choice and interpretation of information transmitted through the airwaves. When used to promote a political cause such as nationalism and reinforced by visual images, messages communicated by television proved the most potent tool of propaganda ever invented. Television, the most influential form of communication, quickly came to play a central role in plans for nation-building in Third World countries. A means everywhere of education and entertainment, television offered a revolutionary means of overcoming the barriers of misunderstanding and prejudice dividing peoples. At the same time, it constituted a potent force for national unification and political indoctrination.

New electronic inventions opened the way for the creation of global networks of television transmission to form what one observer termed a "global village." Communications satellites, relaying signals from one continent to another or between distant regions of one country, first went into service in 1965. Ten years later, they were in place over the Atlantic, Pacific, and Indian Oceans. Small, inexpensive satellite dishes afforded access to these programs for viewers even in countries that censored news and television programs. The booming economy of the People's Republic of China gave millions of Chinese families the means to purchase satellite dishes to view international television. The Chinese Communists objected bitterly to this "poisonous foreign cultural invasion," issuing in 1993 a law outlawing private ownership of satellite dishes. Similarly, Iran's Islamic Republic ordered Iranians to scrap their satellite dishes, used there to bypass the stultifying propaganda and heavy-handed censorship of the Muslim clerics. Both laws proved a failure. Even dictatorial regimes could not overcome the popular desire for a television window onto the outside world.

Transnational communication emphasized entertainment above all. Sports competition was especially popular. An estimated three billion viewers watched the 2002 World Soccer Cup matches. The principal source of foreign programs was the U.S. television industry, generating films, songs, sports competition, celebrities, and dress fads. National television networks attempted with their own programming to stem the flood. They created their own "soap operas," adapting the hugely successful American formula of TV serials dramatizing everyday life to their own social and cultural conditions. Yet the global popularity of the basketball player Michael Jordan and international markets for Hollywood's entertainment industry gave strong

evidence of the alluring power of Western television. The last empires of the late century were media empires.

Global Energy

Global economic growth and improved living conditions for the population depended in large measure on the availability and efficient use of energy. New forms of transportation, industrial production, lighting, and communication required ready access to energy sources. The global demand for energy expanded after the Second World War at an extremely high rate until the late 1970s, when it was four times greater than in 1950. Industrial regions had high consumption level, but developing areas of Latin America and in the newly industrialized countries of Asia soon shared this distinction.

In a fundamental shift in energy sources, coal, principal fuel for the Industrial Revolution, took second place to petroleum after 1960. Access to oil became vital to the well-being of the global economy, but only a few countries possessed major oil fields. At the beginning of the century, the United States had been the chief source of petroleum; sixty years later its oil fields were running dry. By the early 1990s, over half of its needs in petroleum products had to be met by foreign imports; by then, the United States alone consumed one fourth of the total world production of petroleum.

The Middle East (principally Iran, Iraq, and Saudi Arabia) became the leading producers of petroleum in the 1960s. Rising demand, the power of the Organization of Oil Producing Countries (OPEC), and periodic wars in the Middle East sent prices soaring from their low level of $2 per barrel to $14 in the mid-1970s. The Iranian revolution and Iran-Iraq war forced prices for a time to $30. Rapid inflation in the developed countries and hardship in the poorer countries were the result. By then, the Middle East had become an area of vital importance to the U.S.

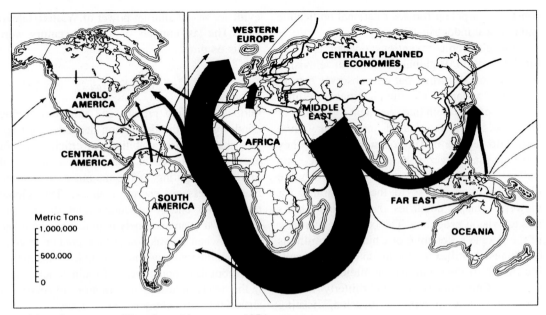

Major International Petroleum Movements, 1974

government, obliged to devise policies to protect the strategic and economic need of the country for stable oil supplies. Its two wars against Iraq (1991, 2003) can best be understood in terms of this overriding interest.

Oil-dependent countries recognized the urgent need to search for other means to power economic growth. For a time, nuclear power appeared the most alluring alternative energy source. Launched in the 1950s by the U.S. government, the program of "atoms for peace" promised technological marvels, among which the most hopeful was electricity generated by nuclear reactors. Nuclear power plants began to appear in large numbers in the 1960s; by the late 1990s, more than four hundred plants were in operation around the world. Their power output represented the energy equivalent to the total yearly production from the world's major oil country, Saudi Arabia. France implemented the most comprehensive program,

obtaining in the late 1980s over two-thirds of its total electricity from nuclear plants.

Many other countries had cut back or stopped nuclear power development by then. The new technology held the risk of grave accidents, and its cost had become appreciably greater than other energy sources for electricity generation. Heightened concern over safety led to complex design changes and delays in plant construction that raised expenses. The nuclear accidents at Three-Mile Island in the United States in 1979 and, most serious of all, at Chernobyl in the Soviet Union in 1986, raised public concern around the world about the very feasibility of safe nuclear power. A few countries, notably France and Japan, with well-run nuclear programs and a great need to reduce oil imports continued their reliance on nuclear reactors. People and states throughout the world confronted painful economic choices touching their everyday lives as a result of their growing reliance on new sources of power to support a satisfactory expansion of production and consumption.

The rising demand for energy posed the crucial problem of the depletion of nonrenewable resources. Two directions were open to make better use of energy, one through conservation and the other through new technology for energy efficiency. The sudden rise of oil prices in the 1970s increased costs to a point where efficiency in energy use became a national priority in the industrial countries. The United States, having for a century expended its coal and petroleum at a prolific pace, began a major program of energy savings in industrial and home use and in transportation. In the decade between 1973 and 1983, it reduced energy consumption (measured in relation to gross national product) by one fourth and curtailed its use of petroleum by one fifth. This trend constituted a Conservation Revolution as important to future world development as the Green Revolution in food production. But the U.S.'s insatiable demand for energy, fueled by its remarkable period of prosperity in the 1990s, produced once again highly wasteful practices, especially in the increased vehicle consumption of fuel oil.

New technology created opportunities for enlarging access to necessary resources and for the substitution of new resources still in abundant supply. The petroleum industry developed complex machinery to move their oil drilling into harsh environments, including offshore areas and sites in Arctic lands. The Alaska and the North Sea oil fields, both developed in the 1970s, became the last great Western oil discoveries. After the fall of the Soviet Union, the new governments of Central Asia invited Western companies to send geologists to search for oil in areas around the Caspian Sea, thought to hold vast reserves. When they had completed their analysis, the oil companies announced that they had discovered oil and natural gas fields with reserves as large as those of North America and Europe's North Sea area combined.

These discoveries promised adequate oil for the first decades of the twentieth-first century. Rising global production combined with conservation policies brought crude oil prices below $20 in the late 1980s. Oil prices remained stable through most of the 1990s and supplies were abundant. In the mid-1990s, the international price of oil was nearly as low (when adjusted for two decades of inflation) as it had been in the early 1970s. Petroleum fueled the global economic boom of that decade. But that period of rapid growth sent oil demand rising. Once again, OPEC was able to use its power as a cartel to help push crude oil prices up, reaching $30 in the early years of the new century.

In the early twenty-first century, the return of high oil prices forced countries to ask the question whether their plans for economic development had hit the barrier of limited resources. The answer at the opening of the new century was encouraging. As a result of technological discoveries, the prices of all basic resources needed for the global economy declined between the 1970s and 1990s. New plastics found many industrial applications in place of expensive metals. The risks posed by wasteful production and consumption were increasingly clear in environmental pollution and periodic shortages. Warnings from scientists of global warming led governments to explore the means of slowing or even reducing energy use from polluting sources, but the cost was high. These troubling conditions made the conservation programs of the 1970s a lesson to be relearned again at the end of the century. "Sustainable" economic growth, defined as growth limited by the need to restrict consumption of nonrenewable natural resources and to protect the human environment, set the sober but realistic limits on the global economy's capacity to offer the world's peoples a better life in the twenty-first century.

HIGHLIGHT: The Global Environment

Economic growth and the rapid expansion of the world's population came at a high price for the earth's environment. Before the twentieth century, the greatest environmental disruptions were caused by natural forces such as volcanic eruptions and severe droughts; humanity acquired the dubious distinction in the last century of becoming itself the principal cause of environmental harm. By the 1950s, the land, water, and air on all continents were showing obvious, ugly signs of serious damage. In turn, this environmental decay contributed directly to loss of natural resources, the spread of infectious disease, and permanent changes in the earth's climate.

The origins of these problems differed substantially between developed countries and the Third World. In the industrial regions of the world, environmental decline resulted primarily from high energy consumption and the wastefulness of consumer societies. In the developing areas, the principal causes lay in unregulated economic development and in the pressures generated by the population explosion, urban overcrowding, and impoverishment. From the beginning of the Industrial Revolution, manufacturers eager for profit had disregarded the deterioration caused by their enterprises. But state-run command economies of the Soviet Union, eastern Europe, and China proved equally destructive of the environment during their decades of intensive growth. Environmental problems intruded on people's lives in ways and to an extent never before experienced. They disrupted the ordinary activities of billions of people and reached into the least populated parts of the globe. Their global character was readily apparent in the pollution of the atmosphere.

The smokestack had been the symbol of the Industrial Revolution from the start. It released the gases produced by coal-fueled steam engines powering factories and lighting streets and homes. In the twentieth-century, the exhaust gases coming from the burning of refined petroleum by internal combustion and diesel engines marked in its smelly way the new consumer societies. The use of these fossil fuels had left visible traces in the smog that was at the origin of London's nineteenth-century "pea-soup" fog, and that hung like a dirty haze over the major cities of the world a century later.

Even in the nineteenth century, a few scientists had pointed out that the accumulation of these gases, consisting primarily of carbon dioxide, would in the long run act like a blanket around the earth, altering the global climate and raising average temperatures. Until the late twentieth century, these forecasts were not substantiated by tangible evidence understandable to governments and to the public alike. Economic growth remained a key to public policy and private investments in the industrial countries. It was a vital goal for underdeveloped nations. Industrialization and rising levels of consumption were impossible without increased energy consumption from fossil fuels. In the global economy of the late century, its use was limited only by market prices and accessibility.

In the 1980s and 1990s awareness of the dangers of atmospheric pollution increased as a result both of the work of scientists and of the concern of populations suffering the painful physical effects of a fouled atmosphere. The chemical process destroying the ozone layer was discernible only to the sophisticated equipment of researchers. By the mid-1980s, they were able to establish the direct link between the diffusion (through evaporation) of manufactured coolants, especially in air conditioning, and the decline of atmospheric ozone vital in protecting the earth from intensive solar radiation. Once understood, the problem became the subject of international conferences. Governments and manufacturers agreed in 1987 to end the production and use of these coolants by the end of the century. Their collaboration produced, for the first time, an international treaty on a critical global environmental issue.

The increase in atmospheric pollution caused by carbon gases raised far more difficult questions. These touched on the very quality of life of both developed and developing countries. The level of carbon dioxide in the air in the 1990s was twenty-five times that of a century before. Western countries bore the major responsibility for this swift rise. Their prosperous economies depended increasingly on road transportation, which was a major cause of carbon dioxide pollution. The United States alone produced one-third of the total carbon emissions in the world. In the last third of the century, Third World countries produced discernable signs of severe air pollution, as evidenced by the great clouds of smog that hung over India's enormous cities. Their lack of modern technology and the pressure for economic growth at all cost prevented them from introducing serious pollution control measures. By the late century, the combined emissions coming from the Third World were nearly equal to those of the Western countries.

In the mid-1990s, scientific findings uncovered clear signs of significant global warning. The evidence revealed a noticeable rise in average summer and winter temperatures throughout the Northern Hemisphere. In 2000, the United Nations Panel on Climate Change published the definitive report on global warming, which it attributed to human deeds. Average air temperatures were rising everywhere, including the Antarctic and Arctic regions. Greenhouse gases, of which carbon dioxide was by far the most damaging, were the principal cause. The consequences were already apparent in the melting of the earth's ice caps, the increasing severity of storms, and the rising level of the earth's oceans.

In this process, the destruction of the tropical forests played its own important part. The causes at work here included both the desperate search for resources on the part of impoverished populations in the Third World, and the appetite for forest products of the expanding global economy. The Brazilian settlers moving into the rainforest areas of Amazonia, and Indonesian migrants starting a new life in the forests of Sumatra, burned millions of acres of forest each year to begin farming. Their action helped to destroy a unique environment, and poured billions of tons of carbon dioxide into the air. Spurred on by the growing demand for wood, international lumber companies purchased enormous rainforest properties, first cutting the trees then burning the undergrowth to sell the land to agribusiness or small farmers. Their destructive burning of Indonesian forests produced severe smog over a vast region of southeast Asia inhabited by more than one hundred million people. In 1997 the government of Indonesia issued an international public apology for the harm done. But its own policies of support for big business and incentives for emigration from its overpopulated central islands to Sumatra and Borneo lay at the heart of this environmental crisis.

The rapid loss of forests around the world was harmful both because it devastated an invaluable resource and because it led to pollution of the air, the land, and the water. In many parts of Africa and Asia, trees and bushes became the sole source of heating fuel as impoverishment and growing rural populations made other sources of heat inaccessible. The disappearance of forests brought decay of farmland, eroded by rains and overworked by struggling farmers, and severe flooding of the lowlands caused by the runoff of rain from deforested slopes. Tropical forests acted as powerful agents absorbing vast amounts of carbon dioxide. Their absence further accelerated the atmospheric accumulation of greenhouse gases. These forests were as well a

Burning Season in the Amazon Basin: Picture, Taken from U.S. Space Shuttle Discovery, of Smoke Cover and Plumes Produced by Fires Burning in the Amazon Forest, September 1988 (*NASA*)

treasure-house of natural products useful to the health and well-being of populations. Once gone, the forests' treasures would be lost as well.

Growing shortages of water in areas such as the Tigris and Euphrates rivers in the Middle East became a economic and political issue. Access to water in semidesert areas of rapid population growth and economic development became so critical that in these places water was "more precious than oil." In the 1980s, the government of Turkey began the most ambitious water control project yet attempted in any non-Western country. It started construction of twenty dams and irrigation canals along the headwaters of the Tigris and Euphrates rivers. Both originated in Turkey's eastern mountains. By the end of the century, this Southeast Anatolia Project had completed half of its major dams. It was already bringing tangible economic benefits to a vast semi-desert region, long stripped of its trees and topsoil by overfarming and deforestation. Land was again becoming fertile through irrigation, cheap electric power was fueling industrialization, and the region's peoples (including millions of Kurds) saw an escape to their age-old impoverishment.

The price of their success was the limitation of water supplies to the downstream regions of Syria and Iraq. Turkey's great dams promised a better life for some peoples, at the expense of others living on the lower reaches of the rivers. The Anatolian Project directors were prepared to sell water (by the boatload) to thirsty Mediterranean lands such as Israel with the funds to afford purchases. Other lands lacked these funds. Collaborative water agreements with Syria and Iraq might protect the well-being of these peoples; war for water was a real possibility too.

Epidemic diseases in the Third World were inextricably bound up with water, air, and land pollution. Rivers filled with silt from deforested lands and from the pollutants of new factories and untreated human waste. Water drawn from these sources became a source of infectious disease and physical deformities for the population living along polluted rivers such as the Yangtze in China and the Ganges in India. Infectious diseases were nourished by the untreated sewage and polluted air in enormous cities such as Cairo and Bombay, to which many millions of rural inhabitants migrated to escape the misery of village life. Countries such as India confronted the recurrence of diseases, such as the bubonic plague, that medical experts had thought forever eliminated by public health and modern medicine. In these terms, the most critical environmental needs at the close of the twentieth century were found in the Third World.

Economic development was a global dilemma as well as a promise. Progress had for a century been defined in large measure as the improvement of economic well-being. The newly independent countries of the Third World subscribed as fervently to that creed as did the West. Their leaders argued in fact that their needs for economic growth were a matter of survival as much as well-being because of the widespread poverty of their populations. They argued that the West had to make the greatest sacrifices for environmental protection. Its total contribution to global pollution was the largest by far and its technological skills were more readily applicable to energy conservation and pollution control. Yet the scale of the problem was so great that no international solution could succeed without the cooperation of all sides.

Two centuries before, an English physician, Thomas Malthus, had warned of a social crisis in his country. He calculated that the population was multiplying faster than food supplies necessary to meet the people's basic needs. The Industrial Revolution and the demographic transition in the West to low birthrates had proven him wrong. In the early twenty-first century, however, the Malthusian trap was closing again. To address the global environmental crisis, effective solutions could come only on a global scale. These had to include both severe population limits and sweeping technological adjustments to restrain energy consumption and to protect the global environment.

Awareness of the crisis brought together representatives from around the world at the first United Nations Conference on Environment and Development in 1992. This so-called Earth Summit, attended by the heads of more than one hundred countries, heard conflicting arguments. Environmentalists demanded immediate measures to protect nature, while Third World leaders insisted that only economic growth could overcome the distress of their peoples and create the financial means to halt pollution. Representatives from developed countries defended the high standard of living of their populations. The conference was unable to agree on measures to halt the degradation of land and water. It did finally put together a Global Warming Convention that called for a halt to the global rise of carbon dioxide emissions by the end of the century.

Measures to achieve this objective had to come from both developing and developed countries. Another conference in 1997 in Kyoto, Japan, produced an agreement by the industrialized states to initiate the difficult process of stopping global warning. Their promise was to reduce by 2010 fossil fuel emissions in their countries to levels below those of 1990. Third World governments agreed to join the effort afterwards. The signers put off until 2000 a specific agreement on how this drastic and painful transformation was to occur. But at the 2000 conference in The Hague, Netherlands, negotiations on measures curtailing greenhouse gases fell apart over disagreements on how each developed country should actually meet the ambitious goal set at Kyoto. Demonstrators there from the world's environmental defense organizations warned that "the earth is in danger!" Negotiators from the United States, which remained the principal source of greenhouse gases, came to the conference knowing that the U.S. Congress was opposed to any treaty curtailing energy so severely as to threaten the country's economic growth. The next year, the new U.S. president, George W. Bush, formally abandoned the Kyoto treaty. The global environment remained hostage to national interests.

Success in saving the earth's environment demanded the voluntary cooperation of states to introduce new energy policies. It also called for the collaboration of peoples around the world to practice conservation in their daily lives. It needed technological solutions for alternative energy sources. The environmental crisis required international collaboration on a scale never seen since the Second World War. The stakes in this crisis were as high as the outcome of the war had been. The consequences of defeat were ominous for the future of humanity.

The Global Market

The global economy of the late twentieth century differed in important ways from the international economy of the early century. For the first time, businesses could disperse their economic activities throughout the world. Corporate headquarters clustered in a small number of cities. Financial operations and factory production gradually moved far from these centers into countries where labor was least expensive and governments granted special benefits to investors. The laboring population of towns in Mexico where factories manufactured car parts were in economic terms neighbors to the Detroit headquarters of the major U.S. automobile corporations.

Because the most inexpensive labor was found in Third World countries, the operations of international corporations—notably those in textiles, automobiles, and electronics—split between executive and research offices in home countries and production in distant lands. These interregional operations were known as "global factories." U.S. corporations tended to look to Latin America for sites for factories. Japan increasingly played the leading trade, financial, and industrial role in southeast Asia. German companies began to move into eastern Europe in the late 1980s. Regional economic formations slowly emerged around one dominant country. These corporate giants operated in a world market but remained rooted in their country of origin.

A second characteristic of the global economy was the decision of all the major developed countries, except for the communist lands, to move toward the reduction or elimination of tariffs on imported goods. The General Agreement on Tariffs and Trade (GATT), formed by the Western countries in the late 1940s to fight a return to 1930s protectionism, played an important role in this process. Its guidelines became the basis for a general reduction in tariffs in the early 1960s. This was followed by an even more substantial international tariff reduction in 1994, when GATT was replaced by the World Trade Organization (WTO). By the turn of the century, membership in the WTO came from more than one hundred countries from around the world, including the Chinese People's Republic. The Chinese communist leaders saw in the global economy the means to sustain the country's rapid economic growth and to find jobs for its 1.3 billion people.

The WTO's goal was to let trading and production be decided not by state regulations but by market forces. Factories would open and close according to profit and productivity. Price increases on goods would be kept in check by foreign imports, helping to reduce inflation and, ideally, the cost of living. World trade doubled in volume in the prosperous last decade of the century. Benefits were unevenly distributed, however. Half of the total world exports originated during that decade from the European Union and the United States. Global free trade was a formula weighted in favor of the industrialized countries.

Opposition to the globalization in trade relations remained strong. Environmental groups protested the weakness in GATT of provisions for environmental protection and pollution control. Political resistance in western countries emerged from the insistence of producers and workers to retain protections from foreign competition, and to receive government financial help to sell their products cheaply abroad. Labor unions objected to competition from lands where wages were low. Agricultural interests in Europe and the U.S. insisted on continued state subsidies for basic crops, such as cotton, though these were produced at lower cost in Third World countries. Global tariff reductions stalled over these issues in the early twenty-first century.

Regional groupings were a better arena of free trade. The expansion of the European Economic Community (European Union) showed the way. Its success led other areas to repeat this formula. Latin America ceased being a continent of hostile states after they moved in the 1980s to free market economies and democratic governments. Economic cooperation was built on these shared values and institutions. Brazil, Argentina, Paraguay, and Uruguay created their own common market in 1995. To the north, the North American Free Trade Agreement (NAFTA, 1994) set in motion the elimination of trade barriers among Mexico, the United States, and Canada.

Regional economic collaboration was risky where economies were underdeveloped and a large portion of the population was impoverished. These dangers emerged within NAFTA shortly after the treaty was signed. Life among the Mexican population of one hundred million resembled in many ways conditions in Third World lands. Its government had grand visions of economic benefits from regional trade and investments from American and Canadian companies. But in 1995, foreign investors (as well as wealthy Mexicans) withdrew billions of dollars from Mexico when they began to doubt the glowing promises of quick profits made by the government. The Mexican currency lost half its value, undermining the government's economic plans, threatening default on the government's international loans, and menacing the value of other Latin American currencies as speculative fears worsened.

This "run" on the Mexican peso created a major international financial crisis. It was so serious that the President Clinton decided to offer a 12-billion-dollar loan from U.S. government funds to bolster the Mexican currency. Nothing like this had ever happened before. The backing of the United States and severe Mexican austerity measures ended the crisis, and the Mexican government repaid the loan within two years. The price was a painful two-year recession in Mexico. This crisis proved a warning that the global economy brought with it the threat of regional financial collapse caused by the rapid movement of speculative and investment funds around the world.

The third new trait of the globalization trend in international economic relations in the late twentieth century was the ongoing policy coordination by the governments of major industrial states in the areas of trade, finance, and economic aid. The well-being of all developed countries depended on the stability of global economic relations. Complex international economic operations in finance and investment were beyond the control of any individual government. Memories of the chaos of trade and finance in the 1930s haunted political leaders and industrialists alike. Regional conflicts and revolutionary movements in the newly decolonized world aroused fears of new obstacles to economic development. To give some order to global economic relations, the leaders of the seven major industrial states (the Western powers and Japan) began in the 1970s to meet regularly to discuss common industrial, financial, and trade problems.

Their basic goal was to keep intact and, when possible, to enlarge the scope of the global economy. These included the relatively free movement of goods and capital, the stability of the most important currencies, and the opening of economies around the world to private investors and industrialists. Their cooperation did facilitate ongoing economic operations. It was based upon a recognition of common economic interests and a shared commitment to liberal capitalism.

Their concerns included economic problems in the Third World. In the global economy, their countries' economic fortunes did feel the impact of prosperity or depression in underdeveloped lands. The unpaid debts owed their banks by Third World states (particularly in Africa) totaled nearly $100 billion by the late 1980s, with no chance of full repayment. In 1996, the "Group of Seven" offered to cancel $25 billion of their debts, on condition the debtor governments adopt free market reforms. Economic aid to impoverished peoples did not drive their efforts. Private investment was the Group of Seven's preferred method of assistance to developing countries. Their financial advisers had become increasingly discouraged by the large amounts of aid wasted in many Third World countries by corrupt regimes. Their choice revealed to what extent the commitment to Third World welfare had been replaced by concern over the well-being of global finances and market economies.

By the early twenty-first century, the term "Third World" best designated those impoverished regions where modern industry was missing and where jobs were either unavailable or insufficient to meet the needs of the growing population. Legally or illegally, people from these poor regions set out for more prosperous lands in search of well-paying jobs. Their presence was felt in countries as small as Kuwait, attracting Indians and Palestinians ready to do unskilled labor, and as large as Australia, one-fifth of whose population were foreign-born in 2000. Gradually the global economy acquired what in essence was a global labor force. The total number of these international migrants was estimated to have reached one hundred fifty million by the mid-1990s. In the previous two decades, more than twenty million people arrived in the United States, most from Third World regions. This sudden influx produced a greater proportion of foreign-born residents than in any comparable period in U.S. history. Comparable trends were apparent in western European countries.

Cities such as Paris, Berlin, New York, London, and Los Angeles were centers for this migration. It put in their midst a Third World laboring population. But these migrants appeared everywhere jobs were available, even though they often encountered prejudice and persecution. In the North African country of Libya, rich in petroleum, migrants from sub-Saharan Africa came in the 1980s and 1990s to fill the menial jobs that Libyans no longer accepted. They stayed until large-scale anti-immigrant riots forced them to flee in 2000. Similar violence against Third World migrants erupted in Europe as well in the 1990s. Social tensions rooted in hostility toward these outsiders exposed the ethnic antagonisms hidden beneath the surface of prosperous countries.

In the expansion of the global economy lay also one hope for finding the means to restrain the expansion of the world's population. Where a better life appears a reality and a family has access to the means to ensure that life, fewer children become a desirable choice. This simple formula was proving its potent effect throughout the world. It depended upon the coincidence of many conditions, including medical care, civil order, literacy, women's rights, as well as a growing economy.

It was an important theme of the 1994 International Conference on Population and Development. Its members, from throughout the world, issued an appeal to include women in all development programs. Without their full participation, the Conference agreed that no effective population limits could come voluntarily. The proposal had the great advantage of relying on the free choice of people given the incentive as well as the encouragement to take control of their personal fate. In doing so, they would contribute to the well-being of their country, and ultimately of the globe. It was a great distance from the global economy to this level of individual choice, but the linkage was already taking shape.

LOCAL WARS AND PEACEKEEPING

The collapse of the Soviet Union left only the United States with the economic resources and the military might of a superpower. At the close of the 1991 Gulf War, the U.S. president sought to reassure the world that his country would not abuse its global dominance. In previous centuries, diplomatic and military alliances had been the principal means for weaker states to protect themselves from the threat of what in German was known as *machtpolitik* ("power politics") inflicted by a dominant state. In 1919, President Woodrow Wilson had proposed a new international system grounded in democratic government, national self-determination, and collective defense against aggression to maintain peace to replace the balance of power system (see Chapter 1, Highlight: "Internationalism"). In 1991, President George Bush took up that liberal idea again, calling for a "new world order" for "peace and security, freedom, and the rule of law," to be achieved through the United Nations, now freed from its Cold War stalemate.

Throughout the 1990s, the U.S. supported collective efforts at peacekeeping. In the Balkans, the Middle East, Africa, and Asia, U.N. peacekeeping forces appeared to control or prevent violent conflicts within or among states. It proved a difficult task, impeded by the limits placed on U.N. forces, and by the temptation among leaders of sovereign states to reject international controls and to rely on their own forces. Violence came as well from terrorist organizations, capable of inflicting terrible destruction on innocent civilians anywhere in the world. The end of the Cold War marked the opening of a new era of international relations.

In the post-imperial age of the 1990s, the new nation-states of the world confronted local and ethnic conflicts in greater numbers than ever before. By one count, they numbered nearly fifty, including civil wars in the former state of Yugoslavia and in Afghanistan, and the civil war and massacre in the African republic of Rwanda. The issue in these, and many other similar conflicts, was struggle for state power among competing ethnic groups. Leaders of the competing movements claimed to speak for their ethnic nation, whose "rights" they defended. At times, war became a way of life for the warriors, seeking only power and wealth. Some conflicts arose out of the brutal efforts by the regime in power to impose dictatorial rule on its peoples. The process of national self-determination proved in these conditions incapable of ensuring elementary conditions of peace and security for the population.

Ethnic Conflict and War in Central Africa

In the new nation-states of Africa and Asia, relations among ethnic groups suffered when, as occurred often in the 1990s, problems of misrule, poverty, and social unrest became acute. When resources were scarce and peoples were forced to move to urban slums in search of a livelihood, the occasions for ethnic rioting multiplied. Social hardship fed rising crime rates, and when the state could not offer protection, tribal solidarity promised the best defense. Incompetent or unscrupulous political leaders could hope to hold onto power by mobilizing their own ethnic or tribal followers against other peoples. Differences that earlier mattered little, such as religious affiliation, became another source of conflict. The variations on the formula for ethnic hostility were many, the result universally disastrous for the peoples touched by the unrest.

In 1994, Rwanda experienced the worst ethnic violence in Africa's post-colonial history. The conflict was in its origins and outcome an exemplary case of the process by which nation-building turned into ethnic exclusion. Rwanda was a small country, but gathered within its borders all the forces capable of igniting ethnic conflict. These included a history of colonial favoritism for a minority people, the Tutsi, at the expense of the other ethnic group, the Hutu, and a population explosion and impoverishment for many of the inhabitants. Under Belgian rule, the Tutsi had enjoyed the position of favored people, whose traditional leaders enjoyed the honors and benefits as collaborators of the colonial rulers, and found ready access to education and jobs in the colony's civil administration.

Belgium's sudden withdrawal in 1962 had stripped the Tutsi of these advantages. In the name of majority rule, the Belgians passed power to the majority Hutu people (90 percent of the inhabitants). The new national leaders forcibly ejected the Tutsi from all positions of authority, from the central government to local administration. They sought the economic and social rewards brought by political dominance with its privileged position, as it became known among the poorer new states, of "gatekeeper" (control over access to state posts and preference in business deals). Political power provided an important source of income in that mountainous land, which had one of the highest population densities (eight hundred per square mile) in Africa.

The new rulers found help from the former colonial rulers of the region. The Belgian and French governments supplied foreign aid to the Hutu leadership, just as they did to Mobutu's government in Zaire. Their goal was to protect their political influence in a region which was rich in natural resources, and where Franco-Belgian economic interests from the colonial period remained strong. Their concerns did not extend to ethnic relations and minority rights.

Hutu leaders retained the colonial system of using identity cards that denoted Rwanda citizens' ethnic origins. They sought to deflect discontent at their incompetent rule by arousing antagonism toward the Tutsi, whose living conditions were usually better than the Hutu. A secret extremist Hutu group even devised plans to eliminate the Tutsi entirely. "Back to Ethiopia" was their slogan. Their propaganda portrayed the Tutsi as outsiders in their own country. Ethnic cleansing was their goal. Periodic attacks on the Tutsi occurred in the following decades. As a result, many Tutsi fled to neighboring states, some to organize for guerrilla war against the Hutu regime in Rwanda.

The escalating ethnic antagonism led to efforts by some Hutu leaders, including the president, to create a coalition government under United Nations supervision. Their efforts were undermined, however, by other Hutu who sought the solution in mass executions. In 1994, the suspicious death of the Hutu president in a plane crash gave Hutu extremists the excuse to claim that the Tutsi were preparing to kill the Hutu. Their accusation was absurd, intended only to mobilize their supporters among armed Hutu militia and the army. They had already laid plans for the mass execution of the Tutsi (and were probably responsible for the plane crash). They could rely on the loyalty of their followers and the hatred felt by many Hutu toward their Tutsi neighbors.

They mobilized their militia forces and broadcast to their followers the message that "the Tutsi

Genocide in Rwanda: Bodies of Massacred Tutsi inside Nyamata Catholic Church, 1994 (*Reuters/Corinne Dufka/Archive Photos*)

need to be killed." A small United Nations peace-keeping force was powerless even to protect its own troops from the mobs, and fled the country. When moderate Hutus attempted to halt the bloodshed and to defend Tutsi, they also fell victims to the killing. In the massacre that followed, one-half (perhaps five hundred thousand) of the Tutsi population in Rwanda were assassinated.

In the decades since the Nazi Final Solution, the Hutu leaders' action was as close as any fanatics had come to implementing a policy of genocide, that is, a conscious, collective effort to exterminate an entire people. And like the Holocaust, it defied rational explanation. A Belgian Catholic missionary, wounded in a vain effort to give shelter to a group of Tutsi children,

explained later to foreign correspondents that "we were overwhelmed by this great evil. There is a madness at work." Faced with such inhumanity, he could find no other answer.

This horrific event set off fighting that led to a major war in central Africa. To stop the killings, Tutsi armed forces in exile in neighboring Uganda invaded Rwanda. They had the backing of the leader of Uganda. Ten years before, he brought his country out of civil war by what he called "no-party democracy" and effective protection of ethnic minorities. Repelled by the bloodshed and fearing that the violence would spread to his land, he gave vital aid in arms and finances to the Tutsi rebel army. His action raised the conflict in Rwanda to an African war. The

Tutsi invaders proved much better fighters than the Hutu militia, who fled Rwanda. They were accompanied by an estimated two million Hutu refugees who feared death at the hands of their former prey. The massacres ended, and a new Tutsi government set out to restore order and to bring to justice the "agents of genocide."

That conflict exploded into an international crisis when the conflict spread to Zaire. The bulk of the Hutu refugees had gathered in vast camps in Zaire bordering on Rwanda. Among them were most of the Hutu warlords and militia responsible for the genocide. They turned the camps into their base of guerrilla operations against the new Rwandan regime. The feeble Zaire government was powerless to maintain order on its own in that eastern region of its vast country. By that time, Zaire had collapsed into disorder and decay. It had experienced three decades of such misrule by Mobutu that it had become one of the worst cases in the postcolonial regions of a failed state. Its bloody "tribal" conflicts revealed it to be a land without order or real state authority (see Chapter 5). In a desperate attempt to maintain some influence in eastern Zaire, Mobutu lent his support the Hutu guerrillas. It was a fatal move, for that action turned the conflict into a regional war.

In 1995 Rwandan government troops, with the backing of an informal regional alliance, invaded Zaire in pursuit of the Hutu militia. Two issues were crucial in this new-style, postcolonial local war. Zaire's internal disorder made it likely that any conflict there would spread beyond its borders without new leadership. Both Rwanda and Uganda confronted this likelihood. In addition, Zaire's abundant natural resources, including diamonds, exercised a strong attraction for neighboring states and for predatory militias seeking to profit from the conflict.

That African war was led by the Rwandan government, desperate to end the constant border fighting with Hutu guerrillas operating from sanctuaries in Zaire. It brought in political enemies of Mobutu, among whom the most capable was an opponent of thirty years named Laurent Kabila. It included the neighboring states of Angola, Zambia, and Uganda. Their leaders had an urgent need to bring some political stability to the region. They anticipated as well substantial benefits to their own economies when their armed forces occupied mineral-rich areas of Zaire.

Working together, these forces succeeded in a remarkably short time in organizing and supplying an army headed by Kabila and trained and led by Tutsi officers from Rwanda. In the summer of 1996, this army swept through Zaire to the capital. Mobutu's army collapsed; he fled the country. Kabila took control of the state, renaming it (as it had been at independence in 1960) the Democratic Republic of Congo. The government of the largest country in sub-Saharan Africa had changed hands in a war launched by what some observers called a "pan-African alliance."

The violence did not end, however. The Rwandan government promised protection for both its Hutu and Tutsi citizens. But the hatred between the two groups flared up repeatedly in sporadic fighting. The Democratic Republic of Congo remained a vast underpoliced land. Fugitive Hutu militia periodically mounted raids on Rwanda, whose forces continued their manhunt for the Hutu responsible for the 1994 massacre. Troops of Uganda, Angola, and Zambia moved into border areas, and soon were fighting not only Congolese troops but also each other to control diamond-rich areas. Civil and foreign war in central Africa continued for years, leading to the death of more than three million people. Only the intervention in 2003 of U.N. peacekeeping forces, and the impoverishment of the region, reduced the fighting to sporadic ethnic rioting. The U.N. organized, under the authority of its International War Crimes Court, trials of thousands of Hutu accused of genocide. The scars of that brutal event made peace in the region a distant goal.

In the early twenty-first century a very fragile peace existed among the states of central Africa. There, the colonial borders remained as the vestiges of imperial rule. Political leaders continued to talk of civic nationalism and the need for an end to ethnic and tribal hostility. The leaders of the Rwandan government, like those in neighboring Tanzania and Uganda, recognized that human rights were a desirable goal. They insisted, however, that their regimes not be measured by Western political ideals. As one said, "the African and the Western worlds are many worlds apart."

Elsewhere in Africa, local wars in the 1990s became a struggle for the spoils of war. The "blood diamonds" of Zaire had to compete in an international market of booty produced by private armies elsewhere in the continent. Civil wars in countries such as Angola and Sierra Leone fed on pillaging by self-styled armies whose warriors knew no other way of life. Precious raw materials were a prime target of these armed groups. The rich diamond mines of Angola sustained a rebel army that had been fighting to seize the central government ever since independence in 1976. Its military backing from foreign sources had dried up at the end of the Cold War, when Soviet and U.S. agents ceased competing for influence there. Control of the diamond trade kept the rebel army fighting through most of the 1990s, as long as it could find buyers for this war booty. One observer concluded that in those areas "diamonds are warfare's best friend."

The Warring Peoples of the Balkans

The end of the Cold War brought brutal ethnic conflict to peoples within the former communist lands. The worst of these occurred in southeastern Europe, in the region known as the Balkans inhabited mainly by peoples of Slavic languages but of divided religious loyalties. The Catholic and Orthodox churches were dominant among Croatians and Serbs, respectively; the Muslim faith had spread among many inhabitants of the region know as Bosnia, as well as in Albania.

The communist rulers of Yugoslavia, heirs to the South Slav (Yugoslav) state formed in 1919, had managed to hold together their various Slavic-speaking peoples in a federal state of "national republics," formed on the model of the Soviet Union (see Chapter 2). Tito, the founder of the Yugoslav Communist Party and head of postwar Yugoslavia, enjoyed enormous personal authority among the peoples there. His death in 1980 left his state without a strong leader; the collapse in 1989 of the other communist states of eastern Europe undermined the very legitimacy of communism in Yugoslavia. The country had to be rebuilt, and the only principle that attracted strong backing was national self-determination.

The conflicts among peoples in the former Yugoslavia proved the tragic consequences of attempting to redraw state borders to appease nationalist passions based on ethnic loyalty. In 1990, the leaders of the major national republics of Yugoslavia agreed to allow the people of each national republic to vote whether to secede from or to remain within the federal state. Their decision was an admission of weakness. They recognized that communism was bankrupt and that their only solution to the political crisis was free elections. Two republics (Slovenia and Croatia) immediately chose to leave. In 1991, their leaders formed independent nation-states, and the other republics soon followed their example (see map of Europe, 1992, p. 198). Each new "nation-state" contained substantial ethnic minorities whose "native" national territory lay in a neighboring republic. The nationalist vision of ethnically pure territory went counter to the realities of ethnic intermarriage, migrations, and the generations-old persistence of ethnically mixed communities in the Balkan region.

This mixing of peoples gave the ambitious leader of the Serbian republic, Slobodan Milosevic, his opportunity. Serbs living in Croatia and Bosnia belonged, according to extremist nationalists, within "Greater Serbia." Milosovic made this rallying cry the basis for his new political agenda. Once an ardent Communist, he used Serbian nationalism as an alternative platform on which to rebuild his power in the post-Yugoslav Balkans. In the First

World War Serbs had fought against the Austria-Hungarian Empire for national freedom for South Slavs. That history inspired Milosevic and his nationalist followers in 1992 to demand that all Serbian people live in one "greater" (i.e., enlarged) Serbian state. Enlarging Serbia was possible only by annexing neighboring territories. The weakness of the other successor states in the former Yugoslavia convinced Milosevic that the plan could succeed. His nationalist ambitions destroyed the last hope for the preservation of peaceful relations among Balkan peoples. War had begun in 1914 when a Serbian terrorist had assassinated the Austro-Hungarian Grand Duke in the Bosnian capital of Sarajevo. War began again in 1991 in the same region over Serbian efforts to expand their rule into Bosnian areas where large numbers of Serbians lived.

Bosnia was a multiethnic, multireligious land. It was divided among a Muslim population (labeled Muslim because they belonged to a distinct community, not because they all were practicing Muslims) in small majority, and large numbers of Serbs and Croatians. In 1992, the Serbian republic and Bosnian Serbs joined forces to seize large areas of Bosnia. Arms and military forces from the old Yugoslav army (largely Serbian) went into Serbian-inhabited areas of Bosnia. Armed groups of Serbs began a systematic effort to expel Muslims from these regions. Their "ethnic cleansing" (a new term referring to the forced removal of an entire people) included killing, rape, and intimidation on a massive scale. Its purpose was to force the bulk of the Muslims to flee into a small territory of their own and leave the Serbs in sole possession of most of Bosnia. The Serb forces put under siege the capital city, Sarajevo (site of the 1984 Winter Olympics). At the same time, the Croatian government launched its own ethnic cleansing campaign, expelling Serbs from its territory and seizing parts of Bosnia where many Croatians lived. The Muslim government of Bosnia organized an army and fought desperately to defeat the Serb and Croat armed groups. Its forces employed at times methods as brutal as those of their opponents. Respect for innocent civilians and simple pity vanished in a ruthless civil war.

A reckless, ambitious political leader started the process leading to civil war in former Yugoslavia. Yet Milosevic's war could not have produced such widespread brutality had antagonism among ethnic groups not revived despite three generations of peaceful life in the federation. Neighbors began to fear one another in a process fueled by demagogic calls for violence. Only small groups of soldiers carried on the fighting. The civilian majority was unwilling to participate for fear of suffering for a cause that was less important than their own safety and well-being. At times, private armies took over large sections of the country. Their warlord leaders justified combat in nationalist terms, but seemed motivated by the sheer love of battle.

Their message of ethnic hatred denied human dignity to their enemies. Women became objects for sexual abuse; men became victims of brutalization. By 1994, one hundred thousand people had died as a result of the fighting throughout the Balkans. A million or more had become refugees, forced to flee their homes to escape the violence of war. The Balkan civil war, on the territory of the former Yugoslavia, embodied the ugliest, most inhuman features of the ethnic conflicts in other parts of the world.

Losing the war, the Bosnian government appealed in 1993 to the European Union and the United Nations for help. Both attempted to find a compromise solution to the conflict, but failed. The Serbian forces in Bosnia continued their expulsion and execution of Bosnians, even those living in U.N.-protected areas. The city of Sarajevo was under constant bombardment by Serbian guns. Only military intervention could halt the bloodshed. That action came in 1995 from the armed forces of NATO. Its leaders finally concluded that the war, which might spread to surrounding states, threatened the interests and well-being of all Europe. Led by the United

States, the NATO air force began the bombing of Serbian positions in Bosnia. The NATO high command warned the Serbian leaders that they risked seeing the war spread to their own territory unless the Bosnian Serbs stopped fighting and agreed to a compromise peace treaty.

The military action by NATO ended the Bosnian war. The 1995 treaty left the militias of the Serbs and the Croatians stationed in the areas that they had conquered. A united Bosnia remained a paper promise. In the Balkans, nationalism had become the tool of unscrupulous political leaders, prepared to inflict death and suffering on innocent civilians. For a time Milosevic and other nationalist fanatics had persuaded their peoples that their new nation-states required an ethnically "pure" land. It was a false message and a human tragedy. Milosevic himself fell from power a few years later. Accused of "crimes against humanity," he was placed on trial in 2002 by an International War Crimes Tribunal, operating under a United Nations mandate.

Internationalism and the United Nations

The determination to restrain these post–Cold War conflicts through international peacekeeping efforts brought together a coalition whose leaders came from humanitarian organizations and from the United Nations. A few peacekeeping missions had been a part of the U.N.'s functions since its founding, although at no point had its members agreed to allow the U.N. command of its own armed forces. Throughout the Cold War, the Soviet Union had refused to approve extensive U.N. military operations, arguing that it was an instrument of the Western powers. The readiness of the last Soviet leadership to collaborate in the United Nations coalition in the Iraq war of 1990–91 proved that the U.N. was freed at last from this constraint on its action.

Influential backing for U.N. intervention in local wars came from the European Union in the 1990s. Once the Soviet threat had disappeared, its member governments, especially Germany and France, became active proponents of the international defense of human rights within Europe, and beyond. They made internationalism an important objective in the E.U.'s foreign relations. They were prepared to use armed forces to halt abuse by Serbs of human rights in Bosnia, supporting first the use of U.N. peacekeeping forces there, and then the dispatch of NATO forces to the Balkans in 1995.

Private groups in the West were instrumental as well in promoting and acting upon this liberal ideology on a global scale. Nongovernmental organizations (NGO) had existed since the nineteenth century. The Red Cross was the first NGO, making medical aid to wartorn lands its primary goal. To avoid taking sides, it had excluded all political judgments from its wartime operations. In the 1970s, this international humanitarianism became the inspiration for an increasing number of organizations. New groups such as the French "Doctors without Borders" and the British "Oxfam" sent their members into areas of violence to bring help to innocent civilians. They did not hesitate to issue public condemnation when they judged governments or armed groups responsible for crimes against humanity.

Their political involvement, based on humanitarian principles, was the grounds on which they appealed for outside intervention. Bernard Kouchner, one of the founders of Doctors without Borders, had worked with the Red Cross in Biafra during the Nigeria civil war (see Chapter 5). His outrage at the crimes committed by Nigerian armed forces induced him to found the new organization in 1971. He openly broke with the apolitical position of the Red Cross. The charter of Doctors without Borders required that they "bear witness" publicly to atrocities and "care for" the sick and the wounded. Their efforts, and those of other nongovernmental organizations, were of enormous assistance to the civilian populations caught in the midst of the violence. In 1990, the U.N. Assembly formally recognized the desirability of their international humanitarian action.

ONGOING U.N. PEACEKEEPING MISSIONS

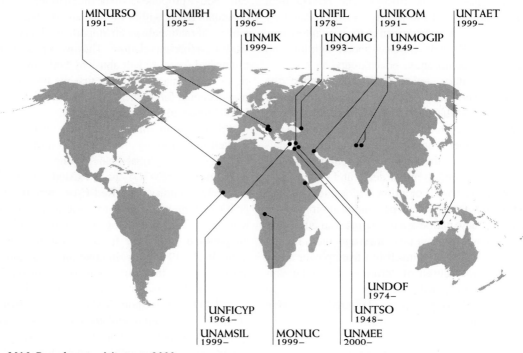

U.N. Peacekeeping Missions, 2000

The local wars of the 1990s drew the NGOs to the most distant parts of the globe. It also placed them in the middle of bitter conflicts where their very presence became a political issue. Kouchner believed deeply in what he called a "right of intervention" by foreign powers, including the United Nations, in wars that inflicted brutal punishment on innocent civilian populations. In 1994, the Doctors without Borders went to Central Africa to assist the millions of Hutu refugees from Rwanda. They soon discovered that Hutu militia, responsible for the Rwanda genocide, controlled the refugee camps of Zaire and were seizing medical and food assistance and aid services. The new Rwanda government protested that the NGOs supplying the camps were helping the assassins of their people, not serving a humanitarian aim. In

disgust at the Hutu warlords' use of their assistance, the Doctors without Borders stopped their lifesaving work there. They were trapped between their hopes of peace and the ugly reality of ruthless power-hungry warlords bent on violence.

The United Nations appeared the ideal choice to all those who believed a truly new world order had to rely on the international community, not on power politics, to resolve the local wars of the late century. The U.N. charter called for peacekeeping action to assist in finding just settlements in the best interests of war-torn countries and contending ethnic groups. This peacekeeping mission fell under the direct responsibility of the Secretary General. The Security Council approved recommendations for intervention and voted the funds to pay for civilian personnel and, if necessary, troops to take charge of the operation. At times, the Security Council authorized member countries to dispatch their own troops to intervene against aggressive states in defense of the victim. The Korean War of 1950–53, and the Gulf War of 1990–91, were fought successfully in this manner. For local wars, U.N. armed forces usually operated directly under the peacekeeping branch of the Secretariat. The Secretary General provided overall supervision of the conduct of the operations.

As a distinguishing sign, the United Nations' equipment bore the distinctive emblem of a white dove over a blue background. The troops made up an unusual military force. They were composed of contingents, including commanding officers, from the member countries whose governments agreed to participate. Their charge in conducting their operations was, until the early 1990s, to use their arms solely for self-defense. No one had an answer to the question of how this armed force was to prevent the militias of warlords or regular armies, if determined at all cost to achieve military victory, from wrecking havoc and death among the populations who got in their way. A U.N. military force of symbolic, not real, might could not be effective in these circumstances.

For the first forty years of its existence, the question of warmaking did not arise. Then, the U.N.'s peacekeeping role had been to enforce peace agreements that the combatants had already put into effect. When the Suez War of 1956 ended in the withdrawal of Israeli troops, the U.N. sent peacekeepers to patrol the Egyptian-Israeli border. They were there to reassure the Israeli government that Egypt would no longer send Muslim terrorists into their land, and to help the Egyptian government respect a peace agreement very unpopular with its Muslim fundamentalists. These operations were useful, though they did not occur frequently. Between 1945 and 1990, the U.N. had sent troops on only thirteen peacekeeping operations. Operating at the invitation (more or less voluntary) of combatants and in

conditions of relative order, the U.N.'s intervention had proven useful and (almost) bloodless.

Its activities accelerated dramatically in the 1990s. Suddenly local wars flared up throughout the world. The Security Council moved to prevent mass killing and atrocities in the spirit of humanitarian defense of human rights. In 1991, it unanimously approved a policy of U.N. military intervention for the sake of "human security" when threatened by wars or ethnic conflict. In the next years, the U.N. found itself engaged in twenty wars requiring the participation of seventy thousand U.N. troops. Some actions involved peacemaking, not just peacekeeping, when the warring parties continued fighting. The U.N. flag flew over military camps in very dangerous parts of the world.

That danger first became apparent in the African country of Somalia. The nomadic peoples there had proven unable to create a stable government after receiving their independence in 1960. It had become a failed state, like other Third World lands where poverty and clan loyalties fatally weakened vital functions of public life. The population's miserable economic conditions worsened seriously when serious drought hit the country in the 1980s. Nongovernmental organizations attempted to help the starving peoples, but were powerless to prevent warlord-led militia from stealing their supplies and fighting each other in an endless civil war.

In 1991, the U.N. responded to the international outcry by approving military intervention to protect the aid activities. In 1992, it accepted the proposal of President George Bush to send U.S. forces, operating on their own, into Somalia. The Muslim warlords united against the "infidel" American occupier, killing eighteen U.S. soldiers in a highly publicized military operation in the country's capital city. The American military and the U.S. Congress raised serious questions why American military should die for a cause of no national interest to their country. Shortly after, the U.S. government ended its "armed humanitarianism," and the

U.N. stopped its efforts at peacemaking in Somalia. The warlords had won; the United Nations (and the people of Somalia) had lost.

International peacemaking failed several times to end ethnic atrocities inflicted on minority peoples in the next years. U.N. troops went to war-torn areas of the former Yugoslavia in 1993 to stop the brutal ethnic cleansing, directed primarily at the Muslim population in Bosnia and the Serbian people in Croatia. In that same year, the Security Council authorized U.N. peacekeepers to go to Rwanda to help enforce a ceasefire between the Hutu government and Tutsi rebel forces. In both cases, the U.N. Secretariat had at its disposal very few troops, armed only with light weapons, to contain heavily armed forces engaged in brutal civil wars against hated minority peoples. The U.S. government refused to participate directly, fearing public hostility to military intervention that might end in bloodshed among U.S. troops. It claimed that the "disorders" there were internal affairs to be resolved by the states themselves. Without U.S. backing, the Security Council and the U.N. Secretariat could not launch real military intervention in these lands.

The result was that the U.N. troops were helpless witnesses to the massacre of Bosnian Muslims and to the Rwandan genocide. Only the NATO intervention in 1995 stopped the Bosnian civil war. In Rwanda, the Tutsi guerrilla forces defeated the Hutu army only after the genocide had ended. "Bloodless" peacemaking in these areas was an absurdity, and the U.N. peacekeepers lacked the military might and the authorization from the Security Council to engage in real warfare. The 1949 U.N. Agreement on War Crimes had obligated the United Nations to take all steps necessary to prevent genocide, but the U.N. failed the test in Rwanda in 1994.

This tragic failure strengthened the resolve of the new Secretary General, Kofi Annan, to ensure that the U.N. act promptly and decisively in areas where violence erupted. He became the U.N.'s highest officer in 1996. His election marked the first time a diplomat from sub-Saharan Africa had served as General Secretary. He made the troubles of Africa his prime concern. He explained that the U.N.'s task had to include intervention in conflicts (including civil wars) where "the main aim is the destruction not of armies but of civilians and entire ethnic groups." It was a goal that went beyond the aims of Woodrow Wilson and other founders of the first collective peacekeeping organization, the League of Nations. But times had changed since 1919. The one hundred fifty new nation-states had found their collective voice within the United Nations. Annan believed deeply that it, better than any outside power, was suited to the task of peacekeeping.

At least once in the last years of the century, his resolve lead to successful military intervention. The people of the eastern half of the island of Timor had received their freedom from the Portugese Empire in 1975, only to be conquered the next year by the Indonesian army. For the next two decades Timorese nationalists fought an obscure, sporadic war for liberation from Indonesia. In the late 1990s, Indonesian militia and military units continued the fight, killing at random Timorese civilians to force their nationalist leaders to abandon the struggle. It was another local war coupled with ethnic massacre.

Under international pressure, a new Indonesian civilian government finally agreed to allow the East Timorese to vote on independence. It reluctantly accepted the presence of U.N. military units whose task was to end the fighting. Australian troops were the first to intervene, capturing and disarming the Indonesian militia. After their combat ended, other U.N. civilian and military personnel supervised the elections. The Timorese people voted for independence. The new government began, with U.N. and NGO assistance, the slow, tortuous work of rebuilding their devastated land and constructing the new nation-state of East Timor. In post–Cold War world, internationalism had become a vital force thanks to the efforts of the United Nations.

TERRORISM AND LOCAL WARS

International relations among nations in the postimperial age evolved at times in directions dictated the old methods of power politics and balance of power. The Soviet Union and the United States had, in the course of the Cold War, created a fragile balance of power (baptized the "balance of terror"). Each had constructed a comparable array of weapons of mass destruction, and each acknowledged limits to its influence created by these terrible instruments of war. The disappearance of the Soviet Union left Russia a weakened player in that diplomatic game.

The United States, with only 4 percent of the world's population, possessed the economic capacity to generate almost one third of the total global production. U.S. military expenditures amounted to more than 35 percent of the total military spending of all the countries of the world at the turn of the century. In real terms, the U.S. military still possessed five thousand intercontinental ballistics missiles, and deployed a multiocean navy. In these circumstances, no global balance of power existed in the world as had been the case in the Cold War. In the years after the fall of the Soviet Union, the United States enjoyed global hegemonic power.

Russia and Inner Asian Wars

In the area once under the rule of the Soviet Union, the Russian Federation used its much weakened military forces to preserve some measure of diplomatic influence. The fate of the successor states to the Union of Soviet Socialist Republics proved, by comparison with the Balkan tragedy, to be far more peaceable. The principal reason lay in the agreement among almost all the leaders of the successor nation-states, most importantly the Russian Federation, not to attempt to alter the state borders put in place when the Soviet government created the ethnoterritorial "national

republics." None of these new nation-states could claim to govern an ethnically "pure" population. All ruled over minority national groups from other, neighboring states. After seventy years of Soviet rule, migration out of the Russian Soviet Republic had left fifteen million people claiming Russian nationality but living in other republics, especially in Ukraine to the south and Kazakhstan in the east. President Boris Yeltsin refused all demands from nationalists within and beyond the borders of his state to create a "Greater Russia." His moderation kept peace in northern Eurasia.

The policy of unaltered borders also meant that no minority within the Russian Federation could secede. The Russian constitution explicitly granted self-rule within the federation to its numerous minority peoples. All accepted Russian sovereignty except the Chechens, a people of Muslim faith living in a small area of the Caucasus mountains. When the Soviet Union disintegrated in 1991, their leaders proclaimed the creation of their own small nation-state. But Russia adhered to the principle of "territorial integrity," sending troops to suppress the uprising. By 2002, its forces had defeated the rebels. In response, Chechen nationalists resorted to terrorist attacks on civilian and military sites in the North Caucasus and even in Moscow. They employed the methods of suicide bombing, whose explosives killed the bombers as well as anyone nearby. They justified their deeds as the work of "martyrs" in an Islamic war to free Chechnya from infidels and colonial oppressors. They fused the defense of Islam and their nation in their struggle for independence.

After 1991, wars among the peoples of the independent states in the Caucasus region presented the Russian government with opportunities to create a new sphere of influence on its southern borders. The state of Georgia, hostile toward its powerful neighbor to the north, discovered that rebellions among its minority peoples were supported secretly by Russia. Failing to defeat the uprisings and impoverished by the collapse of its economy, it had to heed Russian requests for collaboration, joining with Russia in repressing the Chechen rebels on their shared mountain frontier.

When Armenia and Azerbaijan fought a small-scale war between 1991 and 1994, Russian support went to the Armenians. The Armenian government fought to occupy a remote mountainous area within Azerbaijan inhabited largely by Armenians. Armenian forces were victorious, forcing Azerbaijan troops to abandon the region. In the course of the war hundreds of thousands of Armenians and Azeris who had living at peace as minorities in the neighboring state during the Soviet period, had to flee to their homes to escape persecution.

Russian backing for Armenia did not arise out of sympathy with the nationalist cause that started the war. In that region, the principal Russian strategic interest was the abundant petroleum reserves of the Caspian Sea. A weakened Azerbaijan government had to cooperate with Russia in developing its petroleum (along with the international oil companies whose presence it had welcomed). A regional balance of power gradually emerged in the Caucasus area, with Russia the most influential diplomatic player in its complex affairs. The Soviet Union had vanished, but a Russian sphere of influence took its place.

In the Central Asian republics, the Russian state became directly involved in a local war in a successful effort to maintain some measure of diplomatic and military influence there. Its principal goal was to maintain political stability and friendly states there after the final Soviet troop withdrawal in 1989 from Afghanistan, just south of the new Central Asian nation-states. The Soviet Union had failed to defeat the Afghan opponents of their client communist regime; their departure left the country in chaos. A powerful Afghan Muslim movement, which took the name of Taliban, carried on the fight, begun against the Communists, to install an Islamic state there. Despite decades of Soviet religious repression, Central Asian peoples had maintained their ancestral Muslim faith. The fervor of the Taliban spread to the north, where

some Muslims hoped to establish their faith as the foundation of the new nation-states.

In the new state of Tajikistan, the transition to independence led after 1989 to a civil war among former communists, clan leaders, and a Muslim movement inspired by the Taliban. The Russian government was determined to make the border with Afghanistan a barrier beyond which fundamentalist Muslims, bitterly hostile to their state, could not extend their influence. It sent armed forces to Tajikistan to guard the frontier and threw its support behind the former communists. With its backing an agreement to share power was finally reached in 1997 among the warring groups. It gave the former communists a major role in the government. Russian troops had permanent garrisons there to help keep this failed state intact. Russia had achieved its goal of preserving a sphere of influence in Central Asia and strengthening secular, not Islamic leadership. The Soviet Union had vanished, but the diplomatic and military influence of Russia along its borderlands continued to hold in place some pieces of the old imperial realm.

Islam in Afghanistan

Across the border from Tajikistan, the Islamic forces of the Taliban grew in strength until they were able to seize control of Afghanistan in the late 1990s. The Taliban ("students") movement had emerged out of the religious schools in Pakistan. It recruited its followers primarily from Afghan refugees who in the 1980s had fled the war against the Communists and their Soviet ally. Within a few years, the Afghan refugee population had climbed to 1.5 million, some in Iran but most in Pakistan. The Soviet army's departure from Afghanistan in 1989 left the country prey to competing armed groups, united earlier only by opposition to the Communists. The Taliban's militant faith had sustained them in the bloody war against the "godless" Communists. They had attracted as well thirty thousand volunteers from other Muslim lands (the "Arab Afghans").

Refugees from Afghan-Soviet War: Refugee Camp, Iran, 1986 (*UNHCR/16045/ 11.1986/A. Hollmann*)

After the Soviet withdrawal, they carried on the struggle for victory over the other guerrilla forces to transform their war-torn country into an Islamic republic. Their skills in fighting improved with time, with special publications such as the *Encyclopedia of the Afghan Jihad* to help train their fighters. The Pakistan government gave them secret military support, hoping to exercise some influence over these religious zealots. Wealthy, pious Muslims such as Osama bin Laden organized financial aid and military supplies.

In 1997, the Taliban finally had sufficient control of the country to form their own state. Although the country was in ruins, they immediately set about laying the foundations for an Islamic republic even more strict than that in place in Iran. They imposed Muslim law on the population. Women were confined to home and the family, forced to leave behind schooling or work. Criminal law followed traditional Muslim rules, with mutilation and stoning for serious offenses. Secular "vices" such as listening to music became a public crime. Opium growing was banned as equally heinous. The people were subjected to a regime of religious purification.

The Taliban government welcomed foreign Muslims who shared a similar hatred of secular-

ism and modernity. Western material civilization, especially American, was an evil force to which it was vehemently opposed. In 1996, Osama bin Laden established headquarters there for his terrorist organization, Al Qaeda. Its goal, like other fundamentalist Muslim movements of the 1980s and 1990s, was the restoration of a "pure" Islamic faith in place of the modernist heresies brought by the West, in all Muslim countries, and the destruction of American political and diplomatic presence there. For that reason he had been expelled from his homeland, Saudi Arabia, whose feudal monarchy relied on U.S. backing. His group was few in number, but prepared to die in a holy war against the United States. But the term "war" meant in reality terrorism, and his targets extended anywhere in the world.

His organization established secret ties with other small terrorist groups in southeast Asia and the Middle East. In Indonesia, fundamentalists set out in the late 1990s on a violent campaign against Indonesian Christian churches located near Muslim communities, and targeted in 2002 a nightclub in Bali popular with Western tourists, killing nearly two hundred people. In the Philippines, insurgent Muslim forces in the southern islands fighting to form their own Islamic

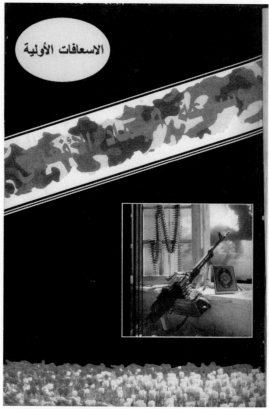

Cover to *Encyclopedia of the Afghan Jihad,* Peshawar,
Pakistan, 1992 (*Hoover Institution*)

state and to expel Christians welcomed foreign
terrorists in the battle. In 1993, yet another
Islamicist terrorist group had done minor damage
when they exploded car bombs in the World Trade
Center in New York City.

The symbolic importance of this skyscraper
made it, along with government buildings in
Washington, DC, a target that the terrorists would
not abandon. Al Qaeda plotted a new, far more
deadly plan of attack. On September 11, 2001,
twenty of bin Laden's followers hijacked four
commercial airliners and turned these planes into
monstrous guided bombs. They piloted two of the
planes into the twin towers of the Trade Center, a
third into the Pentagon building in Washington,
and intended the fourth to hit the White House
(the plane crashed earlier, as a result of the resistance of passengers). The collapse of the towers,
killing nearly three thousand people, was captured in film and shown on television throughout
the world. The terrorists had brought their "holy
war" to the very center of Western civilization.

SPOTLIGHT: Osama bin Laden

Osama bin Laden (1957–?) never used the word "terrorist" to describe his activities organizing attacks on Middle Eastern governments, and on American targets inside and beyond the borders of the United States. He believed himself a warrior in a holy war ("jihad" in Arabic) against the enemies of Islam. His claim to defend their religion made him a hero to many Muslims. His violent campaign against the U.S., culminating in the destruction of the New York World Trade Center in 2001, made him a hunted man with an enormous price on his head.

His personality, and his conspiratorial activities, are shrouded in mystery. In public, he spoke of himself only to restate, in lengthy proclamations, his vow to bring death and defeat to all those who threatened the Muslim faith, welcoming death in this battle. He was reported to have explained in 1998 that "I am fighting so I can die a martyr and go to heaven to meet God." He cultivated an aura of great conspirator, claiming or implying that members of his organization Al Qaeda ("The Military Base") were responsible for bombings in South Asia, the Middle East, Africa, Europe, and the United States. He welcomed this violence for the good that it supposedly brought his cause. His conviction that these deeds were the righteous acts of true Muslims marked him as a religious fanatic. His readiness to inflict indiscriminate death and destruction as a means to intimidate and weaken his enemies placed him among the practitioners of terrorism.

Holy war in defense of Islam became the center of his life from the moment in 1980 when he joined the forces in Afghanistan fighting the Soviet invaders. Before then, he had distinguished himself only as a pious son of an extraordinarily wealthy Saudi Arabian businessman. His father's construction business flourished, for the Saudi monarchy favored it above all other enterprises in the mammoth projects for the reconstruction of the holiest of Muslim sites, Mecca and Medina. Bin Laden perfected his business and engineering skills as a student at a Saudi university in the 1970s. Once in Afghanistan, he put them to use in gathering funds and constructing impregnable defenses for the Afghan guerrillas. The son, like the father, practiced an austere, rigorous version of the Muslim faith called Wahhabism. He understood the Afghan war in these strict Islamic terms. Muslims were once again, as in the time of the Crusades, under attack from infidels.

Bin Laden was persuaded that this war in defense of Islam required the participation of the faithful throughout the Islamic world. Many volunteers (the "Arab Afghans") did come to Afghanistan, mostly from Arab-speaking lands. He set up special military camps to train them in the skills of modern warfare (with weapons supplied secretly by the U.S. government). He learned the meaning of holy war, Islamic warrior, and martyrdom in the midst of those bloody battles. In 1988, these comrades in arms became the core group of his new conspiratorial organization, Al Qaeda. Bin Laden gloried in the victory in 1989 of the Afghan guerrillas, who had defeated "the largest heretic power on earth." He was convinced that he had witnessed there the disappearance of "the myth of the superpower in the face of the outcry that 'God is Great' [Allah Akbar]." He became a Muslim warrior by conviction and his lived experience in the Afghan war. Those years were his apprenticeship as a terrorist.

Afghanistan was only one site of the holy war in which he was engaged. In the 1990s, it had to be fought throughout the Muslim world against the remaining superpower. He became convinced of that danger in 1990, when American military forces moved into Saudi Arabia in preparation for the war against Iraq in defense of Kuwait. He publicly condemned the Saudi monarchy as "agents of the United States" for permitting the infidels into this Muslim holy land. For that, in 1991 the Saudi government expelled him and stripped him of his citizenship. In his eyes, the evil power behind his own persecution, and behind the "crusade" against all Islam, was the United States. He found refuge in Sudan, where an Islamicist regime had taken power. There he set about organizing his "warriors" for the new war against America. His life from this moment on was entirely absorbed by his secret terrorist activities.

By the early 1990s, small terrorist groups had emerged in many Muslim lands to pursue the battle against the evils of secularism and modernity. They formed a loose network of organizations which shared a common goal and collaborated in carrying out their terrorist actions. Bin Laden's Afghan work had brought him fame and followers among these extreme Muslim fundamentalists. With this backing, he made Al Qaeda into one of the best organized and funded terrorist groups. He was already responsible for bombings in Saudi Arabia, and was pursued by agents from Saudi Arabia and the United States. To find a more secure refuge, in 1996 he moved his operations from Sudan back to Afghanistan. There, the Taliban movement was close to winning the civil war that followed the Soviet withdrawal. Its leaders shared his religious zeal. As a result, he quickly became a close collaborator of the new regime, and was permitted to use his old military bases as the center for his battle against the United States.

His notoriety as a terrorist organizer and spokesman dates from these years. He had no serious training in Islamic theology, but this lack did not weaken his eagerness to claim to understand religious truth. Twice while in Sudan he appeared in videotapes (his preferred means of communication) to call for war on the U.S. In early 1998, he issued in the name of "The International Islamic Front for Holy War against Jews and Crusaders" a religious declaration stating that "the individual duty of every Muslim" was to "kill the Americans and their allies, civilians and military" in "any country in which this is possible." His bombastic tone, typical of earlier political terrorists claiming that their deeds constitute the will of their community, was a sort of declaration of war. That fall, the bombs that destroyed the U.S. embassies in Kenya and Tanzania, almost certainly the work of Al Qaeda members, proved to the world that he belonged in the forefront of international terrorists.

The success of his September 11, 2001, attacks on U.S. targets was a moment of triumph for his cause and for him personally. The operation that he had planned required years of meticulous preparation. Al Qaeda members had to be trained as pilots, and the four separate terrorist squads had to hijack their planes in a coordinated move to reach their targets at nearly the same time that day. He rejoiced in the terrible destruction wrought by the three planes that did reach their targets, declaring it a "success beyond my wildest dreams." Yet it was successful only in provoking another Afghan war that ended the Taliban's rule. That conflict did serious damage to Al Qaeda, and perhaps to him. U.S. bombing attacks destroyed the cave shelters that he had built ten years before in the war with the Soviet Union, and where Al Qaeda had created its center of operations. Many of its members were buried alive there, and he himself may have died or been wounded. A few tapes purporting to be his speeches from the next years suggested he had survived (although they might have been composed from earlier tapes by Al Qaeda survivors). His action brought a worldwide repression of Muslim fundamentalists. In the end, his so-called triumph proved once again that terrorism is a self-destructive movement.

Cover to Al Qaeda book *And America Trembled*, 2002 (*Hoover Institution*)

The Local Wars of the United States

The international outrage and horror created by terrorist attack on the U.S. brought together an international coalition of states united in their determination to destroy the Al Qaeda movement and its Taliban backers. The United States government, with the support of the United Nations Security Council and of the North Atlantic Treaty Organization, organized an anti-Taliban military coalition of Western air and land units collaborating with several Afghan guerrilla armies. Russia and the Central Asian states gave their backing to the action. Even Pakistan, once the secret patron of Taliban forces and sanctuary for fundamentalist Muslims, publicly backed the war. The coalition's attack in late 2001 proved a remarkable success in overthrowing the Taliban and destroying the Al Qaeda camps. The success was due in good measure to the dislike among Afghans for their ruthless Muslim leaders. This war of intervention was only partially successful, though. It could not wipe out the network of Al Qaeda terrorist cells, for many operated secretly in other countries; it could not bring stability and political unity to a country where nation-building had never overcome clan, tribal, and religious quarrels. In world affairs, its most notable feature was the war's demonstration of the overwhelming military might of the United States. The superpower had global reach.

Yet to those who believed that the balance of power determined success or failure in global relations, the United States appeared even after the Afghan invasion a weakened superpower. Among leaders of this persuasion was the new U.S. government under the presidency of George W. Bush. Muslim terrorists had demonstrated to the world that they could destroy strategic civilian sites and inflict grave damage to the U.S. economy. The message had particular importance in the Middle East whose petroleum was vital to the global economy, and to U.S. economic interests in

particular. The U.S.-led coalition of 1990–91 war in Kuwait had defended those interests by defeating Saddam Hussein's armies. The war was fought under the U.N. flag, and ended on a compromise peace that left Saddam Hussein' regime in power. Enforcement of the peace was the responsibility of the U.N. Its inspectors insured the elimination of Iraq's weapons of mass destruction (until their expulsion in 1997). The Security Council authorized Kurdish autonomy in northern Iraq and U.S. air protection for this semipartition of the country. Its officials monitored the partial embargo on Iraq oil exports. This peace arrangement used methods of containment, similar in intent to those first directed by the U.S. on a global against the Soviet Union, to limit the power of Saddam Hussein's regime, ruling a drastically weakened country (see Chapter 6).

After the September 11, 2001, attack, President Bush and his advisers decided to force Saddam Hussein's regime out of power. Their calculation rested on the assumption that the diplomatic and military influence of the United States in the Middle East could only recover from the damage inflicted by the Al Qaeda attacks by its destruction of the Iraqi regime. Saddam Hussein's government had no role in the Al Qaeda attack, nor did it possess weapons of mass destruction or pose a clear and immediate military threat to the region. Saddam Hussein was a symbol of anti-U.S. resistance. The U.S. leadership calculated that his removal would demonstrate that in the Middle East the balance of power was dominated by U.S. military might. To them, this goal was worth the cost in lives, both Iraqi and U.S., and in damage to the Iraqi economy and society.

Bush was prepared to act without the sanction of the United Nations Security Council. There, a new war lacked the support of key members, including Germany, France, and Russia. Their leaders favored continuing the policy of containment. With the backing among major states only of Great Britain, the United States invaded Iraq in 2003. Its forces easily destroyed the regime of

Saddam Hussein, and proclaimed the liberation of Iraq from dictatorship. It had no viable plans for a "liberated" Iraq, for no peace treaty followed the war (as had been the case even against Nazi Germany) and no unified Iraq coalition was prepared to take control. Widespread international criticism focused on the invasion and military occupation of Iraq. The Russian president observed that the war was not intended to "combat the evil" of terrorism, but was an effort to expand the U.S. "zone of strategic influence" in the Middle East through the use of its "strong and well-armed national army." He saw in the war a U.S. act of power politics. The U.S. unilateral action had intentionally excluded an internationalist strategy of maintaining peace under the auspices of the United Nations. It made clear that no "new world order" yet determined international relations in the post-Cold War era.

SUMMARY

The early years of the twenty-first century bore little resemblance to earlier decades. Communism had disappeared from Europe, and remade itself in China into a free-market political dictatorship. Empires had vanished, and so, too, had the Cold War. The newly elected leaders of the former communist states began to restore free-market economies and liberal democracy. It proved to be a difficult transition. Western societies had moved in the half-century since the Second World War into a new industrial revolution and new global economy. Their living conditions were far different from those relics of outdated industrial life left behind by the communists.

The closing years of the twentieth century were a time of ethnic conflicts so severe that they threatened the very survival of some new nation-states. The responsibility for these tragic events lay in large measure on ambitious leaders determined to seize and hold power regardless of the human consequence. Fearful people, often suffering hardship with little hope for the future, turned

in desperation to political movements that seemed to offer easy solutions to complex social and economic problems. Extremist nationalist leaders appeared most often at the end of the century to hold that key. Their appeals to nationalist passions fanned the flames of ethnic hatred and at times heightened the risk of war with neighboring states. The work of the United Nations offered some hope that these conflicts could be contained, yet the poisonous effects of hatred and intolerance among peoples did not disappear.

After the 2001 terrorist attacks and the 2003 Iraq war, the world remained a very unstable and violent place. The United Nations attempted with only limited success to control local wars. Leaders of powerful nation-states had in their hands still the power to wage war or to join in collective peacemaking policies. In the new nation-states, their readiness to promote civic nationalism could restrain ethnic hatreds and war. But ethnic nationalism was still a potential force for violence. The United States, whose empire had never rivaled that of other Western powers, employed in 2003 the methods of power politics when its leaders judged its national interests at stake, relying on war instead of collective methods of containment of Iraq. President Woodrow Wilson's 1919 appeal for peace protected by a "community of nations," not power politics, remained a wish, not a reality.

DATES WORTH REMEMBERING

1964 Integrated-circuit computers
1965 First communications satellite
1971 United States abandons gold standard
1973 Oil crisis and global recession
1978 Beginning of market reforms in China
1986 Chernobyl nuclear accident in Soviet Union
1980–97 Asian economic boom
1991–95 Civil war in Yugoslavia

1990–91 United Nations war against Iraq
1992 Global Conference on the Environment
1994 North American Free Trade Agreement
1994 Massacre of Tutsi people in Rwanda
1995 Mexican financial crisis
1996–2002 War in Central Africa
1998 World population approximately six billion
1997 Asian financial crisis
1997 Taliban forces conquer Afghanistan
2000 Global warming confirmed by U.N. Conference on Climate Change
2001 Al Qaeda terrorist attack on United States
2001 Defeat of Afghan Taliban regime by U.S-led invasion
2003 U.S. conquest of Iraq

RECOMMENDED READING

Global Economy, Global Environment

John McNeill, *Something New Under the Sun: An Environmental History of the Twentieth-Century World* (2000). A carefully balanced study of what humanity did to the global environment in the twentieth century.

Anthony Sampson, *The People and Politics of the World Banking Crisis* (1983). The best account of the fragile global financial network in the recession of the late 1970s–early 1980s.

Peacekeeping, Local Wars, and Ethnic Conflict

Christopher Bennett, *Yugoslavia's Bloody Collapse: Causes, Courses, Consequences* (1995). A brief account of the complex political and ethnic origins of Yugoslavia's civil war and the agony of ethnic cleansing.

Walter Laquer, *No End to War: Terrorism in the Twenty-First Century* (2003). An inquiry into contemporary global terrorism by an author well versed in the subject.

Clyde Prestowitz, *Rogue Nation: American Unilateralism and the Failure of Good Intentions* (2003). A thoughtful, critical study of failures of U.S. global leadership in the post–Cold War era.

Ahmed Rashid, *Taliban: Militant Islam, Oil and Fundamentalism in Central Asia* (2000). An informative study of the Afghan regime from a journalist with a thorough knowledge of the complex politics of the region.

William Shawcross, *Deliver Us from Evil: Peacekeepers, Warlords and a World of Endless Conflict* (2000). Despite the title, an optimistic view of the achievements of the United Nations in the 1990s in dealing with the mass mayhem of civil wars and local conflict.

Travelers' Tales and Visual Aids

*Michael Ignatieff, *Blood and Belonging: Journeys into the New Nationalism* (1993). Firsthand account, by a thoughtful observer of political violence, of the human side to nationalism of the 1990s in Europe and the Middle East.

*Fergal Keane, *Season of Blood: A Rwandan Journey* (1995). A BBC correspondent's vivid story of the 1994 Tutsi massacre, viewed at the very moment of the tragedy.

"The Last Just Man" (2002). A powerful documentary on the Rwanda genocide, focusing on the Belgian general who tried, and failed, to bring international intervention.

<http://www.un.org>. A Web site, compiled by the United Nations, containing a rich array of information on its current and past activities.

Index